Fields of Folklore

FIELDS OF FOLKLORE

Essays in Honor of
Kenneth S. Goldstein

Edited by Roger D. Abrahams

Michael Robert Evans, Charles Greg Kelley, & John McGuigan
Associate Editors

Trickster Press

BLOOMINGTON

CONTENTS

Tabula Gratulatoria

Roger D. Abrahams
Philadelphia, Pennsylvania

Wanni W. Anderson
Providence, Rhode Island

Samuel G. Armistead
Davis, California

David S. Azzolina
Philadelphia, Pennsylvania

Robert Baron
Brooklyn, New York

Peter Bartis
Washington, D.C.

İlhan Başgöz
Bloomington, Indiana

Richard Bauman and
    Beverly J. Stoeltje
Bloomington, Indiana

Dan Ben-Amos
Philadelphia, Pennsylvania

Regina Bendix
Philadelphia, Pennsylvania

Robert D. Bethke
Elkton, Maryland

Deborah Bowman and
    John McGuigan
Bloomington, Indiana

Charles L. Briggs
Poughkeepsie, New York

Saul Broudy and
    Elisabeth H. Null
Philadelphia, Pennsylvania,
    and Washington, D.C.

Mary Ellen Brown
Bloomington, Indiana

Jan H. Brunvand
Salt Lake City, Utah

David D. Buchan
St. John's, Newfoundland

Anne C. Burson-Tolpin
West Orange, New Jersey

Carole H. Carpenter
Toronto, Ontario

Tom Carroll
Pittsburgh, Pennsylvania

Carter and Kay Craigie
Paoli, Pennsylvania

Daniel J. Crowley
Davis, California

Barry Dolins
Chicago, Illinois

Thomas A. Dubois
Seattle, Washington

Susan Adair Dwyer-Shick
Seattle, Washington

J. Joseph Edgette
Glenolden, Pennsylvania

John Eilertsen
Southampton, New York

Burt Feintuch
Durham, New Hampshire

Edith Fowke
Toronto, Ontario

Hugo A. Freund and
    Susan L. F. Isaacs
Philadelphia, Pennsylvania

Angus Kress Gillespie
New Brunswick, New Jersey

Henry Glassie
Bloomington, Indiana

Archie Green
San Francisco, California

Helen (Brad) Griebel
St. Paul, Minnesota

Herbert Halpert
St. John's, Newfoundland

David J. Hufford
Hummelstown, Pennsylvania

Dell H. and Virginia D. Hymes
Charlottesville, Virginia

Edward D. Ives
Orono, Maine

Roger L. and Dawnhee Yim Janelli
Seoul, South Korea

Deborah A. Kapchan
Austin, Texas

Barbara Kirshenblatt-Gimblett
New York, New York

Hilda Adam Kring
Grove City, Pennsylvania

Yvonne Lange
Santa Fe, New Mexico

Denis Mercier
Pitman, New Jersey

Wolfgang Mieder
Burlington, Vermont

Margaret Mills
Philadelphia, Pennsylvania

Mick Moloney
Philadelphia, Pennsylvania

Lynwood Montell
Oakland, Kentucky

Eric L. Montenyohl
Lafayette, Louisiana

Kathryn L. Morgan
Swarthmore, Pennsylvania

Linda Morley
Manchester, New Hampshire

William R. Murphy
Nokomis, Florida

Peter Narváez
St. John's, Newfoundland

Venetia Newall
London, England

Wilhelm F. H. Nicolaisen
Aberdeen, Scotland

Dorothy Noyes
Philadelphia, Pennsylvania

Malachi and Bonnie O'Connor
Wenonah, New Jersey

Elliott Oring
Los Angeles, California

Gerald Pocius
St. John's, Newfoundland

I. Sheldon Posen and
  Maxine Miska
Ottawa, Ontario

Leslie Prosterman
Washington, D.C.

John W. Roberts
Philadelphia, Pennsylvania

Warren E. Roberts
Bloomington, Indiana

Dan Rose
Haverford, Pennsylvania

Jack Santino and Lucy Long
Bowling Green, Ohio

Peter I. Seitel
Mt. Rainier, Maryland

Shalom Staub
Harrisburg, Pennsylvania

Robert Blair St. George
Philadelphia, Pennsylvania

Janet S. Theophano
Philadelphia, Pennsylvania

Gerald Thomas
Torbay, Newfoundland

J. Barre Toelken
Logan, Utah

Jack Truten
Meadowbrook, Pennsylvania

Mark E. Workman
Jacksonville, Florida

Steven and Amanda Zeitlin
Hastings Hudson, New York

Charles G. ("Terry") Zug III
Chapel Hill, North Carolina

Rosemary Levy Zumwalt and
  Isaac J. Levy
Davidson, North Carolina

Essays in Honor of
Kenneth S. Goldstein

INTRODUCTION

Kenny Goldstein and the Pursuit of Folksong

Roger D. Abrahams

Every collection—itself an island—needs an island.
—Susan Sontag, *The Volcano Lover*

KENNY GOLDSTEIN is the great theorist of intermediacy. His record producing and collecting placed him in a position to understand how traditional performers and performances were usefully enhanced by modern technological devices. He has come to be known, then, for his remarkable achievements as a collector and as one who brought theoretical concerns into the process of collecting. I have known him for nearly forty years, and I like to think that our relationship is special. As graduate students, we talked and read and collected and searched many bookstores together, and even started a business of our own, Folklore Associates.

Early in our relationship I learned that he burned with a different kind of flame than I did. Our differences were not political, though they might have been had we talked through that subject. Nor were they social or cultural in spite of the differences in our backgrounds and our take on life. Our divergences and our disagreements were stylistic. I came into folklore scratching a generalized itch. Looking for an excuse to address my nervousness by searching for interesting things out there. Singing and finding songs worth listening to fueled my desires to be on the go.

Kenny, too, can't sit still very long, but he came into the profession as an organizer, a producer, a collector. Kenny showed by example that I am really not a collector in the deepest sense. A real collector must be pure of mind, able to screen out everything else from life in the moment of getting the scent and moving out toward the prey, bagging it, bringing it back and putting it in its proper place. Collecting involves constructing a world that only resembles other constructed spaces in superficial ways. This is a personal memory garden, whole unto itself, one whose interior arrangement is in great part unsharable.

Like cabinets of curiosity, it attracts an audience because of its bizarre particularity. The power and the integrity of the collection appeals to the outsider nonetheless. The accumulation of things within such a space accounts for itself in its own terms; it grows or it dies. It has no sense of itself except as it illustrates a process.

Kenny Goldstein has been a collector all of his professional life. To be on the hunt with him is a unique experience. Whether in the southern mountains of the United States or the Newfoundland outports, or at Papermania or another book and ephemera show, his engagement in the task is complete. Do not expect idle chatter for the sake of conversation itself. Wait until it is over when you can get in on a catalog of the catches-of-the-day.

Of course, folklorists know Kenny best for his folksong hunts. This is not only because of the size of the collection or the duration over which it has been collected, but for the theory that he developed out of the practice ever since his work in Scotland in the late 1950s. His mastery of the new technology of data gathering and amplification led him to consider just how much more data might be recorded in the field, and how much larger the number of features of the performance situation might make it into the record, thus enlarging the very idea of context.

By the middle of the 1950s technological innovations in amplification, recording and sound reproduction had led fieldworkers to wrestle with such questions. The mobile directional microphone made it possible both to get closer to artists as they were recording. In combination with the tape recorder, it freed the collector to go into the field and to bring back tape-recorded performances of sufficient quality to be issued commercially. Moreover, the use of vinyl acetate in producing these records made it economically feasible to produce limited-run recordings.

These developments affected the folksong revival in many ways. New audiences with new ears came forth for this old-timey music. Folksingers, like other popular entertainers, felt challenged to come up with new 'material' all of the time, either new songs, or old songs in new versions. Even for someone who was not a star performer themselves, a *folknik* revival singer might discover the song that everybody else started singing or the song that would become a fixture on the folk festival circuit. In producing records and involving himself in festival presentations, Kenny found himself at the center of this system of popular performance.

Folk festivals brought together traditional musicians, scholar-collectors, and revival singers: in Philadelphia, with the creation of the Philadelphia Folksong Society; at the University of California in both Berkeley and Los Angeles; at the University of Chicago; and, with truly national notice, the Newport Folk Festival. These differed from earlier folk festivals in featuring scholar-collectors as presenters and interpreters, introducing singers and their songs, and holding interviews on stage and in the smaller workshop venues. The new microphones and other devices of amplification, and the recording equipment that was taking it all down for posterity, helped develop a large and well-informed audience. (One of the major ironies of that era was that folksingers decided that *not* amplifying their instruments would be the way in which they distanced themselves from 'commercial' music.) This was an alternative popular music, we know in retrospect, but one that introduced a more accurate understanding of alternative song traditions and styles.

Moe Asch and his great Folkways project must be credited with first bringing the new technology to bear on these old musics, developing a rich catalogue of traditional musics. But no one was more central to the development of these new audiences than Kenny. Before he had stormed the academy, he was the folksong record producer extraordinaire—I think he points to having produced more than 520 long-playing records. In addition, no scholar has lent his name and his presence to more festival and folk concert performances than Kenny. When he went to make his mark as a folksong scholar, it was as a collector and a theorizer of the process of collection. His dissertation and first book, *A Guide for Field Workers in Folklore* (1964), were given over to this. He brought the practicalities of the field experience and the presentation needs of the festival presenter to bear on the concepts of fieldwork, traditional performance, and repertoire. Only someone with his drive, patience, imagination and yes, *chutzpa,* would have been able to think about the range of songs, song-types and styles in the Anglo-American song traditions.

His article on "The Induced Natural Context" (1966) affected the way in which everyone who sought to collect by modern standards of authenticity and excellence set up their recording sessions. He created the workshop singing discussions and other festival sessions that gave those attending some idea of how folklorists and traditional musicians interacted in the field. His writings on active and passive tradition bearers (1971) in the issue of the *Journal of American Folklore* commonly referred to as "New Perspectives" called attention to the role of the collector in ascertaining the range of songs that a traditional performer might have learned in a lifetime. Kenny put forth several standards that have become accepted practices in field collecting today, not only in folklore study but in anthropological studies of performed traditions (though these fieldworkers, as often as not do not know the source of the criteria for capturing "the authentic sounds.")

At the historical moment in which Kenny and many others of his generation were making the switch from the commercial to the academic worlds, the basic terms in the discipline of folklore were undergoing change from within. Surveying definitions of folklore by American folklorists, Francis Lee Utley (1961) had noticed, for instance, that the concept of tradition itself underwent change. Prior to World War II, texts and objects exhibiting the characteristics of lore through variation had provided the basic materials of the discipline as it was pursued by comparatists. Their primary aim was to explain the life history of items of lore in international circulation: stories, proverbs, ballads, whatever. In the postwar era the core of the discipline shifted to the study of memorial transmission itself. Folklorists looked for the ways in which the individual tradition-bearer might affect the life-history of the song or story.[1]

The ideas generated by comparatists now were tested in field situations. Traditional singers themselves were asked questions about why certain songs or types of songs were sung, and how individuals developed their repertoires. In the repeated interactions between singer and collector, asking questions concerning the who, where, why, and how of song learning and remembering, a greater respect for the singers themselves developed. This new regard was translated into stage representations when the best of these performers were put onto the festival stage and subjected to the rigors of making high fidelity recordings. Here, Kenny's work with the Stewarts of Fetterangus and Sara Cleveland were central in developing our contemporary notions of how to present and study repertoire.[2]

As he shifted his activities somewhat away from the commercial world and into academia, Kenny brought much of his earlier experience to bear on the institutions with which he now contended. In the many edited volumes produced during the mid-sixties and the mid-seventies, he introduced contextual features into discussions of performance events and repertoire analysis. Among the theoreticians gathering to read papers to each other at various meetings, Kenny brought a kind of practical experience to the endeavor. He had been to the field more than anyone else and had used his personal enterprise and his technological expertise to ensure that the songs were sung as naturally as possible and the singers made to feel most comfortable and most fully involved in the production themselves.

Until the early 1960s, a division existed between folklorists who saw themselves involved in a great international and comparatist "scientific" enterprise and those who were primarily concerned with the ways in which folklore gave nations, regions, or locales their special character. The former tended toward being library and archive scholars, while the latter were theorists who had also been involved in field collecting who were as interested in the singers and storytellers as the songs and the stories.

The comparatist perspective, once associated with Stith Thompson and his students and colleagues at Indiana University, focussed on the materials of tradition. They study lore in the manner of the natural historian, through taxonomic distinctions and through a mapping that might reveal both historic and geographic patterning. Regionalists and those involved in creating the idea of the plural nation, were convinced that in lore might the secret of folk creativity and endurance be comprehended. They approach folklore as part of the enterprise of place and people, scholarship involving a set of political activities that would bring folklore study again into the mainstream descriptions of the national experience.[3]

From this perspective, the ascension of Richard M. Dorson to the chair of the Indiana's Folklore Institute, on Thompson's retirement, signaled the beginning of the end of this face-off, for Dorson had made his name as a regionalist and an Americanist.[4] But in his capacity as head of the leading comparatist program, he developed a middle way. He encouraged hard-line fieldwork, historically situated and presented so that the reader would come to know that he or she was dealing with materials important in the formulation of locale, region, or nation. Yet he also demanded that each item of lore be footnoted in such a way that the reader would know that it was drawn from the great ocean of story and song and proverb and riddle that flowed around the world on the tongues of traveling tradition bearers.[5]

Dick Dorson, in many ways the intellectual, saw that folklore could be a discipline of disciplines; it could draw on the insights and even methods of other disciplines. Even the students at the University of Pennsylvania, the other major graduate program in the United States, saw in his work a model for developing transdisciplinary perspectives that might well be emulated. In contrast to Thompson, Dorson encouraged dissertations involving insights and techniques of analysis from different disciplines so long as they brought new understandings to the life of the materials of tradition. Unlike Thompson, Dorson himself had actually carried out fieldwork. He based his writings on his observation of people engaged in telling stories to each other for entertainment and instruction.

His opposite number at Penn, MacEdward Leach, also had found his way into fieldwork after developing his reputation as a library scholar. He came into folklore as a literary historian and comparativist. He was a member of the English Department at Penn for most of his life. At a crucial time in mid-career, Mac had been persuaded by his friend Horace Beck to carry out fieldwork with traditional performers, first with Frank Speck, then later with Horace himself. This experience caused him to recognize that texts fixed in literate formulation did little to extend our understanding of the construction and uses of lore as employed by groups entertaining and instructing each other. His frustration with library scholarship, then, emerged from the limitations this method imposed in getting at the folk character of the folk.[6] Leach valued the contribution in this area of those who had carried out fieldwork of any sort, even if it resulted in belletristic and journalistic renderings of the lore.

By contrast, Dick Dorson seized upon this theme as a way of continuing to distance the Indiana approach from the rest of the discipline. Fiercely loyal to his institution and its reputation, he wanted to maintain its primacy in folklore studies in the minds of the rest of the world. Even more important, he did not want to have the name of folklore sullied in any manner because of nonacademic—especially journalistic—usages. It was out of these fears that he developed his argument concerning the difference between fakelore and folklore.[7]

The folklore program at Indiana had prospered because of its claim to international and scientific power. If the membership of the American Folklore Society did not fully accept the position that Indiana had taken, at least that institution was accorded its due place as the center of folklore studies in America. Leach, as Secretary-Treasurer of the Society during the 1950s, had come to represent those who stood in opposition to the claims of Thompson, and then Dorson, to scientific purity. Attracting a number of students to his courses in folksong and ballad from the ranks of song scholars (first John Greenway, William Simeone, Tristram Coffin and Malcolm Laws; then Kenny, myself, Robert Byington, and Ellen Stekert), Leach was able to declare departmental independence from the Department of English early in the 1960s. This was about the same time that other programs (at Texas, Western Kentucky, Berkeley, and UCLA) were in formation. Because of Leach's preeminence as a teacher, a ballad scholar, and a diplomat within the profession, the program at Penn quickly achieved an important position within folklore studies.

Once the opposition between Indiana and Penn was articulated, the students at the two institutions made a promise to each other not to perpetuate this division. Kenny had attended the Folklore Summer Institute at Indiana in 1958 and had already established the lines of connection. He saw that the rising primacy of fieldwork in the future of folklore study was going to provide the glue for the discipline no matter what form a publication might take afterward. Along with D. K. Wilgus and Archie Green, he brought attention to the importance of folk music on commercial recordings as a research and a teaching tool.

This sense of bringing together the various folkloristic perspectives with a carefully worked out social agenda and an address to issues of folklore as a set of communicational devices was strengthened as Kenny's ascencion to the department chair in the mid-sixties pulled the program at Penn together and enlisted the talents of Don Yoder and Dell Hymes in teaching for the growing department. More than this, first as secretary-treasurer of the American Folklore Society and then as the editor of the Society's various publications, he could draw upon his abilities to recognize the capacities of the new technology in producing books as well as phonograph recordings. Among other things, he put the Society in a positive financial condition by the end of the 1960s.

Finally, Kenny should be credited with being one of the first to recognize the developing consensus occurring within the profession regarding the study of folklore as communicative systems. He participated in many of the most interesting conferences out of which some important documents of the profession emerged. This was the world that Kenny Goldstein had done so much to construct, one in which scholars coming into the discipline got nothing but encouragement to do our best work as quickly as possible. Kenny was especially artful in bringing the proceedings of these conference into print.

The organizational and disciplinary coherence initiated by the development of the university programs now resulted in conferences and symposia that became important books. If *Toward New Perspectives in Folklore* (1972) is the most celebrated of these—it was the arena in which Kenny published his theory of repertoire analysis—it should be read in conjunction with a number of other similarly energized gatherings of essays, especially *Folklore: Performance and Communication* (1975), edited by Kenny and Dan Ben-Amos. This work was issued in 1975 but consisted of papers read at the 1969 annual meeting of the American Folklore Society. Under the impact of these changing viewpoints, a reexamination of the basic terms of the field occurred. The feeling then, as now, was that the term *folklore* could not bear up under the weight of the attention being given to performed traditions. The perception emerged that the confrontation between literary comparatism and the anthropological study of tradition was outdated with regard to the ways questions were formulated. Only the adherence to the words and actions recorded directly from tradition bearers remained to connect the older ways of studying with the new concerns.

Not only were field collecting and theory brought together in new ways, but the very idea of fieldwork became subject to theorizing. Here, of course, Kenny's dissertation and book, *A Guide for Field Workers in Folklore* (1969), provided the center of gravity for the practice for the next generation. Fieldwork was now installed as the *sine qua non* of folklore study as it had been in cultural anthropology and other ethnographic disciplines. This was true not only with the verbal arts but also with the study of material culture, as was demonstrated by Henry Glassie in his *Pattern in the Material Folk Culture of the Eastern United States* (1968). Glassie's work carried the stamp of European folklife notions and the influence of his mentors Don Yoder and the cultural geographers E. Estyn Evans and Fred Kniffen. Both folklore and folklife studies, then, were recognizably after the same range of data, using the same styles of observation and organization, and calling for the same careful attention to the ways in which items of traditional design were collected, arranged, and subjected to theoretical discussion.

The term *folklife,* was brought into play from Europe in the late 1960s out of the synthesis that had taken place at Penn under Kenny's guidance. In conversations held primarily in Washington in 1967–68, academic and public sector folklorists introduced the term into the discussion as a means of suggesting the breadth of interests of the field. The term addressed multiple needs. Using it provided a way of dodging the political opprobrium of the term *folklore* that had developed among politicians. The aversion to folklore among some of those in power arose from the widespread idea that folklore was being carried out by amateurs. Folklore had been tainted because of its use in political propaganda by, among others, Hitler and Stalin. At the very moment when Penn was changing the name of its program to Folklore and Folklife, because Don Yoder had joined the program, the Smithsonian Institution was developing the Festival of American Folklife, soon to be followed by the creation of the American Folklife Center at the Library of Congress. Throughout, the impact of Kenny and his colleagues Don Yoder and Henry Glassie on the thinking of those instigating the federal presence—Ralph Rinzler, Archie Green, and others—must not be overlooked.

These various strands came together in the idea that folklorists of the future must concern themselves with the creative dimension of individuals who reveal themselves as operating within specific traditions as observed in particular cultural milieux. These practices would be approached as organic phenomena expressive of the human creative response to group life. The stuff folklorists studied, then, were items that called attention to themselves because they carried the stamp of tradition through their stylization and usage in particular social circumstances—they communicated messages between makers and users, performers and audience. Arguments for the distinctiveness of *folklife* in any realm depended on the ways in which expressive and material traditions operated in counterpoint to both official or mass-produced forms.

At this point the fieldwork revolution was completed to all intents and purposes, or at least it was domesticated and made a part of the routine of practicing as a folklorist. It owed its genesis and development to the individual whom we honor in these pages. Let me record my gratitude, and that of the profession as a whole, to Kenneth S. Goldstein, the collector, the organizer, the man.

Notes

When I began this article, I wanted to weigh the contributions of Kenneth S. Goldstein in the history of folklore study and presentation in the thirty-some years he has been in the profession. The bulk of these remarks were prepared for presentation at the 1992 annual meeting of the American Folklore Society in Jacksonville, Florida, at which the first draft of this festschrift was presented to Kenny. They were made as part of the survey of the profession over the past twenty-five years. Some of these papers, including a revision of my remarks, have been published in a special issue of *Western Folklore,* edited by Amy Shuman and Charles Briggs (1993). A few of the sentences, even paragraphs, from that essay are repeated here, now in an entirely altered context.

1. The document that most fully reviewed the question of memorial transmission was the introduction to Tristram Potter Coffin's *The British Traditional Ballad in North America* (1950; rev. ed. 1963). Ruth Finnegan's book, *Oral Poetry: Its Nature, Significance and Social Context* (1977), provided an excellent survey of all of the issues surrounding memorial transmission and oral-formulaic composition, a controversy that was not waged by the folklorists featured in the present argument, but by those arguing for or against the Parry-Lord hypothesis concerning epic composition.

2. The development of folk festivals that brought together traditional performers on the same stage as folk-revival singers became common during the early 1960s because so many of the traditional singers were brought to national attention through commercial recordings. These were anticipated by folk festivals in the 1930s that involved a similar congeries such as the National Folk Festival, first held in Nashville in 1935. See here David Whisnant, *All That is Native and Fine: The Politics of Culture in an American Region* (1983:245), and Archie Green, "The National Folk Festival Association" (1975).

3. Here the historical portrayal of American folkloristics put forward by Alan Dundes and his student Rosemary Levy Zumwalt, which describes a conflict between the anthropological and the literary approaches to folklore, is primarily an exercise in academic politics concerning the relative weight given members of anthropology or literature faculties in carrying out the business of the American Folklore Society and its publications. But, as both Dundes and Zumwalt recognize, the academic folklorists, no matter their departmental affiliations, were essentially comparatists. The primary guardians of the romantic nationalist perspective in its American formulation were belletrists, journalists, or the leaders of the local folklore societies who were involved in collecting folksongs and ballads. See Rosemary Levy Zumwalt, *American Folklore Scholarship: A Dialogue of Dissent* (1988), and D. K. Wilgus, *Anglo-American Folksong Scholarship Since 1898* (1959).

4. Thompson's choices for his successor did not include Dorson. He preferred the Europeans Kurt Ranke and Reidar Christiansen, but they declined to stand for the position, as did the Germanist Wayland Hand. Dorson, conscious of Thompson's attitude, did as much

as he could under the circumstances to allay the latter's fears that Indiana's international comparatism would disintegrate when he assumed the chair. Dorson, to that point severely American in his interests, by force of will (and he had a lot of that) became an internationalist, pursuing area studies interests on the Americanist model throughout the world. Through the assistance of the Ford Foundation, he was able to bring scholars from all over the world to get advanced degrees at Indiana. He himself arranged significant professional encounters with Japanese, English, Yugoslavian, and Latin American scholars, in addition to editing the great Folktales of the World series for the University of Chicago Press. He once told me that he would feel the complete folklorist when he could edit a collection for that series of the folktales of every existing country.

5. For an assessment of Dorson's career and impact, see the special issue of *Journal of Folklore Research* edited by Robert Georges (1989). For an overview of his career in relation to public sector folklore, see my article "The Public, the Folklorist, and the Public Folklorist" (1992).

6. This breakthrough was not Leach's alone. The field research of Milman Parry and Albert Lord brought about a rereading of Homer and a rethinking of epic compositional technique during this period as well. Lord's *The Singer of Tales* (1960) was as avidly read and discussed in folklore as in other disciplines.

7. The European concept of *folklorismus,* which does not carry the same political charge to it, has come into use instead in discussions of how traditions may be manipulated for official purposes by government or the commercial sector. See here Regina Bendix (1988). Dorson's student Alan Dundes has written a definitive piece, entitled "The Fabrication of Folklore" (1989:40–56), on the failure of the concept to distinguish between accepted folklore classics and manufactured lore.

References

Abrahams, Roger D.
  1992 The Public, the Folklorist, and the Public Folklorist. In *Public Folklore*. Eds. Robert Baron and Nicholas R. Spitzer. Washington, D.C.: Smithsonian Institution Press. Pp. 17–27.

Ben-Amos, Dan, and Kenneth S. Goldstein, eds.
  1975 *Folklore: Performance and Communication.* The Hague: Mouton.

Bendix, Regina
  1988 Folklorism: The Challenge of a Concept. *International Folklore Review: Folklore Studies from Overseas* 6:5–15.

Briggs, Charles, and Amy Shuman, eds.
  1993 *Theorizing Folklore: Toward New Perspectives on the Politics of Culture.* Special issue of *Western Folklore* 52:109–400.

Coffin, Tristram Potter
  1950 *The British Traditional Ballad in North America.* Rev. ed. Philadelphia: American Folklore Society, 1963.

Dundes, Alan
  1989 The Fabrication of Folklore. In *Folklore Matters.* Knoxville: Univ. of Tennessee Press. Pp. 40–56.

Finnegan, Ruth
  1977 *Oral Poetry: Its Nature, Significance and Social Context.* Cambridge: Cambridge Univ. Press.

Georges, Robert, ed.
   1989   *Richard M. Dorson's Views and Works: An Assessment.* Special issue of *Journal of Folklore Research* 26:1–80.
Glassie, Henry
   1968   *Pattern in the Material Folk Culture of the Eastern United States.* Philadelphia: Univ. of Pennsylvania Press.
Goldstein, Kenneth S.
   1964   *A Guide for Field Workers in Folklore.* Hatboro, Pa.: Folklore Associates.
   1966   The Induced Natural Context: An Ethnographic Folklore Field Technique. In *Essays on the Verbal and Visual Arts.* Ed. June Helm. Seattle: Univ. of Washington Press. Pp. 1–6.
   1971   On the Application of the Concepts of Active and Inactive Traditions to the Study of Repertory. *Journal of American Folklore* 84:62–67. Also in Paredes and Bauman (1972:62–67).
Green, Archie
   1975   The National Folk Festival Association. *John Edwards Memorial Foundation Newsletter* 9:23–25.
Lord, Albert B.
   1960   *The Singer of Tales.* Cambridge, Mass.: Harvard Univ. Press.
Paredes, Americo, and Richard Bauman, eds.
   1972   *Toward New Perspectives in Folklore.* Austin: Univ. of Texas Press.
Utley, Francis Lee
   1961   Folk Literature: An Operational Definition. *Journal of American Folklore* 74:193–206.
Whisnant, David
   1983   *All That Is Native and Fine: The Politics of Culture in an American Region.* Chapel Hill: Univ. of North Carolina Press.
Wilgus, D. K.
   1959   *Anglo-American Folksong Scholarship Since 1898.* New Brunswick: Rutgers Univ. Press.
Zumwalt, Rosemary Levy
   1988   *American Folklore Scholarship: A Dialogue of Dissent.* Bloomington: Indiana Univ. Press.

"INDUCED NATURAL CONTEXT" IN CONTEXT

Dan Ben-Amos

FOLKLORE STUDENTS of several generations have grown up on Kenneth Goldstein's *A Guide for Field Workers in Folklore* (1964). When they prepared to go into the field, they used his *Guide*, and they consulted it again when they arrived there. His cogent advice followed them, tucked conveniently in their pocket or pocketbook, reassuring them in doubt and offering solutions in uncertain situations. In the loneliness of the field, the *Guide* became a companion to which researchers turned in crisis and in joy. Make "safety copies of all recordings and notes" (p. 143), Goldstein's sound advice followed them wherever they went. If pay an informant you must, consider it as a gesture of "good will and friendship" rather than "a payment of incentive" (p. 170); and for your own sake stay away from any "hostile factionalism" that is inevitably present in any community (p. 73).

When the *Guide* first appeared, one reviewer welcomed it as "an attempt to bring together ideas, suggestions, and theoretical statements which reflect a needed cross-disciplinary point of view," and "highly recommended" it as "stimulating and provocative" (Black 1966:353). Another hailed it as an "excellent field manual" that "is designed to make [the field work] experience . . . much richer," noting his "praiseworthy ethnographic bias" (Dundes 1965:547). And in the *Journal of American Folklore,* Arthur J. Rubel emphasized the significance of the book for anthropologists: "It reflects current anthropological interest in cultural cognitive systems" (1965:359). Almost thirty years later in a book devoted solely to research and method in oral traditions and the verbal arts, in the midst of a list consisting of the the most recent books in the field, Ruth Finnegan mentions Goldstein's *Guide* and comments parenthetically that it "is still useful despite its date" (1992:57). Later she points out that his "categories of 'natural', artificial', and 'induced natural' contexts . . . can be criticized and extended, but are still extremely illuminating distinctions to start from" (1992:76).

Both reviewers and casual commentators singled out the *Guide's* contribution to the practice of fieldwork in folklore. They welcomed its interdisciplinary nature. However, in the hindsight that thirty years may provide, it appears that they failed to fully apprehend the range of Goldstein's disciplinary borrowing. In most cases they have been misled by Goldstein's own explicit statements, focussing on his synthesis between methods in folklore and anthropology. A closer reading, however, reveals another discipline looming right behind these two academic siblings in the study of culture. Its presence becomes apparent in Goldstein's casual statements, anecdotal examples, and formal methodological concepts. Consequently, in practice and in purpose, the *Guide's* contribution to folklore extends far beyond fieldwork, implicitly proposing a research direction that was new at the time of its publication. Since Goldstein himself has hardly pursued this direction systematically, and since others have not joined him with sufficient vigor to form a scholarly trend, the novelty of this direction has not worn off and its promise awaits fulfillment.

Goldstein alluded to the rudiments of such a research direction in his *Guide*. At the same time he clouded them with some ambiguity and a certain degree of duality of purpose inherent in the book that has obscured his ultimate vision of folklore. Every guide book or manual has by definition an ideal addressee. A tourist guide's readership is self explanatory; a sex manual aims at the inexperienced, unimaginative, or simply bored lover. Goldstein wrote his book for the consummate folklore collector: "He is the most important element in the scholarship of folklore" (p. 2), because all further "evaluation, interpretation and analysis" (p. 2) are dependent upon the materials the collector harvests in the field. For Goldstein, folklore collecting is the ultimate scholarly experience, and although he realizes that its enjoyment depends on temperament, he implicitly hoped that the book would make all folklorists of varying persuasions converts to collecting. Realistically yet optimistically he states:

> This book cannot make a folklorist a collector. A methodology is only one of the requirements for successful collecting. More important is the individual who would become a collector. If he does not have the inclination, temperament, or personality for collecting, he will not become a successful field worker merely by using the methods and techniques given here. While it is true that his inclination can be changed by inspired instruction, temperament and personality go so much deeper that it is unlikely that they could sufficiently affected. Still, any one is capable of doing a certain amount of collecting, though not in the "field." One can collect from family, friends, and neighbors, and to such collectors the basic requirements for obtaining data will apply as much as they do to qualified field workers. (p. 9)

Goldstein's message filters through the conditionals, the "if," the "while," and the "still": collecting folklore itself will be an inspirational experience. Although he knows otherwise, the initial negative statement that opens the quoted paragraph transforms at the conclusion into an expectation that all folklorists will discover the joy of collecting. The "collector" is both the main protagonist and the addressee of the *Guide*. Goldstein advises him; evaluates his action; places him in real, fictive, or hypothetical situations; rescues him out of complex relationships; and weaves both story and theory around his personality.

At the same time Goldstein cast his ideal collector in another role—that of a scientist. He prepared the *Guide* out of "a concern with the status of the discipline of folklore. It is part of a larger effort to raise the discipline to the level of a science (a social science retaining close ties with the humanities, to be sure)" (p. 13). The *Guide* would clearly spell out the principles for adequate description of folklore processes:"Such documentation, which is essential if folklore is to achieve scientific status, can be supplied only by trained professional folklorists guided by a body of theory, or by amateurs trained by such professionals" (p. 14). In short, Goldstein's collector has a dual mission: not only does he have to save folksongs, folktales, proverbs, riddles, and customs from real or alleged oblivion, but he has to conduct his rescue operation along scientific principles.

According to the views that dominated folklore research up to the forties and the fifties, lagging behind other disciplines in the social sciences, there was a clear distinction between collecting, which still had to be accurate and detailed to have any value, and analysis, which ensued as the scientific research stage, involving primarily type classification and motif identification. Such a division is clearly apparent in the discussions in a mid-forties conference (Anon. 1946), and in a set of four mid-century symposia (Thompson 1953) from which Goldstein quotes, and in several studies to which he refers (Addy 1902; Burne 1902; Crooke 1902; Dorson 1953, 1957a, 1957b, 1964:1–20; Dundes 1962; Grainger 1908; Jones 1946; Leach 1962; Lindgren 1939; Opie 1953; Seligmann 1902; Skeat 1902).

However, for Goldstein these two roles were inseparable. He recognized that the scientific process began in the field and before, and could not be delayed until the material reached the archive. The formulation of the research problem, the selection of informants, the questions posed to them, and the context of collecting all have direct bearing on any procedures to which a subsequent scientist would subject the collection. Goldstein thus removed the scientific work in folklore from the desk to the field. Goldstein would have agreed with his contemporary, the philosopher of science Norwood R. Hanson, who, in the course of discussing another discipline, point out that "by the time a law has been fixed into an [hypothetico-deductive] system, really original physical thinking is over" (Hanson 1969:70).

But where could Goldstein find the necessary models for such a conception of the collector as a scientist, for they were absent from folklore scholarship? MacEdward Leach, Goldstein's mentor, wrote about the problems of collecting oral literature (1962), but he defined his issues in historical, not scientific, terms, assessing, among other things, the impact of the collector's historical assumptions concerning the origin of folklore in a specific region on the data that he recorded (quoted in Goldstein 1964:19). Anthropology, with its emphasis on the exotic, could have been helpful, but not sufficiently so, particularly since Goldstein is emphatic that his *Guide* would serve the fieldworker in "essentially rural, agriculturally-based, non-industrial communities" (p. 10), and he has taken a guarded attitude towards "its application to non-folk, aboriginal, non- or pre-literate areas of the world" (p.10). In short, Goldstein requires of his fieldworker to act in the dual roles of collector and scientist, yet at the same time he is rather vague about the models of scientific folklore toward which he aspires.

Yet, although Goldstein did not articulate his sources of scientific inspiration, his *Guide* provides some preliminary clues, which he amplified in some of his later works. In his introductory presentation to his book, Goldstein states: "The *Guide* is based on collecting experiences and experiments conducted in "folk" communities" (p. 10). Now, Goldstein's prose is rarely alliterative, and the phrase "experiences and experiments" immediately stands out. Historically, folklore has not been an experimental science. Occasionally some field workers came upon experimental situations serendipitously—a classic case is the Zuni rendition of the Italian version of "the Cock and the Mouse" (Tale Type 2032, "The Cock's Whiskers") that Frank Hamilton Cushing told them and a year later recorded as a native Zuni tale (Cushing 1901:411–22; reprinted in Dundes 1965: 269–76; see Cushing 1979, 1990). The few occasions in which experimentation has been used in folklore deliberately occurred when psychologists applied their trade to tales and songs (Bartlett 1920, 1932), or when folklorists sought to confirm or refute the role of memory in oral transmission (see Dundes 1965:246–47).

Therefore, the apparently casual use of the term "experiments" is deliberate and symptomatic, indicating some notions Goldstein had in mind but did not make sufficiently explicit, and revealing his orientation toward experimental psychology. Indeed he clearly lists books in "the fields of psychology" (p. xiii) among the works that he read in preparing his *Guide,* and he defers to psychology as the only field in which he feels a lack of competence, yet recognizes its import to his scientific field work. He states:

> The present work does not include methods requiring special training and techniques, such as psychological or projective tests designed to obtain information about personality functioning. When a revised edition of this book is made, it should include one or more chapters on such techniques by persons properly qualified to instruct in them. (p. 11)

Until Albert Lord had fully developed Perry's formulaic theory (1960), memory had been thought to have a central role in oral transmission, and hence experiments concerning the remembrance of things past seemed to test the central process of oral transmission. But Goldstein wished to extend the role of experimentation in folklore to other area, such as creativity, rise and decline of tradition, aesthetic principles, and the role of the individual in the formation and continuation of tradition. For him the field was for the folklorist what the laboratory for the psychologist. While he glorified collecting, his *Guide* put an equal emphasis on experimentation with oral tradition. In that sense Goldstein was a proponent of experimental folklore. In a later study that resulted directly from his fieldwork "experiences and experiments" in Scotland Goldstein specifically cast the scientific procedures of folklore in these terms. His essay "Experimental Folklore: Laboratory vs. Field" (1967) not only set up a pair of opposition that had been crucial to his conception of folklore, but actually named as "experimental folklore" the direction that he implicitly outlined for the discipline in his *Guide*.

From such a perspective, the *Guide* is not just a handbook for fieldwork, but a proposition for the construction of folklore on the basis of experimental principles. Goldstein prefers the kind of scientific psychological methodology that develops and confirms knowledge through experiments. He tends to formulate folklore as a positivistic science, and in spite of his academic background in statistics, he does not select analytical models from sociology, in which quantitative statistical analysis has provided the positivistic scientific basis, but rather turns to psychology—and specifically cognitive psychology—as the more appropriate and more relevant model for the science of folklore.

Some European folklorists—Wesselski (1931:127–31), Anderson (1951), and Ortutay (see Anderson 1956:5–6)—preceded Goldstein in conducting experiments in folklore. While he acknowledged and criticized them (1967:73), it is necessary to point out a major difference between Goldstein's experimental folklore and the experiments that preceded him. Anderson, Wesselski, and even Ortutay conducted their experiments within the framework of the historic-geographic method. The first sought to confirm, and the second to falsify, the theory of oral diffusion of narratives. Memory, forgetfullness, and narrative re-creation have been some of the core concepts of a diffusion theory that presupposes exclusive reliance on oral transmission. Therefore, when Anderson sought to validate such a theory he considered it necessary to confirm the reliability of memory in narrative recall. In contrast, Wesselski, who considered print to be the stabilizing factor in folktale transmission, set out to demonstrate the unreliability of memory.

But Goldstein took a completely different path of research. He was not so much concerned with the diffusions of tales or songs, nor with the possibility of the dependence of this process exclusively on oral means, memory, and recall. Rather, he sought to examine experimentally the dynamics of folklore in society. For Goldstein folklore is a science of social and verbal interaction. To be sure, memory, recall, and verbal creativity are part of his concerns, but he regards them as significant processes in and of themselves and not as instruments in the diffusion of texts. Furthermore, the folklorists and the psychologists before him experimented with folklore in situations that were analogous to the psychological laboratory, whereas Goldstein has preferred the natural context of folklore performance in society. For him, this was the only context in which experiments could be valid. In spite of Goldstein's personal and emotional attitude toward field collecting and his many singer-friends, he conceives of the field as the science laboratory of folklore, and his "natural context" as the ideal situation for experimental folklore.

Significantly, Goldstein illustrated his typology of contexts (pp. 80–87) with only two specific examples. The first of them, which involves an experiment, concerns the question of recall:

> For many informants the loss of situational familiarity and meaning is so great that they cannot perform effectively. One of my informants in northeastern Scotland could not recall his songs in an artificial context. Outside of his shoe repair shop he felt lost when attempting to sing his songs. I brought him his shoe-mending equipment and asked him to fix my shoes and sing his songs. The attempt was a failure. I took him at his word when he told me: "If you come tae me shop, I'll fairly fill yer tape wi' song while I mend yer sheen there." In the natural context of singing while working in his own shop, he performed some thirty ballads without pause, hesitation, or memory loss; in the artificial context I was able to garner only imperfect and fragmentary texts and tunes. Needless to say, the only meaningful observations of his performance style worth reporting would be those made in the natural context of his shop. (p. 85)

The second example, in which Goldstein addresses the impact of natural context on the singing style of another Scottish informant, illustrates his division between the roles of scientist and collector that a field worker may have. "My duty," Goldstein states "obviously, is to describe her performance styles as observed in natural context; the artificial context was valuable only for obtaining the texts and tunes of the material themselves" (pp. 86–87). The scientist, in other words, must conduct his observations and experiments in the natural state of folklore; for the collector, on the other hand, the artificial context may do.

When natural context is unobservable, the experimental scientist can resort to the manipulation of situations and induce the natural context (Goldstein 1964:87–90; 1968). Logically, the concept "induced natural context" is an oxymoron. "Induced" labor, as many mothers know, is no longer natural, even if it is distinct from some more radical medical interventions. But in the context of experimental folklore the concept makes sense. It is an experimental situation in which the field worker, as scientist, manipulates his informant, causing harm to none, in order to simulate a situation that takes place in society without the field worker's presence. It is a collecting situation that is natural and in which the collector minimizes his presence so as to minimize, in turn, his influence on the data to be collected.

Ruth Finnegan, who is sensitive to the ethical issue of "covert" actions by a field worker, finds it a valuable concept and method. She writes:

> But there is also a variety of "natural induced" contexts in which the performers know their performances are being recorded but do not find performing in this kind of situation strange. Thus researchers sometimes exploit local conventions by inviting a praise singer to perform at a party,

contributing towards the cost of putting on a memorial ceremony, or acting as host for a regular session of riddling and story-telling, whilst not concealing the presence of a tape-recorder in the background (often ignored). Since, after all, performances regularly depend on the instigation of groups and individuals it may not seem unnatural for the researcher to take and overt role. Such settings clearly have some advantages over fully "natural" contexts. Merely waiting around hopefully may mean never having access to certain genres or events. The practice of induced settings may even be a locally recognized one, as in putting on displays for a visitor or for special occasions. Compared to "artificial" settings, "induced" performances may be closer to the normal interactions, particularly if involving an audience—often important for performance. (Finnegan 1992:80–81)

Goldstein himself offers two examples of 'induced natural context' taken from his own "experiences and experiments":

Having found out what the normal context for riddling was in northeastern Scotland, I invited six of my informants over for a social evening on Saturday night. When the moment seemed appropriate, I led the conversation in the directions of riddles and posed one that I had heard from an informant who was not present. I then took the role of a participant observer and was able to study the situation in depth during the two hours that the riddling session went on. In the meantime, my wife sat in the background and made notes on each of the riddles posed. Since there was usually five or six minutes [break] between the time when a riddle was recited and the answer was given, she had sufficient time to write out each riddle and indicate the name of the poser. I made notes on my observations of the riddling context immediately after my informant friends left the house later that evening. By playing the role of the instigator, I was able to hide the real purpose of the evening from every one of the other participants, thereby assuring a more natural context.

I have also been able to avoid using accomplices from among the folk by having a member of my own family play that role on certain occasions. Wishing to observe marbles games in action as played by the children in the neighborhood, I had one of my daughters bring several of her schoolmates to our home so that I could observe them while they played on our rear lawn. Generally, such games were never played in the presence of adults because most of the home owners on the block were angered by the children digging holes in their lawns in order to play their marbles games. My daughter introduced her friends to me and asked if it was all right to play marbles. After I gave my permission, my daughter dug the hole for the game about 15 feet from where I was sitting (according to a pre-arranged plan), so that the game would be in full view to me. I busied myself pretending to be writing letters, but actually was taking notes on the situation. (Pp. 89–90)

The natural and the induced natural contexts are methodological concepts in Goldstein's experimental folklore. Yet a method without a theory is like a play—actions without a purpose that have no consequences. What, then, are the theoretical foundations of the science of folklore that Goldstein builds in his *Guide?* Having broken with the diffusion theory of folklore that the historic-geographic school addressed, and not having embraced the literary-historical approach that his mentor, MacEdward Leach, taught, Kenneth Goldstein set in his *Guide* the foundations for a new folklore theory, a theory of cognitive folklore. Goldstein's theory of cognitive folklore seeks, in a sociological-psychological and interactional tradition, to infer from human actions how people process their traditions in their minds and how they apply these traditions in their daily lives and culturally defined specific occasions and social events. While the *Guide* reflects a certain degree of preoccupation with the adequacy of documentation as a basis for the formation of folklore as a science, the details Goldstein asks his fieldworkers to note indicate his goal of establishing folklore as a social science that deals with psychological issues of tradition. 'Natural' and 'induced natural' contexts are the only situations that will yield reliable scientific observations having any value toward the formulation of a theory of cognitive folklore. While such a theory may, in the final analysis, offer some universal principles, Goldstein conceives of human cognition as cultural dependent and situationally conditioned. Therefore it is necessary to observe traditional performances and actions within their cultural and situational contexts. His *Guide* spells out the basic requirements for scientific observation, documentation, and experimentation that would establish cognitive folklore as a social science.

References

Addy, S. O.
    1902   The Collection of Folklore. *Folk-Lore* 13:297–99.
Anderson, Walter
    1951   *Ein volkskundliches Experiment.* Folklore Fellows Communication, vol. 141. Helsinki: Soumalainen Tiedeakatemia.
    1956   *Eine neue Arbeit zur Experimentellen Volkskunde.* Folklore Fellows Communication, vol. 168. Helsinki: Soumalainen Tiedeakatemia.
Anonymous
    1946   Conference on the Character and State of Studies in Folklore. *Journal of American Folklore* 59:495–527.
Black, Robert A.
    1966   Review of *A Guide for Field Workers in Folklore,* by Kenneth S. Goldstein. *Ethnomusicology* 10:352–53.
Burne, Charles S.
    1902   The Collection of Folklore. *Folk-Lore* 13:299–302.
Crooke, William
    1902   The Collection of Folklore. *Folk-Lore* 13:302–7.
Cushing, Frank H.
    1901   *Zuni Folk Tales.* New York: G. P. Putnam's Sons.

1979 *Zuni: Selected Writings of Frank Hamilton Cushing.* Ed. Jesse Green. Lincoln: Univ.of Nebraska Press.

1990 *Cushing at Zuni: The Correspondence and Journals of Frank Hamilton Cushing, 1879–1884.* Ed. Jesse Green. Albuquerque: Univ.of New Mexico Press.

Dorson, Richard M.

1953 Collecting in County Kerry. *Journal of American Folklore* 66:19–42

1957a Standards for Collecting and Publishing American Folktales. *Journal of American Folklore* 70:53–57.

1957b Collecting Folklore in Jonesport, Maine. *Proceedings of the American Philosophical Society* 101:270–89.

1964 *Buying the Wind.* Chicago: Univ. of Chicago Press.

Dundes, Alan

1965 Review of *A Guide for Field Workers in Folklore. American Anthropologist* 67:546–47.

Finnegan, Ruth

1992 *Oral Traditions and the Verbal Arts: A Guide to Research Practices.* London and New York: Routledge.

Goldstein, Kenneth S.

1964 *A Guide for Field Workers in Folklore.* Memoirs of the American Folklore Society, vol. 52. Hatboro, Pa.: Folklore Associates.

1967 Experimental Folklore: Laboratory vs. Field. In *Folklore International: Essays in Traditional Literature, Belief, and Custom in Honor of Wayland Debs Hand.* Eds. D. K. Wilgus and Carol Sommer. Hatboro, Pa.: Folklore Associates. Pp. 71–82.

1968 The Induced Natural Context: An Ethnographic Folklore Field Technique. In *Essays on the Verbal and Visual Arts: Proceedings of the 1966 Annual Spring Meeting of the American Ethnological Society.* Ed. June Helm. Seattle: American Ethnological Society. Pp. 1–6.

Grainger, Percy

1908 Collecting with the Phonograph. *Journal of the Folk-song Society* 3:147–62.

Hanson, Norwood R.

1969 *Patterns of Discovery: An Inquiry into the Conceptual Foundations of Science.* Cambridge: Cambridge Univ. Press.

Jones, Louis C.

1946 A Student Guide to Collecting Folklore. *New York Folklore Quarterly* 2:148–53.

Lindgren, Ethel J.

1939 The Collection and Analysis of Folk-Lore. In *The Study of Society: Methods and Problems.* Eds. F. Bartlett *et al.* London: Routledge & Kegan Paul. Pp. 328–78.

Lord, Albert

1960. *The Singer of Tales.* Cambridge, Mass.: Harvard Univ. Press.

Opie, Peter

1953. The Collection of Folklore in England. *Journal of the Royal Society* 101:697–714.

Rubel, Arthur J.

1965. Review of *A Guide for Field Workers in Folklore. Journal of American Folklore* 78:359–60.

Seligmann, Charles G.

1902. The Collection of Folklore in England. *Folk-Lore* 13:310–12.

Skeat, W.
  1902. The Collection of Folklore. *Folk-Lore* 13:307–10.
Wesselski, Albert
  1931. *Versuch einer Theorie des Märchens*. Reichenberg, i.B.: F. Kraus.

MORE ON "MARY HAMILTON"

Tristram Potter Coffin

THE TRADITION of the song "Mary Hamilton" has been subjected to a great number of articles and a great deal of speculation. Starting with Charles K. Sharpe in the early nineteenth century, through such distinguished scholars as Andrew Lang, Francis James Child, and Albert H. Tolman, down to Carlos Drake summing things up in the 1969 *Southern Folklore Quarterly,* there have been attempts to pinpoint the age of the ballad, the origin of the story, and the relationship of the lyric "last nicht" stanzas to the full song.[1] Still, in spite of all the writing, few conclusions have been drawn.

The consensus is that the "Mary Hamilton" ballad (Child 173) is an eighteenth-century remodelling of a sixteenth-century Scottish broadside about the court of Mary of Scotland. Without real evidence, common sense has proclaimed that after a 1719 scandal at the court of Peter the Great news of a Scottish lady-in-waiting's transgressions with an aide-de-camp, Ivan Orloff, travelled from St. Petersburg to Edinburgh where it was fitted to a similar circumstance concerning long-ago goings on at Holyrood.

Capitalizing on an up-to-date scandal by superimposing it on an older ballad was certainly the way of the shops. No one will argue with that. But at this point, everyone has pretty much given up. I, for one, do not feel that matters have been examined in an imaginative, much less exhaustive, fashion. Further speculation on Child 173 is in order.

The background of the ballad ultimately involves the tragic, complex story of Mary, Queen of Scots.[2] Named to the throne when six weeks old, she was sent to the French court when five and married the future Francis II of France at sixteen. Widowed just after Francis assumed the throne, she returned in 1561 to Scotland, stressing her not insignificant claims on the English crown of her cousin, Elizabeth.

Naive and strongly Catholic, she was immediately embroiled in Protestant resentments (especially those of John Knox), various struggles for control of the court, and the machinations of Elizabeth's advisers who feared both Mary and her Papish leanings. Eventually, a marriage between Mary and an English Catholic, Henry Stewart or Stuart, Lord Darnley, was engineered, certainly with Elizabeth's consent; and it is ironic (or should one say appropriate) that the son of Darnley and Mary was to succeed Elizabeth.

It is important to know that the handsome Darnley became almost immediately *de trop* as a husband. Machiavellian, a wencher (if charming), involved in the murder of Mary's confidante, David Riccio, he was himself murdered after a botched explosion plot that most historians believe Mary knew about. After Darnley's death, one of the main instigators of that crime, the ambitious James Hepburn, Earl of Bothwell, literally forced Mary to marry him to the result she entered a further power struggle with her relatives and lords. She lost and foolishly fled to England where she believed Elizabeth would protect a cousin and fellow queen. Elizabeth had her arrested, house imprisoned, and nineteen years later beheaded for scheming to take over the throne. Mary died in 1587.

This unfortunate queen had four maids-in-waiting, each with the name Mary. These young ladies were called "maries," which is an old North Germanic word for maid or virgin applied by the Scots to royal maids-of-honor. The four, as little girls, accompanied the five-and-one-half-year-old Queen to France, which added an additional twist to the double-entendre of the names. Exactly what the symbolism was in having the four maids all named Mary is a matter of dispute. It probably was but a happy whim. On the other hand, it has been pointed out that four Marys ministered to Christ: his mother, Mary mother of James, Mary Magdalene, and Mary of Bethany. At any rate, these four girls were Mary's closest friends growing up at the French court, and they returned to Scotland with her as eligible young ladies.

They were from very good families. Mary Fleming, the prettiest, was a cousin of the Queen, which gave her a certain precedence over the others. She eventually married William Maitland, a powerful political figure at court and a man deeply mixed up in the intrigues involving Darnley and Bothwell. Without going into detail, suffice it to say his role in the events often confused the relationship between Mary Fleming and her Queen.

Mary Beaton of Creich in Fife was from a French family, the Bethunes, who had migrated to Scotland where they reached prominence in court, church, and foreign affairs. A handsome woman, but without Mary Fleming's vivacity, she married Alexander Ogilvy of Boyne. To complicate matters, Ogilvy's real love was Jean Gordon, who made a political marriage to Bothwell and was divorced by him when she got in the way of his plans for Mary. Romantically, years later, after Mary Beaton's death, Jean Gordon and Ogilvy did marry.

Mary Livingston, referred to by John Knox as the lusty, was the lively daughter of the Queen's guardian, Lord Livingston. She was the first of the group to drift away, marrying John Semple or Sempill in March 1565, the year Darnley came north.

Mary Seton was the daughter of Lord Seton of West Niddrie, and her mother had been a French lady-in-waiting. While Mary Seton seems to have had a number of opportunities to marry, for one reason or another she remained chaste and loyal to the Queen, following her into captivity. In 1583, four years before Mary's execution, her health failing, she was allowed to enter a nunnery in Rheims where she lived out her life, surviving at least thirty years beyond the beheading and dying "decrepit and in want," to cite the words of Mary Fleming's son, James Maitland.

There were other maries, some of them named Mary. One, Mary McLeod, a ward of the Duke of Argyll, is mentioned in Sir Walter Scott's *Tales of a Grandfather*. But until time and wedding bells broke up the quartet, the original "four maries" were the inner circle, the intimates.

Child 173 does not seem to concern these four maids, although the names Seton and Beaton are present in the famous "Four Maries" refrain:

> Last nicht there were four Marys,
> This nicht there'll be but three.
> There's Mary Seton and Mary Beaton,
> Mary Carmichael and me.

Fleming and Livingston (with one exception) are dropped. Mary Carmichael has defied all efforts of this and other scholars to identify her. Moreover, as Carmichael or Michael was almost always a Protestant name in Scotland, it seems an unlikely name for any marie. We may never know why she has her steady presence in the song. There is also no record of a Mary Hamilton at the Scottish court, although the Hamiltons were a powerful Catholic family at the time. But the Mary Hamilton or Hambleton who was beheaded in 1719 in St. Petersburg was well-born and from a Russian branch of a Scottish family.

In the ballad, the Scottish Mary Hamilton, a marie, enters into an affair with Mary's consort, "the highest Stewart of all" (i.e., Darnley). A baby results and is cast out a window or set adrift. Mary is caught, accused, tried, and hung, with the Queen an active participant in the apprehension. The king or prince, as he is usually called, suffers no punishment.

Regardless of those who make up the cast in the song, we know at least one court maid did get in well-publicized trouble at Holyrood. In 1563, the puritanical John Knox, who had little use for the Catholic Mary and her French-trained entourage, reported with obvious relish a scandal involving the Queen's apothecary and a foolish French maid-in-waiting:

> In the very time of the General Assembly, there comes to public knowledge a heinous murder committed in the court, yea, not far from the queen's own lap; for a French woman that served in the queen's chamber had played the whore with the queen's own apothecary. The woman conceived and bare a child, whom, with common consent, the father and mother murdered. Yet were the cries of a new-born bairn heard: search was made, the child and mother was both deprehended and so were both the man and the woman damned to be hanged upon the public street of Edinburgh. (Child 3:382)

Later Knox points out that

> Yet was not the court purged of whores and whoredom, which was the

fountain of such enormities; for it is well-known that shame hastyed marriage betwixt John Semple, called the Dancer, and Mary Livingston, surnamed the Lusty. What bruit the Maries and the rest of the dancers of the court had, the ballads of that age did witness, which we for modesty's sake omit. (Child 3:382)

Knox was not fabricating scandal (the event is also reported in the *Calendar of State Papers, Foreign Series, of the Reign of Elizabeth*, 1563). The affair of the French girl and the apothecary is a historical fact, as is another salient point. The young maids at the court (like the pretty Mary Fleming and the lusty Mary Livingston) were being courted and tempted by the various gentlemen present, and broadsheet ballads documenting the excitement were being hawked. Lord Darnley, who was hand picked to court Mary, and who successfully married her, did not arrive in Scotland until February 1565, well after the execution of the apothecary and the French girl and just before the marriage of Mary Livingston. It is unlikely he was ever involved with a marie.

Nonetheless, Darnley was a most prominent man, associated with the killing of Riccio. Killed while fleeing a spectacular explosion in 1567, Darnley also was notorious as a wencher. Legend, like gossip, will gravitate to an appropriate and prominent figure when it can. Thus, it is quite natural that Darnley would enter the story of the compromised court maid. Furthermore, as the apothecary seems to have been referred to as "the highest steward of all," the understanding of that phrase as "the highest Stewart of all" developed. And, of course, that Stewart was the king or prince (i.e., Darnley).

In similar fashion, it seems likely that the seduced French girl would be thought of as one of the four maries. After all, the four maries grew up in France, had known the French court, and so (to the popular mind) were probably easy marks. It was far more interesting that one of the four maries be guilty than just a silly court maid. The evolution of the ballad from one about a scandal involving an apothecary/French girl to one about a Darnley/marie scandal is to be expected. Later, the introduction of the Scottish/Russian Mary Hamilton into the affair calls for little adjustment. Knowing the way the print shops worked, there are no surprises here.

One just about has to believe that the ballad originated in 1563 when the trial of the French girl and the apothecary was going on, and that it was adjusted, perhaps by the shops, perhaps by tradition, to include Darnley and one of the four maries in 1565–67 when "the highest Stewart of all" was in the news. The question then is: do we have any ballads available that trace back beyond 1719 to such broadsides? And the answer may well be yes.

The variants listed in Child as E, F, P, Q, T, U, V, and Y can be called the "Duke of York" variants. Perhaps J should be added. They form a loose group somewhat separate from those opening with the cliche

There lived a lord in the north (west, south)
And he had daughters three.

Except for T (where the opening is also this cliche) and V, they have not had the name Mary Hamilton introduced into them. Two are most interesting: F and U, but especially F, which retains the name Lady Livingston, though the maid's lover is called the trite "Sweet Willie." With the names Seton, Beaton, and Livingston present, it implies the sinning marie to be Mary Fleming. From the Skene Ms. (Child 3:389), the first three stanzas are significant:

> My father was the Duke of York,
> My mother a lady free,
> Mysel a dainty demosell,
> Queen Mary sent for me.

> The queen's meat, it was sae sweet,
> Her clothing was sae rare,
> It made me lang for Sweet Willie's bed,
> And I'll rue it ever maer.

> Mary Beaton and Mary Seton,
> And Lady Livinston three,
> We'll never meet in Queen Mary's bower,
> Now Maries tho ye be.

Stanza 12 reads:

> Get up, Lady Beaton, get up, Lady Seton,
> And Lady Livinstone three,
> An we will on to Edinburgh,
> An try this gay lady.

Nobody, certainly not Darnley, is known to have had an affair with Mary Fleming, though her eventual husband, William Maitland, was enamored of her long before he could marry her. Pretty as she was, she seems to have remained free from scandal. However, as the prettiest marie she is a likely candidate to be the girl who replaced the apothecary's girl in "the news." She was still single in 1565–67, and the print shops had no scruples that might prevent them from linking her loveliness with the notoriously unfaithful king.

Variant U mentions the pottinger (apothecary) as lover, which is historically accurate, but also introduces the name Mary Carmichael:

> Yestreen the queen had four Maries,
> This night she'll hae but three;
> There was Marie Seton, and Marie Beatoun,
> And Marie Carmichael, and me.

> My love he was a pottinger,
> Mony a drink he gae me,
> And a' to put back that bonnie babe,
> But alas! it wad na do.

These are stanzas 12 and 13 from the mouth of Jean Milne as communicated to Sir Walter Scott (Child 4:509).

These two texts, F and U, are probably much like the oldest forms of the song, harking back to the original Edinburgh broadsides. There is no way Mary Livingston's name could replace Mary Carmichael in a text after she married Semple in March 1565, nor is it likely the pottinger would enter the U song after the king, the infamous Darnley, had established himself in it. That would be contrary to all the laws of both gossip and legend.

However, the "Duke of York" variants are scarcely pure. It is quite clear the more modern popularity of the "Mary Hamilton" variants and the lament stanzas have found their way into some of them: for example, stanza 12 of U printed above. Nor is there any explanation of who the Duke of York might be. The lines "My father was the Duke of York, / My mother a qay ladie (ladie free)" imply the girl to be well-born, called to the court at the Queen's request. Mary Fleming (if she is the sinner of the F song) was from a prominent family, that of Lord Fleming. Her father was not a duke, and her mother was the natural daughter of the Earl of Buchan. Certainly, the five-year-old Queen did not request her presence at court. The opening seems a commonplace; the Duke of York, an impressive name. There is nothing to tie this material to the history of the events.

Finally, I believe that the famous "last nicht" lament stanzas are a relatively late interpolation, probably a skillful and polite rewriting of less artistic stanzas such as these from F:

> O had you still, ye burgers' wives,
> An make na meen for me;
> Seek never a grace of a graceless face,
> For they hae nane to gie.

> Ye merchants and ye mariners,
> That trade upon the sea,
> O dinna tell in my country
> The dead I'm gaen to die!

As a "last goodnight," it smacks of the eighteenth century and most likely was composed at the time the name Mary Hamilton was introduced. Usually framed by the repetition of the first stanza at the end, it is literary to say the least and by the nineteenth century was widely known, circulating in a number of songsters. Moreover, Phillips Barry (1929) has shown that given additional, nontraditional lines it was popularized as an Edinburgh broadside and by use as a concert piece at the end of the nineteenth century. As it carries the "emotional core" of the story, it eventually dominates the tradition of the full ballad and is today the form widely encountered (Coffin 1957). The popularity of this lyric (what Barry [1929] calls the "secondary tradition" of the song) undoubtedly accounts for the widespread introduction of the name Mary Hamilton and the inappropriate Protestant name Mary Carmichael throughout the extant texts.

So, it is fair to say some things have been overlooked or looked at too casually in the studies of Child 173. And I am willing to state with reasonable confidence the following:

1) that the song descends directly from the Edinburgh broadsides, and the full ballad is essentially the song of 1563;
2) that Lord Darnley and by implication Mary Fleming were substituted for the apothecary and his French maid-in-waiting long before the ballad was called "Mary Hamilton";
3) that the introduction of Mary Hamilton into the song about 1719 is little more than the introduction of a newsworthy name;
4) that there is a good chance that the "last nicht" lament, with the inappropriate name Mary Carmichael, dates from the texts of the story circulated from 1719 on;
5) that the popularity of this lyric lament enables it to enter most variants and so solidifies the names Hamilton and Carmichael in the circulating texts of the song, even corrupting those that had come down from the sixteenth century and survived in tradition into the eighteenth;
6) and finally, that because the lament carries the "emotional core" of the story, it eventually becomes the dominant form of the ballad, causing almost all other forms to die out.

At least such a history of Child 173 is logical, in keeping with the way the print shops and legendary history work. Given the mists of time, this may be the best one can do—short of revelation!

Notes

1. Bibliography for Child 173 and its history and scholarship can be found by consulting Francis James Child's *The English and Scottish Popular Ballads,* especially 3:379–99; 4:507–15; and 5:298–99 (1882–98); my article "'Mary Hamilton' and the Anglo-American Ballad as an Art Form," which discusses the "emotional core" of the ballad; my *The British Traditional Ballad in North America* (1977); and Carlos Drake, "'Mary Hamilton' in Tradition" (1969).

2. For background about Mary, see Antonia Fraser's *Mary, Queen of Scots* (1969). This is the standard biography and a thorough study.

References

Barry, Phillips, Fannie H. Eckstorm, and Mary Winslow Smythe
    1929   *British Ballads from Maine.* New Haven: Yale Univ. Press.
Child, Francis James
    1882–98   *The English and Scottish Popular Ballads.* 5 vols. Boston and New York: Houghton Mifflin.
Coffin, Tristam Potter
    1957   "Mary Hamilton" and the Anglo-American Ballad as an Art Form. *Journal of American Folklore* 70:208–14.
    1977   *The Traditional Ballad in North America.* Rev. ed., with a Supplement by Roger deV. Renwick. Austin: Univ. of Texas Press.

Drake, Carlos
    1969 "Mary Hamilton" in Tradition. *Southern Folklore Quarterly* 23:39–47.
Fraser, Antonia
    1969 *Mary, Queen of Scots.* London: Weidenfeld and Nicolson.

AT WORK IN BURSA

Henry Glassie

KENNETH S. GOLDSTEIN is the author of one of the few books essential to the folklorist's art. In English it is *A Guide for Field Workers in Folklore*. In Turkish it is *Sahada Folklor Derleme Metotları,* and one young folklorist from Turkey, Özkul Çobanoğlu, who is working to reshape the discipline in his land, calls it his bible.

I was lucky to be a young folklorist in the days when the American discipline was being reconstructed into the pattern of its current practice. My students hear a simple tale of those days. The revolution in study was created by thinkers who brought the recreational reading of their undergraduate years into their scholarly work. They had read Camus and Sartre, or novels and poems and essays by people who had read them, and the modernist message of existentialism was being naturalized in folklore by 1960. (Scholars in some disciplines have gotten the news so late, so long after the formation of the modern movement by the likes of Joyce, Kandinsky, and Duchamp, that, missing the connection, they are tempted to give the old idea a new name and call it postmodernism.) The philosophers follow the artists, and Jean-Paul Sartre, the philosopher of modernism, said that the essence of existentialism is imagining a world without gods. Adjusted for scholarly consumption, that means imagining a world in which the active agents are not superhuman forces but people like us. The basic idea is responsibility. Once, the makers of folklore could be described as bearers of tradition, trudging under burdens they did not create, and power was attributed to forces beyond them, to history, culture, the economy, the laws of tradition in motion. Comparably, it could once be said that individual scholars had minor, restricted codes within patterns scaled beyond their reach; they could make contributions, but power lay in an abstraction called the discipline. In America, all that was changed utterly by a few thinkers, many with new doctorates in a new discipline, in the middle of the 1960s; to say it exactly, 1964 was the year.

Sandy Ives published a biography of the man who made the songs in 1964, mobilizing humanistic tradition to render full monographic treatment to Larry

Gorman, as though he were Dante or Milton. In 1964, Dell Hymes published two in the series of essays through which he worked valiantly to formulate an idea, consolidated later in *Foundations in Sociolinguistics,* and speakers of language ceased being animals occupied by machinery for grammar making; they became human beings who used innate potentials to communicate, to express themselves and connect with others. The old philosophical problem of will and conditions, the old anthropological problems of structure and function, of culture and action, had solutions. Folklore gained its dominant paradigm, performance, and the carriers of folklore became creators, historical actors.

The people we studied became real, wise and foolish in their own dilemmas. They became like us; we became like them. Scholarly practice was simultaneously marked by responsibility. Sartre argues that disciplines are necessary (as strict workshops are necessary for apprentices) to teach discipline itself, but the person whose mature practice is confined by the discipline is a technician, not an intellectual. The intellectual moves from the discipline into interdisciplinary interaction, and then drives past that phase into a serious, disciplined amateurism, because individual disciplines, the constructs of custom, the casualties of battles over budgets, never stretch to match the wondrous wildness of reality. And by the middle of the 1960s, Alan Dundes had pressed bravely into new interdisciplinary territories. Alan Merriam had brought ethnomusicology into conjunction with anthropology to write the key historical text for modern students of nonwestern music. Once upon a time, it was possible for folkloristic roles to be divided, for some to be hunters and gatherers, for others to be cosmopolitan theorists in lofty castles of knowledge. But in those days, in the middle of the sixties, works by Roger Abrahams and Dan Crowley offered models of responsible integration. Folklorists could be— should be—theorists, interdisciplinary theorists, and fieldworkers too. Fieldwork was more than gathering information to be processed later. It was guided by theory, and the obligation to fieldwork, more than anything else, engendered the power and spirit of the folklorist's discipline in the 1960s. Kenny Goldstein's *Guide,* despite passages he would like to purge, was the inspiration for that crucial and highly productive period in American folklore study.[1]

All this happened when I was lucky and just beginning my training in folklore; the implications of the revolution were becoming clear when I was Kenny Goldstein's student, and the author of a few small articles based on folklore collecting, in 1965. At my first American Folklore Society meeting, I watched as Kenny Goldstein, Alan Dundes, and Roger Abrahams debated in the halls the matter of the definition of folklore. It was like witnessing a heroic struggle from some elder epic, and it surely confirmed my commitment to the study of folklore, begun in childhood, nurtured by recordings of folk music edited by Kenneth S. Goldstein, and given its first shaping in the affectionate hands of the great geographer Fred Kniffen.

There are annual calls in folklore for new theories, as though newness itself held virtue, as though sciences need fashions. But I am convinced that those in the disciplines around us, from whom we are accustomed to borrow new ideas, are only now learning what folklorists, because they were (and are) humanists as well as social scientists, learned nearly thirty years ago, and I am convinced that we do not need new theories. We need to test and modify those we have, and above all, I believe, we need more—and more intense and expansive—fieldwork, more long experience in the reality that theories help us enter, that becomes, once we are there, too big and fine and strange for any ideology. Kenny Goldstein's *Guide,* read with empathy because it is no longer a new book, but a text in our necessary history, remains sturdy enough to get us going, to aid us while we do what we must do, and that is to get on with our work.

For twelve years my work has been in Turkey. I went there by accident, then I learned the language and returned with purpose because Turkey offers excellent ground for an ethnography of art. Art, like culture, society, and history, is a concept that folklorists are obliged to address, with strength gained from empirical pursuit, to prevent thought from closing down around one of the world's many ideas of human worth. Modern Turkey is good for study because fine objects abound; there is no need to tax theory to compensate for weak data. Art is a vital part of common life; objects remain in the hands of their creators who willingly, articulately guide study. The dominant arts are not figurative; the analyst is denied an easy retreat into facile iconography.

My study began in the artisans' district, where things are made and sold on the slope descending to the Golden Horn in İstanbul. It expanded in the city of Kütahya, where one-third of the 120,000 people are involved in the manufacture and sale of an elegant kind of pottery that has been made in the city since the beginning of the sixteenth century. It expanded in the mountain villages of southwestern Çanakkale, where women, two or three together, weave today at a thousand looms the rich carpets for which the region has been famed since the fifteenth century. Bursa, the major city of northwestern Anatolia, was another of my stops, and in homage to Kenny Goldstein, teacher, friend, fieldworker, I offer a fragment of my work in progress, set in the green city of Bursa.

Bursa is built on the hip of Ulu Dağ, the Mount Olympus of antiquity. A beautiful city of more than a million, it was, before Edirne and İstanbul, the Ottoman capital. Modern life still flows around two grand Ottoman monuments. Near the city's center spreads the massive, vast Ulu Cami, built amid a series of military victories to the order of Sultan Beyazit I, called the Thunderbolt. Across a ravine, uphill stands the glittering jewel of early Ottoman architecture, Yeşil Cami, the Green Mosque, built by artists assembled by Beyazit's son, Mehmet I, early in the fifteenth century. Below Ulu Cami, there is the Covered Bazaar, a wide, roofed market for commerce, and below it a district for artisans, for wood turners, coppersmiths, saddlers, and basketmakers, drifts into neighborhoods of pretty, jettied, half-timber houses. Eastward out of the Covered Bazaar, a long street runs by the silk market into a second district for artisans. Past open, smoky shops, through banging and clanging, the street goes toward the little Kayan Camii, where the workmen come to pray and rest.[2]

I will tell you about Bursa by telling you about one intersection just down from Kayan Camii. Next to each other, on one corner, stands a pair of blacksmiths' shops. My work depends on my keeping a notebook in which I write a few things as I go, which becomes a garrulous diary as I fill it each night with the day's detail, not stopping to worry about future use. When I came there first (I know it was December 1, 1984), the masters of the forges were Ahmet Çelikkıran and İbrahim Çıkıkçı. I was always a surprise. Foreigners might get lost and wander through on their stroll from Ulu Cami to Yeşil Cami, but they do not know Turkish, do not stop for long. Language and time are the keys to the experience my diary records. I lingered, and while I watched the work displayed to the street, I fell into conversation with the sons of the old masters, men of about my age who were the heirs apparent, and I can read now what they said to me first.

İbrahim, the son of Ahmet Çelikkıran, said his father did not have a name as great in Bursa, nor so many connections beyond, as his neighbor İbrahim Çı-kıkçı. (Indeed, an axe from the Çıkıkçı forge that I saw for sale in Tahtakale in İstanbul led me to Bursa.) But, İbrahim continued, there was no blacksmith in the world better than his father. Then, stiffening against prejudices that I as a tourist, and therefore wealthy, might hold, he said that the old man, his father, might seem simple, but he was wise. "He knows more than all of us," İbrahim asserted.

Halit, the son of İbrahim Çıkıkçı, paused from his work in the larger forge on the corner and, projecting upon me antiquarianism rather than class preju-dice, told me how the framed shop in which they worked was a piece of real old Ottoman architecture, dating back a century and a half. But the most historical artifact of all, he said with a twinkle, was his own big father. He twitted my interest in history in a warm manner (as it turns out, he shared it), and then the first question he had for me was whether Americans, like Turks, love Mevlana, the great Sufi poet of thirteenth-century Konya. Disappointed with my answer, he shifted the topic, and after a long discussion of American Indian culture, he turned back to the forge, reminding me that Islam is everyone's religion, that all are welcome at the mosque.

I came back often, watching in winter while they made tools for farriers and carpenters, in summer while they made tools for farmers. I watched how work was organized and conducted. The American business might be arranged to maximize profit by operating with a minimum of help, but the Turkish business, restaurant or forge, maximizes power in the form of employees. Each of these small shops contained four men. The workers shifted easily among themselves to fill set roles. The master, the *usta*, Ahmet in one shop, İbrahim in the other, tonged the piece, cherry red, from the forge and placed it over the anvil, directing with his hammer, or his motions, the quick rhythmic blows of his *kalfa*, his journeyman, Recep in one shop, Salih in the other. A third man, the son of the *usta*, İbrahim in one shop, Halit in the other, took on the master's role in his absence, added a third hammer early in the sequence of work, and freed the master to concentrate on creation by handling the commerce when people stopped by the shop. They worked mostly to fill large orders, but retail customers also came to them, here in the middle of the Kayan Blacksmiths'

Halit Çıkıkçı, 1990 (Photograph by the author)

Yakup and Halit Çıkıkçı, 1994 (Photograph by the author)

Market. A fourth man, Kâzım in one shop, Halit's younger brother Yakup in the other, raised a hammer when needed and performed tasks around the edge. Yakup ground blades sharp, did the welding, packaged shipments, and dealt with customers when Halit was leading the banging.

Both shops had a forge in the rear, a curtain of axe heads and adze blades hanging in front. Men from each would wander into the other to borrow tools without a need for a word of request. They were old competitors, neighbors, colleagues, makers of axes, adzes, drawshaves, and gimlets, shovels, hoes, mattocks, and sickles, scrapers for ovens, latches for doors.

I was there often enough to become a small part of life. On a bleak February day, I sat in the cold shop with Halit and Yakup, holding hands, sharing in the grief of their mother's death. I was there often enough to see change. In 1990, both shops had added pneumatic power hammers to help with the rough pounding. Ahmet Çelikkıran was away on the pilgrimage to Mecca. His son, İbrahim, worked as master. İbrahim Çıkıkçı had retired. The shop, formerly Halis Çelik, had been renamed Hacı Oğulları, Sons of the Hacı. Halit was master, but the old master, now remarried and looking wonderfully fit, would wander down during the day, take a seat in the shop and watch. He wore a brilliant white shirt, not the thing for work at the forge, a sure sign of his leisured status, but when a small interesting job would appear—little repairs break the day's rhythm—he could not resist. He would hammer away for a minute in an exhibition of old skill and undiminished strength before taking a seat in the shade, across the street in front of the shop of a maker of stoves, resting to smile in greeting to old comrades, to watch while Halit and Yakup filled a big order of sickles for Trabzon, far away on the Black Sea coast.

Halit told me business was good, but not so good that life had become easy. The explanation for his limited success had nothing to do with fate. I have not found that the Turkish worker's deep faith connects to a concept that might be called fatalism. Fate might be raised in a retrospective account or in a dream of the future, but it does not figure in explanations of daily conditions; it is no check to industrious commitment. Instead, Halit said, the poor were poor because of an economic system controlled by people who rob you, not with a gun, but with a pen. The people who benefit most from the system tell you the economy rewards industry: work hard and you will become wealthy. He works hard. He is not wealthy. But business is good, their quarters seem cramped, and he is planning to move the operation to a suburban location. There they will have wider space for working and easier access to the highways that carry their handmade products throughout Turkey.

In 1994 they were still at work in the old location. I had sent Halit a copy of the small book in Turkish I had prepared to explain my work to those who had helped. I also sent a copy of the large book from which I adapted this paper when Roger Abrahams invited contributions for Kenny Goldstein's festschrift.[3] Early writings on fieldwork stress the difficulties of making contact and recording data. As important is making sure that people receive the results of research; more important—and difficult—than establishing rapport is preserving connections once the work is done, and, a decade after my first visit, I was back in Bursa to thank my friends and catch up. We reminisced, laughed, and hugged, and the workers of the street gathered, Turkish-style, for collective, commemorative photographs.

One night we went home with Halit for dinner. He lives with his wife and children in a wide apartment on the mountainside above the city. We looked through his library of books on Ottoman history, then after a delicious meal of potato soup, salad, and tender lamb, we gathered to watch television. It was the first time I had ever seen a VCR; in my notes I call it a TV you can put tapes in. Halit said it was good because you can borrow video cassettes that are better for family viewing than the shows the stations broadcast. They were married young, and all the children were present, from the daughter, then sixteen, who was born before he went into military service, down to the baby. The film showed lovely pictures of the world, of mountain streams and fields of wild-flowers, of birds and bees and farmers working, of men delivering a load of wood to a poor neighbor. The film's voice said that experience of the world teaches a simple message. All is interdependent. Nature's parts build into a beautiful whole, the whole is God's design, and the message for people is that they should work cooperatively, in peace and love, contributing to unity.

Art is a contribution to unity. It is, said Avni Sefa, the master of a little factory for knitting socks in İstanbul, the sympathy between worldly and divine creative force. The film's message, reinforced by the smiles with which Halit directed me silently to certain passages, organized anecdotes in my mind. I thought of a cab driver in İstanbul who came from the Black Sea region and told me I should not waste time in meditative introspection. I should conduct research, opening my eyes to common experience, and God would be revealed. I thought of an old man in Ulu Cami who came upon me pondering an enormous calligraphic work. He told me that food growing from the ground was proof enough of God's existence. His idea was like Walt Whitman's contention that there is miracle enough in a mouse to stagger sextillions of infidels. It was like the Koran's example of the cow. There is no need to wait for aberrant wonders, for marvels philosophy cannot encompass, science cannot explain. God works through the common goodness of the normal world. That it all fits together through patterns of recurrence and interdependence, I had seen depicted abstractly in the repetitive arrangements of Turkish art, in interlocked stars and buildings compounded of identical bays, and I had seen it enacted by artisans working cooperatively to produce objects to serve others. The things hammered out of daily work at Halit's forge come of interdependence, and they serve interdependence. Working with his mates, collaborating with natural forces, with muscles and heat and refined ores, Halit positions himself within God's design to accomplish God's design.

It is one smooth unity, a perfect fusion of parts. Halit stands in the glow. An axe head lies buried in the coals. He waits, motionless, resting, then quickly drives the tongs into the fire and in one silky gesture pulls the work to the anvil. Salih and Yakup stand ready, sledge hammers raised. They pivot from the bottom hand, swing from the top, hammering down, one after the other. Quick while the piece is hot, rhythmically to coordinate their speed, Salih then Yakup bang down to the tempo that Halit sets as he shifts the axe head over the anvil. There is no pausing, no time or energy wasted. Every motion is swift, practiced, efficient, sure. Halit shifts, one hammer falls, then another, he shifts, the hammers fall, click, bang, bang, a steady rhythm of three beats repeats, unifying them as they crouch and swing around the anvil. The piece is exposed and hit and hit, flipped and hit, then cooling it is thrust back in the coals. Yakup returns to other work, ready to intercept customers. Salih stands until Halit pulls the axe head over the anvil again. This time, while he steadies the work with the tongs, Halit places upon it a blunt, flat hammer while Salih lowers his sledge. Through a smooth series, the small hammer is set, the big one bangs down: set and hit, set and hit, the hammers move over the faces of the axe and bevel the edge. It returns to the fire. They wait. Again it appears and Salih lowers the sledge onto the tool Halit places, first a pointed hammer to perfect the shape, then hammers that stamp the trademark and a series of decorative motifs on the axe face. The eye is stretched with a series of blows and checked for symmetry. The piece returns to the fire. When it reappears, Halit works alone, bouncing a small hammer over the steaming head, checking to be sure it rings true, hammering to sharpen the edge. Then he drops it into a bucket of water. The sizzling ceases, and soon the axe head lies on the ground, purple and black, rose and blue, waiting to be sharpened on the electric wheel.

Three men blend in the process directed by the master, required by creation. A single hierarchical order unifies their interaction. The process has four steps, marked by time in the fire. The first uses three men, the next two use two, the fourth is the master's solo moment for checking and refinement. The process is confined by physical laws and driven by the wish to make a strong and useful tool, but its third step is ruled by taste. At this point, overall form is perfected. When I first encountered hand-forged axes in a hardware store in Tahtakale in İstanbul, Özkan Aydoğan told me that all the axes did the same job, they all worked equally well, but you could tell whether they were from Tokat, Balıkesir, or Bursa, by the form of the head, and his store had to stock them all because men preferred certain shapes. When I asked Yakup what made an excellent axe, he did not comment on utility. He assumed they were all strong and sharp. Instead, he drew carefully in my notebook the shape of the axe head, emphasizing the pert curve of its upper line, the long run of its edge. Form is refined in the third step, and decoration is applied. Halit uses the old word *nakış,* rather than the usual modern word *süs,* to describe form's ornament, the star-like "flowers" he hammers into hot steel. Three men, four steps, one result: an axe that melds men and matter, use and beauty.

Halit's is the last in the long line of ringing, smoking blacksmiths' shops. The next block east is for makers of harness and saddles. In front of the Çelikkıran and Çıkıkçı forges, black and bright axe heads hang. Behind, sharing their rear wall and reverberating to the sound of their hammers, there is a shop where goat hair is spun and woven into cinches and saddlebags. The entry is around the corner, between the end of the Çıkıkçı forge and the *depo* where finished work by Ahmet Çelikkıran is stored. The window is blocked by harness. The front door gives into a long narrow shop like a miniature rope-walk. It is dark, but once your eyes adjust, you see on the left a man walking backward, feeding goat hair to spinning wheels. To the right, beyond the pile of finished work, two looms stand against the wall. Between them, a charcoal brazier supplies heat in the winter, and one bulb hangs above the bowl for the shop cat's milk.

The shop works on a system of two masters. Necati Haksöz is the *patron*, the boss. He manages the business and prepares the material. All day he walks backward into the darkness. A rope around his waist spins the wheels, while he pulls goat hair out of the pouch on his belly with both hands. The strands lengthen between him and the wooden wheels turning in the front of the shop until he is nearly lost in the gloom, then he rolls up the yarn and begins again his backward march. Muhittin Güloğulları is the weaver. There are others. Necati has an assistant, Zeki Erterek. Occasionally an old man appears to weave a bit at the second loom. When school is out, Necati's grandson and a chum come to work. Cahit Haksöz and Serkan Akman sit in the sun outside, folding the ends of long woven strips and stitching them into saddlebags. But Necati handles the commerce, Muhittin is the master craftsman.

Muhittin Güloğulları told me that when he was a boy there were sixty weaving shops like this one in Bursa. He worked in one until he went into the army. After his military service, he worked for twenty-five years weaving fine cloth. Then power looms put hand-weavers out of work. There are men his age, he said, who enjoy sitting all day in the teahouse doing nothing. Not him: he was fifty-six when we met in 1984, and he was still hard at it six years later. He does not smoke or drink, his health is excellent, he loves to work, so he did not retire when he lost his job. He returned to the work of his youth, weaving goat hair. He does not admire the rough work he has to do and would prefer the challenge of fine weaving. I heard similar sentiment from İhsan Bolamat, a turner two years younger than Muhittin, who works in the district below the Covered Bazaar. İhsan said that when he was young the wood turner took on a wide variety of difficult tasks. The market now has been reduced to a few simple objects, but he has his trade, and he does what he can to make the things he must sell beautiful. His spindles are elegantly shaped and ornamented with turned banding. Muhittin's work is similar. Not so interesting as it once was, it could be better, but this is what remains, so there is nothing to do but do it as well as it can be done. Muhittin weaves with celerity and great mastery in the last shop in all of Bursa where goat hair is woven and sewn into cinches and saddlebags, nosebags for horses, mittens for currying.

Across the street from the shop where Necati spins and Muhittin weaves, there is a narrow space where tea is brewed. A boy runs through the streets bringing tea to the workers who pause briefly, standing to drink, to pass a few words, before returning to their hammering and grinding, their spinning and weaving, their stitching of leather.

Mehmet Tosun, 1984 (Photograph by the author)

In the middle of the next block, a few paces beyond Halit's forge, is the shop of Mehmet Tosun. He makes the *semer*, the framed and upholstered saddle for donkeys. On the corner and across the street are shops full of men who do the same work. Next to him on one side is the shop of Hüsnü Altıparmakoğlu, where knives are made. On the other side is the shop of the saddler, Ahmet Abraşoğlu, maker of harness for horses, blue-beaded bridles for oxen.

Mehmet Tosun has worked at this trade in this shop since 1928. When he began, he told me, there were forty shops of *semerciler,* of makers of the semer, in Bursa. The count is down to six: three in this block, three in the area below the bazaar. His craft, he says, is peculiar to his nation, unknown in Europe or America, and it is five hundred years old in Turkey.

Mehmet Tosun's shop is a two-man operation, one *usta*, one *kalfa*. The *kalfa* is Mehmet Turan, who, at thirty-five, has spent twenty-six years at the trade. His job is to stuff and stitch the pad beneath the frame the master builds of hornbeam.

The sun falls in through the small panes of glass in the front wall. Mehmet Tosun sits to the right by the window on a chair covered with a sheepskin. Behind him, tools hang on the wall with a photograph of a calligraphic master-piece from Ulu Cami. Before him stands the wooden block on which he works. He leans over the block to shape a curved piece of hornbeam with an adze, steadying it with his feet. Then he saws it in half to get an identical pair which he couples at their crossing to create an arched unit, analogous to the bent in a crucked frame. He joins two such units (the rear one taller and wider) with three slats sprung in mortises on each side. To size the elements of the frame and control their relationships, he uses a measuring stick. I once wrote a book about old houses in Virginia, and I imagined the carpenter of the past using such a ruler, but I had never seen one until I came to Mehmet's shop. Dark, smooth and shiny with use, it is square in section. Each face carries a rhythmic program of scribed lines, slashes, and x-marks. There are no numbers. The stick does not relate the work to an external numerical system; it contains its own system of incremental proportion. Relations between the marks along each face govern all the elements in frames of different sizes. Now he lifts the stick, using it to measure diagonally, checking the frame's square and depth. He saws a bit from the bottom of one foot, checks again, hammers and wedges the frame tight, and tumbles it across the floor toward Mehmet Turan.

To the left of the door, Mehmet Turan sits on the floor by a low hinged window through which he talks to customers and receives tea for the shop. He cuts and bundles reed, stitching it with a long needle into a pad, which he covers with burlap. Then he covers the pad with leather above, felt below, and stitches it under the frame. The last step is decorating the rear of the *semer*. He sews red, green, and blue yarn around the arc of the form; then he gathers and stitches pompons of colored yarn, which he calls flowers. Halit Çıkıkçı called the asterisks he hammered onto the axe face flowers. It is not that these circular shapes represent flowers. Rather, they are like flowers in their symmetrical form and decorative presence. Turkish weavers gather small circular geometric motifs under the name *flower,* just as they gather small square ones under the name *stone.* They are not depicting flowers and stones; they subdivide geometrical shapes into soft and hard categories that they name by reference to real things in their experience, rather than by abstract concepts. Widely in the world—in the embroidery of Scotland, for example, or the painted barns of Pennsylvania—the decorative is identified with the flower that ornaments nature. Americans call fancy speech flowery, not meaning that it is full of flowers, but that it is full of the flower's decorative qualities. In Bursa, the tool's ornament is its flowering.

It is a low gray day. Snow falls thick. The domes and roofs are caked with white, the buildings lie black beneath them. Along the rutted street, a faint pinkness marks the forges. Amber dots of electric lights glow dim in the low darkness. Mehmet Tosun's shop is warm and full. He is a *hacı;* he has been on the pilgrimage to Mecca, and he is a teacher who attracts men to his shop for earnest religious discussion. In a few years he will cease working, but he will still come into the old shop every day. While workers across the street in the shop of his neighbor, Halil Semercigil, continue to make the *semer*, he will sit and talk with the men gathered around him. Today I have listened. Men have come and gone, drinking tea, trading simple deep precepts, planning ways to help people in need. The framed couple for a *semer* leans against his chair. Woodchips scatter the floor. The steady snow drops a pale film beyond the windows.

The door slams open and shut. A whisper of cold and a red-cheeked boy burst in. Wet and winded from running, the lad addresses quiet words to the old man. He is told to sit next to the stove. Mehmet Tosun rises and throws in a handful of chips to increase the heat. He hands his grandson his own glass of hot, sweet tea. The boy, Faruk is his name, sits silently among the men. School ended finally, the snow still fell, and he ran to his grandfather with a request. He wants a sled.

Mehmet Tosun finds a stout, short board among the scraps, sits again, and notices the puddle under the boy's boots. He tells his grandson to take them off and asks if they feel small or large. "A bit big," the boy answers in a small voice, and his grandfather tells Mehmet, his *kalfa*, to cut pieces of felt to fit inside. He had done the same for me when I appeared in his shop, cold and wet, two months earlier. Faruk sits by the stove, sipping his tea. Behind him rows of completed saddles are stacked up the wall. Big men press around him in the small shop. Mehmet Tosun settles with a piece of wood, adzing the curve of one runner. "Your socks are wet," he says, "take them off." The boy does, dropping them beside his chair, shifting his bright pink feet nearer the stove. His grandfather takes up a second board and, using the first as a template, draws the profile upon it, notches the top with a saw, and then hews a matching curve.

Faruk sits, sips, glances out the window. The light holds. Thick snow falls. His grandfather notices the thin black socks, crumpled into a wet wad on the floor, and tells his grandson to wring them out and hang them over the stove. Then he holds the runners together, using the adze to perfect the match of their curves, to knock a nick off the rear above and below.

The boy is quiet. His grandfather rests the runners on his chair and rises to feed another handful of chips to the stove. A visitor enters. Another round of tea arrives. The boy sips. The men talk. His grandfather pulls an old gray board out of the scrap pile, marks a point with his thumbnail, saws straight down, and begins to adze its face. Pale light from the street outlines his noble brow and full white beard, while he bears down, concentrating, worrying the board smooth. Then he rummages up a second board, saws it to the length of the first, and sets about adzing its surface. With four long nails and a battery of short ones, he nails the boards over the runners, and feels the strength of their unification in his hands.

The boy sits. His tea is done. The sled seems done. His grandfather takes up a rasp, handmade by a man in İstanbul and wonderfully sharp. With it he softens all the edges, down along the runners, all around the top. The conversation in the shop turns to a comparison of our age with ages past. "Today," his grandfather says, "it is all done with machines. In the past they lacked such, but look at the wonders they created." The sled waits on his lap while he gestures uphill with the rasp. "Look at Yeşil Cami. It is a wonder. In those days they did not build with machines. They built with the help of God. No building in these times can begin to compare with the works of the old masters, and they worked only with their hands. It makes you think."

The sled seems done. His grandfather lifts an electric drill and it screams, driving holes down through the tops of the runners. The boy is quiet. His grandfather asks if he is warm and stokes the stove with another handful of chips. It is very hot. The sled rests on his grandfather's chair, its smooth graceful runners ready to speed through the snow. At last his grandfather finds a pair of old toggle rings, which he taps and swivels free of rust. While the call to prayer begins from Kayan Camii, he hammers the toggles through the holes, clinching them tidily below. The boy has his warm socks on, his boots lined with felt, and he is standing. His grandfather holds the sled, brushing hard over the surface with his hand to be sure no splinters remain. He sights down the runners, gives one a bash with the hammer, sights again, brushes it again, feeling the smooth wood under his hands, and he passes it to the boy. He is turned toward the door, listening while his grandfather fastens the top button on his coat, tight under his chin, and warns him against getting too cold, and explains in detail how he should find a rope and tie it firmly to the rings with good knots so he can pull the sled behind him. The boy kisses his grandfather's hand, touches it to his forehead, the door bangs, and he is gone in the snow, running with the new sled. His grandfather buttons his overcoat and leaves for prayer.

I am the grandson of a carpenter, and I watched as though a film of my past were running before my eyes. I remember the concern, the waiting. Grandfathers do nothing perfunctorily. I remember my grandfather marshaling the accumulated experience of a lifetime to fulfill my little requests with deliberate, scrupulous skill. Like Faruk's, the wooden toys of my boyhood were unnecessarily excellent, because grandfathers love grandsons, because carpenters love wood, because artists cannot help but do things well.

Notes

1. The reference is to these works: Goldstein 1964, 1977; Sartre 1963, 1976; Ives 1964; Hymes 1974 (full citations for the crucial works of a decade before can be found on pp. 220–21); Dundes 1964; Dundes, ed. 1965; Merriam 1964; Abrahams 1964; Crowley 1966. My aside on postmodernism was quick but serious: in August 1992, at a conference held in Portland, Oregon, to commemorate thirty years of his contribution to the ethnography of communication, Dell Hymes said of postmodernism that he saw no reason to give a new name to the ideas he learned years ago from Kenneth Burke. It is not my intention, of course, to tell the history of American folklore in a couple of paragraphs. With appreciation, I wanted to set Kenny Goldstein's work with that of his colleagues to sketch the moment that has proved so influential upon my cohort. As I say in *Passing the Time in Ballymenone* (1982:721–23), looking backward we can recapture many who anticipated current work before 1960, Jeremiah Curtin in the nineteenth century, for example, John and Alan Lomax in the twentieth. I end this with reference to one short article that exhibits both awareness in the earlier generation and the importance of the field experience in exposing limitations in the older paradigm. MacEdward Leach taught Kenny Goldstein (as well as Roger Abrahams and me); this paper of his was crucial for me at least: "What Shall We Do with 'Little Matty Groves'?" (1963).

2. For Ulu Cami and Yeşil Cami, Bursa's great mosques, see: Kuran 1968:114–23, 151–53; Goodwin 1971: 51–55, 59–71. The writing on Turkish art of the sixteenth century is excellent; for examples: Atıl 1987; Petsopoulos, ed. 1982. Turkish writing on recent vernacular architecture is superb, but the bibliography on other twentieth-century traditional arts is not extensive; however: Kenan Özbel wrote a series of descriptive pamphlets on crafts in the late 1940s, gathered as *El Sanatları* (c. 1982); there is a good survey of modern

earthenware, Güner 1988; there is a good survey of recent carpet weaving in eastern Turkey, Görgünay (c. 1972); and modern calligraphy is treated as the latest link in an unbroken chain of masters and followers, stretching back through the sixteenth century, in Rado (c. 1983). My paper for Kenny Goldstein is adapted from the middle of chapter 12 of *Turkish Traditional Art Today* (1993b). That book's prelude, in which I argued around the scholarly matter of folk art in preparation for a descriptive and analytic confrontation with Turkish art, is *The Spirit of Folk Art* (1989). In this paper, I chance to refer to my book, *Folk Housing in Middle Virginia: A Structural Analysis of Historic Artifacts* (1975:22–25).

3. Glassie 1993a and 1993b.

References

Abrahams, Roger
  1964   *Deep Down in the Jungle: Negro Narrative Folklore from the Streets of Philadelphia.* Hatboro: Folklore Associates.
Atıl, Esin
  1987   *The Age of Sultan Süleyman the Magnificent.* New York: Abrams.
Crowley, Daniel J.
  1966   *I Could Talk Old-Story Good: Creativity in Bahamian Folklore.* Berkeley: Univ. of California Press.
Dundes, Alan
  1964   *The Morphology of North American Indian Folktales.* Helsinki: Suomalainen Tiedeakatemia.
———, ed.
  1965   *The Study of Folklore.* Englewood Cliffs: Prentice-Hall.
Glassie, Henry
  1975   *Folk Housing in Middle Virginia: A Structural Analysis of Historic Artifacts.* Knoxville: Univ. of Tennessee Press.
  1982   *Passing the Time in Ballymenone.* Philadelphia: Univ. of Pennsylvania Press.
  1989   *The Spirit of Folk Art.* New York: Abrams.
  1993a *Günümüade Geleneksel Türk Sanati.* İstanbul: Pan Yayıncilik.
  1993b *Turkish Traditional Art Today.* Bloomington: Indiana Univ. Press.
Goldstein, Kenneth S.
  1964   *A Guide for Field Workers in Folklore.* Hatboro: Folklore Associates.
  1977   *Sahada Folklor Derleme Metotları.* Trans. Ahmet E. Uysal. Ankara: Başbakanlık Basımevi.
Goodwin, Godfrey
  1971   *A History of Ottoman Architecture.* London: Thames and Hudson.
Görgünay, Neriman
  c. 1972 (n.d.) *Doğu Yöresi Halıları.* Ankara: Türkiye İş Bankası Kültür Yayınları.
Güner, Güngör
  1988   *Anadolu'da Yaşamakta Olan İlkel Çömlekçilik.* İstanbul: Ak Yayınları.
Hymes, Dell
  1974   *Foundations in Sociolinguistics: An Ethnographic Approach.* Philadelphia: Univ. of Pennsylvania Press.
Ives, Edward D.
  1964   *Larry Gorman: The Man Who Made the Songs.* Bloomington: Indiana Univ. Press.
Kuran, Aptullah
  1968   *The Mosque in Early Ottoman Architecture.* Chicago: Univ. of Chicago Press.

Leach, MacEdward
1963   "What Shall We Do with 'Little Matty Groves'?" *Journal of American Folklore*
76:189–94.
Merriam, Alan
1964   *The Anthropology of Music*. Evanston: Northwestern Univ. Press.
Özbel, Kenan
c. 1982 (n.d.)   *El Sanatları*. Ankara: C. H. P. Halkevleri Bürosu. Reprint of c. 1948.
Petsopoulos, Yanni, ed.
1982   *Tulips, Arabesques and Turbans: Decorative Arts from the Ottoman Empire*. New
York: Abbeville.
Rado, Şevket
c. 1983 (n.d.)   *Türk Hattatları*. İstanbul: Yayın Matbaacılık.
Sartre, Jean-Paul
1963   *Search for a Method*. New York: Alfred A. Knopf.
1976   *Between Existentialism and Marxism*. New York: William Morrow.

THE DEVIL, THE FIDDLE, AND DANCING

Herbert Halpert

"THE DEVIL'S in the fiddle" and "The fiddle is the Devil's instrument" were remarks heard so often in my fieldwork in various parts of the United States that I assumed they were common proverbial sayings reflecting a familiar folk belief. As a result I rarely noted where and when they were said. Other fieldworkers have told me that they too had heard these dites,[1] but like me had not written them down. Surprisingly, neither saying is listed in standard dictionaries of American and English proverbial sayings.

Various legends and dites about the Devil's connection with the violin and other instruments are well known in North America and in Europe. The Devil is known for his skill in playing the fiddle, an instrument which some reports say he invented. Sometimes he has contests with human fiddlers. If he teaches people to play, they become superlative performers. When he or his pupils are invited to play at dances, their music may be compulsive; people who hear it are forced to dance. Sometimes they cannot stop dancing until they die—unless the spell is broken, frequently by religious means. Instruments he or his pupils have played may continue to play by themselves after the pupil's death. (See Halpert 1943:39–43; Hand 1964:151–53, No. 5772; Christiansen 1958:77–80, Type 4090; Moriarty and Moriarity 1974:2–9).

This paper will discuss the two belief sayings cited at the outset, illustrating through anecdotes and personal experience stories how widespread these beliefs were, and how they both dictated and controlled social behavior. The documentation of these sayings is based on published sources mainly from the United States, with some citations from Canada, Scotland, and Scandinavia. It will demonstrate their pervasive role in the prohibition of social dancing, and also the negative attitude toward violin playing and fiddlers. The examples illustrate also how belief in these sayings has led both lay individuals and clergymen either to destroy violins or to exert strong social pressure on musicians to destroy or dispose of their own beloved instruments.

The first four of the following comments on "The Devil's in the fiddle" indicate that in a few instances clergymen have played the violin in spite of this belief and their parishioners' disapproval. They also show how strongly people believed that dancing was sinful.

In a 1942 interview, the former Dean of the Music School at Indiana University, who had been a violin teacher for many years, told me:

> I grew up in Chicago and Aurora. And one of the earliest things I can remember about my fiddle, that my old uncle told me "the Devil was in the fiddle. He was my guardian, and he wouldn't let me take lessons.
>
> When I was eighteen, I had two students: one was a Presbyterian minister and one was a Congregationalist. The Congregational minister told me that in his ministerial life it so shocked some of his parishioners that he played the violin that he was obliged to play it to himself, and he urged me not to let it be known that he was taking lessons; and the Presbyterian minister said the same thing. One of them said, "Not that there's anything wrong in playing the fiddle, but you know how people will talk." And for a girl to play the fiddle! She was on the way to perdition. (Halpert 1943:39–40)

In an article about Texas fiddling and fiddlers, J. Olcutt Sanders summarized a section of a newspaper story about a Texas minister who had fought in the Civil War, served as sheriff of Madison County, Texas, "during its wildest days," and eventually became a minister of the Church of Christ, preaching for 25 years in the South, Southwest, and far West. The minister's own remarks about his fondness for the fiddle are quoted from that article.

> I learned to fiddle . . . from a Negro slave belonging to my grandfather. During my 25 years of preaching I did not touch a fiddle; not that I thought there was a "Devil in every fiddle," but because of my constant study of the Bible and my devotion to the work of preaching. But after I began to feel old and dwelt much in the past, I took to the fiddle again. I derive much pleasure from it. (Sanders 1941:86)

In an interview first published in 1928, an 87-year-old woman, born in Indiana, whose family went to Oregon in 1851, said: "No, my folks wouldn't let me go to dances. They held that the Devil was in the fiddle and that if a girl danced, she was dancing her way to hell" (Lockley 1981:142).

In Oklahoma in 1929, B. A. Botkin had a long interview with a man, born in the Ozarks, who came from a family of musicians and had played at entertainments and square dances in Southern Oklahoma and Norman. Here are excerpts from that interview:

> The church's attitude was against dancing. The church at present is more lenient than it was at that time. How could a man reconcile religious scruples and dancing? He didn't. The active church members didn't go to dances. If a boy or a girl belonging to any church danced, the saying went round that they had danced themselves out of the church. . . .
>
> I can't understand why it was but in my boyhood days—I don't know how to express it—but the fiddle was the instrument of Satan. The Devil was in the fiddle—that's the saying exactly. (Botkin 1963:21)

I am surprised that I found so few published comments on "The Devil's in the fiddle." I am convinced that it has a considerably wider distribution than the present evidence shows, but further investigation would be required to demonstrate this. The preceding quotation includes also an example of the second saying, "The fiddle is the Devil's instrument," which will be further documented in the next group of references.

The authors of an interesting Canadian article entitled "The Fiddle in Folklore" comment: "Both European and American rustics believed that the fiddle was the Devil's instrument and that Satan himself was the master fiddler." Unfortunately, they do not provide specific references (Moriarty 1974:3).

After describing a fiddling contest in Brooklyn, New York, between a black fiddler and the Devil, C. M. Skinner, an early compiler of American legends, added the following remark: "there are fewer fiddlers among the negroes than there used to be, because they say that the violin is the Devil's instrument" (1896:133–35).

Herbert Walker, in his article on Pennsylvania lumberjacks and raftsmen, discussed some of the amusements of the lumberjacks on winter evenings and Sunday afternoons, and then noted: "There was also a good deal of fiddling—the woods were full of fiddlers, righthanders and southpaws. Some church people in the towns regarded the fiddle as the Devil's own instrument, but that did not worry the fiddlers" (1949:341). Art Galbraith, a well-known fiddler in the Ozarks, has written about fiddle playing there: "In spite of the opposition to the 'Devil's Own Instrument,' fiddling has continued to flourish" (1977:21; courtesy Gordon McCann).

Describing entertainment in the early days in Cape Breton, Nova Scotia, Francis MacGregor observed: "The milling frolics were not frowned upon by the Church as was dancing. Some of the old timers looked upon the violin as the Devil's instrument. Nevertheless, at a wedding dancing was enjoyed for two nights" (MacGregor 1976:12–13).

After a vivid description of the popularity and power of fiddle playing and fiddle music in the South at the end of the nineteenth century and in the early years of the twentieth, Howard W. Odum added:

> The old revivalists, who wished to wean their converts from the vanities of the balls, felt compelled to proscribe the fiddle as the Devil's instrument. When I was a boy it was a general religious tenet, that playing it was a sin equal to dancing, horse-racing, cock-fighting and gambling.
> Fiddling and dancing just naturally seemed to go together. (1947:185)

Before 1932, Arch Bristow interviewed two people over ninety years old in northwestern Pennsylvania, both of whom said they had never danced:

> Dozens of other men and women who can look back on lives reaching ninety years back, never indulged in dancing, they were strictly raised in the church, when that religious organization looked on the dance and most of its concomitants with a forbidding frown.

The fiddle was an instrument of the Devil, the dance was a lure to catch the unwary, a paper bound copy of "From the Ball Room To Hell" lay on the parlor table, this of course at a later date. (Bristow 1932:309)

Commenting on a North Dakota tale which reflects a Norwegian community, Barbara Woods observed:

As a result of this terrifying encounter the fiddler gives up his playing (as do his cousins in Norway, usually after perceiving the Devil among the dancers for whom they are playing). Basic to the whole story, of course, is the popular notion that the fiddle is the Devil's own instrument, and therefore playing it involves one with the Devil himself. This idea of fiddling as wicked is prevalent in Norway and Scandinavia in general as well as among some fundamentalist sects in the United States (cf. the development of play-party games as a substitute for dancing to fiddle music). (1958:197)

The relation of fiddling to play parties is discussed in detail later in this paper.

Fiddling was not always totally proscribed by religious persons. Attitudes depended on the occasion and the kind of music played. After noting that in New Hampshire in the mid-1850s dancing was considered "awfully wicked," Wilson Palmer commented:"They didn't dance in those days,—I mean the church people. To them, the violin, as a translator of music other than 'Old Hundred' and other tunes that stretched themselves out in prolonged notes, was the Devil's own instrument" (1905:293–94).

But New Hampshire people were more liberal than many others about accepting the violin if it played religious music. Compare their attitude with the following report from the Annapolis Valley of Nova Scotia:

I think it was in the summer of 1910, we had as our guest for a few weeks a nephew of Elva's who was a fairly distinguished fiddler. He played in the first-fiddle section of the Boston Symphony, and was no slouch. He made such a hit during this visit that he was besieged with requests to play at a church service. He agreed, and I remember that his number was to be Schubert's *Ave Maria*. Well, all the arrangements had been made except for one little detail. Deacon Allen had given his consent. A local accompanist had practised her head off. A neighbor of ours had moved his piano into the meeting house. But there was no performance. When the Reverend McNeil got wind of what was afoot he blew higher than a kite! He would have none of it!

Says he, "No instrument of the Devil will be played in my church!" (Foster 1976:172)

Equally violent was the reaction of an old woman in a small town church in the Ozarks. A young woman visitor one Sunday sang beautifully, accompanied on the violin by her cousin. When they resumed their seats, before the pastor could speak,

Grandma Graves rose as if ascending into her own private heaven and in a high-pitched voice of self-righteous indignation exhorted:"Brethren and Sisters! Are we so spiritually weak that we're afeared to speak out in the Lord's house. . . . Lord have mercy that I should live to see the day that arch instrument of the Devil, that dancin' fiddle of sin and shame, should be brought into the Lord's house. I beseech you let us kneel and pray." (Guy 1976:15)

The stringent opposition to the fiddle often went much further than forbidding its use in church. Fathers forbade their sons to play it at home, and enforced their prohibitions firmly. Here are three illustrative narratives from the United States:

1) In a West Virginia story told by Patrick Gainer, a boy borrowed a fiddle from his maternal grandfather and secretly practised on it despite his father's warning that if he ever played the fiddle, he would have to leave home. The father returned home unexpectedly and heard his son playing:

Peter opened the door and walked slow-like into the room without sayin' a word. Then he took the fiddle out of the boy's hands, and he took his knife and cut all four strings. He took that fiddle and hung it on a nail just to the left of the fireboard. . . . Then Peter turned and spoke: "There hangs the instrument of the Devil. I would a-broke it in a hundred pieces, but I want it to hang there as a lesson to all of them who will not obey. I have said that my son could not live in this house if he ever brought such an instrument under this roof. Now let him go to his grandpappy's and see if he has another fiddle. Let him go now, and let him stay there." (Gainer 1975:37–44)

2) The son of a strict Quaker father in Indiana secretly acquired a fiddle on which he practised in the hay-loft. One day his father overheard the noise and proceeded to investigate. The boy was startled to see his father's stern face at the top of the ladder. Years later the young man described to a friend what followed:

Father said to me "What is that thing with which thee is making such unearthly noises?" I answered, "It is a fiddle." He said, "Whoever thought thee would bring that instrument of the Devil here, give it to me," which of course I did. He then ordered me to follow him and we marched up to the house where a good fire was burning in the large fireplace. He directed me to a chair while he placed the fiddle and bow in the roaring flames. We watched them burn and listened for the strings to break. The E string broke first and the others in order, and as the bass string broke I seemed to feel my heart break too. (Charles 1961:63–64)

3) Jean Ritchie has written about a Kentuckian who had a large family of boys, all of whom, to his grief and shame, "loved playing the fiddle." The father "at last put it against the law for them to play a fiddle any more, and he broke up every one the boys had made." They, however, made other instruments and hid

them in hollow logs in the woods, where they would go to fiddle and sing. One evening when the father heard"that Devil's music" come rolling down the mountain, he followed the sound and found one of his sons lost in playing. He "beat him with a big oak limb. Then he smashed up the fiddle, too." On another occasion the whole family were rolling logs to clear some newground. The boys seemed reluctant to tackle one huge, nearly rotten log, till the father forced them to work on it. When the log went leaping down the mountain side, fiddles began to fly out of it—"strings a-popping, gourds a-busting." Eight or ten instruments had been hidden in it. The father is reported to have said that "he personally tore up Hell in the newground that day!" (Ritchie 1955:145–46).

An equally violent opposition to the fiddle was shown by one Catholic clergyman in Nova Scotia. Elizabeth Beaton, in a written contribution made to me September 23, 1977, wrote [I have condensed her paper]:

> About 100 years ago in Mabou [Nova Scotia], the parish priest gathered all the violins in his parish, [and] took them down to the wharf where he smashed and burned them.
>
> I have heard this from priests and lay-persons, musicians and non-musicians. The priest who destroyed the violins was Father Kenneth MacDonald, who was born in Antigonish County, Nova Scotia. The incident happened about the year 1865.

In a published article referring to this incident, Beaton commented:"The Mediaeval suspicion that the pipes and the fiddle were instruments of the Devil was generally held by some of the early parish priests of the area" (Beaton 1977:8).

Although there are reports of ministers and elders in Scotland burning musical instruments, they frequently achieved the same result merely by applying social pressure. In 1875, W. Anderson Smith commented on the disastrous effect the church had had on the musical life of the Isle of Lewis in the Outer Hebrides:

> Then there are no musicians whatever among the people, as the ministers and elders as a rule proscribe such pure enjoyment. One lame lad at Shawbost had bought a fiddle to solace himself during the long winter evenings, but the elders forced him to dispose of it, and now not a man plays anything but a Jew's harp among the natives of the west. (1875:165–66)

Alexander Carmichael, one of the greatest collectors of Scottish Gaelic folklore, described what happened to one old musician. I give within quotation marks Carmichael's English translations of two Gaelic sections:

> A famous violin-player died in the island of Eigg a few years ago. He was known for his old style playing and his old-world airs which died with him. A preacher denounced him, saying: "Thou art down there behind the door, thou miserable man with thy grey hair, playing thine old fiddle with the cold hand without, and the devil's fire within." His family

pressed the man to burn his fiddle and never to play again. A pedlar came round and offered ten shillings for the violin. The instrument had been made by a people of Stradivarius, and was famed for its tone. "It was not at all the thing that was got for it that grieved my heart so sorely, but the parting with it! the parting with it! and that I myself gave the best cow in my father's fold for it when I was young." The voice of the old man faltered, and a tear fell. He was never again seen to smile. (Carmichael 1972:xxxii)

Smith's explanation for the lack of musicians on the Isle of Lewis is amplified in frightening detail by Carmichael. The following is excerpted from Charmichael's English translation of a much longer interview he had with a woman from the Isle of Lewis:

"In my young days there was hardly a house in Ness in which there was not one or two or three who could play the pipe, or the fiddle, or the trump. And I have heard it said that there were men, and women too, who could play things they called harps, and lyres, and bellow-pipes, but I do not know what those things were."

"And why were those discontinued?"

"A blessed change came over the place and the people, . . . and the good men and the good ministers who arose did away with the songs and the stories, the music and the dancing, the sports and the games, that were perverting the minds and ruining the souls of the people, leading them to folly and stumbling. . . . They made the people break and burn their pipes and fiddles. If there was a foolish man here and there who demurred, the good ministers and the good elders themselves broke and burnt their instruments, saying:

'Better is the small fire that warms on the little day of peace,
Than the big fire that burns on the great day of wrath.'

The people have foresaken their follies and their Sabbath-breaking, and there is no pipe, no fiddle here now," said the woman in evident satisfaction. (Carmichael 1972:xxix–xxx)

The nineteenth-century religious opposition to playing the fiddle was not limited to North America and Scotland; it was also found in Scandinavia. In 1880, Rasmus Anderson observed:

Those who read "The Spell-bound Fiddler" will notice that there still lingers a good deal of prejudice among certain classes in Norway against all other than church music, and especially against the violin. There are a great many so-called pietistic (puritan) priests and laymen in Norway who oppose, in season and out of season, the singing of popular airs, dance music, and the use of the fiddle. . . . While the fiddle is the national instrument of Norway, these serious people look upon it as the instrument of the Devil, and in many descriptions of hell the Devil is represented as playing cards and the fiddle. (Anderson 1880:42)

In the United States, one of the major effects of this belief in the Devilish nature of the fiddle was the development of the play-party in which young people managed to dance to their own singing, without any instrumental accompaniment. A baker's dozen of books and articles on the play-party document the widespread prohibition against dancing. I have limited my citations to those that clearly stress the relationship between the prohibition of dancing and the belief in the Devilish nature of the fiddle and fiddling.

Writing about the play-party in the Caney Fork country of Tennessee, the McDowells pointed out:

> Parents who would not for a moment consider allowing their daughters to attend a dance might let them play an innocent game in the home of their friends. Likewise a "fiddle" was considered an instrument of Satan for the destruction of the young people, but if these same young people only sang the music instead of hearing it played, then they could presumably march around in some simple manner made necessary by the game. (McDowell and McDowell 1938:4; reprinted in McDowell n.d.:19)

Vance Randolph commented, in describing the social pleasures of the early settlers in the Ozark mountain region:

> Most of the old-timers thought that dancing was immoral, and regarded the fiddle as the devil's own instrument. . . . I myself heard one of our leading citizens declare that he would rather see his daughter dead than to have her dance, even in her own home. But the play-party, it appears, is a different matter altogether, and even the most fanatical religionists see no particular harm in it. (1929:201; reprinted in Randolph 1931:138)

In discussing the play-party in Texas, William A. Owens remarked:

> In practically all communities predominantly Protestant, dancing was, and is, taboo. The fiddle was the "instrument of the devil," and all who danced to its strains were unfit for membership in the community church. (1936:xxi)

The foregoing examples make clear the disapproval of dancing to the fiddle, and the acceptance of the unaccompanied singing of play-party games. How strictly this distinction was adhered to is seen in the following quotations. In Botkin's early discussion of the play-party in Oklahoma he observed:

> In the eyes of many church people the music was—and to some extent still is—the most objectionable feature of dances, fiddlers and fiddles having been looked upon for generations as the devil's own agents. For that reason, I am informed, "many of the girls of the pre-statehood days believed it a sin to dance but not to go to a play-party. Consequently they would do the regulation square dances as long as the accompaniment was sung, but if a fiddle was sounded they would stop immediately." (Botkin 1928:12; partly reprinted in Botkin 1963:23)

S. J. Sackett, discussing the widespread popularity of the play-party on the American frontier, makes the same points even more vividly:

> Many individuals and religious groups believed that dancing was sinful. Probably the chief reason for this belief was that they thought dancing afforded a young unmarried couple too much opportunity for physical contact; but also strong in its effects was an ancient European superstition that the fiddle was the devil's instrument.

Furthermore, Sackett quotes an informant who described

> an occasion on which a group of young people were playing play-party games in the barn when one of the young men present took out his fiddle and joined in the same tune which the players were singing. Immediately the outraged parents rushed in and broke up the party, sending the guests home. (1961:5)

Clearly, these two sayings, "The Devil's in the fiddle" and "The fiddle is the Devil's instrument," have been reported from many parts of the United States. The latter one, by far the more common, is also known in eastern Canada, Scotland, and Scandinavia. More important than their distribution is the demonstration, by anecdotes and personal experience stories, that these sayings were not merely casual comments but strongly held beliefs which have led to dramatic action by the believers. Fiddles were banned in many homes and in churches, and often were actually destroyed by both laymen and clergymen. In the United States the strength of these beliefs was particularly shown by the widespread religious prohibitions against dancing to the music of the fiddle, the Devil's instrument.

Notes

There is no doubt in my mind that the wild assemblage of references in this paper will charm my fellow book hunter, Kenneth Goldstein. I can vouch for the fact that his pleasure in reading it has been greatly enhanced by the stringent editing of my wife, Violetta M. Halpert.

1. The term *dite* was introduced and discussed in detail by the Swedish scholar, C. W. von Sydow, in the English translation of his earlier article in Swedish (1948:106–26). Laurits Bødker summarized the English article and included von Sydow's definition of a dite as a saying "without characterizing that which is said as true or false, believed or fictitious" (Bødker 1965:70; Alver 1967:67). A dite is thus an admirably neutral term that applies to a great variety of statements. Although I refer to the two discussed in this essay as "belief sayings," this does not imply that other dites mentioned in the second paragraph are of the same nature.

References

Alver, Brynjulf
    1967 Catergory and Function. *Fabula* 9:63–69.
Anderson, Rasmus B.
    1880 Introduction. In Kristofer Janson, *The Spell-Bound Fiddler: A Norse Romance.*

Trans. Auber Forestier. Chicago: S. C. Griggs. Pp. 11–59.

Beaton, Betty
1977   The Role of the Parish Priest in Maintaining Ethnic Tradition in Eastern Nova Scotia. In *Highland Heritage*. Port Hastings, Nova Scotia, and Mabou, Nova Scotia. Pp. 8–9.

Bødker, Laurits
1965   *Folk Literature (Germanic)*. Vol. 2 of the *International Dictionary of Regional European Ethnology and Folklore*. Ed. Åke Hultkrantz. Copenhagen: Rosenkilde and Bagger.

Botkin, B.A.
1928   The Play-Party in Oklahoma. *Publications of the Texas Folklore Society* 7:7–24.
1963 [1937]   *The American Play-Party Song*. New York: Frederick Ungar.

Bristow, Arch
1932   *Old Time Tales of Warren County: A Collection of the Picturesque and Romantic Lore of Early Days in Warren County, Pennsylvania*. Meadville, Pa.: Privately printed.

Carmichael, Alexander
1972 [1900]   *Carmina Gadelica: Hymns and Incantations. With Illustrative Notes on Words, Rites, and Customs, Dying and Obsolete: Orally Collected in the Highlands and Islands of Scotland and Translated into English*. Vol. 1. Edinburgh and London: Scottish Academic Press.

Charles, Helen White, coll. and ed.
1961   *Quaker Chuckles, and Other True Stories about Friends*. Richmond, Ind.: Privately printed.

Christiansen, Reidar Th.
1958   *The Migratory Legends: A Proposed List of Types with a Systematic Catalogue of the Norwegian Variants*. FF Communications, no. 175. Helsinki: Academia Scientiarum Fennica.

Foster, Malcolm Cecil
1976   *Annapolis Valley Saga*. Ed. Howard L. Trueman. Windsor, N.S.: Lancelot Press.

Gainer, Patrick W.
1975   *Witches, Ghosts and Signs: Folklore of the Southern Appalachians*. Grantsville, W.Va.: Seneca Books.

Galbraith, T. Arthur
1977   The Devil's Own Instrument. *Ozarks Mountaineer* 25(9):21.

Halpert, Herbert
1943   The Devil and the Fiddle. *Hoosier Folklore Bulletin* 2:39–43.

Hand, Wayland D., ed.
1964   *Popular Beliefs and Superstitions from North Carolina. The Frank C. Brown Collection of North Carolina Folklore*, vol. 7. Durham, N.C.: Duke Univ. Press. Cited as Hand-Brown.

Howard, Guy
1976 [1944]   *Walkin' Preacher of the Ozarks*. Springfield, Mo.: ABC Publishing Services.

Lockley, Fred
1981   *The Lockley Files: Conversations with Pioneer Women*. Comp. and ed. Mike Helm. Eugene, Oreg.: Rainy Day Press.

McDowell, Flora L.

n.d.   *Folk Dances of Tennessee: Folk Customs and Old Play Party Games of the Caney Fork Valley.* Delaware, Ohio: Cooperative Recreation Service.

McDowell, Lucien L., and Flora Lassiter McDowell

1938   *Folk Dances of Tennessee: Old Play Party Games of the Caney Fork Valley.* Ann Arbor, Mich.: Edwards Brothers.

MacGregor, Francis

1976   *Days That I Remember: Stories with a Scottish Accent.* Windsor, N.S.: Lancelot Press.

Moriarty, Norma Catherine, and Sirri Kathleen Moriarty

1974   The Fiddle in Folklore. *Anthropological Journal of Canada* 12(3):2–9.

Odum, Howard W.

1947   *The Way of the South: Toward the Regional Balance of America.* New York: Macmillan.

Owens, William A.

1936   *Swing and Turn: Texas Play-Party Games.* Dallas, Tex.: Tardy Publishing Co.

Palmer, Wilson

1905   *Reminiscences of Candia.* Cambridge: Riverside Press.

Randolph, Vance

1929   The Ozark Play-Party. *Journal of American Folklore* 42:201–32.

1931   *The Ozarks: An American Survival of Primitive Society.* New York: Vanguard Press.

Ritchie, Jean

1955   *Singing Family of the Cumberlands.* New York: Oxford Univ. Press.

Sackett, S. J.

1961   Play-Party Games from Kansas. *Heritage of Kansas* 5(3):2–61.

Sanders, J. Olcutt

1941   Honor the Fiddler! *Texas Folklore Society Publications* 17:78–90.

Skinner, Charles M.

1896   *Myths & Legends of Our Own Land.* Vol. 1. Philadelphia and London: J. B. Lippincott.

Smith, W. Anderson

1875   *Lewisiana, or Life in the Outer Hebrides.* London: Daldy, Isbister and Co.

von Sydow, Carl Wilhelm

1948   Popular Dite Tradition: A Terminological Outline. In *Selected Papers on Folklore: C. W. v. Sydow Anniversary Volume.* Ed. Laurits Bodker. Copenhagen: Rosenkilde and Bagger. Pp. 106–26.

Walker, Herbert J.

1949   Lumberjacks and Raftsmen. In *Pennsylvania Songs and Legends.* Ed. George Korson. Philadelphia: Univ. of Pennsylvania Press. Pp. 326–53.

Woods, Barbara Allen

1958   The Norwegian Devil in North Dakota. *Western Folklore* 17:196–98.

THE EXPERIENCE-CENTERED
ANALYSIS OF BELIEF STORIES

A Haunting Example
in Honor of Kenny Goldstein

David J. Hufford

Purpose

IN THIS PAPER I shall present and analyze a set of stories[1] about a house believed to be haunted, in order to illustrate some aspects of my theory about belief in the existence of the supernatural.[2] This theory grows directly out of my work on beliefs about "supernatural assault" (1982) and the mystical experiences of ordinary people (1985). It is an "experience-centered" theory—for ease of reference, "the Experiential Theory." The Experiential Theory asserts that it is possible to derive inductively a set of experiential categories that can be shown to underlie many widespread supernatural beliefs. These experiential categories exhibit stable pereceptual patterns that are independent of cultural patterning and that seem to the subject to directly suggest the idea of "spirits." Stating that these experiences "directly suggest the idea of spirits" is not a naive claim that such experiences are *unmediated*, but rather that, like many ordinary perceptual experiences, *they are not necessarily mediated by the concepts to which they give rise.* This issue of the mediation of experience is constantly debated in the philosophy and psychology of mysticism. (See, for example, Katz [1978] and Proudfoot [1985] to the effect that "religious experience" can only be ordinary experience interpreted in a religious way, and therefore is invalid [circular] as evidence for religious belief. Arguments to the contrary are summarized in Davis [1989].)

An experience refers intuitively to spirits if it involves a perception that seems to force a choice between "I must be hallucinating" and "I am perceiving a 'spirit.'" These experiences constitute an important empirical basis for rationally developed systems of belief. I call these categories "core supernatural experiences."[3] This understanding of widespread supernatural beliefs accounts, at least in part, for similarities among such beliefs in different cultures and for their persistence in the modern world. This theory is intended to be paradigmatic in that it suggests an entire program of research that is different from what has been done previously on this subject.

Two terms that are obviously central to the Experiential Theory are *supernatural* and *belief*. My definitions are as follows:

> Stipulated Definition of *Supernatural*: By supernatural I refer to a domain that a) contains persons who do not require physical bodies for their existence (i.e., spirits), b) is objectively real (meaning only that it is not entirely imaginary), and c) interacts with the ordinary world.

It could be added that this domain is different from the ordinary world of matter and energy—nature, but the presence of spirits assures that difference and constitutes the minimum difference. On the other hand, without spirits, differences from the ordinary world are readily assimilated by postulating previously unknown phenomena of the ordinary world. The exact nature of the supernatural domain, its interactions with the ordinary world, and the persons it contains are left entirely open in this definition.

Reference to the term *supernatural* is always understood to be contestable. For example, when I use the phrase *supernatural experience*, I mean "an experience believed (by someone) to have been really supernatural." I will not use *alleged* repeatedly, although *all* claims about the world in this discussion (those of folklorists as well as folk) will be understood to be "alleged," and none is privileged.

> Stipulated definition of *Belief*: Belief is the holding of something to be true. This is belief in the cognitive sense, and it implicitly refers to propositions.

Inevitably, *belief* is also used as a shorthand reference to believed propositions, as in "the belief that ghosts exist"—*that ghosts exist* is a proposition, *that that proposition is true* is the belief. The common term "religious beliefs" also refers as much to what is held as to the holding of it. These terminological nuances are unavoidable in discussion, but the distinction between a proposition and the believing that it is true must be kept in mind. Otherwise one may fall into the habit of referring to certain propositions as "beliefs," even in situations where they are not believed.

The cognitive definition does not imply that people hold their beliefs as a list of articulated propositions as some critics have suggested.[4] *Beliefs in propositional form are to be understood as constructed by the investigator in an attempt to refer to the truth ideas of those from whose speech and behavior they have been inferred.*

Experience and Culture

I have sometimes found folklorists and anthropologists puzzled by my approach. They are accustomed to viewing experience through culture, while I spend quite a bit of energy on separating the two, and my primary focus is on the experience itself. Some colleagues have said that they are concerned with the *meaning* of beliefs, not with the alleged events to which they refer. After all, the events themselves are not available for inspection. My purpose includes a better understanding of the "meaning" of beliefs. But when scholars study food traditions or folk costume or architecture—folklife—it is understood that the endeavor requires a knowledge of the materials and the technology involved—how, for example, the flax is grown, processed, spun, woven, and made into clothing. Every step is described and placed within the context of the lives of those who wear the clothes.[5] Studying the material thus enhances the understanding of the meaning of the clothing. The symbolic and emotional and social meanings are not obscured by knowing as much as possible of what lies behind them. Similarly, the processes by which folk literature is created, the innovation, the social forces shaping its expression, and the structure of the stories all enhance efforts to understand folk narratives. The raw materials of folk literature lie in the social world and the creativity of narrators.

The Experiential Theory asserts that folk belief and the stories associated with it have been, in a sense, implicitly mis-classified. Understanding folk belief requires the folklife approach in which the entire environment, not just the social environment, is taken into account. The "core supernatural experience" categories are raw materials analogous to the farmer's experiences with soils, the weaver's experiences with fibers, and the hunter's experience with animals. The development of coherent systems of belief in which these "core supernatural experiences" are integrated with everyday life, language, emotion, symbol and social action is analogous to all sorts of making from farms to clothing and meals. We need to know the raw materials and the process for our account of the meaning to be valid. We do not need to know the "ontological status" of the "objects" of these experiences—whether the beliefs are true—any more than the folklife scholar needs to know the molecular structure of building stones or the evolutionary history of flax, in order to understand their traditional use and meaning. Such an inquiry would certainly be useful in some instances, for example in explaining the superior durability of some structures or tracing the historical use of flax. But it is not necessary in order to understand the current maker's use of tradition and materials. By the same token, the truth of supernatural beliefs is certainly important, and may (or may not) be a factor that can be determined with confidence, in a scholarly fashion. But regardless of such uiltimate determinations, we must begin the study of these beliefs with an account of how they arise from the experiences of those who hold them.

Inferring Beliefs and Reasons

Most people (philosophers and theologians aside) do not consciously hold their "beliefs" in a highly articulated form, certainly not as a list of propositions. Even if one knows, accepts and has reflected on an official religious creed, as may (or may not) be the case for a Christian who recites the Nicene Creed or Apostles Creed in church, that creed is unlikely to contain all that one believes to be true about the supernatural. This is not, however, to say that most people do not know what they believe. Rather, people's beliefs are embodied in their "stories" and their actions, from which they must be inferred by the interested observer. Stories and their discussion, then, are the natural currency of belief traditions. And these stories that center on the description of events also embody the arguments and counter-arguments by which people support their beliefs. But like the assertion of the beliefs, the arguments are often tacit, packed into various descriptions of the events themselves. Beliefs in propositional form are to be understood as constructions of the investigator, inferences of truth drawn from the speech and behavior of those observed. Such beliefs have the same status as the values, symbols, and other abstract entities that scholars infer from the behavior and statements of people.

Because descriptions of belief in the cognitive sense are inferred from believer utterances and refer to aspects of the cognitive worlds of believers, the validity of those descriptions requires an empirical check based in those worlds. I call this requirement the *principle of local acceptance*: a valid belief description must be acceptable to the one to whom it is attributed.

Using the cognitive meaning of belief, it makes no sense to speak of "unconscious beliefs," etc. The simplest check on the validity of a belief description is to offer it to the one thought to hold it, and ask if it is acceptable. If it is not acceptable it must refer to a belief the inquirer held about the believer, a belief that should now be corrected. The fact that a believer may lie about a belief poses an important problem in belief study, but it does not override this principle. Neither does this view exclude "covert beliefs." For a discussion of this important point see Robert Hahn's "Understanding Beliefs" (1973). We will consider the methodological issues raised by this principle below, under "Constructing Belief Statements."

Belief descriptions must also be carefully scrutinized for ambiguous terms. Until all terms have been properly defined, *in ways acceptable to the believer*, a valid description has not been established. Even if the inquirer finds local acceptance of the belief "that this house is haunted," the possibility of serious error exists until the meaning of *haunt, to the believer*, has been properly stated.

Stories may be very private, but the justification and development of belief is naturally a social matter, because inter-subjective checking is one of the most basic tests of the veridicality of a perception—that is, its faithful reference to something external to the observer. Sometimes one is readily convinced without inter-subjective support. I do not, for example, need to ask others whether I seem to have a computer on my desk in front of me. But even apart from the question of whether the object of perception exists, conclusions about the "meaning" of a perception are often part of a social process. And when a perception appears to run counter to what one's culture has taught one exists, then even the basic observational features cry out for social confirmation: "Did you see *that*!?"

A Haunting Example

The following example is a complex account involving two major speakers, an audience, and testimony ranging from first to third-hand and beyond. The beliefs and interpretations to be inferred are correspondingly complex. Perhaps most importantly, this example involves a variety of experiences, most of which do not qualify as "core supernatural experiences," but at least one of which does, and *all* of which the speakers take to refer to a related set of facts.

The set of stories involves a house in Georgia that its inhabitants believe is haunted. A variety of kinds of experience are described, most of which are not the "core supernatural experiences" of my theory. The one clear core example given here will be used to illustrate how such experiences function within cumulative cases for belief. This account is itself a cumulative case for the family's beliefs, and from a broader view this family's account is part of the larger cumulative case that is folk tradition.

Many of the narrative elements in the family's account have also been documented in tradition. To facilitate comparison with traditional narratives, I have provided motif numbers for these elements, at the end of the account. I have also provided a list of entries in the "Index of Features" in *The Terror That Comes in the Night* (pp. 267–70). This will make it possible to easily compare relevant aspects of Alice's experience with those that I reported and analyzed in that book.

Interview Context

In April of 1981 I received a phone call from a man in Georgia. He said that his niece had been attacked that morning by a ghost. This happened in his house, a house that had long been considered haunted. She was badly frightened, and he and his wife had spent the day trying by telephone to find someone who could help them come to terms with her experience. During this effort they had made contact with Lynwood Montell in the Folklore Department at Western Kentucky University, and knowing my work he had suggested that they call me. When I had heard the details I was able to recognize the major features of their account and at least let them know that what had happened to them was parallelled, in considerable detail, in the experiences of many others. I was fortunate in that this family, including the niece, was planning to come to the Washington, D.C., area on July 4th to visit relatives. Their trip made it possible for me to arrange to interview them in person. What follows is taken from the transcript of that interview, which lasted several hours and involved six family members.[6] What is presented below is a continuous block that centers on the niece's "attack."

    Dramatis Personae
        Jane & Richard (own the house)
        Sam   (family friend)
        Alice   (niece, victim of attack; daughter of Jane's sister)
        Kate   (Jane's mother)

The Account

The interview took place in Kate's home. Asked simply to begin at the beginning, Jane started the session by telling the history of the house, including a story of its purchase years ago by a man who paid eighteen sheep for it and then disappeared. The original owner then returned and took possession of both the sheep and the house. She went on to say that her husband (Richard) had purchased the house shortly before their wedding in 1968. In the weeks before the wedding she often spent Sunday afternoons there. On one such afternoon:

JANE: I was running my mouth and Sam was there and Richard was there, and we were the only ones in the house. . . . And I was talking and then all of a sudden I noticed that the men were looking up like that [she demonstrates] and just kind of listening. They weren't listening to me, and I stopped talking. And I could just hear the footsteps. . . . And it just sounded like someone was walking around up there. And I don't know how long it lasted. A couple of minutes probably. But it was—it was so normal that it didn't sound out of the ordinary until we realized that we were the only ones in the house. . . . Sam had one (other) experience with—with the uh—other than hearing what we heard. One night, for some reason, both he and Richard were sleeping in this room, and Sam's bed was along the attic wall. And Richard . . . had a bed over here. . . . And they both woke up at the same time, and they heard the footsteps. And—they don't know what woke them up, but they both realized they were awake. And the footsteps came directly toward Sam, and he said that he could hear them coming towards him, and . . . he could not move. Whether it was from fright or if there was some physical reason he could not move, he didn't know. But the footsteps walked towards him, under his bed and into the wall, into the attic.
HUFFORD: So he heard the footsteps pass right under where he was lying? [Right.] . . . . And at the same time did your husband Richard hear the footsteps?
JANE: Yes, they both heard them. . . .
ALICE: When I was baby-sitting Alan one day (in the spring of 1981), the first time I heard the ghost it was real, sort of creaky. Not quite footsteps. But it was upstairs, around the top of the stairs. And in my doorway. [M-hm.]
HUFFORD: Did you hear this from downstairs?
ALICE: Yes. In the living room, sitting by the window. And I turned the TV off, or down, and just listened to him walk around the stairs, at the top of the stairs. Um. Sitting in the living room you can't see all the way up the stairs, so I couldn't see anything, but I could hear him walking around. And I think it was a week and a day later, I heard him walking again. But it was real loud. It was, again, like she said, there wasn't anybody in the house, and it was around 9 o'clock in the morning, and I realized there was somebody upstairs walking around. And I—Loud steps, just like I said. And I realized I was alone, and he walked around my bedroom . . . for about 20 minutes. . . .
JANE: (Our hearing of the footsteps) started in August and it went through December (of 1968). We were married in December. One of these Sundays . . . the three of us were in the house. . . . A doorbell rang, and we don't have a doorbell! . . . It was the kind of doorbell—the old fashioned kind. Something like a bicycle bell.
UNIDENTIFIED SPEAKER: Where you turn it?
JANE: Yeah. And it goes, brringg, brringg, like that. And it did it two or three times. But it sounded just like an old-fashioned doorbell.
    Jane then described events during her wedding rehearsal in the house, in

December of 1968, when the ghost was seen—appearing as an old man. Also at this time several people claimed to have knocked on the walls of the house—obviously the story of the haunting was well-known—and to have received answering knocks.

Then Jane and Richard moved away for several years, renting the house to a family from Florida, not returning until 1978. Their tenants told them that they considered the house haunted and had heard footsteps, but no one in the family heard them from the time of the wedding rehearsal until Alice came in 1981 to baby-sit Jane and Richard's new baby:

ALICE: . . . . When I moved in, within the first day or so, I would go up into my room—which is the ghost room—the top one, up here—and I'd knock on the wall three times, and I'd talk. I mean, I figured if anyone was there they'd listen. And I would say, "I don't mind you being here. As a matter of fact I'd like you to be here. But I don't want to hear you at night, because night's the only time that I'm afraid." And I could spend fifteen minutes just talking, or saying who I thought he was. I think you're John Smith—John. And I was really proud that this guy, even though he was killed, would stay to claim his property. And I thought that was pretty neat. And I said, "If you heard me, make some kind of sound or noise, or let me know you heard me." And I went back downstairs, and within fifteen minutes—I was sitting with Richard in the living room—and we heard a big bang in my room upstairs. And it was as if somebody had jumped with, you know, their two feet and just hit down hard. And Richard looked over at me, and I didn't say anything really. I just looked at him, and he—I guess he knew it was the ghost. And, so I was glad, I guess, that he heard me.
HUFFORD: M-hm. Did you like the idea? [ALICE: Of talking to the ghost?] Yeah, and having it there. . . .
ALICE: It was—Something to be sort of a friend to me. Or, something to talk to, that I could relax and talk. [HUFFORD: M-hm.] And if nobody heard me or somebody heard me it didn't make that much difference.
HUFFORD: Well, how did you feel then when you heard the—
ALICE: I was real happy, because I had said what I wanted to. [HUFFORD: M-hm.] And I felt that I wouldn't have to worry at night. And I never was worried after or afraid.

There followed a pause while the tape was turned over, and further description of the house, its history and family reactions to it followed. Jane said that her mother-in-law has always explained the ghostly footsteps as "squirrels in the attic." But she has never heard them, and those who have heard them reject this explanation. Then Alice picked up the narrative with the events of the night of her "attack by the ghost":

ALICE: It was June 2nd, or the morning of the 3rd. And I went to bed. I had fallen asleep downstairs on the couch, and it was hot. And I went upstairs, and it was around 1:15. And I went to bed. It was hot, so I slept in the nude. But I turned off the light, and I remember walking through the middle of the room where the light was, it was a string, over to my bed. And I could imagine seeing myself walking over. I don't know if you've ever—If you just think of, like, riding your bike down the street, and seeing yourself ride down the street. That's your feeling. Well, I felt like I watched myself walk over, or—I don't know about being watched or seen, but—It wasn't—I was really thinking about how I looked walking across. I don't know why. And I went to bed, and I had my sheets pulled up under my arms. . . .

KATE: Explain to him what the light looks like.

ALICE: It's in the middle of the room. Just a light bulb with a string, and you just pull the string. And I was probably in my room for a minute before I went to bed. And I probably just sat down on the edge of my bed. And turned on the radio and adjusted it so that it would go off in an hour. [HUFFORD: Yeah.] And I'd taken off my clothes because it was hot. And one leg, my right leg sort of out of the sheets over the covers. And the door was open, I guess about an inch—two inches—opened, so the light came in. The hall light . . . That light was on. It's always left on, for the boys and for me just to get down the stairs. And so I fell asleep, and it was—probably about 1:30. And I woke up, because I heard steps coming up the stairs. Fast steps. Four fast steps. They didn't make it quite to the top. They missed probably the first—the top two steps they missed, or so. And I heard the steps, and they frightened me, because—one was I had a lot of trust in the ghost and I didn't expect to hear anything from him at night, and the other one was, I didn't recognize the steps. I think you can, just while you're asleep, you can tell who walks around and you won't wake up unless, you know, it's somebody who's not supposed to be there. [HUFFORD: M-hm.] And so I heard the steps, and I looked toward the foot of my bed. My head, the headboard's against the attic. [HUFFORD: OK.] And, you know, the footboard is right by the door. [HUFFORD: M-hm.] So I looked down towards my feet, at the light at the door. And as soon as I motioned to sit up . . . sort of tensed my muscles to sit forward to see who was coming or what was going on, I realized something was at the end of my bed—standing on top of it, over my feet. And I—I got real mad at first. Just extremely mad, because I knew—Like, I had said, "This is my space and my time, and I don't want anything to do with the ghost." And I—Then I was frightened. It was all in an instant. The steps and then somebody at the end of my bed. And I knew that it *couldn't* be the ghost, because he wouldn't do that. I had enough trust and faith in him, and I figured that he just wouldn't do that. And I motioned to sit forward or get up, and I was thrust back into my bed and had a great pressure on my chest and my forehead. And then the sheets were ripped—were just jerked straight down from under my arms to my waist level. And the pressure was still just on my chest and my forehead. And I tried yelling, tried saying, "Goddamit leave me alone!" It was something Barbara had heard—Barbara, Jane's younger sister, had talked to somebody and they said, "Get mad at ghosts and tell them just to leave you alone." But I couldn't get anything out. There wasn't any words or any air. And so I tried calling for help. Tried calling for Jane. And I couldn't get anything out yet. And so then I started—I physically couldn't move. It was like I didn't have any arms or legs. I hadn't even thought of using them. It was more just my body trying to sit forward. And my arms and legs were just dead weight. There wasn't anything to them. And I stopped really struggling, because I couldn't get any air. And I started concentrating, I think, on crosses. I wanted a cross. I wanted something religious. I wanted a cross, and I was just imagining a cross and I then passed out and had dreams—I knew they were dreams—about getting help. . . . And I realized I was really asleep, and that if I were going to do anything I had to wake up. And I woke up, and my radio was still playing like I had left it. It was set on "doze" so it would go off within an hour of when I set it. And I just grabbed my nightgown and ran downstairs, and spent the rest of the night in Jane and Richard's bedroom. And I stayed up until 5 when I called my mother. . . .

Alice then explained that at first she told her mother she had to come home immediately; she could not spend another night in the house. However, on reflection she became convinced that she must have been attacked by a "different ghost," an interpretation the entire family came to accept, because the regular haunt had always been so harmless. She forced herself to stay the remaining two and one-half weeks, and even spent the last six days in "the ghost room." All of the family present at the interview, and by report most of those not present, believed Alice's report and saw a connection with the haunting of the house despite the attribution of the attack to a spectral interloper.

Although naturally all of the family had heard of ghosts, they were not familiar with other accounts or traditions about attacks of the kind experienced by Alice, and this was their only experience with a full-scale haunting. They are a middle class, college-educated family. They denied being "into" parapsychology, spiritism, and so forth.

Motif Numbers (Thompson 1966)

E235.3. Return from dead as punishment for trying to raise ghost.
E261. Wandering ghost makes attack.
E279.3. Ghost pulls bed clothing from sleeper.
E281.3. Ghost haunts particular room in house.
E334.2.1. Ghost of murdered person haunts burial spot.
E338.1(ab). Ghost causes bell to ring. E402.3(a) Sound of ghost bell.
E338.1(ad). Occupants hear ghost fall on floor of room above them.
E421.5. Ghost seen by two or more persons. . . .
E434.8.1. Ghost cannot harm person wearing a cross.
E544.2. Ghost pulls blanket from sleeper.
F470.1. Spirits pull off person's bedclothes.
F471.1. Nightmare (Alp) presses person. . . .
F473.5(a). Knockings and rappings that cannot be traced.
J1782.3. House noises thought to be ghosts.

Index of Features (Hufford 1982)

I.A. Impression of wakefulness.
I.B. Paralysis. 2. perceived as restraint.
I.B. Paralysis. 3. uncertain or variously perceived.

I.C. Real setting accurately perceived.
I.D. Fear
II.A. . . . subjective impressions. 10. other. . . . f. out-of-body sensations.
II.A.2.b. Footsteps (heard).
II.A.6. motion. c. covers pulled off bed
II.A.7. pressure. d. feels like . . . being pushed.
II.A.7. Pressure. a. on chest & c. on head.
II.A.8. respiratory difficulty.
II.D. Termination of attacks. 4. prayer.

Comments on the Haunting

This account of a haunting (called hereafter the *Haunting*) concerns folk beliefs that have little part in most official, institutional religions: returned spirits of the dead, ghosts. Returned spirits, however, constitute the most basic spirit category in folk traditions about the supernatural. Whether a tradition contains demons, shapeshifters, vampires, fetches, or angels, almost all include spirits of the dead. Nonetheless, we can see here some of the interaction of religious and non-religious, supernatural beliefs.

An Account of Supernatural Experience

This account illustrates each of the elements in my definition of *supernatural*. The house is thought to be haunted by the discarnate spirit of its previous owner. In establishing this as a ghost, the stories[7] describe characteristics that distinguish a spirit from physical persons—for example, invisibility and the ability to pass through solid objects, as when the footsteps pass under Sam's bed and through the wall of the room. The objective reality of this spirit is attested by the multiplicity of witnesses, some of whom make their observations simultaneously. The stories also specify several kinds of interaction between the spirit and those living in the house: causing a sound like a doorbell, hearing Alice's speech and responding with a noise heard by Alice and her uncle, appearing visibly to Alice, pulling down her covers, and holding her powerless. These vary in the directness with which they support the implicit claim involved in calling an event supernatural, and they illustrate the difference between "direct supernatural experience" and "interpretive supernatural experience," a crucial difference in the Experiential Theory, because *core supernatural experiences* are by definition *direct supernatural experiences* that also possess a cross contextually stable perceptual pattern.

> Stipulated definition: A *direct supernatural experience* is one in which identifying characteristics of a spirit(s) (i.e., persons not requiring physical bodies, as given in the definition of *supernatural*) are perceived. Such an experience seems to force a choice between "I must be hallucinating" and "I am perceiving a 'spirit.'"

> Stipulated definition: An *interpretive supernatural experience*[8] is one in which identifying characteristics of a spirit(s) are not perceived, but a believed supernatural connection is made in some other manner, as by inference.

This distinction is not simple, and I fully recognize that observation and interpretation cannot be rendered truly dichotomous. However, the Experiential Theory does not require any strong or controversial view of this distinction. The distinction to which the theory refers is exactly like that which exists between seeing a friend sitting on his porch and therefore believing that he is home (direct experience), and seeing that the lights are on in his house and therefore believing that he is home (interpretive experience with regard to your friend's location).

Inferring Beliefs

While the stories that make up the *Haunting* share a common focus, there are many events, many actors, several speakers, and many implicated beliefs to consider. In such a situation the process of inferring unstated beliefs requires close attention.

In the *Haunting* the words "belief" and "believe" were not used even once by family members. Instead, the speakers describe events in a way that implies their beliefs and tacitly makes a case for them. For instance, Jane, in her description of the anomalous footsteps, did not state *any interpretation* or use the word *ghost*. The closest she came to *ghost* was "Sam had one (other) experience with—with the uh—Other than hearing what we heard." Yet the context of the discussion and the implication of the observations she reports make it clear that she is offering reasons to believe that the spirit of the murdered owner resides in her house.

Accounts such as this one implicitly support and carry forward both argument and counter-argument, as in the report of Jane's mother-in-law's belief that the footsteps are "squirrels in the attic," and the rebuttal that *she* has never heard the footsteps. Stories about belief serve a variety of functions, including entertainment, and if they were not interesting, they would not be retold. However, they obtain much of their interest from the claims they make about the world. When these stories are in oral circulation, they are among what folklorists call legends. A legend, it has been observed, "always *states* something and often attests its statements. In some cases, it formally relates statement and attestation in the manner of deductive reason" (Dégh and Vázsonyi 1976:116). I find that the reasoning is often informal and that it involves induction as much as deduction, especially in the absence of a well-developed institutional tradition of theory building. But the general point is the same: beliefs about the supernatural and the reasoning by which they are derived and applied are to be found in stories. They are not *hidden* in these stories, because the stories are constructed specifically to carry on a discussion, even a debate, about the beliefs. They are therefore displayed quite prominently.

The analysis of stories about beliefs begins by inferring the beliefs and supporting reasons. The study of language provides a useful analogy. Official ("correct") English has a rigorous and highly complex system that can be found codified in books. There are official English speakers/teachers who can recite the rules and can correct inaccurate usages. Practically all American children are exposed to much of this official system (and some in fact learn it). Informal speech (e.g., local dialect, slang) does not have such a prominent and codified system, but linguists have demonstrated that a complex grammatical system is nonetheless present and acted upon. Speakers speak correctly (depending on their competence) and recognize errors, although they generally find it difficult to state the rules behind the distinctions. However, a linguist can infer the rules through observation, analysis, and the questioning of speakers. Systems of belief operate in the same fashion. Just as speech implicitly carries the rules of grammar, accounts such as the *Haunting* implicitly carry beliefs, evidence attesting to their truth, and the rules of evidence and reasoning that relate evidence and belief. This analogy reminds us that "beliefs" are inferences, constructs. They are not like the vocabulary in language, because they are not usually given explicitly in the text. Rather they, as much as the rules of reasoning, are implicit within the text and must be derived by inference by the analyst. This is why catalogs of beliefs are so inadequate as representations of tradition.

The setting in which the *Haunting* was recorded was not a natural one, inasmuch as the assembled family was telling me, an outsider, about the haunting. However, I imposed no structure and the resulting group effort was typical of sessions in which belief stories are told. What emerged was not a single story, but rather a series of related stories, of which I have given ten that were told contiguously, seven told by Jane and three by Alice. Everyone present had heard some of these stories before, and several of them said they had heard the footsteps or witnessed other evidence of the ghost's presence. But in this session the other four family members primarily served to corroborate the belief that these stories are true and that the inference of haunting is reasonable and valid.

The Stories in the Haunting

The following is a list, not necessarily exhaustive, of the stories present within the *Haunting*. I have roughly indicated the sources and the directness with which they attest the various claims. Notice that the claims include both what people have *said* and what they have *experienced*:

1. A man buys the house for eighteen sheep; it is implied that he was then murdered by the seller. (Jane, from oral tradition)
2. Jane, Richard, and Sam hear the footsteps together. (Jane, first hand [that she heard this] and second hand [that Richard and Sam heard this])
3. Richard and Sam hear footsteps that pass under Sam's bed. (Jane, second hand)
4. Alice hears the footsteps for the first time. (Alice, first hand)
5. Jane, Richard, and Sam hear the nonexistent doorbell. (Jane, first and second hand)
6. At the wedding rehearsal knocking is heard and the ghost of an old man is seen. (Jane, first [Jane heard the guests say they heard raps], second and third hand [the hearing of raps])
7. The tenants state that the house is haunted, and they have heard footsteps. (Jane, first [that they said they heard] and second hand [the hearing itself])
8. Alice communicates with the ghost by knocking on the wall and talking, setting rules. Subsequently a loud 'answer' from the ghost is heard by Alice and Richard. (Alice, first hand)

9. Jane's mother-in-law says the sound is caused by squirrels in the attic, but those who have heard the footsteps reject this explanation. (Jane, first hand)

10. Alice describes her attack and subsequent decisions. (Alice, first hand)

Some of these stories have enough independent interest to stand alone. For example, I have heard stories similar to the wedding rehearsal and Alice's attack told separately. However, some of these stories would not only lack interest but would not make much sense alone. The fact that the man who bought the house disappeared or that Jane, Richard, and Sam heard a bell where there was none, gain their significance from their relationship to the other stories. This set of stories actually operates as a cumulative case for a set of related beliefs by organizing and presenting a variety of experience claims and implicit interpretations. This organization is as important as the individual elements, because it elucidates the belief system within which this family makes sense of these events.

The Ghost of a Previous Owner Haunts the House

The most obvious belief displayed and attested by this account is that the spirit of a deceased man frequents Jane and Richard's house, that he haunts the house. For convenient reference, I will refer to this belief as *The Owner Haunts*. This belief is asserted and supported by the description of a variety of events. Each of the nine stories listed above attests this belief. All of the stories of footsteps, the ghostly bell, and so forth make and support the claim that the ghost is. The story of the purchase of the house for eighteen sheep, and the buyer's disappearance, suggest who the ghost is. The description of Jane's mother-in-law's squirrels-in-the-attic explanation shows a consideration of possible alternative explanations and implicitly rejects them. *The Owner Haunts* is supported by a variety of kinds of reasons, some very direct and some very indirect. The belief that the owner was murdered after paying eighteen sheep for the house, one premise of *The Owner Haunts*, came to the family as oral history. They accepted it as true on the authority of tradition, having no personal knowledge about the matter. Other beliefs serving as premises to *The Owner Haunts* were derived from experience—some direct and some interpretive—and by inference.

The Implicit Belief System

The Owner Haunts is an easily inferred belief that illustrates some of the ways that beliefs may relate systematically to one another. The concept of belief systems is generally recognized, but has not been consistently applied to the study of supernatural folk beliefs.[9] The Experiential Theory requires that the systematic relationship of beliefs be a central issue. The rationality of these beliefs is found in their systematic relation to each other and to experiential reports. These systems, it must be remembered, are hypothetical constructs inferred from the accounts and conversation of believers. The relationships that I will illustrate here are those that are inherent within each belief, so that part of the structure of the system to which they come to belong is intrinsic within each member. These relationships illustrate the ways that core supernatural experiences and beliefs underlie and change the implications of other, less direct, experiences and beliefs. There are many other, more complex relationships that develop when these or any beliefs come into a broad belief system or world view. The minimal systematic ordering of beliefs to which these basic relationships give rise may be called the implicit system of that set of beliefs. I will call the basic relationships *entailment, enablement,* and *suggestion.* Beliefs related in these ways may either support or conflict with each other.

Entailment

If it is true that *The Owner Haunts*, then it must also be true that people (at least, and at least some) have souls (definition: personal elements that can survive death). Either of these beliefs requires that the supernatural (by my definition) exists objectively. The belief that souls exist and that the supernatural is real are entailed by *The Owner Haunts.*

> Stipulated Definition of *Entailment*: Belief B is entailed by belief A, if A cannot be true unless B is also true.

This is not a symmetrical relationship. Believing that souls exist and survive death does not require a belief that such souls ever haunt.

Enablement

The belief that people have souls *enables The Owner Haunts*, by establishing one of the minimal conditions required for that belief to be true. An entailed belief *enables* the belief that entails it. That is, it asserts grounds that are necessary for the enabled belief to be possible. These are not necessarily sufficient grounds. A belief that souls exist enables *The Owner Haunts*, and many other beliefs, without necessarily suggesting them. That souls exist is not the only condition necessary for *The Owner Haunts* to be true; it is not sufficient grounds.

> Stipulated Definition of *Enablement*: Belief A is enabled by belief B, if B makes it possible for A also to be true.

Suggestion

Suggestion is more general than entailment, which it includes (any entailed belief is suggested), and more specific than enablement (one belief may enable another without suggesting it). The beliefs that (a) an earlier owner was secretly murdered, and that (b) the house is haunted, presented together, suggest that *The Owner Haunts*. More generally, they suggest that violent death and injustice can lead to haunting. None of these beliefs entail each other. That the house is haunted enables *The Owner Haunts*, because the latter could not be true without the former. That an earlier owner was murdered does not enable any of the other beliefs, because they could be true without that premise. The owner's death does, nonetheless, suggest *The Owner Haunts.*

> Stipulated Definition of *Suggestion*: Belief A is suggested by any belief or set of beliefs that imply or propose "that perhaps A is true," raising A for consideration.

Beliefs Embedded in Perceptual Experiences and Their Descriptions

The implicit relationships among beliefs also exist between some experiences and beliefs, and among *many* descriptions of experience and beliefs. The distinction between experience and descriptions of experience is very important, because our access to descriptions is direct but the characteristics of experiences are always inferred (except by the subject). When entailment, enablement or suggestion of beliefs are inferred from descriptions of experience, they may be said to have been embedded in those descriptions. Even minimally ramified[10] descriptions of perception embed some elements of belief. The sentence "I look at the computer on my desk," embeds both the belief that there is a computer there (a belief about the world) and that I see the computer there (a belief about my experience).[11] In the case of the computer on one's desk, it is unlikely that most people would stop to reflect on the belief that perception was occurring, but when the percept is very unexpected such reflection is common. That is why people pinch themselves or look away and look back or say "Did you hear that?" In any event, even very simple statements, unless loaded with cautionary hedges beyond those ever found in normal discourse and thought ("I seem to see something before me that looks like what I think a computer looks like."), carry such embedded beliefs. Thus, we may speak of experiences and experiential reports as entailing, enabling and suggesting beliefs just as we have spoken of beliefs having this relationship. This does not mean that any experiences are "self authenticating"[12] in a generally compelling way. That is, no experience makes any incontrovertible claim on anyone other than the subject of that experience, and many experiences do not even establish claims for the subject. That is why the experiences may cause subjects to "pinch themselves." Nonetheless, some experiences do, for the experiencer, entail belief. For example, speaking of the "sense of a presence," C. Thompson observes that the experience is characterized by an "over-riding sense of reality," that amounts to "an 'imposed sense of conviction'" (1982:628). The same might be said of my experience of seeing my computer. This is a characteristic that some supernatural experiences share with many natural experiences, presumably because of the recognizable "mental texture" of reality. But the existence of hallucinations and delusions guarantees that this texture is sometimes a counterfeit. We infer that some experiences entail belief, but we may directly observe that many experiential reports, descriptions of experience, do so as well.

Direct supernatural *experiences* (including core experiences) *entail* some supernatural *beliefs* by definition, because the definition of *supernatural* includes "objectively real." Thompson's point concerning the "sensing of a presence" illustrates this. Descriptions generally entail, enable and suggest more beliefs than do experiences *per se*. The more ramified a description of experience is, the greater the variety of embedded beliefs is likely to be. Alice said, "The first time I heard the ghost it was real, sort of creaky. Not quite footsteps. But it was upstairs, around the top of the stairs." Alice's description is only moderately ramified, by the use of the term *the ghost*. By employing that term within her description, Alice embeds the beliefs that *The Owner Haunts* and the more general beliefs that ghosts exist and that they make noises that people can hear.

We could redescribe this experience in a less ramified manner as "Alice heard 'creaky sounds, not quite footsteps'. She interpreted these as being caused by the ghost of whom she had heard." With this redescription the beliefs about ghosts and this particular ghost cease to be embedded. This permits us to see that the embedding in this case was in the description rather than the experience. Alice interpreted the sounds as caused by the ghost.

Next consider Jane's description of her first hearing of "the ghost's footsteps":

> And I could just hear the footsteps. . . . And it just sounded like someone was walking around up there. And I don't know how long it lasted. A couple of minutes probably. But it was—it was so normal that it didn't sound out of the ordinary until we realized that we were the only ones in the house. . . .

No supernatural beliefs are embedded in this experiential report. The belief that these footsteps were ghostly is derived by inference from "hearing footsteps" and "we were the only ones in the house."

But there is still an important embedded belief in what is a moderately ramified description. The word footstep reaches beyond what was observed. Jane's phrase "I could just hear the footsteps" describes hearing a sound that is like the sounds that she commonly associates with footsteps. To say that one has a "direct experience of footsteps" we would want at least an observation of the feet striking and the sounds following. In *The Terror that Comes in the Night* (1982), I reported my surprise at realizing what a variety of perceptual details are covered under the word footsteps (89 ff.). As I sought less ramified redescriptions from subjects, new and significant perceptual patterns began to emerge.

It is always possible to reduce the ramification of an experiential report. Theoretically the ultimate endpoint of this process would be an atomistic account of sensations and other discrete "appearances in the mind." Practically, the language and methods that would allow such a description to be derived with confidence do not exist.[13] The closest useful approximation that I have found is the eliciting of sensory analogies, when the subject can provide them. For example, one subject in *The Terror* redescribed "whooshy footsteps" as like "the sound of a block of wood being rubbed repeatedly over a piece of velvet." But the process of developing phenomenological descriptions of perceptual elements in an experience should not be overdone. The fact that observation statements can be endlessly redescribed until their meaning is lost in a subjective haze merely reminds us of what has already been granted regarding experience and reason, observation and theory: they are *not* dichotomous. The terms of description always embed theory, and theoretical statements always (except in metaphysics) refer to observations.

From the subject's viewpoint, and for our understanding of the believing process, the important boundary comes where conscious inference and interpretation stop. Beyond that point we have perception. Judging from the descriptions, it seems that Alice engaged in some conscious association of the vague sounds with "the ghost" she had heard about. Jane, however, seems to have "heard footsteps" before she began to think about their implications.

From the analyst's viewpoint, seeking perceptual elements is useful even beyond the perception-inference boundary, to the extent that the resulting descriptions are clear and that significant patterns emerge. This search for perceptual details makes it possible to inquire in detail, for example, into claims that two different subjects have "had the same experience." Perceptual details may also suggest explanations or may even rule out some explanations. To assess Jane's mother-in-law's squirrels-in-the-attic explanation, perceptual details from several hearers of footsteps, together with detailed knowledge of the sounds made by squirrels in attics, might be very helpful. It is also useful in studying the reasoning of subjects to discover the extent to which belief discussions reach behind ramification in an effort to establish inter-subjective support. When this is not done, the ambiguity of ramified descriptions can itself account for apparent correspondence when in fact little or none exists.

However, we are not justified in asserting that the ramification of description renders experiential reports unintelligible or constitutes an overwhelming bias. I have already noted that observation, belief, and argument are bundled together in folk tradition. Given the normal rules of informal discourse, the giving of minimally ramified descriptions communicates uncertainty about the meaning of events. This is a consequence of what H. Paul Grice calls "conversational implicature" (1975). In ordinary conversation the strongest statements consistent with belief are used. "I heard a sound like footsteps" would mean that the speaker is not sure that the sound *was* footsteps. The extent to which conversations about supernatural experience seek to develop belief or simply to communicate it or even merely to entertain will determine the care with which speakers permit ambiguity or strive for specificity.

The development of careful phenomenological descriptions often has the effect of showing that the experiential reports by subjects of supernatural experience are careful and represent patterns that are actually supported by perception and reasonable inference. We could note Jane's reluctance to use the word "ghost" and Alice's specification that the first time she "heard the ghost" it was "real creaky. Not quite footsteps." We will also see that we can have good reason to believe that Alice's description of her attack is very accurate and not heavily ramified. The assumption of many scholars that there are no clear perceptual patterns to be found behind ramified descriptions focuses analysis on the wrong level if we wish to understand how ordinary discourse carries and develops the significance of experiential reports. If the ordinary listener gives too much credit to the specificity and coherence of traditional supernatural references, then the scholar typically gives too little. It is no wonder the overall interpretations diverge so sharply. But the analysis of conversation *by itself* cannot be confused with the analysis of experience. And it must be remembered that the traditions within which the conversations of interest arise are about experiences, not about other conversations. Believers are seeking to make sense of experience. To understand them, scholars must attempt to do the same.

The Implicit Belief System and the Background Belief System

Belief systems, like the beliefs of which they consist, are hypothetical constructs. Their scope is determined by the level and intent of analysis. The implicit belief system is found in a very close analysis. At a much broader level we may speak of cultural belief systems representing the relationships among the beliefs held by many individuals. But even within the individual we may infer various levels of systematic organization. The inherent relationships of supernatural beliefs and experiences must be understood within the broader system of beliefs, meanings, and values of their holders. Even such a strong relationship as entailment can be transformed by differences in the meaning of terms. For example, the entailment of a belief in souls by the belief *The Owner Haunts* can be canceled by some meanings for *haunting*. Some parapsychologists have suggested theories of hauntings that involve something more like an emotional echo in which haunting apparitions appear to be insensible automatons rather than the persons like whom they appear.[14] This is a reminder that the relationships outlined are among concepts, but the expression of those concepts in words is frequently misleading because of ramification and other sources of ambiguity.

A less direct relationship, such as enablement, is quite dependent on other beliefs within the system. Within many belief systems a belief in souls enables a belief in ghosts. But when the belief in souls is accompanied by a belief in the fate of souls that precludes their communication with the living, as in the theology of Jehovah's Witnesses or Seventh Day Adventists, the belief in souls does not enable a belief in ghosts. In fact, we may say the belief in "soul sleep" held by these groups disables belief in ghosts (Rosten 1975:135–36, 247).

Background Knowledge of Beliefs

In speaking of background knowledge, we use *knowledge* in its second sense of familiarity. We do not grant certainty to this information. In the *Haunting* we can see the operation of a variety of background ideas and beliefs. For example, the idea of "ghost" is a very important background element here. We do not know whether any of the actors *believed* in ghosts and haunting before their experiences in the house, but we can be confident they knew of such an idea. Being familiar with a belief and holding it are obviously very different things. And yet just knowing a belief can be a powerful factor in shaping reactions to experience. Jane's reaction to footsteps when she believed no one was there to make them was obviously shaped by her awareness of the ghost idea. When people sort through explanatory possibilities, they draw their hypotheses from their background knowledge of beliefs about the world. Those beliefs that they do not yet hold will be farther down in the hierarchy, but they are there.

It is probably the case that most people are familiar with more beliefs than they hold. Quite probably most readers do not believe that blood-sucking, supernatural vampires exist, but they know many beliefs about such entities. If faced with the right circumstances, they would know how to employ garlic and a crucifix as protection! By the same token we have no reason to believe that Alice held any particular beliefs about communicating with ghosts before coming to the house, but she knew "what to do" when convinced that her room was haunted. She communicated with the ghost as if she had had spiritualist training. Then, when she awoke paralyzed and threatened, she knew that she wanted crosses for protection. There is no need to assume that she had ever held the belief that crosses will repel evil spirits—but most people in the United States today are familiar with the idea. I very often find such background knowledge, not previously believed, being pressed into service in such circumstances.

This account demonstrates a variety of other examples of background knowledge of supernatural beliefs. It is unlikely that the family "made up" the idea that violent and unjust death can result in haunting. Almost certainly this background possibility was one premise in the inference that the murdered owner is the ghost. This background idea, together with the experiences that suggested the house was haunted, gave credibility to the legend that the earlier owner had been murdered. The legend and the experiences in turn transformed what may have been a belief known but not held, that violence and injustice can cause haunting, into a confirmed belief for the family members.

Non-supernatural Beliefs and Values

Beliefs and values about personality underlie part of Alice's reasoning that her attacker "*couldn't* be the ghost, because he wouldn't do that. I had enough trust and faith in him, and I figured that he just wouldn't do that." This particular belief entails the general belief that different ghosts have different and consistent personalities, but it arises from a much more general set of ideas about personality that has no special reference to ghosts.

Beliefs about Beliefs

More generally we can also see the operation of background "beliefs about beliefs." When Jane describes the first time that she heard the ghostly footsteps, she includes a description of Sam and Richard "just looking up . . . kind of listening." When she describes Sam's paralysis experience, she specifies that both he and Richard were awake and both heard the footsteps. Alice notes that Richard also heard the "loud bang" that answered her request that the ghost show that he had heard her. Jane notes that the tenants who rented the house at one point also heard the footsteps. These features draw their significance from the belief that beliefs are better supported by the observations of numerous witnesses. This is not a "supernatural belief"; rather, it is an epistemic belief, part of the same background of rules of reason that would be used to advance any argument.

Direct Experiences in the *Haunting*

Most of the events recounted in the *Haunting* involve interpretive supernatural experiences. Footsteps, the phantom doorbell, raps on the wall, all of these suggest that the house is haunted. Or conversely, the belief that the house is haunted suggests and enables the belief that these anomalies have a ghostly source.

There are three events described that are direct supernatural experiences, one of which is the appearance of the ghost as an old man, at the wedding rehearsal in

1968. None of those present during my interview of the family were sure who had seen the old man—none of them had. So this event is described third hand at best. It is obviously implied that the witness had good reason to believe that the old man was not a flesh and blood being, so the description is a very incomplete account of some sort of direct supernatural experience. The description may be wrong, and perhaps there was no direct supernatural experience of this kind at that time. But, nonetheless, *the description* is of a direct supernatural experience.

Jane's account of when Richard listened with Sam as "the footsteps walked towards him, under his bed and into the wall, into the attic," is a direct supernatural experience. Although they may have been mistaken—perhaps a squirrel *under* the floor this time—they "heard footsteps" in a place where they could see that there was no one to make them, and the "footsteps" passed under and through solid objects. We may add to these details the fact that Sam "couldn't move." In this account we have multiple witnesses, Richard and Sam, although we have the story second hand from Jane.

And third, we have Alice's account. I reproduce it here, retaining only the descriptive elements.

> And I woke up because I heard steps coming up the stairs. . . . and they frightened me, because . . . I had a lot of trust in the ghost and I didn't expect to hear anything from him at night;—and . . . I didn't recognize the steps. . . . And so I heard the steps, and I looked toward the foot of my bed. . . . towards my feet, at the light at the door. And as soon as I motioned to sit up. . . . sort of tensed my muscles to sit forward to see who was coming or what was going on, I realized something was at the end of my bed—standing on top of it, over my feet. And I—I got real *mad* at first. Just extremely mad, because I knew—Like, I had said, "This is my space and my time, and I don't want anything to do with the ghost." Then I was frightened. It was all in an instant. The steps and then somebody at the end of my bed. And I knew that it *couldn't* be the ghost, because he wouldn't do that. I had enough trust and faith in him, and I figured that he just wouldn't do that. And I motioned to sit forward or get up, and I was thrust back into my bed and had a great pressure on my chest and my forehead. . . . And then the sheets were ripped—were just jerked straight down from under my arms to my waist level.

This description is only moderately ramified. The use of the term *footsteps* goes somewhat beyond Alice's direct observation. The rest of the account, though somewhat incomplete, stays very close to the way that the event *appeared* to Alice. Something that rushes into your room in the night, suddenly appears over your feet, and produces an invisible pressure that forces you back into your bed provides a good fit with my definition of supernatural without need for inference or reflection. Alice's account is a perceptual experience that intuitively refers to the supernatural; there is no claim that this experience is "unmediated" or completely "uninterpreted." We have already noted that all perceptions involve some level of (incorporated) interpretation. I do not propose to hypothesize how a "really supernatural perception" would be mediated. Neither does tradition specify this process, except to suggest that it is different from but analogous to physical sense perception.

A Core Supernatural Experience

Alice's "attack" experience clearly belongs to the class of experience that I documented and analyzed in *The Terror* (1982), what Newfoundlanders call "the Old Hag," and what physicians call "sleep paralysis." To avoid the burden of local theory carried by each of these terms (such as the inaccurate gender implication of "hag" and the physical reductionism of sleep paralysis), I have chosen to use the old Anglo-Saxon word for the experience, *mara* (see Hufford 1982:53–56, 125). By this term I refer simply to the experience of finding oneself awake and paralyzed in the presence of a frightening being. Nothing more, neither interpretation nor cause, is implied. The following is a list of some of the common features of Mara attacks that occur in Alice's experience:

1) She was lying down in a supine position and had been asleep.
2) She was awakened by the sound of footsteps.
3) She was sure that she was wake and perceiving her natural environment in the ordinary way.
4) She saw an anomalous "something" approach.
5) She felt paralyzed.
6) She felt intense pressure.
7) Her sheets were pulled down.
8) She could not cry out.
9) She was subsequently certain that she had been awake during the experience. (This is not redundant with #3, because it is needed to set this experience apart from false awakening dreams which are subsequently recognized as dreams.)

These features constitute a cross-culturally stable pattern, as documented in *The Terror*,[15] so Alice's attack is an example of a "core supernatural experience."

It is interesting that neither Jane nor Alice specifically associate Sam's experience with Alice's. Nonetheless, in what description we are given, we find items 1, 2, 3, 5, 7, and 10 to be stated or implied. It too took place in what Alice calls "the ghost room," and Alice's bed like Sam's is described as being against the attic wall. Apparently, Alice's experience serves somewhat to confirm Sam's experience. But Sam's experience is presented as a part of the "regular haunting," while the entire family has come to agree that Alice's experience must have been caused by a "different ghost," not the murdered owner.

When these paralysis attacks occur in the midst of haunting, I have several times found that the people involved do not separate these attacks from the other events.[16] In this case the family, and especially Alice, have additional reasons not to associate them. The family seems quite pleased with the haunting by the murdered owner. As Alice said, "I was really proud that this guy, even though he was killed, would stay to claim his property. And I thought that was pretty neat." But a malevolent ghost that paralyzes, presses, and torments would not be "neat."

The relationship that the family has developed with "their ghost" and the desire not be afraid of their own home both constitute "non-rational reasons" for believing that Alice's attack was carried out by a different ghost, just as they suggest non-rational reasons for them to want to believe *The Owner Haunts*. Non-rational reasons are generally emotional or motivational "biases." They are reasons to *want* to hold a belief, as opposed to reasons that others should accept a belief as true. Non-rational reasons include "irrational" (cognitively disordered) reasons, but they are not limited to them. Obviously, many people have non-rational reasons that support (but do not necessarily determine) the holding of beliefs generally accepted as true. For example, doctors and patients have many non-rational reasons to believe in the efficacy of antibiotics, that is, to *want* antibiotics to effective. But these are not their only reasons nor do these reasons invalidate their scientific reasons. Non-rational reasons must be sought in studying beliefs, but they cannot be *assumed* to the "real explanation" of the beliefs. Scholars very often assume that supernatural beliefs are based on non-rational reasons, without ever seeking any other grounds. This assumption, concerning beliefs not held by the investigator, constitutes overwhelming bias and creates an impenetrable barrier to understanding.

Cumulative Cases

Carolyn Franks Davis (1988) discusses at length the idea of cumulative arguments, both for and against the evidential force of religious experience. This important concept goes right to the center of a complaint long made by believers of all sorts, that detractors of a position often proceed by attacking each observation and each bit of reasoning in isolation from all others. Davis is especially even-handed, pointing out that believers have the same tendency, responding to individual criticisms and counter-examples one at a time. This one-at-a-time approach, unfair in several regards, makes it easier for the one contending to focus on weak evidence and bad logic. There is generally a very large supply of faulty arguments for any position, so successful sniping can go on interminably but without any decisive outcome. Furthermore, some weak evidence gains support from independent stronger evidence. Franks uses the example of a ship's officer on watch in stormy weather who reports having glimpsed a lighthouse. The observation seems impossible because the navigator's reckoning places the ship hundreds of miles from land. If the sighting was uncertain and brief, and confidence in the navigator's reckoning is high, the sighting is likely to be discounted as an error. However, if additional observations from other crew members, each one somewhat uncertain, begin to consistently suggest that the ship is approaching land, at some point their cumulative strength will overturn the confidence in the navigator's placement of the ship.

In the *Haunting* we can see the same cumulative effect. In part this cumulative effect seems related to a "belief about beliefs" that Richard Swinburne calls "the principle of credulity":

> it is a principle of rationality that (in the absence of special considerations) if it seems (epistemically) to the subject that x is present, then probably x is present; what one seems to perceive is probably so. (1979:254)

The matter of "special considerations" is obviously crucial, and Swinburne discusses several that are often involved in assessing perceptual claims. One that he discusses is especially pertinent here, the counter-claim that x was not present. The belief that ghosts do not exist is a general special consideration that is advanced against the credibility of a claim to have perceived a ghost (if they do not exist they cannot have been there). This attributes to the believer the informal fallacy of *non causa pro causa*, "there is no cause of the sort that has been given as the cause" (Angeles 1992:108). For the belief scholar, this position has the defect of operating only within the framework of a shared set of beliefs. To use it one must privilege the negative beliefs, *a priori*, as *knowledge* in the strong sense. Doing so merely expresses personal beliefs about reality rather than carrying out an inquiry. A more limited claim is also encountered, that ghosts may exist, but no ghost was present in this case. It is a common and interesting aspect of the social processes of believing that very different beliefs and disbeliefs can cooperate in connection with particular instances; for example, some Christians share with atheists their grounds for disbelieving the claims of non-Christian religions.

In the *Haunting* account both Jane and Alice make it clear that they are aware of the existence of the "no ghost was there" counter-claims, and they address them by supplying the same sort of evidence that would be supplied in arguing a natural observation: multiple witnesses, many separate observations, and finely detailed descriptions.

In this account it is clear that once these counter-claims have been addressed, the principle of credulity is taken to apply; that is, if their evidence demonstrates to the listener that ghosts exist and that a ghost was indeed present, then it can be assumed that each description of similar encounters does not have to re-establish its truthfulness and veridicality. Under the argument that ghosts do not exist, each claim may be explained separately in different ways: squirrels in the attic, children playing a prank, Alice having a nightmare caused by stories about the ghost, etc. Because of the principle of credulity, once the boundary of special considerations has been crossed, the multiple events cohere and acquire a cumulative effect. This change is subjective and depends on one's viewpoint. The skeptical listener still hears a jumble of unrelated alleged anomalies, while one who takes the haunting as established hears an account of various experiences having the same or very similar referents.

The place of Jane's attack in this account is best understood as a part of a cumulative case. Outside a cumulative case, her attack, if the family's interpretation that this was "a different ghost" is correct, is extraneous—having nothing obvious to do with *The Owner Haunts*. But if satisfying the conditions of the "principle of credulity" is considered, then Alice's attack is pertinent as the family's most direct experiential support for the belief that ghosts exist. Further, since they include footsteps, which are a cardinal feature of the haunting, Alice's observations support the inferential association of mysterious footsteps with a ghost. Alice's experience puts the entire discussion of ghosts and ghostly footsteps into a new, better attested context. Conversely, the background of a believed haunting provides the same assurance for Alice's assertion that she "was attacked by a ghost."

The risk of cumulative arguments is that they may draw in spurious evidence and make it seem credible. Even if the house echoes with truly mysterious sounds, the cumulative effect of the haunting accounts practically guarantees that if there are squirrels in the attic, they will be occasionally mistaken for ghosts. In turn, the squirrel noises will add to the accumulated weight of the testimony. This pattern illustrates how cumulative arguments can accidentally draw in a circular use of evidence. Skeptics often implicitly treat belief traditions as a cumulative case, but then explain their apparent weight *entirely* on the basis of circularity.

Granting that cumulative assessment will inevitably involve some spurious evidence, my theory holds that the most compelling and interesting characteristics of supernatural belief can only be assessed by a cumulative view that goes beyond individual cases. That should not be surprising, because the same is true of all efforts to create knowledge. It is very rare, even in the laboratory, for a single instance to be decisive. That is more often an appearance that develops with hindsight, in the context of justification. Outside of the laboratory it is even more rare. The usefulness of inter-subjective checking in establishing claims about the world *requires* the concept of a cumulative case. If we treat the claims of individual subjects in isolation, we will never have a view that includes what in ordinary reasoning we consider to be corroboration. The cross-cultural distribution of core experiences constitutes cumulative corroboration of local beliefs of which even their most ardent holders are often unaware. For the *Haunting*, we might note that in *The Terror* I presented two first-person descriptions of hauntings. In both of them mysterious footsteps heard by multiple witnesses were a notable feature, and in both there were repeated paralysis attacks. In one (Case 20) the paralysis attacks involved several different people. The similarities among the three independent accounts from different parts of the country (Georgia, Kentucky, and Pennsylvania) has the effect of supporting Jane and Alice's account. Of course, these similarities might also call into question their grounds for treating Alice's attack as unrelated to the other events in the house. For the skeptic the existence of such accounts is problematic, which is a corollary to the observation that multiple accounts support the claims of believers. If paralysis attacks were traditionally described within American traditions of haunting, the skeptic would have no major obstacle. But such is not the case. And in each of these three accounts the principals involved had never heard of such attacks before.

Spontaneous and Elective Experiences

Part of my definition of core experiences is that they are independent of the subject's intention. In this sense they are spontaneous rather than elective, following from my claim that they are independent of psychological set in general. In order to intend to have a particular experience, one must know what the intended experience entails. Because psychological set, usually provided via culture, is so widely assumed to explain the patterns occurring in supernatural experience, the spontaneity of core experiences is a crucial piece of evidence for the Experiential Theory. The fact that an experience has been sought by no means proves that the seeker's intention *caused* the experience to be as it was. But if prior knowledge and intention are always present, it becomes impossible to show that they did *not* cause the experience. However, when the same perceptual pattern recurs in different subjects, who have no prior knowledge of it, prior knowledge and intention cease to be explanatory options. Therefore, the Experiential Theory does not rule out the authenticity of elective supernatural experiences, but it does give theoretical primacy to spontaneous ones.

Jane and Richard do not appear to have purchased their house with the intention of being haunted. Some people do buy houses *because* they are supposed to be haunted, but that does not appear to have been Jane and Richard's motivation. We do not have an indication that Alice went to their house in order to "see a ghost" either, but we do know that she was aware of and had heard about "the ghost" before. The experience that in Alice's case *was* clearly elective involved her communication with the ghost. When she asked for a response to show that he had heard her request to stay away at night, she was intentionally trying to have a supernatural experience—which any answer from a ghost would be. The same may be said of the wedding guests who rapped on the wall and received answering knocks. This kind of intention obviously changes interpretations of subsequent events.

As Alice sat with Richard in the living room subsequently, she says that

> We heard a big bang in my room upstairs. And it was as if somebody had jumped with, you know, their two feet and just hit down hard. And Richard looked over at me, and I didn't say anything really. I just looked at him, and he—I guess he knew it was the ghost. And, so I was glad, I guess, that he heard me.

If she had heard that noise under other circumstances, we may presume, she might well have had a different reaction, such as "What was that?" Richard's interpretation, even if Alice is right that he "knew it was the ghost," was different from Alice's. He didn't know that "this was the ghost saying, 'OK, I won't come around at night'." That interpretation was enabled and suggested by Alice's attempted communication and request for an answer.

Elective experience creates conditions within which the salience and meaning of events is changed. Alice's request was ambiguous as to what would constitute a response, so a great many subsequent events might have been interpreted as such by her. If Richard was not overly surprised by the "loud bang" without knowing of

Alice's request, then we must assume that such noises were not rare in the house, whatever their source. Alice's confidence that she had been "answered" and even that Richard "knew it was the ghost" are all produced by the conditions that she intentionally created. She may be right on all counts, but her intention has given a great deal of significance to inherently ambiguous events.

The conditions of elective experiences undercut their evidential force in two ways: (1) they provide an alternative psychological explanation, even if its use requires us to invoke "mass hallucination," and (2) they multiply greatly the opportunities for interpretive supernatural experience.

Alice did not intend to be paralyzed and attacked by a malevolent ghost. She did not know that such an attack would be likely to involve the features that she ultimately described. We can be confident, therefore, that she did not impose the terrifying perceptual pattern on her experience. Her description specifies an experience that is directly and obviously supernatural in perceptual terms. Jane's mother-in-law is unlikely to say that the squirrels in the attic did *this*! Or is she? "Bad dreams" confused with or interpreted as real are a common parallel to the squirrels explanation. Such an explanation might be especially tempting in Alice's case, because she "passed out and had dreams" before getting up and running downstairs. Might the entire event have been a bad dream, perhaps beginning with the incorporation of squirrel sounds into a dream shaped by the talk of haunting?

Alice argues to the contrary by showing that she "knew they were dreams" and that she "realized I was really asleep." But this internal appearance is not compelling on the skeptical listener. Ironically, the outside observer, aware of the sleep paralysis literature *and* the experiential features of sleep paralysis (which is largely missing from that literature) *and* the global distribution of traditions about that experience, is in a position to provide inter-subjective confirmation of the accuracy of Alice's report, confirmation of which she herself is unaware. This cross-contextual distribution of the recognizable perceptual patterns in core experiences means that they serve in the same way as other empirical "anchors." As Alice and Jane's family talk and read about the experiences that others associate with ghosts, they will recognize patterns that they did know existed. These independent accounts will not only add support for their own beliefs, but they will enter into their assessment of the truth of the beliefs of other individuals whom they encounter. The cumulative case for their own haunting experiences will expand and come to include entirely independent observations.

Disbelief as a Kind of Belief

Beliefs about ghosts include such propositions as 'ghosts do not exist.' Such disbeliefs share the characteristics described regarding positive beliefs, entailing, enabling and suggesting other beliefs. For example, that 'ghosts do not exist' entails disbelief in *The Owner Haunts*.

The relationship of beliefs and disbeliefs is not symmetrical. Being in the house and 'not seeing the ghost' does not carry the same force that being in the house and 'seeing the ghost' does. Most disbeliefs are less direct, understandably, than positive beliefs.

Contradicting a Belief

Jane's mother-in-law's belief that 'the alleged ghostly footsteps are the misinterpreted sounds of the squirrels in the attic' conflicts with *The Owner Haunts*, and related beliefs in these accounts. As stated, this belief entails the conclusion that 'people in the house do not hear footsteps caused by a ghost.' When a belief conflicts with another by entailing that it is wrong, the beliefs *contradict* each other.

> Stipulated definition of *Contradiction*: One belief contradicts another if it is impossible for them both to be true.

If we restated the disbelief more generally as 'Natural sounds in old houses are easily mistaken for ghostly manifestations by believers,' it would not *contradict* the belief in ghostly footsteps, but it would *suggest* that the belief is false. The more general statement still, that 'old houses are full of sounds that are hard to identify,' *enables* the more directly conflicting beliefs, but does not in itself imply them. In fact, such basic positive beliefs about the world held by disbelievers are often shared by believers.

In order for an *experience* (as opposed to a belief) to directly support a disbelief, it must entail a belief that contradicts the competing belief. Such contradiction is usually possible only for very specific and therefore limited beliefs. For example, it would be possible to do a title search for the house and look into the biographies of previous owners. If the search resulted in observations that directly supported the belief that all of the owners are accounted for, and all died of natural causes, that would contradict the belief that *The Owner Haunts* because he was murdered. Any dispute from the believers would have to be mounted by redescribing the disbeliever's claim. Perhaps the title search missed someone (not *all* owners) or perhaps the murder was made to look like natural causes (all owners *appear* to have died naturally). But even if the disbeliever's claim stands up, it will not contradict the belief that the house is haunted.

Two other common direct challenges to belief involve either redescription of the experience claimed to support the belief or redescription of the belief itself.

Controversial Redescriptions of Experience

When Jane's mother-in-law explains the footsteps as squirrels-in-the-attic she is implicitly redescribing the experience. Obviously the believers would not say, "I heard a sound like squirrels in the attic. I think it must be a ghost." And she claims to have had "the same experience" (hearing animals in attics) but reached a different conclusion. It is very difficult to achieve a minimally ramified experiential report. Even having such a report, establishing that it and another report refer to the same, or the same kind of, experience is more difficult. Therefore, this kind of challenge deserves very careful scrutiny. It is not surprising that such challenges are loosely constructed in ordinary discourse. Many traditional "anti-legends" or disbelief stories hinge on such redescriptions.[17] It is unfortunate that the same looseness is often found in scholarly interpretations.[18] All theoretical considerations that obscure the possibility of deriving highly specific reports of perceptual experience, or that such reports are connected with supernatural belief, encourage this looseness.

Controversial Redescriptions of Belief

Opposing a belief can easily be aided by redescription of the belief itself, a technique employed by both believers and disbelievers alike. For example, "She believes we are all crazy" might be an exaggerated misrepresentation of the mother-in-law's claim that could serve to discredit her. However, the asymmetry of pro and con argument, in which believers can cite direct experiential support of their belief but disbelievers must often be less direct, makes the construction of expedient but inaccurate belief descriptions somewhat more common among disbelievers. Jane and Alice can dispute the mother-in-law's explanation by reference to what they heard. The mother-in-law can only refer to her own redescription of the experiences or the beliefs that are attested by them. More often disbeliefs are supported by beliefs about believers or about the beliefs they hold, and these beliefs are the ones which are attested by experience—for example, that believers fail to consider natural alternatives carefully. These are epistemological beliefs.

Constructing Belief Statements

The construction of belief statements inferred from accounts and conversation is a central methodological issue in the study of belief, although rarely discussed in explicit terms. The risk of biased redescriptions of beliefs just discussed should indicate the importance of careful criteria for stating inferred beliefs. I have chosen to state the beliefs that I have inferred in a moderately simple form, but not in the smallest possible units. This approach is helpful in meeting the test of *local acceptance* noted above. My intention is to create propositions that would be recognized and accepted by the family members. If one disagrees with the description of a belief attributed to him, he cannot be said to hold that belief. A believer need not agree with the *explanation* of his belief, or an account of its implications. But the belief itself is different. A belief is a proposition held to be true. If I look at a proposition, whether it is attributed to me or not, and do not consider it true, then I do not hold it as a belief. The ultimate justification of a claim to have accurately represented a belief, obviously, is empirical: what does the believer say about the description? Although this method permits some latitude in developing these statements, it also imposes important constraints. Failure to use statements that would be accepted by the believer, at this stage of analysis, is a methodological error that will invalidate any subsequent effort to understand *why* this person holds these beliefs. In his criteria for understanding a belief system, Martin Hollis emphasizes this important relationship:

> I take there to be understanding, when he [an enquirer] knows what his subjects believe (identification) and why they believe it (explanation). But let no one forget that the two go together, lest we propose a canon for explaining beliefs, which would make it impossible to identify them. (1982:72)

I would go further. If the belief is misidentified by being given in a form that the holder would either not recognize or not agree with, then subsequent explanations will be about a false belief that the interpreter holds about the believer. Unfortunately, such mistaken interpretation happens all too often.

Jeff Todd Titon gives an example of such inaccurate redescription in *Powerhouse for God* (1988), where he criticizes Kaplan (1978) for saying that Pentecostals have to be "saved over and over again," a practice that would be nonsensical. Titon points out that *saving* only happens once but that the backsliding Christian must nonetheless ask forgiveness and be returned to a proper relation with God. This practice is not nonsense, and it conforms with Pentecostal belief. Titon's redescription of the basic belief not only provides a more accurate representation of Pentecostal belief and practices, but it allows the *non*-believer to understand the meaning of the practice. It now makes sense in a way that bridges the belief-nonbelief boundary. Titon's redescription did not have to be constructed in the words of a Pentecostal believer, but rather in words recognizable and agreeable to such a believer.

Kaplan's error is a common one. He misused a believer's term. Attributing false but apparently plausible meanings to terms is a common source of inappropriate belief descriptions in the service of negative interpretations. (From the believer's viewpoint, any interpretation showing that a held belief is unfounded, inconsistent, or false is a negative interpretation, no matter how sympathetic the account.)

Some analyses of mystical experience misrepresent belief by the way they employ the term *ineffable*. William James, in his classic *Varieties of Religious Experience*, used this term, reasonably enough, to refer to the difficulties of description so frequently expressed by mystics in connection with their experiences, a common feature of descriptions by those claiming all sorts of "core supernatural experiences." However, many commentators arguing against the possibility that mystical experiences have any specific meaning or can support any particular belief take the mystical belief to be that *nothing* can be said about these experiences. For example, Steven Katz says that

> to take the mystic's claim seriously, i.e., that his proposition "x is PI" ["x is paradoxical and ineffable"] is a true description, turns out to have the damaging implication that one cannot make any reasonable or even intelligible claim for any mystical proposition. (Katz 1978:56)

If the experience cannot be described at all, then it cannot support any statements. True enough, but despite all of the mystical insistence about the difficulties of reducing these experiences to words, is it accurate or fair to attribute to them the belief that nothing meaningful can be said in describing them? The mystical literature contains constant efforts at description of mystical experience by mystics even though such descriptions are always said to be inadequate. If Katz is right, then the descriptions of mystics are meaningless and the beliefs of mystics are irrational. But the fact of descriptive efforts and the drawing of conclusions from them suggests that Katz's rendering of ineffability (after all, James's word, not theirs) misrepresents the beliefs of many mystics. The case for a redescription of the "ineffability" of mystical experience is elaborated by Caroline F. Davis (1989:14–19). Essentially she contends that the ineffability claim, read in context, is a combination of "poetic hyperbole" like "unbearable pain" (about which we would not say the victim "lied," simply because he did in fact bear it) and the impossibility of completely describing any experience that one's listener has not shared. For those mystics whose accounts are properly read by Davis, Katz is explaining a belief they do not hold. The investigation of direct supernatural experience in folk tradition supports Davis's conclusion. The struggle for words is constant, but one never finds a simple assertion that "no words can be given that describe this experience at all."

Another common form of misrepresentation is the attribution of a belief description that is absurd on its face. For example, Carl Sagan, a frequent debunker of all sorts of religious and spiritual beliefs, says that

> Some people think of God as an outsized, light-skinned male with a long white beard, sitting on a throne somewhere up in the sky, busily tallying the fall of every sparrow. (1980:330)

But Sagan proceeds as though all beliefs in a personal God could be addressed under this description of a crude, sexist, and racist belief. And he does so without a single empirical case to show that *anyone* holds that belief.

One reason that misrepresentations of supernatural belief are not more obvious is that they are often implicit. Many accounts of belief seem to assume that there is a consensus about the nature of the beliefs to be explained. For example, Judith Devlin, in *The Superstitious Mind*, begins her section entitled "Ghosts" by saying that "Belief in ghosts also exemplifies the complexity of legendary beliefs of the rural poor" (1989:88). The discussion that follows gives a variety of theoretical and interpretive statements, together with brief sections of several accounts. But she does not state what she takes to be covered by the ambiguous phrase "belief in ghosts." Attempting to describe what is believed, she relies largely on the comments of scholars. These descriptions are so highly ramified that we can be sure that a nineteenth-century peasant would not recognize them. On one occasion, for example, she notes that

> there were two ways of believing in apparitions of the dead: the 'horizontal' vision, which was naturalistic and traditional, and which implied that the dead person lived on; and the transcendental conception of the theologians. (1987:90)

Granted, the inference of accurate belief statements is not always simple, and the analyst may often be wrong. But there is no doubt that much of the literature on these topics undertakes to *explain* beliefs or to interpret images and values that are associated with beliefs. If this is done without a clear, even if tentative or hypothetical, description of the beliefs at issue, how can the results be well supported? In the absence of such description the reader must actually infer the beliefs entailed in an interpretation from *the interpretation itself*. As a result, in the absence of clear and supported statements of the beliefs to be explained, interpretations of belief tend to be viciously circular. That is why an interpretation of the stories in the *Haunting* cannot properly begin until the beliefs that constitute its central message have been carefully inferred and described.

Conclusion

The Experiential Theory requires the scholar studying folk belief to take seriously the same issues that arise in the study of formal, official knowledge claims. As the *Haunting* illustrates, when such an approach is embraced, the founding of such belief can take on an entirely new appearance. I do not propose that the experiential approach should replace other approaches, but I do argue that where belief is concerned the experiential approach requires a certain methodological primacy. There are all sorts of analyses that could be productively performed on the *Haunting*—structural, functional, ethnopoetic, and so on. However, if any of these analyses aspired to causal explanations ("They believed the house was haunted because. . . ."), they would almost certainly be wrong if they did not first take into account the experiential grounding and rational (though implicit) elaboration of the beliefs. Let us return to my example of my seeing the computer on the desk in front of me. My belief that a computer is there has important functions for me: the computer itself is a powerful symbol in my life and work, and I tell a variety of stories about my computer, each of which could be analyzed. But if I were said to believe that I have a computer on my desk because that makes me feel a participant in modern scholarship, if my stories about my computer were said to be produced by modern scholarly traditions about personal computers and our ambivalence toward them, all such interpretations would be at best incomplete, at worst incoherent, if they omitted the fact that I believe I have a computer on my desk because I see a computer on my desk. To understand stories about the supernatural we must recognize that many of them are experientially warranted in the same way and that some of the experiences that produce them display a stable perceptual pattern that constitutes persuasive evidence for some of the beliefs involved. That understanding does not require the scholar to share those beliefs. However, it does require the scholar to recognize the beliefs and their grounds, and to take both seriously.

A Personal Note

In 1966 I entered the University of Pennsylvania Folklore and Folklife graduate program essentially because Ken Goldstein had told my undergraduate departmental chairman, Bob Byington (English, Lycoming College), that doing so would not prevent me from eventually finding gainful employment. From the day I entered the program, through the present, Kenny has been one of my closest friends and most trusted advisors. He is my daughter's Godfather, and Rochelle is my son's Godmother. In graduate school Kenny showed me how to transform a populist bias combined with a love of folk tradition and of books (almost an oxymoron, but as Kenny showed me, *not*) into the opportunity to spend my life studying the human condition in a way that has enriched my understanding of myself, my family, and my world; in a way that has been a good living and an opportunity to work with students who also want to understand. Sunday breakfasts at the Goldstein's in Mount Airy, hours spent working in Kenny's personal library, the chance to meet folklore scholars from around the world at Kenny's home—all of these things and more Kenny used to show me that a love of learning and a love of ordinary people could not just co-exist, but could support and augment each other. I had hoped as much, but not all academic experiences had nourished that hope. All of my experiences with Kenny and his family have.

Kenny taught me always to take seriously the people from whom I sought to learn. He taught me that hours in the field and hours in the library complement each other. He showed me that theory and method are not alternate choices, but that they are two sides of the same path. And when we spoke together of the study of belief, Kenny helped me to see that taking our informants seriously is not the opposite of performing belief scholarship. The summers that he spent with my family and myself at the shrine of Ste. Anne de Beaupre provided invaluable support, emotional and intellectual, for the understanding of folk practice within official institutions and for a view of belief and experience that cannot be summed up in the expression of "religious preference." Kenny's work with religious balladry helped me in my conviction that the separation of "belief"—as if it constituted a genre—is counter-productive. Just as much, his earlier writings about levels of belief had underlined the dynamic nature of believing, making "belief" a roving target that can never be pinned down but must be studied on the move.

Kenny's entry into the life of my family showed me that the academic world is still the place I hoped it might be. The acceptance of my family into his has forged a tremendously rich and constant link between ourselves and folklore, a link that a peculiar person such as myself, with a decidedly eccentric career, has needed.

I wish Kenny were not retiring, but I know that he will not stop being my teacher and my friend. Perhaps when I retire we will have the time to go to some more Sixer's games or make another field trip to Ste. Anne's. Whatever Kenny does, he will never cease to be a help to my believing and my knowledge, he will always be *compadre*, and I will always love him. Without Kenny I would not have been able to write the essay above—because without Kenny I would not be in folklore. Thank you Kenny.

Notes

1. Because my interest here is in the beliefs carried by these stories, I will not enter into the issues surrounding classification of these stories as memorates or legends.

2. Hereafter simply called "supernatural belief." I supply a detailed definition of my meaning for *supernatural* on the following page. For a presentation of other features of my theory, see Hufford 1995.

3. For my useages of these terms, see the following pages.

4. This fact has been ignored in the publication of lists of "beliefs" with no indication of the strength with which they are held, if at all; see, e.g., Hand 1961 and 1964.

5. As Jane Schneider notes, in the introduction to *Cloth and Human Experience*, among

the "domains of meaning" concerning cloth, the "first is the domain of cloth manufacture itself" (Weiner and Schneider 1989:3).

6. In editing this transcript I have followed the same procedure that I used in *The Terror That Comes in the Night* (1982). All omissions are marked by ellipses. Dashes (——) are used to indicate pauses. On those rare occasions where it has been necessary to add a word to make sense of a passage (usually this indicates an inaudible word or several people speaking at once), I have put the added words in parentheses. I have added my own descriptions occasionally for reasons of space. I have strictly preserved the anonymity of my subjects by changing all names and disguising other personal information that might identify them.

7. I use *story* in its most basic sense: "1. The narration of an event or series of series of events, either true or fictional" (*American Heritage Dictionary* 1991:1201). I will use *story* and *account* interchangeably. The term *narrative* has come to be used in a very narrow, technical way by some scholars, so I will refrain from using it to avoid excess theoretical connotations. Although *legend* and *memorate* are also applicable to most of the accounts I consider, their customary usage is too strongly associated with falsity to be useful in this approach, which seeks to avoid peremptory assumptions about truth issues.

8. This is patterned after Davis's "interpretive religious experience" (1989:33–35).

9. For a discussion of health belief systems and their rational organization, see Hufford 1988:253–63.

10. *Ramification*, of either an experiential report or an interpretation, refers to the extent to which the report or interpretation reaches beyond what is directly observed. In ordinary discourse extensive ramification is the norm, while minimally ramified sentences are a technical accomplishment, as in phenomenological descriptions. I have adopted this very helpful use of *ramification* from Carolyn Franks Davis (1989:24–25).

11. For a discussion of these relations of perception and belief, see Audi 1988, especially beginning at page 8.

12. Skeptics often attribute the notion of self-authenticating experiences to believers. For example, see Anthony Flew, *God & Philosophy* (1966:132–33).

13. The phenomenological psychologist Edward Titchner was reaching toward a method for such descriptions early in this century. However, contemporary psychology has been less interested in pursuing subjective report.

14. See, e.g., Tyrell on some ghosts as "collective 'idea-patterns'" (1953:163–65).

15. Examples of each of these elements may be readily found in *The Terror That Comes in the Night* (Hufford 1982) by using that book's "Index of Features."

16. For a particularly rich example, see Case 20 in *The Terror That Comes in the Night* (Hufford 1982).

17. See, e.g., the motifs listed by Thompson (1966) under "Fools; Absurd Misunderstandings; J1780 Things thought to be devils, ghosts, etc."

18. See, e.g., Zusne and Jones 1982.

References

Angeles, Peter A.
1992   *Dictionary of Philosophy*. New York: Barnes and Noble Books.
Audi, Robert
1988   *Belief, Justification and Knowledge*. Belmont, Cal.: Wadsworth Publ. Co.
DeVinne, Pamela B., ed.
1991   *The American Heritage Dictionary of the English Language*. 2nd college ed. Boston: Houghton Mifflin Co.

Davis, Caroline Franks
    1989   *The Evidential Force of Religious Experience*. Oxford: Clarendon Press.
Dégh, Linda and Andrew Vázsonyi
    1976   Legend and Belief. In *Folklore Genres*. Ed. Dan Ben-Amos. Austin: Univ. of
            Texas Press. Pp. 93–123.
Devlin, Judith
    1987.   *The Superstitious Mind*. New Haven: Yale Univ. Press.
Flew, Antony
    1966   *God & Philosophy*. London: Hutchinson.
Grice, H. Paul
    1975   Logic and Conversation. In *Syntax and Semantics*. Vol. 3. Eds. Peter Cole and
            Jerry L. Morgan. New York: Academic Press. Pp. 41–58.
Hahn, Robert
    1973   Understanding Beliefs: An Essay on the Methodology of the Statement and
            Analysis of Belief Systems. *Current Anthropology* 14:207–29.
Hand, Wayland D., ed.
    1961, 1964   *Popular Beliefs and Superstitions from North Carolina*. In *The Frank
            Brown Collection of North Carolina Folklore*, vols. 6 and 7. Durham, N.C.: Duke
            Univ. Press.
Hollis, Martin
    1982   The Social Destruction of Reality. In *Rationality and Relativism*. Eds. Martin
            Hollis and Steven Lukes. Cambridge, Mass.: MIT Press. Pp. 67–86.
Hopkins, Budd, David Michael Jacobs and Ron Westrum, et al.
    1992   *Unusual Personal Experiences: An Analysis of Data from Three National Sur-
            veys Conducted by the Roper Organization*. Las Vegas: Bigelow Holding Corp.
Hufford, David J.
    1982   *The Terror That Comes in the Night: An Experience-Centered Study of
            Supernatural Assault Traditions*. Philadelphia: Univ. of Pennsylvania Press.
    1985   Commentary: Mystical Experience in the Modern World. In *The World Was
            Flooded with Light: A Mystical Experience Remembered*, by Genevieve Foster.
            Pittsburgh: Univ. of Pittsburgh Press. Pp. 87–183.
    1988   Contemporary Folk Medicine. In *Unorthodox Medicine in America*. Ed.
            Norman Gevitz. Baltimore: John Hopkins Univ. Press. Pp. 228–64.
    1995   Beings without Bodies: An Experience-centered Theory of the Belief in
            Spirits. In *Out of the Ordinary: Folklore and the Supernatural*. Ed. Barbara
            Walker. Logan: Univ. of Utah Press.
Katz, Steven T.
    1978   *Mysticism and Philosophical Analysis*. London: Sheldon Press.
Proudfoot, Wayne.
    1985   *Religious Experience*. Berkeley: Univ. of California Press.
Rosten, Leo, ed.
    1975   *Religions of America*. New York: Simon and Schuster.
Sagan, Carl
    1979   *Broca's Brain*. New York: Ballantine Books.
Swinburne, Richard
    1979   *The Existence of God*. Oxford: Clarendon Press.
Thompson, C.
    1982   *Anwesenheit*: Psychopathology and Clinical Associations. *British Journal of
            Psychiatry* 141:161–65.

Thompson, Stith. ed.
1966 *Motif-Index of Folk-Literature*. Bloomington: Indiana Univ. Press.
Titon, Jeff Todd
1988 *Powerhouse for God*. Austin: Univ. of Texas Press.
Tyrell, G. N. M.
1953 *Apparitions*. Rev. ed. London: Duckworth.
Weiner, Annette B. and Jane Schneider, eds.
1989 *Cloth and Human Experience*. Washington: Smithsonian Institution Press.
Wright, Lawrence
1993 (A Reporter at Large) Remembering Satan—Part I. *The New Yorker*. May 17. 69 (13):60–66, 68–74, 76–81.
Yoder, Don
1974 Toward a Definition of Folk Religion. *Western Folklore* 33(1):1–15. Reprinted in Yoder 1990:67–84.
1990 *Discovering American Folklife: Studies in Ethnic, Religious, and Regional Culture*. Ann Arbor: U.M.I. Research Press.
Zusne, Leonard, and Warren H. Jones
1982 *Anomalistic Psychology: A Study of Extraordinary Phenomena of Behavior and Experience*. Hillsdale, N.J.: Lawrence Erlbaum.

READING TAKELMA TEXTS

Frances Johnson's "Coyote and Frog"

Dell Hymes

I. Introduction and Contents

THIS MYTH is one of those transcribed by Edward Sapir in July and August 1906 at the Siletz Reservation in western Oregon from Frances Johnson. Sapir was able to prepare the texts for publication as holder of a Harrison Research Fellowship in Anthropology at the University of Pennsylvania (1908–9), and the texts appeared as vol. 2, no. 1 of the Anthropological Publications of the University of Pennsylvania, The Museum, in the latter year (1909). Until recently one could buy a copy at The Museum.

Sapir collected meticulous texts in several Native American languages, and transmitted zeal for such work to students. In most cases these texts are the basis of what can be known of aboriginal verbal art among the peoples in question. Such a text is appropriate to honor Kenneth Goldstein, an indefatigable collector who has guided and inspired many others.

The text is Sapir's inasmuch as it would not exist if he had not sought out Takelma and written it down, and it would not be possible to grasp its implicit form were it not for the accuracy made possible by his training and skill. The text is first of all the words of Frances Johnson (*Gwísgwas-hä·n* 'Chipmunks'), of whom Sapir says: "It is largely to her patience and intelligence that whatever merit this volume may be thought to have is due" (1909:5). I hope that this presentation will enhance appreciation of Mrs. Johnson's gifts as a narrator, and of the art of the tradition she represents.

Scholarly detail is required, to be sure, in the service of those aims, and my title, "Reading Takelma Texts," is intended to be taken in two ways. Here is an example of what it can be like to read (or hear) Takelma narratives in English, approximating the original as closely as one can. Here is an example of what is involved in attempting that approximation.

This essay is reworked from one that I wrote in 1978–79, relatively early in my exploration of Native American narratives as a kind of poetry ("measured verse"), organized in groups of lines.[1] I remember working out relations and details, looking out through trees, toward trees, across a mountain stream, in the Oregon forest. I began this revision there in less happy circumstances, but at least can finish it also looking through trees toward a mountain ridge.

Let me give first a brief overview of the myth, then the new translation, and corresponding text. Coming first, the myth can be more easily found and returned to in relation to discussions that follow. The English and Takelma versions are on alternating pages to aid comparison.

The translation and text result from three kinds of consideration. One has to do with philology in the narrow sense: How are the words to be shown (orthography)? What is to be said about the role of sounds of the language (expressive features)? Are the words as printed the same as those first written down (field notebooks)?

A second consideration has to do with retranslation, of words and of form. Choices have had to be made with regard to English wording, and with regard to relations of form, of arousal and expectation, implicit in the text. A good deal can be said separately about translation of words, and general observations can be made about indications of form. Still, questions of one can involve the other. Something about form may arise under the heading of translation (e.g., *ganga* and how act VII ends). Something about translation may arise under the heading of form (the meaning and status of *-hi'*).

Translation and formal relations involve a third consideration, interpretation of action and expression. Ultimately one has to develop a sense of what Mrs. Johnson intended. Some points arise in discussing translation, more in discussing form. Yet others arise in connection with features of the narrative discussed in a further section, essentially in the order of their occurrence. Some of these features are in effect themselves small genres (titles, headings, song burdens, formal close). The rhythm of the first act seems to belong here as well. In sum, the linearity of this study is partial. Like Mrs. Johnson's myths as a whole, and Sapir's grammar, one has to read back and forth and read again, and make connections. In other words, descend into details, and return to the story itself.

At the end there is a detailed account of the form of the story ("Profile"), which may help, and the contents of this study are outlined at the end of this section. Finally, a portion of another myth that uses much the same theme as the beginning of this one, but in a different formal pattern, is shown in an appendix.

Two audiences are addressed in this study: those interested in how such a narrative achieves its ends, and whoever may take up the study of Takelma itself. For the latter especially, I must justify each choice that is made. I hope someone else indeed will take up this work, finding helpful what I have done. I hope that others can skim such passages, noting their nature, and find rewarding what is said about the art itself.

Contents

I. Introduction and Contents
II. Overview of the Myth
III. English Translation and Takelma Text
IV. Philological Background
  1. Introduction
  2. Takelma Orthography
    A. Vowels (phonemic status, accent, rhetorical length)
    B. Consonants (expressive contrast, useful symbols)
  3. Field Notebooks
    A. Rhetorical Markers
    B. Missing Lines
V. Translation of Words
  1. Constant Particles
  2. Two Verbs "to sing"
  3. Graphic Marks and Degrees of Force
  4. Segmenting Time
  5. Hearing
  6. Dancing
  7. Probably?
  8. Here
  9. Start Again
  10. Chieftainness?
  11. Songs
  12. *ganga* 'always' (and scene vii)
  13. In Vain
  14. Latin
  15. Verb of Pronouncement
VI. Translation of Form
  1. Distinguishing Lines
  2. Distinguishing Verses: Initial Particles and Other Markers
    A. Rhetorical Questions
    B. Quoted Speech
    C. Other Particles
      a. Terms of Time, Terms of Location
      b. Names
      c. Postpositions (1) *-si'*
      d. Postpositions (2) *-hi'* 'quotative'
        (a) Verse-marker?
        (b) Quoted speech
        (c) Traditional speech?
      e. Lists and Couplets
      f. Expressive Role

II. Overview of the Myth

The published text occupies 86 printed lines, printed as 10 paragraphs. Analysis indicates that it has 245 narrative lines, organized in 97 verses. The verses occur mostly in pairs, grouped in 41 stanzas. The stanzas make up 8 scenes (i-viii), with 5 "subscenes" (designated by Arabic numerals) in scene ii. The scenes are paired, forming four acts (I-IV).[2] In brief:

      I. *Coyote goes to a puberty dance*
        [i] Alone, he hunts gophers
        [ii] He hears and hurries to the dance
      II. *The girls and Coyote sing*
        [iii] Frog and Coyote sing
        [iv] Bluejay, Mouse and Coyote, Swan sing
      III. *Singing brings bears*
        [v] Goose sings and Brown Bear comes
        [vi] Some keep singing and Grizzly comes
      IV. *Coyote finds out about Frog*
        [vii] Grizzly Bear breaks up the dance
        [viii] Coyote runs off with Frog
        [Close]

III. English Translation and Takelma Text

Translation

[I] [*Coyote goes to a puberty dance*]

[i] [Alone, he hunts gophers]

There was a house.   (A)

Coyote would set traps for gophers all by himself every day.

When it became morning,   (B)

    again he set traps for gophers;

        there were no people,   5

        he was all by himself.

In the evening he brought them home.

Then again,   (C)

    a different dawn,

        he would set traps for gophers.   10

How long did he not set traps for gophers every day?

When it became morning,   (D)

    again he set traps for gophers.

Then,

    when it became evening,   15

        he counted gophers,

            how many he caught.

[ii] [He hears and hurries to the dance]

[1] [He hears the dance]

Now he heard something,

    the puberty dance for girls being danced.

Now he listened.   20

Then

    "S'a! Where is the puberty dance being danced?"

        said Coyote.

Now he suddenly discovered (in which direction)

    the puberty dance was being danced.   25

"Sh'a! That's where I'll go."

[2] [He runs]

Now he went,   (A)

    he threw away the gophers.

Now he ran,

    was tired;   30

        stood still,

            listened.

Takelma Text

[I] [*Coyote goes to a puberty dance*]

[i] [Alone, he hunts gophers]

Wili· yowó'.³   (A)

Sgisi à·kda'x tì·s lok'òlha be·wì'.

Dewènxa la·lí·ta',   (B)

   honò' tì·s lò·k;

      àni·' kì yap'a,   5

        à·kda'xí.

Dahó·xa liwìlhak".

Gane·hi' honò',   (C)

   wi'ìn wè·giauda',

      tì·s lok'òlha.   10

Gwi·'nè dì wede tì·s lòu'k be·wì'?

Dewènxa la·lí·ta',   (D)

   honò' tì·s lòuk.

Gane·hi',

   dahó·xa la·lé·,   15

      tì·s má·n,

        mìxal halohounanà'.

[ii] [He hears and hurries to the dance]

[1] [He hears the dance]

Mi· kai dà·'agán,

   wù·lham hoyodagwán.

Mi· da·sgèk'i·.   20

Gane·hi'

   "S'à! gwìdi wù·lham hoyodagwán?"

      nagàihi' Sgìsi.

Mi· da·t'ayàk

   wù·lham hoyodagwànma'.   25

"Š'a! Ge ginìkde'."

[2] [He runs]

Mi·hi' yà',   (A)

   tì·s he·k'u·wu·.

Mi· hò'k,

   hu·línt;   30

      sasini·,

        dà·sgek'í·.

Then now again he rushed off,   (B)
    he ran.
Then now again he rested.   35
Still the puberty dance was danced nearby.
Then
    "Ah! Must be here the puberty dance is danced."
There he arrived,
    no people.   40
"S-where *is* this dancing?"   (C)
    he said,
        he spoke to himself.
It was as if they were dancing the puberty dance right nearby.
"It's must be here upriver."   45

                 [3] [How long does he not run?]

Now again he ran,   (A)
How long did he not run?
It was if they were dancing nearby.
Then again he rushed off,   (B)
    he ran.   50
He would name the name of the land,
"They must be dancing there,"
    said Coyote.
Then again he rushed off,   (C)
How long did he not run?   55
    he was tired,
        he kept resting.
Always as they sing,
    it is (as if) right at hand.
Then again he went,   (D) 60
    he rushed off,
How long did he not go?
"S-where *is* the puberty dance being danced?"
    he said;
        he listened about.   65
Then,
    "S'à! Must be here upriver",
And indeed the puberty dance was being danced in the east.
Now again he ran there,   (E)
How long did he not run?   70

                 [4] [Almost there]

Then how long it was.   (A)
Now he was tired;
    there he was *just* nearby.

Gane·hi' mi· hono' he·bilìu',   (B)
    hò'k.
Gane·hi' mi· hono' ligí·nt;   35
Hàwi wu·lham hoyodagwàn da'ól.
Gane·hi'
    "Ah!   Emè' mì·'wa wu·lham hoyodagwàn."
Ge wó·k,
    àni·' kai yàp'a.   40
"S-gemè'di aga'à hoidiáuk?"   (C)
    nagàihi',
        à·ki wahimitgwit.
'Alí· da'ól wu·lham hoidiàuki' na'nagài'.
"Emè' mì·'wa hìnwadá."   45
                        [3] [How long does he not run?]
Mi· hono' hò'k.   (A)
Gwi·'nè di wede hòk?
Da'òl hoidiàuki' na'nagài'.
Gane·hi' honò' he·bilìu',   (B)
    hò'k.   50
Tga· kwedèi p'u·wù·'auk,
"Ge mì·'wa hoyodiàu',"
    nagàihi' Sgìsi.
Gane·hi' honò' he·bilìu',   (C)
Gwi·'nè di wede hòk?   55
    hu·lìnt,
        lìgilagánt.
Ganga heleliàuda',
    ali· nà'nagài.
Gane·hi' honò' yà',   (D) 60
    he·bilìu',
Gwi·'ne dì wede yanák?
"S-gemè'di aga'a wu·lham hoyodagàn?"
    nagàihi';
        da·sgek'eí·ha.   65
Gane·hi',
    "S'à! Emè' hinwadà mì·'wa",
Agàsi' gwentga·bòkdanda wu·lham hoyodagwàn.
Mi· hono' ge hiwilìu',   (E)
Gwi·'ne dì wede hók?   70
                        [4 [Almost there]
Gane·hi' gwì·'ne la·lé·?   (A)
Mi· hu·línt;
    ge' yà·hi da'òl la·lé·.

Then he started up again.   (B)
Then he ran from below [downriver] near   75
   (where) the puberty dance was being danced.
Now again he ran.   (C)
Then he stood still,
   was tired,
      listened.   80
                        [5] [He arrives]
Then now there he arrived.   (A)
Ahhh, girls in great numbers were dancing the puberty dance,
   many kinds of girls,
      Swan,
         Goose,   85
            Bluejay,
               Mouse,
                  Frog.
What kind did not dance the puberty dance?   (B)
Many kinds were standing there.   90
Coyote now arrived;   (C)
   he looked around,
      the puberty dance was being danced.
                [II] [*The girls and Coyote sing*]
                [iii] [Frog and Coyote sing]
Then one girl,   (A)
   chiefly,   95
      wore many kinds of garments,
         rattling.
"S'a! I'll take s-that one there,"
   he said.
Then he went among them,   (B) 100
   he seized the hand of just that one,
      the chief's girl.
"Then begin the song,
   "Begin it!"—
      the chief's girl was told that.   105
Then she began it: (C)
   "Like something indeed,
      "I strut about sticking out my br*ea*st!
   "Like something indeed,
      "I strut about sticking out my br*ea*st!   110
         she said.
   "I have warts on my back,
      "I blink my eyes,"
         said Frog,

Gane·hi' ba·dè'yeweyák^w.   (B)

Gane·hi da'o·l dì·'hiwilìu'   75
    wu·lham hoyodagwànma'.

Mi· honò' hò'k.   (C)

Gane·hi' sasiní·,
    hu·lìnt,
        da·sgèk'í·.   80

               [5] [He arrives]

Gane·hi' mi· gè wó·k.   (A)

A····· waiwì neyè·da' wu·lham hoyodák^w,
    kài gwala waiwì·,
      Bélp,
        Hà'ka·,   85
          Ts'ài·'s,
            Ts'amá·l,
              Lapá·m.

Kài nàk'a di 'ànì·' wu·lham hoyodák^w?   (B)

Kài gwalá sasiní·.   90

Sgìsi mi· wó·k;   (C)
    alxik'ìxa',
    wu·lham hoyodagwànma'.

         [II] [*The girls and Coyote sing*]

         [iii] [Frog and Coyote sing]

Gane·hi' mì·sga' waiwì·,   (A)
    da'à·nau,   95
      kaì gwala du·gwì· di·t'u·gu·í·,
        čelè'm.

"S'à! s-gà ge 'i·gì·'nan,"
    nagàihi'.

Gane·hi' ganau ginì'k,   (B) 100
    ga yà·hi 'ì·t'aut'au i·ù·xda,
      da'à·nau waiwì·.

"Gane· baimàsga hè·l,
    "Baimàsga!"—
      da'ànau waiwì· ga nagàn.   105

Gane·hi' bàimats'ák: (C)
    "K'i-xin-hi,
      Gel'-wi-liu-te····!
    "K'i-xin-hi,
      Gel'-wi-liu-te····!"   110
        nagàihi'.

    "Di·-tbo·-k'àlx-de',
    "Al-twa-p'à-twap-na'n,"
      nagàihi' Lapá·m,

           as she sang.   115
"I bubble under water,
    I'm lean in the rump,
        I have no fat in my legs and feet,
            Frog indeed,
                Poor me,   120
                  Poor me,"
                    said Frog,
                      she called herself that.
Then he for his part sang like this: (D)
    "For me,   125
        for *me,*
    "For me,
        for *me,*
    "For me,
        for *me,"*   130
        he sang out only half right.
                [iv] [Bluejay, Mouse, Swan and Coyote sing]
Then many kinds sang.   (A)
    "You begin your turn!"
        Bluejay was told that.
Then Bluejay sang: 135
    "Jay-jee-ay,
        her brush, her brush,
    "Jay-jee-ay,
        her brush, her brush."
Then now again,   (B) 140
    "You begin your turn!"
        again one girl was told,
            Mouse.
Then now she began:
    "Ruh-ruh-roo-shes-*roo*-a,   145
        "Ruh-ruh-roo-shes-*roo*-a,"
        that is how Mouse sang.
Coyote for his part sang it only half right: (C)
    "*S-ruh*-ruh-roo-shes,
        "*S-ruh*-ruh-roo-shes,   150
           "*S-ruh*-ruh-roo-shes,
               "*S-ruh*-ruh-roo-shes."
Then,   (D)
    "You begin your turn!"
        they said that to one another.   155
Then Swan began:
    "Pretty Swanny, put it to sleep,

helèlda.   115
"Da-bo-k'op-na'n,
   Di·-k'a-las-na'n,
      Gwel-sal-t'ees-na'n,
         La-pa·m-hi,
            'O-šu,   120
               'O-šu,"
                  nagàihi' Lapá·m,
                     a·ki ga nagaí·kwit.
Gane·hi' à·k'a gana'nèx helèl':   (D)
   "'ùsi,   125
      'ù·si,
   "'ùsi,
      'ù·si,
   "'ùsi,
      'ù·si,   130
         dayawànt'ixihí yonó·n.
                  [iv] [Bluejay, Mouse, Swan and Coyote sing]
Gane·hi' kài gwala helèl'.   (A)
   "Màsi' baimàsga!"
      Ts'ài's ga nagàn.
Gane·hi' helèl' Tsài's: 135
   "Č'ai-č'i·-a,
      gwa-ča, gwa-ča,
   "Č'ai-č'i·-a,
      gwa-ča, gwa-ča."
Gane·hi' mi· honò',   (B) 140
   "Màsi' baimàsga!"
      nagán mì·'s hono' waiwì·,
         Ts'amá·l.
Gane·hi' mi· bàimats'ak:
   "Be-be-bi-ni-bi·-a,   145
      "Be-be-bi-ni-bi·-a,"
         gana'nèx helèl' Ts'amá·l.
Sgìsi à·k'a dayawànt'ixi helèl':   (C)
   "S-be-be-bi-ni,
      "S-be-be-bi-ni,   150
         "S-be-be-bi-ni,
            "S-be-be-bi-ni."
Gane·hi',   (D)
   "Màsi' baimàsga!"
      ga nagàsa'n à·ihí.   155
Gane·hi' baimats'ák Bel`p:
   "Be-lel-do· wain-ha,

      "Pretty Swanny, put it to sleep,
        "Pretty Swanny, put it to sleep,
          "Pretty Swanny, put it to sleep,"   160
        said Swan,
          she sang that way for her part.

            [III] [*Singing brings bears*]
        [v] [Goose sings and Brown Bear comes]

Then,   (A)
    "You begin your turn!"
      said the girls to one another,   165
        Goose was told that.
Then she began:
    "Put to sleep Brown Bear's anus,
      "Put to sleep that old one's anus,
    "Put to sleep Brown Bear's anus,   170
      "Put to sleep that old one's anus,"
        Goose sang that way.
Then,   (B)
    "S'a! Where are they talking about my anus?"
      said Brown Bear.   175
Then *again* they said *that,*   (C)
    that song was sung:
      "Put to sleep Brown Bear's anus,
        "Put to sleep that old one's anus,
      "Put to sleep Brown Bear's anus,   180
        "Put to sleep that old one's anus."
Then now he heard it.   (D)
    "Where are they talking about my anus?"
      he said.
Now Brown Bear went.   185
Now he went where he heard
    the puberty dance being danced,
      right by (there) he went.
Now,
    "S-hau,   190
      hau,
        hau,
          hau,"
    right by where the puberty dance was being danced
      went Brown Bear.   195

      [vi] [Some keep singing and Grizzly comes]

Then some of the girls heard,   (A)
now Grizzly Bear was coming.
"No matter what, don't sing,"   (B)

"Be-lel-do· wain-ha,
    "Be-lel-do· wain-ha,
        "Be-lel-do· wain-ha,"   160
            nagàihi' Bel`p,
                helèl' gana'néx à·k'a.

[III] [*The singing brings bears*]

[v] [Goose sings and Brown Bear comes]

Gane·hi',   (A)
    "Masì' baimàsga!"
        nagàsa'n waiwì·tan,   165
            Hà'ka ga nagán.
Gane·hi' bàimats'ak:
    "Wain-ha· Mè-na dol-ki,
        "Wain-ha· i·-dol-ki,
    "Wain-ha· Mè-na dol-ki,   170
        "Wain-ha· i·-dol-ki,"
            Hà·ka· gana'nex helèl'.
Gane·hi',   (B)
    "S'a! Gwidi dòlkinitk yawayagwàn?"
        nagàihi' Mená.   175
Gane·hi' honò'hi gahi neyè',   (C)
    ga hè·1 yononàn:
        "Wain-ha· Mè-na dol-ki,
            "Wain-ha· i·-dol-ki,
        "Wain-ha· Mè-na dol-ki,   180
            "Wain-ha· i·-dol-ki."
Gane·hi' mi· da·'agán.   (D)
    "Gwidì dòlkinitk yawayagwàn?"
        nagàihi'.
Mi·hi' yà' Mená.   185
Mi· da·yehé·í·
    wu·lham hoyodagwànma',
        gada· ginì'k.
Mi·,
    "S-hau,   190
        hau,
            hau,
                hau,"
wu·lham hòidigwia gada·
    ginì·k Mená.   195

[vi] [Some keep singing and Grizzly comes]

Gane·hi' da·'agàn waiwì·tan dal'wì',   (A)
mi· Xámk baxàmda'.
" `I·si' wede he·lát,"   (B)

```
          they said to one another.
                 It indeed was heard,                                    200
                     Grizzly Bear was coming.
     All the same the dancing goes on.
     Still some among them:                                    (C)
             "Don't sing,
             "A dangerous being comes,"                                  205
                 girls did say to one another.
     All the same the puberty dance kept being danced.
     Then,                                                    (D)
             "Hàu,
                 hàu,                                                    210
                     hàu,
                         hàu"—
         they stopped dancing suddenly.
     Now Grizzly Bear had gotten right here.
```

[IV]. [*Coyote finds out about Frog*]

[vii] [Grizzly Bear breaks up the dance]

```
     Then,                                                (A) 215
             "Hàu,
                 hàu,
                     hàu,
                         hàu,"
                             he said.                                    220
     Now he jumped among them;
         they flew right up,
             he killed no one.
     Coyote, though, ran off with this chief's girl.           (B)
     *That* was all.                                                     225
```

[viii] [Coyote runs off with Frog]

```
     Now they flew off in a bunch,                             (A)
         Grizzly Bear scared the people all about.
     Now this Coyote, for his part, ran off into the brush with the chief's girl.
     Then,                                                     (B)
             a little while,                                             230
                 "Are you female?
                 "Must be female,"
                     he kept saying.
     Coyote, for his part, now wanted to sleep with her.
     Then he did not find his "kinswoman's" private parts.     (C) 235
     "What did *I* get?
             "I thought you must be a woman,"
                 he said to her.
```

nagàsa'n.
    Dà·hi'aganìn,   200
        Xàmk baxàmda'.
Gangàhi' hoyodiàu'.
Dal'wìsi':   (C)
    "Wede he·lát,
    "Kài'wa baxà'm,"   205
        nag`asa'nhi' waiwì·tan.
Gangàhi' wu·lham hoyodagwàn.
Gane·hi',   (D)
    "Hàu,
      hàu,   210
        hàu,
           hàu" —
ba·salxòxigin.
Mi· yaxa 'alí· la·le· Xámk.

[IV] [*Coyote finds out about Frog*]

[vii] [Grizzly Bear breaks up the dance]

Gane·hi',   (A) 215
    "Hàu,
      hàu,
        hàu,
         hàu,"
          nagàihi'.   220
Mi· dàlxabilìu';
    ba·yà·domò'siau',
      àni·' nék t'omò·m.
Sgìsisi' aga da'à·nau waiwì 'i·hougwák[w].   (B)
Gàhi' ganga.   225

[viii] [Coyote runs off with Frog]

Mi· k'u·wù·',   (A)
    Xámk yap'a daxoyòxi.
Mi· aga Sgìsi à·k'á da'ànau waiwi· dàlhiwilí·k[w].
Gane·hi',   (B)
    bou né·xada',   230
      "Waiwì· di eí·t?
      "Waiwì· mì·'wa,"
        nagàihís.
Sgìsi'a mi· gelwaí·nia gelgulúk[w].
Gane·hi' àni·' tayák gwi·'nèi hawùxda·.   (C) 235
"Kàdi gi·'á?
    "Kailà·pa mi·'wa nagàsbi'n,"
      nagàhi'.

Coyote threw Frog into the water.   (D)
"Do you think you will be a woman?   240
    "You will always be called 'Frog',"
        he said to Frog.

It goes just up to there.   [Close]
It's finished,
    go gather and eat your baap seeds.   245

Sgìsi Lapá·m xamgwidík^w.   (D)

"Ma dì kai'là·pa yuda'?"   240

   "'Lapa·m' nànsbina',"

     nagàhi' Lapá·m.

Gé de'winìthí.   [Close]

Gweldi,

   ba·bi't lè·plap.   245

IV. Philological Background

1. Introduction

The Takelma text and English translation just given are not identical with those published by Sapir. The Takelma orthography has been revised. Two previously unpublished lines are incorporated. Implicit rhetorical form has been made apparent. Translations have been changed. The reasons for these changes are taken up in the four sections that follow. Interpretation and assessment of the narrative occur along the way in connection with features involved.

The present section (IV) has to do with philology in a narrow sense—how are the words to be shown (orthography); is there more to be said about the role of the sounds of the language in narrative (expressive features); are the printed words the same as those first written down (field notebooks)?

Translation has to do with both words and form. The two can be interdependent. Some changes from the original publication in English wording involve the makeup of Takelma words in relation to concern about rhetorical form. (Note "Hearing," "Probably?" and *"ganga"* 'always', sections 5, 7, and 12 in part V.) Because of concern to represent the form of the original as accurately as possible, words that are the same in Takelma are the same in English insofar as possible. Such repetition is part of form, signalling relationship.

Part V takes up matters that have to do primarily with words. Part VI takes up matters that have to do primarily with form in the sense of sequence. Part VII takes up maters that have to do primarily with form in the sense of minor forms employed in the myth.

2. Takelma Orthography

Sapir recorded Takelma in exquisite detail. It is fortunate that someone with his gifts did so. In particular, others might have missed the contrast in tonal accent. The field work became the basis of his doctoral dissertation, and was undertaken before he and others developed phonemic analysis.[4] In later years Sapir himself devised a phonemic representation, which he used in classes at Yale. It was recorded in class by Mary Haas, and is reproduced by Shipley (1969:227), which should be consulted by anyone interested in Takelma.

The orthography used here is almost isomorphic with Sapir's phonemic analysis and the slightly different research orthography adopted by Shipley. All three are of course a simplification of that used earlier in the published texts, particularly through elimination of many non-phonemic distinctions in regard to the quality and placement of vowels.

A. Vowels. Three aspects of vowels need to be mentioned: phonemic status, accent, rhetorical length.

(a) Phonemic status. Takelma has a phonemic difference between long and short vowels, and a variety of ways in which the two are manifested. There appear to be five phonemic vowels and five long counterparts (Shipley 1969), essentially (i e a o u) and (i· e· a· o· u·).

(b) Accent. Takelma has a significant contrast of pitch accent, falling versus rising. Sapir published the texts and grammar with an acute accent (´) for the falling accent, and a grave accent (ˋ) for the rising accent, contrary to usual practice (see G22, n. 1). The research orthography (Shipley 1969) reverses this to accord with common practice, and so do I. Two accent marks are found here, then, acute (´) for a rising accent, and grave (ˋ) for falling accent.

In the texts and grammar there is a third accent mark, a circumflex (~). It represents a rising accent found only on long vowels and dipthongs. Sapir himself observes that (~) and what is here written (´) are variants of a single unit. (´) is "found on short vowels or unitonal long vowels and diphthongs (generally in last syllable of word)," and "is best considered an abbreviated form of ~, i.e., the vowel or diphthong reaches its higher tone immediately instead of sliding up to it" (1909:11). This audible difference in the two forms of the raised, or rising, accent understandably led to writing them differently in the field.[5] The other phonemic accent, falling, also occurs with both short and long vowel nuclei.

(c) Rhetorical length. Sapir used a plus sign (+) for more than normal length. In the Takelma text I substitute repeated raised dots (····). In the translation I either repeat a letter ("Ahhhh!" in line 82), or underline ("br*east*" in lines 107, 109). (Underlining is also sometimes used for the effect of emphasizing affixes.)

B. Consonants. The orthography used here differs from Sapir's phonemic analysis and Shipley's research orthography in two principal respects. One has to do with a principle (a), one with practical convenience (b). Labialized stops (c) and characterizing prefixes (d) should also be mentioned.

(a) Expressive contrast. Both sibilant (s) and shibilant (š) (analogous to the initial sounds of English "sip," "ship") occur in Takelma, but the difference is not phonemic. It does not distinguish words with different reference. It does, however, have relevance. One and the same word can be said with one or the other sound to convey an expressive difference. When Coyote first hears the sound of the puberty dance, he exclaims "*S'à*" (22); a moment later, he exclaims "*Š'à!*" (26). I take the latter to be more affirmative.

Again, Frog sings '*O-šu* (120); Coyote imitates her with '*ùsi* (125ff). Frog's words have been vaunting, and here too, even though this word can be interpreted as "Poor me," the shibilant conveys the augmentation of a show-off. When Coyote imitates Frog, he is only "half-right," and the sibilant, a sound characteristically associated with him, seems appropriately diminishing. The different sounds seem part of the contrast between the singing of the two.

In a song sung by another girl, the same difference appears in the corresponding affricate (always glottalized, and usually written (ts'). Bluejay's name is regularly *Ts'ài's*, but the self-referring first word of her song plays upon her name with *Č'ai-č'i̇-a* (line 136). The song can be taking as vaunting, and the phonetic difference as appropriately expressive.

In this text, then, the sibilant forms (s, ts') appear to express a diminishing, the shibilant forms (š, č') augmentation (cf. Hymes 1981:75). That is the case in Wasco-Wishram Chinook, and in some other languages of the region.

These cases illustrate a general principle. There is not just one dimension of contrast in phonology (and the rest of language), there are two. Elements can contrast with regard to referential function (better, "propositional function"). Elements can contrast with regard to expressive function (better, "presentational function"). That is an elementary dimension of language also, interdependent with the other. The point was made more than thirty years ago by Roman Jakobson (1960:354), and I have tried several times to enunciate it (e.g., Hymes 1972:xxv–xvii, 1974:146, 160–61, 1984:54–59). Linguists continue to ignore it, missing generalizations and scope in consequence, but folklorists need not.

(b) Useful symbols. Other departures here have to do with choice of symbols. The choice of the usual symbols for rising and falling accent (´ `) has been indicated above. The notable other choice has to do with the three series of stops.

Takelma has three series of stops: intermediate, aspirated, and glottalized. Sapir wrote these as b d g, p' t' k', and p! t! k!, respectively. Shipley (1969) substitutes p t k for the b d g of the first series, while retaining marks of aspiration (ph th kh) and glottalization (p' t' k') to distinguish the second and third. The use of (p t k) in all three series makes visible their phonetic and phonological relationship. None of the three series is voiced.[6] The first series, weakly articulated, does sometimes sound voiced to an English ear, but the actual differences reside in the aspiration and glottalization of the other two.

This reasonable orthography unfortunately makes use of the published material more difficult. The texts (T) and grammar (G) could be written with (p t k), instead of (b d g), perhaps more efficiently. But as first published, and as republished, the texts, grammar, and vocabulary (verbs and nouns are at the end of the texts, other sets (numerals, adverbs, etc.) at the end of the grammar) have the first set (b d g). Unless and until the texts, grammar and vocabulary are published with the later (p t k) of both Sapir and Shipley), use of the sources is facilitated by retention of their (b d g). Otherwise, one would have to remember to look up "p" under "b," "d" under "t," and "k" under "g," and be continually converting. That is a lot to ask of anyone not a specialist. With (b d g), morphemes retain in the mind's eye the shape in which they are cited and discussed by Sapir. To be sure, the (p t k) symbols would avoid a temptation to mispronounce the intermediate stops with voicing, like English (b d g); but it may be better to avoid a temptation to pronounce them with aspiration, like English (p t k). That would eliminate the Takelma contrast between [p t k] and [p' t' k'].

Given (b d g) for the intermediate series, it is unnecessary to set the aspirated series apart with a mark of aspiration. (p t k) will do. Only one stop series, then, has a diacritic here, the glottalized series (here p', t', k'). That may make forms more perspicuous.[7]

(c) All the orthographies presented by Shipley (1969:227) distinguish a labialized order, represented with a raised w following k, g, k' (kʷ, gʷ, kʼʷ). The raised w indicates the voiceless variant of (w) which occurs only with k at the end of a syllable. Before vowels, a full w is heard; that is easier to write and print and is used here.[8]

(d) Takelma makes use of two expressive prefixes, (s-), commonly preposed to words said by Coyote, and (ɫ-, "L" in Sapir), commonly preposed to words said by Grizzly Woman. Sapir indicates the expressive prefixes by a hyphen before what follows in the translation. I add a hyphen in the Takelma text as well (lines 41, 63, 98, 149–52, 190).

The two prefixes are not used exclusively by Coyote and Grizzly Woman, respectively. Others may use them. From the use of the "Coyote prefix" not only by Coyote, as in this myth (149–52), but also by Brown Bear in this myth, by Grizzly Woman, and by ten Bear brothers, I have inferred an expressive contrast (1981:71–72, 73–74). Both prefixes convey something diminutive or depreciating; (ɫ-) indicates greater distance, and (s-) less. When contrasted to (ɫ-), the (s-) prefix indicates relative closeness. In contrast to its absence, the (s-) prefix indicates relative lack of respect, as in Coyote's use of it in this myth. The same is probably true with Brown Bear, who uses it before *hau* (190), as against Grizzly Bear, who does not (209).

Sapir does not suggest a translation for the interjection (s'à ~ š'à), used by Coyote in this and other myths (Sapir 1922:279, where the citations to 71.14 and 90.12 of the published texts refer to this form), and I leave it untranslated also. It may consist of the *s-* characteristic of Coyote and a variant of ('a), "sudden surprise at new turn, sudden resolve" (1922:278).

3. *Field Notebooks*

Interpretation of the verbal artistry of Native American narrators such as Frances Johnson depends on philology. In the broad sense of the term, interpretation of meaning, this entire essay is philological. In the narrow sense of the term, establishment of written records, it must also be philological. The sad fact is that one cannot assume that published texts are entirely accurate in relation to the manuscripts on which they are based (let alone contain all the narrative material). Analyzing Louis Simpson's Wishram narrative, "The Deserted Boy" (Hymes 1976), I was able to explain one discrepancy, and correct another, by consulting Sapir's field notebooks. In both cases, analysis into verses pointed up discrepancies from expected poetic pattern. Recourse to the original transcription accounted for both.

We are fortunate to have Sapir's field notebooks for Takelma, and I am indebted to Daythal Kendall for information about the rhetorical markers and the very existence of lines 74 and 75. Their role in the organization of the story is discussed just below ("Missing lines") and under Analysis.

A. Rhetorical Markers. In the notebook recordings Sapir abbreviated the frequent initial particle *gane·hi'* as "g." (g plus period). This was no doubt due to a attempt to keep pace with the flow of speech. (In his Wishram Chinook notebooks, he abbreviated the frequent particle pair *Aga kwapt,* "Now then," as "A.K.".) The difficulty is that the word has two elements, *gane·-* and *-hi'*, and can sometimes occur without *-hi'* (G274). One can not tell if a "g." indicates *gane·*, or *gane·hi'*. Perhaps it usually indicates the longer form, since that is the form Sapir usually prints.

This uncertainty does not affect the form of a text. Both *gane·hi'* and *gane·* mark verses. But tone and expressive emphasis might differ.

Something that is not hidden, but might be, has to do with the sibilant and shibilant distinction. The sequences of Coyote's expressive particle, for example, or repetition of Frog's words and Bluejay's name (discussed above), can be considered rhetorical marking also. The spoken shape is taken as given. What is different here is interpretation of the phonetic difference as significant. Had Sapir transcribed the text phonemically, rather than with phonetic detail, such expressive movement would be invisible.

B. Missing Lines. Kendall has discovered that the field notebooks have two lines not in the published text. They appear here as lines 74 and 75.

Perhaps in preparing the texts for publication the two lines were overlooked because of repetition of *da'òl* 'nearby'. That word is penultimate in what precedes the missing lines, and penultimate in the missing material as well (cf. 73, 75). The eye of Sapir, or someone else, might have passed from the first occurrence to the phrase (76) that follows the second. Such a collocation in fact occurs earlier in the scene (cf. lines 36, 44). The resulting passage would be intelligible.

What difference does the presence or absence of the two lines make? Is the text so integrated that the pair of lines affect its formal coherence? Omission of the two lines would indeed present difficulty, both for the analyses of the scene that preceded this one (cf. 1979a ms, p. 35; 1980b) and the present analysis. This is discussed with the analysis of scene ii, 4.

V. Translation of Words[9]

1. Constant Particles

A principle of a presentation such as this is to be true to the form of the original. That entails consistency in the use of English equivalents for Takelma words. Certain Takelma words are signals of sequence, of the rhythm of the action, particularly *gane·hi'* 'then indeed', *mi·* 'now', *honò'* 'again'. The usual practice in English writing is to vary such terms, but here they are constant.

In the same spirit, parallelism in word-order is maintained as much as possible; repetitions not in the original are avoided if possible, as are false repetitions. All these points arise in scene iv.

2. Two Verbs "to sing"

The published translation has "Then Bluejay sang" (135), "Thus did Mouse sing" (147). In Takelma the order is the same (and normal), verb + name, in both cases; I give the second in normal English order as well, "That is how Mouse sang."

With Swan, the published translation has "Then Swan started in to sing," but the Takelma has only "started in"; I omit "to sing."

When Coyote takes up Mouse's song half-right, the verb phrase following his effort has *dayawànt'ixi helèl'* 'half he-sang' (148). The first time he takes up a song, that of Frog, however, what he does is framed between two different verbs: *helèl'* (124) precedes his effort, and *dayawànt'ixi-hí yonó·n* (131) follows. Both *helèl'* and *yonó·n* are translated with forms of 'sing' (the latter with 'sang'). Now in the vocabulary, the stem *helel-* is glossed as 'sing', *yonon-* as 'sing (a song)'. The noun for 'song' is *hè·l*. With *hè·l-* as incorporated prefix, the ablaut form *yunun-* is 'sing a song'. All this suggests that *helel-* is intrinsically 'sing a song', and *yonon-* is not. Given that, and given that it is Coyote singing half-right in the line in question (131), the best way to differentiate the two verbs would seem to be qualification of *yonon*. The best I can suggest is 'sing out'.

A second principle is to reconsider English renderings generally. It is in fact difficult to shake off the English with which one starts. It becomes familiar and somehow natural. As a result, it may unwittingly influence analysis. I have gone to the grammar and dictionary as much as possible to overcome this, but instances may remain. A virtue of analysis of rhetorical form, such as this one, is that it does bring one or another word or phrase into focus, and leads to new renderings.

One instance of this involves supplying an English translation that was not given. Another involves omitting English that was. The first instance is discussed below in regard to scene vii. The second instance, having to do with the postposed particle, *-hi'*, is analyzed in connection with verse marking in section VI.

3. Graphic Marks and Degrees of Force

Sometimes the force of a form can best be conveyed by adding a graphic mark. In scene viii, lines 228 and 234, "Coyote" occurs twice with the suffix *-'a'*, translated by Sapir as 'for his part' (*Sgìsi ak'-'a* [he-for his part] [228], *Sgìsi-'a* [234]). Sapir comments (G250) that the suffix "differs from the exclusive *-ta* in being less distinctly a part of the whole word and in having a considerably stronger contrastive force." Sapir suggests (G246) that *-ta* is "not susceptible of adequate translation into English, the closest rendering being generally a dwelling of the voice on the corresponding English word." Presumably, English "for his part" conveys the stronger force of *-'a* in the two lines. In the first occurrence (228) I have also underlined "<u>his</u>" to bring out what seems a yet stronger degree of contrast, indicated by the presence of the pronominal marker (*ak'-*) (as against the presence just of "Coyote" [234]). Stronger contrast makes sense in the first occurrence. What coyote does is being established against the background of the preceding line, which tells what everyone else does (Grizzly Bear and the people). The second occurrence comes when only Coyote and Frog are left on stage. Similarly, lengthening in Coyote's second "for me" when he responds to Frog is indicated here by underlining to focus attention better on the pronoun.

Again, the two occurrences of *ga-hi*, literally 'that-indeed', seem best served by underlining of 'that' (176, 275). Sapir translates the first 'just that', and does not translate the second at all (see below with scene vii). Emphatic *-hi* in fact has occurred already in the sentence, the first time being the only time in this text that it occurs with *honò'* 'again'. That suggests that emphasis was indeed on Mrs. Johnson's mind at this point. Two occurrences of "indeed" in the English seem too many. Two uses of underlining seem tolerable. And it is possible to treat the other occurrence of *ga-hi* (275) aptly in the same way: "*That* was all." ("That indeed" would be tolerable in both lines, but in the latter "just that" ["Just that was all"] would not.)

Sometimes there seems to be no way to convey by translation a degree of force indicated in Takelma. Such is the case in Act V. Goose sings, Brown Bear hears; the girls sing, Brown Bear hears and comes. In the first pair of turns each verse is introduced by *gane·hi'* 'then'. In the second pair, the singing of the girls is doubly marked by *gane·hi' honò'hi* 'then again-indeed', and the four verses of Brown Bear's response are distinguished by a run of *mi·* 'now' three times. In the first verse *mi·* follows *gane·hi'*; in the second it begins, followed (unusually) by *-hi'*. This weighting of both initial elements seems to anticipate and underscore the arrival of the outcome. One can translate the particles with "indeed," but that is a somewhat artificial diction. To recognize what is happening in terms of expressive force, one has to become alert to small changes, indeed, it seems to me, to consult and follow the original text.

4. Segmenting Time

A pervasive consideration has to do with the difference between Takelma and English in grammatical categories. Takelma has six tense-modes, distinguished by two forms of stem and five sets of pronominal suffixes. The common tense-mode is the aorist; its stem is derived by augmenting the non-aorist stem in various ways. Sapir translates the aorist as past or imperfect. That seems normal in a myth, but it is important to realize that the temporal range is broader: not only past, but also present, and immediate future (G94, 197). The other five tense-modes—a future distinctly apart, a future imperative, a present imperative, an inferential, a potential—use the plain (non-aorist) stem. Four of these tense-modes each has its own set of pronominal endings (G157); the potential uses those of the aorist. In Takelma, then, verbs mark actions first of all in terms of certainty and uncertainty of occurrence (*realis, unrealis*). A bare stem supports what is expressed as uncertain, because it has not happened or might not have happened. A derived stem supports what is expressed as certain event: what has occurred, what is occurring, what is about to occur.

In lines 58–59 of this myth it seems appropriate to remember the full range of the aorist and to translate in English with the present tense. The two lines use aorist stems, and Sapir does translate in the past: "Whenever they sang, it was as though right at hand." Notice, however, that the import of the lines is almost gnomic, describing a recurrent state. The relative abstractness of the Takelma verbs fit this. In the first clause, the subject of the verb for singing is a collective impersonal suffix, -*iau*, equivalent to German *man*, French *on* (G156); in the second clause the verb is a pro forma general form for activity (G185).

Sapir's "Whenever," as frame for the sentence, seems to come from two features of the first phrase, its verb ending and its initial particle. The verb is marked as a subordinate transitive by -*da'*, whence presumably "when-"; Sapir usually uses "when" to distinguish dependent verbs. The particle *ganga* can be seen to have a sense of "always," whence perhaps the "ever." (See below with respect to scenes vi and vii.) Sapir himself elsewhere (G276–77) notes a connotation for of continuance for *ganga*). "Whenever" has a connotation of intermittence, however, which seems inappropriate. Using "always," which seems preferable for *ganga* here, one can reflect the subordinate marker with "as" (cf. G190 "as they were talking" [line 9 up]). With "always" the present tense seems more appropriate than the past, as in lines 58–59:

> Always as they sing,
> > it is (as if) right at hand.

Let me now take up other examples in the order in which they occur, numbering them for later reference.

5. *Hearing*

Scene ii tells of Coyote hearing the sound of the girls' puberty dance being danced. The terms in which he perceives it, and the term for the dance itself, require consideration.

The published translation says that Coyote heard, listened, heard (lines 18, 20, 24). Repetition of "heard" obscures an incremental series. In the published text the last of these lines is translated "Now he heard the menstrual dance being danced." Its verb-stem, *da·-t'ayag-*, however, is identified in the vocabulary as 'discover by hearing, hear all of a sudden' (T228). These specifications make sense at this point. The hearing follows Coyote's question, where? (22). In effect, "Now he suddenly discovered it," where "it" is an answer, not to what (the puberty dance), but to where. In English a parenthetic phrase is needed to convey the relationship: "Now he suddenly discovered (in which direction)/ the puberty dance was being danced."

That what Coyote discovers is the correct direction is implicit in the fact that his subsequent mistaken judgments all have to do with how close he is, not with the direction in which he is going. Near the end of his series of overly optimistic judgments Mrs. Johnson in fact reassuringly remarks (68) that the dance was indeed being danced in the east (which on the Rogue is the same as upriver). We have in effect three stages in Coyote's perception: what (puberty dance), where (east), how far (nearby).

The verb in line 24 is in fact the third of a trio of verbs which have initial rhyme. Each begins with the same body-part prefix, *da-* 'ear, with ear (referring to hearing)' (G77); each has a different root. The first, *-'agan,* appears to have a connotation of 'to sense'. The second, *-sgèk'i-,* has no attested meaning apart from occurrence with *da-,* but this passage suggests 'to attend, focus, concentrate'. The third, as said, has the basic meaning 'to find, discover'. The sequence as a whole conveys 'to sense by ear', 'to concentrate by ear', 'to discover by ear'. A revised translation, "hear, listen, discover" can convey the presence of an incremental series, if not the ringing of changes on a common form.

The incremental series is one strand of the tight interweaving of this scene (for which see discussion of it as part of consideration of relations of rhetorical form [VI below]).

6. Dancing

The girls' dance (*wù·lham*) is identified as "menstrual round-dance" (T260) in the lexicon accompanying the texts; it is just "round dance" with the burdens of the singers (G280–81); "menstrual dance" is used throughout Sapir's translation of the myth (19, 22, 25, 36, 38, 44, 63, 68, 76, 82, 89, 93, 186, 194, 207). I have substituted the now common term, "puberty dance."

7. Probably?

Coyote's running to the dance is intense in subscenes 2 and 3, and he repeatedly anticipates being almost there. Twice in 2, twice in 3, he says "probably here" (38, 45, 52, 67 ("there" in line 52)). The term of expectation, *mi·'wa,* is glossed (G276) as probably, perhaps', and Sapir uses "probably" for it in this act. Given the many stories in which Coyote is sure of something mistakenly, it is tempting to substitute "must be." Lines 231–33 and 236–38 in the last act seem to require it.

Coyote has run off into brush with Frog, and says,

> "Are you female?
> Must be [*mi·'wa*] female,"
> he kept saying.

What must be taken to happen here is that Coyote immediately attempts to copulate and is trying to find the spot. The verb of saying implies an intention that fails to be realized, i.e., a process. "Probably" seems inadequate. All the effort makes no sense if he has been unsure. The girl's puberty dance itself would have defined the participants as marriageable females with normal parts. "Must be female" seems in keeping with the situation and Coyote.

In lines 236–37, Coyote says,

> "What did I get?
> Woman *mi·'wa* you were"

Sapir translates the second line, "That you were a woman I thought," as *mi·'wa* has no English equivalent. "I thought" makes sense here, but is not present in the verb; perhaps the implication carries over from line 234, where the verb of saying can be taken that way as an idiom. Still, a literal translation makes sense as well. The verb is a transitive passive aorist, with the one pronominal ending, "you (sg.)," its logical subject (G180). If Coyote is taken to be expostulating, "You must have been a woman" fits (cf. 13, 15).

In both passages the joke is not that Coyote has been estimating probability, acting on a percentages, but that he has been sure and is proven wrong. These passages seem really to require "Must be," and support taking the earlier passages in the same way. Coyote is repeatedly sure that the dance is nearby and proven wrong.

8. Here

The term glossed 'here' in the expressions in scene ii is the demonstrative adverb *emè'*; it is part of a series with *i·deme'* 'right around there', and *hè·me'* 'yonder' (near first, second and third persons, respectively). A term used to similar effect is the corresponding demonstrative pronoun *alí·* (44, 59) (G252); it is part of a series: *alí·* 'this here', *i·dalí·* 'that there', *ha·'lí·* 'that over there' (near first, second, and third persons). In this myth Sapir renders it "it was right here" (44), "it was as though right at hand" (49). Related is the local adverb *da'òl* 'nearby' (36, 44, 48, 75) (G270).

9. Start Again

In subscene 4 it is helpful to realize that the verb in line 74 (missing from the printed text) is not the same as verbs that have been translated "he ran" earlier on. Its root, *yewei-*, is glossed 'go back, return' (T238). The two prefixes used with it here, *ba·-* 'up' and *de-* 'in front, ahead', give a sense of 'start up again' (presumably, go back in the sense of go back to what one was doing). In the myth of "Daldal the Transformer" indeed, Sapir translates it as "continued travelling," "started travelling again" (cf. G77). This fits the slackening pace of the scene here, with Coyote tired.

10. Chieftainness?

In scene iii *da'à·nau* 'chief' (95) was translated as in apposition to the preceding "one girl," and as a noun, "chieftainness" (95). A girl just reaching maturity would not have that status; I substitute "chiefly."

11. Songs

Scenes iii, iv, and v have the songs of the girls at the dance. I have translated them (as Sapir did not) and tried to emulate the playfulness involved. It seems best to present that as part of discussion of features in the course of the story (VII).

12. ganga 'always'

In scenes vi and vii *ganga* occurs three times. It is a modal adverb (G271) whose citations there to the texts include English equivalents 'only', 'anyhow', and, with postposed -*si'* (no citation), 'just so, for fun'. At the beginning of line 58 in scene ii, subscene 3 (see discussion above), Sapir translated it "whenever." At the beginning of the two sentences in scene vi, both with postposed -*hi'*, it is translated once as "yet" (202) (T106:16) and once as "still" (207) (T106:17). With preceding *gàhi'*, as if beginning a sentence (225) (T106:21), it is not translated at all.

It is possible to find a semantic link among these uses. A check of the citations and some other uses leads to the conclusion that the essential element of meaning had to do with totality. When an actor in a myth is rendered as saying "only" a certain thing, he could be taken as "always" saying that thing. The first use of *ganga* (58) was translated by Sapir as "whenever," but the story implies that Coyote runs toward a continuing source of singing (and dancing). When he pauses to listen, he is concerned, not with if there is singing, but where or how near (see discussion above).

The uses of *ganga* for dancing (and singing) in scene vi (202, 207) certainly involve continuous activity. That is the point: despite warnings, the girls keep on. Sapir's translations of the lines, "Yet they went on dancing," "still the puberty dance kept being danced," are reasonable, but the continuity is in "went on" and "kept." Initial "yet" and "still" come from the situation (warning ignored), not from anything we know about *ganga*. Its sense of "always" fits. One can combine continuance and situation (warning ignored) in "All the same."

(Scene vii). A sense of "always" also makes it possible to understand the structure of scene vii and the role of *gàhi' ganga* (225) in it. Sapir's translation of this part of the story omits the two words. They are not reflected in what follows or precedes. The *mi·* ('now') that follows starts the next verse. Indeed, the following verses turn out to be a neatly integrated set of four pairs, constituting, in fact, scene viii. Nor is there any connection with what precedes ("Coyote, though, ran off with this chief's girl" [224]).

Syntactically, the two words are orphans. Rhetorically, they fit. They are not part of what happens, but part of what gives the story shape. They provide a temporary close. The preceding act ends with Grizzly Bear's arrival, just as the act before that had ended with the arrival of Brown Bear. Now Mrs. Johnson describes in three verses how it all comes out. Grizzly Bear repeats *hàu*; he jumps among them, they fly up, no one is killed; Coyote runs off with the chief's girl. Then she says *gà-hi'* 'that-indeed' and *ganga,* in effect, 'that was all'. As a fourth verse, it completes an expected pattern.

It is possible that Mrs. Johnson here found herself in the midst of the outcome without having it fully in mind. Or that she wanted to emphasize it by doubling part of it, giving a sketch of the end of the dance, and then, with repetition of that (226–68), going on to the delicious quotation of Coyote. Whether improvised or deployed, this intermediate *finis* maintains immediate form, and, by delay, provides a bit of heightening.

All this about *ganga* is in accord with an insight of Sapir himself in the context of discussion of another adverb, *yaxa* (G276–77), its force being often so weak as hardly to allow of an adequate rendering into English. It often does not seem to imply more than simply existence or action unaccompanied and undisturbed. It is found often with the scarcely translatable adverb *ganga* ONLY, in which case the idea of unvaried continuance comes out rather strongly.[10]

The new translations take advantage of that insight in specific cases.

13. In Vain

In scene viii, line 232 has the suffix *-his*, 'nearly, almost, trying', which "implies that the action which was done or attempted failed of success" (G276).

A frequent idiom is the use of *his* with the verb of saying, *nag-*, as here, to imply a thought or intention that fails to be realized (*idem*), and Sapir translates the line in question as "he thought" (T109:5). I think it desirable to convey the implication of failing to be realized, partly because I suspect such a meaning to be an areal pattern (cf. Chinookan *kinwa* 'in vain'). "He kept saying" has the underlying meaning of "say," and the repetitiveness suggests lack of success (cf. 7 and 15).

14. Latin

Line 235 in scene viii is translated in Latin: *Tunc nihil vulvae repperit* 'Then nothing of-her-private-parts he-discovered'. Latin was often required when such texts were published, although even in 1959, half a century later, Cassell's *New Latin Dictionary* lacked the offending word. The recently republished texts do give a translation in editorial notes: "Then he discovered she had nothing for a vagina" (Golla 1990:578).

Sapir's Latin omits a Takelma word, not for propriety, but uncertainty (so also n. 8 of the Collected Works). In Takelma one has "Then not he-discover *gwí·'nèi* her-private-parts." The omitted word is found in the lexicon (T245), but with a question mark. It is glossed '(her) thing (?)' with a reference to this line. In his Vocabulary Sapir put it under *gwi'neí·-x-* 'relative' (presumably connected with *kwinax-* 'kinsman, relative' [T247]). I take it that in this line the word should be translated as "relative" or "kinswoman." A spouse would be a relative, and perhaps something about in-laws lies behind the form. Because of her wealth and chiefly status, Frog would be attractive (at least temporarily) as a spouse, and a term for relationship itself underscores Coyote's impetuous way of entering into one. Perhaps something expressive of the immediate situation attaches to the form as well. One speculation is that *gwí·'nèi* involves or echoes the copula *ei-* 'be', added to first and second person subjective forms of the conditional (G). If so, an expanded translation might be: Then he did not find his would-be kinswoman's private parts. I have settled for just "kinswoman" with ironic quotation marks.

15. Verb of Pronouncement

Line 237, "You must have been a woman," has been discussed in connection with *mi·'wa* 'probably, perhaps' (7), and 'In vain' (13) above. The passive construction of 237 is paralleled in 241. The Takelma *Lapa·m' na-n-sbin-a'* is literally 'Frog say (intransitive)—causative—you (passive sg.)—future', equivalent to "you will be said to be 'Frog'." The causative element (G135) appears to imply a subject not expressed (G180–81), which in this case would be "I" (Coyote). In effect, not merely "Frog you will always be called" (T108), but "I cause you to be called 'Frog'," literally, "I cause 'Frog' to be said to you." There is a verb 'to name, call by name' ($p'u\cdot wu\cdot k'$-), but the construction used here may be a characteristic way of pronouncing a person's name and nature in myths. The same construction is used when the transformer Daldal places Evening Star in the west and tells him that is what he will be (T33:2). (Cf. 7, 13 above and the end of vii.)

VI. Translation of Form

The fundamental hypothesis is that Takelma narratives are organized in lines and verses, verses forming stanzas, stanzas forming scenes, scenes forming acts. It is assumed that each predicate is likely to constitute a line, but that within that framework other expressions might constitute lines as well. The texts contain particles that frequently occur at the beginning of sentences, and it has been assumed that they would be keys to identifying verses. When work began, it was also assumed that verses, and longer units, would show relations of two and four, rather than of three and five. (These are the common alternatives found in Native American and other traditions.) There are a number of indications of such a principle in this and other myths: in the myth of the wives Grizzly Bear and Brown Bear each has two children, whereas in Clackamas Chinook each has five; in the opening of this myth, Coyote sets traps four times (once generically, then three successive mornings); as he goes to the dance, the question "How long did he not run?" recurs four times; when Brown Bear and Grizzly Bear exclaim, each repeats *"Hau"* four times.

It is difficult to reconstruct the steps by which lines and verses were first arrived at. An initial analysis in the spring of 1978 was taken up again in the summer of 1979, and reworked twice. One reconsideration of the patterning of scene ii was published as part of a paper on this kind of analysis (Hymes 1980b). Reconsideration of points of diction, proportion, artistry, led to refinements and revisions. A number of such reconsiderations are part of this presentation. Several of them emerge from immersing oneself yet again for this purpose. (Some conclusions remain constant after trial of others.) Later insights obscure earlier perceptions. The essential point is that the hypothesis of lines and verses, involving sentence-initial particles, has been sustained. (See also now Hymes 1990.) It led to a blocking out of the organization of the myth that has been repeatedly adjusted, but not fundamentally altered.

The process of discovery, then, is akin to what Kenneth Pike has called "spiral procedure" in grammar. One works back and forth between levels. There is no algorithm of automatic steps, no single criterion (such as certain initial particles) which guarantees a satisfactory outcome. The criterion is the adequacy of the outcome in the light of all that one has come to understand about the particular text. It is essential to remember that one is disclosing the architecture of a performance. The narrator worked with certain devices and patterns, which can be shown to be indeed at work, but there are options in their use. Different performances might generate somewhat different profiles and degrees of elaboration, choices of pattern (cf. scene ii, subscenes 2-4, and the Appendix). We can discern the form of the performance whose text we have, and should. Its considerable regularity indicates that the narrator had in mind canons of organization, both locally and overall. Still, there was not a fixed frame to be filled, like the fourteen lines of a traditional sonnet, or the assigned repetitions of a villanelle. The classical sonata would be an apt analogy, if we keep in mind how freely its inventor, Haydn, used the form.

1. Distinguishing Lines

Lacking recordings and intonation contours, some decisions as to what constitutes a line might be made differently by others. Three kinds of case deserve comment.

(a) Putting verbs of saying on a separate line is a convention of my own.[11] In speech the verbs might precede or follow what is said without pause. Here I substitute a visual frame for what can be marked in performance by quality of voice.

(b) A decision to treat subordinate verbs as lines emerged from wrestling with the text. It arises particularly with the phrase for dancing the puberty dance (lines 19, 22, 25, 36, 38, 44, 63, 68, 76, 82, 89, 93). It is possible to take the two words as the entire predicate of a line, as in 22: "Where is the puberty dance being danced?" It is also possible to take the two words as themselves a clause that is object of another word. That occurs in lines 44 and 48, when the verb "to dance" has the non-aorist stem and the subordinate marker -ki', which forms dependent clauses of unfulfilled action, most frequently forming conditions (G189–90). The operative verb in these lines is na'-nagài' 'it was done' (G187, 286).

When the two words first occur, however, they cannot be taken as object of dà·'agán 'he heard'; the object of "he heard" has already explicitly preceded it (kai 'something'). "The puberty dance was being danced" is syntactically distinct, and seems to require a separate line. This sense of it is supported by the third occurrence in the scene of the two words (25).

Absence of kai 'something' might seem to indicate that this time the object of da·tayàk 'he discovered' is "the puberty dance is being danced." But this time the verb has the suffix -ma', subordinating the passive aorist. I take it that 18–19 and 24–25 are parallel, that Mrs. Johnson has foregrounded "the puberty dance was being danced" as a separate line in each, but by different means: an indefinite pronoun as object in one case, a subordinated verb in the other. I have taken the use of -ma' to indicate a separate line for "the puberty dance was being danced" at lines 76 and 93 as well.

The same reasoning has been followed with regard to Xàmk baxàm-da' 'Grizzly Bear was coming' (201).

(c) The rhythm of lines in the first scene reflects my sense of its phrasing, of detail being lingered upon. These choices have grammatical and rhetorical support, but someone else might not share the same sense of balancing among phrases.

2. *Distinguishing Verses: Initial Particles and Other Markers*

In many languages initial particles having to do with time indicate narrative units. The two most salient instances in Mrs. Johnson's narratives are *gane·* 'then' and *mi·* 'now'. *Gane·* commonly occurs with the suffix *-hi'*; *mi·* does so occasionally. Each invariably marks a verse.

Words with the meaning 'again' are frequently indicators of narrative units. In this narrative *honò'* 'again' is never initial and does not mark a unit by itself, but its occurrence is significant for relations among units. It is part of the initial marking in the second and fourth stanzas in scene i; it is the key to recognizing the five stanzas of the extravagant subscene 3 of scene ii; it helps single out the onset of Coyote's run in stanza B of subscene 2, the second song which Coyote takes up (stanza B in scene iv), the second time Goose sings about Brown Bear (to which he responds by coming).

A. Rhetorical Questions. This myth (and that of Coyote and Fox [see Appendix]) makes use of a type of rhetorical question that constitutes a verse in itself. The general form is *Gwi·'nè dì wede . . .* 'When, how long + interrogative + negative (with inferential and potential, not with aorist) + X' (G201, 269, 271). It occurs in line 11 with regard to gophers, and in lines 46, 55, 62, 70 with regard to running. Without the full phrase, and initial position, *gwi·'nè* itself seems not to be a marker (cf. line 70). As a verse, the whole appears always to occur as second (or third) verse in a stanza (cf. lines 6, 29, 35 in the appendix).

The question in line 89, *Kài nàk'a di 'àni·' wu·lham hoyodák"?* 'What kind did not dance the puberty dance', appears to be another instance of this pattern. The question has to do with "what kind" (*kai nàk'a* [255, 277]) rather than "where," the interrogative marker is the same, and the negative particle *'àni·'* is the one required with the aorist (G271).

B. Quoted Speech. Quoted speech always constitutes a verse, even if there is no other indication. There are twelve instances in this myth. (See the entry --- in the left-hand column of Appendix II.) In half the cases such speech ends scenes and stanzas in which Coyote declares himself (ii-1A, 2C, 3B), and it completes stanzas in iii (ABC) (Coyote and Frog sing), and viii (CD) (Coyote addresses Frog). All this suggests that the use of quoted speech by itself can be expressively motivated.

These recurrent features (and where the particles are concerned, combinations of them) account for about three-fourths of the verses of the myth, seventy-one of the ninety-five: *gane-* 'then' (36), *mi* 'now' (17), initial quoted speech (12), rhetorical question (6). (See Appendix II for their distribution.)

C. Other Particles. Other verses are marked by infrequent particles of similar meaning, and the status as verses of some of them depends on the patterning of which they are a part. Especially in regard to scene ii, rhetorical shape may promote, as it were, a line and a possible marker to the status of verse.

a. Terms of Time, Terms of Location. Other *terms of time* and, less often, *terms of location* may mark verses. In this myth the first scene has three line-initial expressions indicating a new day (3, 7, 12). Each fits into a pattern of verses. A word found to convey a sense of "always," *ganga*, also appears to mark verses three times (58, 202, 207). The shaping of II [ii] indicates that *hawi* 'still, yet' (G270) also marks a verse at that point (36). With regard to location, the generic term for "there" (*ge*) initiates verses three times (39, 73, and at the end as part of the close [243]). Three other terms of location seems also to do so as part of the development of II: *ali* 'this here' (44), *da'ol* 'nearby' (48; cf. 75), and *tga* 'land' (51).

b. Names. The name of Coyote, *Sgisi*, six times begins a line (2, 91, 148, 224, 234, 239). In two of these (91, 234) it precedes *mi·* 'now'. That could be taken as placement before an initial marker (that itself can occur non-initially) for emphasis. The parallel to "Then now" does seem to confer a verse-marking role on *Sgisi* itself.

In one of these two cases (234), and two others (2, 148), *Sgisi* is followed by a pronoun or suffix emphasizing that it is Coyote himself, for his part. In (234) the marking is parallel to a non-initial marking of the same kind in a preceding verse (228) that is structurally equivalent. In another case (224) a postposed discourse marker, *-si'*, would suffice to mark the verse, but co-occurrence with Coyote's name may be part of the marking. Only the last instance (239) is without other support, and it is structurally embedded in a tight alternation of verses. (See discussion of the last stanza under "Formal Close" [in regard to "Formal Place"].)

The use of Coyote's name as an initial marker seems motivated. In Part One it brackets, but does not interrupt, the long saga of his rushing to the dance (lines 2, 91). In the extended sequence of songs at the dance, it occurs just once, when he follows Mouse half-right (147). The remaining occurrences all have to do with his running off with Frog. Quoted speech, or song, would itself indicate a verse, but the pervasive attention to the first element of a verse throughout the myth reinforces a sense of Coyote's name as a marker. His name, after all, need not be given, once the story is under way. A third person pronoun would suffice, and Kendall has come to the view that the myths are so tightly structured syntactically that it is possible to decode them and know who is doing what on linguistic grounds alone. This may be overstated—one would have to know the story already to know which girl sings which song. Still, knowing the characteristics of the actors, and who is likely to do what, would further anchor identification. Takelma seems to be a language, like Chinookan, in which pronouns are not dependent on nouns and names, but in which nouns and names elaborate pronouns, in which the naming of an actor is not a grammatical requirement, but an expressive option.

Occasionally other narratives have seemed to use a personal name or reference as a marker (e.g., Louis Simpson's "A personal narrative of the Paiute war" (Sapir 1909:205–27, Bright 1990:231–53). This narrative by Mrs Johnson seems a particularly clear case.

c. Postpositions (1) *-si'*. The postposition *-si'* occurs once with Coyote

(224), and twice appears by itself to have the weight of a discourse marker that signals verses (*aga-si'* 'and this, and indeed' (68), *dalwi-si'* 'still' (203). Sapir comments (G274):

> This is one of the most frequently occurring particles in Takelma narration, its main function being to bind together two clauses or sentences, particularly when a contrast is involved. . . . *gasi'* and *agasi'* serving to connect two sentences, the second of which is the temporal or logical resultant or antithesis of the first [G has "second" here instead of "first," obviously a slip].

d. Postpositions (2) *-hi'* 'Quotative'? The postposition *-hi'* occurs frequently in this and other texts. Sapir writes (G274): "As no definite meaning can be assigned to it, and as it is found only in myth narration, it is highly probable that it is to be interpreted as a quotative." Sapir in fact translates occurrences of *-hi'* with "it is said." I have not. The reasons follow.

First, a clarification: *-hi'* is not found only in myths. To be sure, it does not occur in the eleven medicine formulas with which *Takelma Texts* ends, nor in generalized descriptions of cultural practices, or Mrs. Johnson's account of being cured by a medicine woman ("Cultural and Personal Narratives" [177–88]). It does occur in "A raid on the Upper Takelma" (189–93), the last text of that section. This suggests that *-hi'* is a diacritic of traditional narrative, both mythical and other. That would fit its presence in a narrative concerning Mrs. Johnson's father's father, but its absence in Mrs. Johnson's narrative of an experience of her own. Interestingly enough, Sapir does not translate *-hi'* in the grandfather's story as "it is said," or indeed at all, and such a translation would seem intrusive there.

A suffix occurring in traditional narrative could well be a quotative. The distribution of *-hi'*, however, suggests that it is not. The issue has three aspects: distinguishing verses, marking quoted speech, marking myth itself.

(a) Verse-marker? If *-hi'* is a quotative, it could be expected to be significant for identifying verses and relations among verses. In the one Bella Coola myth analyzed in such a way a quotative suffix is the key marker. In a Hopi myth a quotative word also is the basis for recognizing patterning. In Tonkawa a quotative suffix interacts with initial particles in a way significant for recognizing relations among verses. In these Takelma texts, *-hi'* occurs most frequently with the first word of a sentence, and with verbs of saying. Occasionally it occurs within a verb, attached to a verbal prefix. In none of these circumstances is it required for the identification of verses, or relations among them.

When *-hi'* follows a word that itself marks verses (*gane·-*, *mi·-*), it of course may participate in such marking, but the marking would occur without it. When it occurs with verbs of speaking, the quoted speech itself would be sufficient to indicate a verse. (The same is true with *-si'* within quoted speech, as in 133, 141, 154, 164, 198.) Such occurrences of *-hi'*, indeed, seem motivated by other considerations, as will be seen.

There is just one possibility of *-hi'* identifying a verse. In scene vi *-hi'* is attached to a verbal prefix in line 200 (cf. G274), and the word in which it occurs is the only candidate for verse marker in a position that might be taken to require one. The matter is a question of the relations one detects in the lines of this scene and act. One might compare 200–201 to 197 and, given repetition of two out of three words, think that the latter pair should be a verse as well. I entertained that possibility, but now see that the full range of repetition involves the next stanza as well (205). All three stanzas of the act refer to Grizzly Bear (or a dangerous being) as coming (197, 201, 205). In the fourth he is there. The middle stanzas (B, C) are alike in having the coming as part of the first verse, preceding the same outcome in the second verse (they keep on dancing nonetheless). The middle stanzas are alike also in having *-si'* at the end of the first word. That seems the respect in which a postposition plays a part in marking them. So understood, line 200 ("It indeed is heard") is not a candidate for beginning a verse.

If *-hi'* does not mark verses, except secondarily, it still might be quotative. There are two possibilities: that it marks quoted speech within the story, and/or that it marks the story itself as told before ("it is said," as suggested by Sapir), as traditional saying. Let me consider each.

(b) Quoted speech. The association of *-hi'* with the verb of speaking, *na-/nag-*, is very strong. In this text all occurrences of *-hi'* with verbs are of this sort, except one, in which it is not final (the case discussed above, "it was heard" [200]). But not all occurrences of verbs of saying have *-hi'*. And the occurrences seem to be motivated by something other than the marking of verses.

In Part One there are no verbs of speaking in scene i, and no occurrences of *-hi'*, except with initial *gane-*. In scene ii there are no verbs of speaking in subscenes 4 and 5 (a second respect, along with recurrence of initial *Sgisi* 'Coyote', in which the end of Part One matches its opening). In subscenes 1, 2, and 3 there is no verb of speaking the last time Coyote speaks in a scene (and the first time in 2). The other four times have the usual verb of speaking with *-hi'* (23, 42, 52, 64).

There is a curious correlation in this. Coyote repeats two things, a question and an assertion. Where is the dance being danced? Must be here. Three times he asks *"Where"* (22–23, 41–42, 63–64), and three times the verb of saying is marked with *-hi'*. Three times he asserts "Must be *here,"* and three times there is no verb of saying at all (38, 45, 67). (There is such a verb, with *-hi'*, when the question is "Must be there" [52–53].) I take this correlation to indicate that an expressive point is being made.

Another pattern of presence and absence appears with the singing of iii, iv, and v. Frog's long song in iii is segmented by three verbs of saying, each with *-hi'*, but Coyote's imitation is described by a verb "'to sing" which has no *-hi'*, and "half-right," which has the emphatic suffix *-hi* (G273).

In iv and v, Bluejay, Mouse, Swan, and Goose are told to begin. None of the verbs of saying, or singing, have *-hi'*. Indeed, in iv only one verb at all has *-hi'*. The last verb of saying (161), following what Swan sings, does. I think this is because her song includes a word that anticipates what will bring Black Bear in the act that follows, *wàinha* 'put him to sleep'. And in the next act the correlation with Black Bear is perfect. Goose is told to sing, and said to sing, without *-hi'* (165, 177). Black Bear responds twice, each time with *-hi'* (175, 184).

In vi the girls twice warn each other not to continue. The first time the verb of saying does not have *-hi'*, the second time it does. It is the second time that brings Grizzly Bear.

In vii the only speaker is Grizzly Bear. He again says "Hàu hàu hàu hàu," and the saying has *-hi'* (220).

In viii the only speaker is Coyote. The first time he speaks the verb has the suffix discussed above, *-his* 'to think that', 'to try in vain'. The final two times the verb of saying has *-hi'*.

In all this there is an indication of singling out certain actions ("Where?" as against "Must be"), certain actors (Frog as against Coyote in iii, Black Bear as against Goose in v), and certain culminations (Swan's "Put him to sleep" at the end of iv, the second warning in vi, Grizzly Bear's second "hàu hàu hàu hàu" (vii), Coyote's concluding statements (viii).

There is an indication of this last in the short myth Sapir analyzes at the end of his grammar, "The Origin of Death" (G290–93). Someone among the Roasting-Dead People asks Coyote to lend a blanket for its dead child. The request is framed within two verbs of speaking. The first (291.2) does not have *-hi'*, the second (291.3) does. At the end of the myth the person twice answers Coyote; the first answer (292.6) does not have *-hi'*, the second, culminating statement (293.2), does.

These observations indicate that *-hi'* is not connected with speaking as such. The postposition does often co-occur with quoted speech, when introduced by the initial particle *gane·hi'*, when followed by a verb of saying, or with both. But quoted speech does not require *-hi'*. Quoted speech can occur by itself (26, 45), or be accompanied in a variety of ways, by something preceding, something following or by both. Not all instances show *-hi'* (103–5, 148–52, 189–95, 198–99) either preceding or following.

The occurrences of quoted speech in this myth (see Appendix II) suggest that the way in which it is accompanied, if accompanied at all, has to do in important part with local emphasis and style. Placement and cooccurrence with specific speech acts (see above) indicate as much. So do instances of parallelism of adjacent occurrences (52–53, 63–64; 112–15, 116–23; 140–43, 144–47; 163–66, 167–72; 176–81, 182–84; 236–38, 240–42). Insofar as *-hi'* goes together with quoted speech, it is likely that it does so to underscore the importance of such speech in the enactment of the story, not to convey the fact of quotation itself.

c. Traditional speech? If *-hi'* indicates the status of what is told as traditional speech, initial particles would be a plausible position, framing what follows. In this text the occurrence of *-hi'* with initial particles is almost entirely with *gane·-* 'then'. Indeed, *gane·-* never occurs without it. The postposition occurs with *mi·* 'now', two of the seventeen times *mi·* occurs in initial position, and once in that position with *gangà-* (207) and once with *ga-* (225). It occurs once in second position with *hono* 'again' (176). A special connection with *gane·-* is indicated also by the distribution of *-hi'* with verbs of speaking. There are fifteen instances (lines 23, 42, 53, 64, 99, 111, 114, 122, 161, 175, 184, 206, 220, 220, 238, 242). All but one (42) occur in a verse introduced by *gane·hi'*. None occur in a verse introduced by any other particle.

If *gane·hi'* framed the narrative from the start, *-hi'* might be a part of it that frames the narrative with a meaning equivalent to "it is said," "they say." That is hard to see. The opening scenes proceed with minor use of *-hi'*. In scene i the marking is mainly in terms of days, and *honò* 'again'. One can see that in this act *gane·-* 'then' might be introduced gradually (9, 14) as one approaches the action of the story proper (ii); *gane·-* 'then' apparently implies sequence. But why introduce gradually the status of the story as something traditionally said? And when sequential action is reached with scene ii, subscene 1, the first verses are not marked with *gane·hi'*, but with *mi·* 'now' (18, 20, and 24) without *-hi'*. This is not because *mi·* cannot occur with *-hi'*; it does so in the next scene (27), and again when Brown Bear comes (185). Why not here?

The use of *mi·* in the opening scene of scene II seems to express a sense that *now* something is happening, and that 'now' is more dramatic than the more common *gane·hi'* 'then'. It is with *mi·* that the three steps of perception occur: hear, listen, discover (verses a b d, lines 18, 20, 24). In the two other verses (c and e, lines 21–23, 25), there is quoted speech at points of culmination. When a tradition uses relations of three and five, the third and fifth point in a sequence is often such. The third point can be both an outcome of three elements (here listen, hear, where?), and an onset of three (here where?, discover, there I'll go). The one use of *-hi'* in this subscene (2) is at such a point. Framing what is said between *gane·hi'* and *nagàihi'* fits this first utterance by Coyote as a point of local culmination. That seems to be what is being done in this middle verse of five, not marking a traditional status for the story.

Again, the use of *-hi'* after *mi·* at the beginning of the next scene, when Coyote first runs, seems for the purpose of underscoring that the long saga of his running now starts.

Altogether, the use of *-hi'* appears to be one way in which point and proportion are conveyed, a way of marking the status of something within the story, not of marking the status of the story as such. This interpretation fits the most likely connection of *-hi'* with what else is known of the language. It is probably linked etymologically with an emphatic enclitic of almost the same shape, *hi*. Sapir remarks, "With *hi* must not be confused: *-hi'*" (G272–73), but examples suggest that the distribution of the two elements may be largely or entirely complementary.

e. Lists and Couplets. In the scene in which Coyote arrives at the dance (ii, 5) the catalog of what he perceives lists five girls. That the number is five, rather than four or some other even number, seems to confirm that the lines indeed continue (and complete) scene ii, guided as it is by relations of three and five. Mrs. Johnson appears to keep in mind that five is the number established here. Just these five appear in the scenes that follow, and their number may constrain the shape of the scenes (which resume relations of four). Conversely, ti may be that an odd number of other singers is agreeable to featuring Coyote twice as an inept singer in stanzas of his own.

The list of girls appears to be part of a verse with the two lines that precede it (82–83), for there is only one predicate for them all (in line 82). There appears to be a pairwise relation between arrival (81) and what is perceived upon arrival (82–88). Within the lines for what is perceived there is doubling at the outset, in the repetition of "girls" with an expression of quantity ("in great numbers," "many kinds").

The next two lines are a concise, more obvious pair, in effect a couplet:

> What kind did not dance the puberty dance?
> Many kinds were dancing there.

The first of the two lines is of course an instance of the rhetorical questions as a marker. Here it marks, not the second line in a couplet, but the second "couplet" in a pair of pairs devoted to the "many kinds" (of girls). Notice that "many kinds" is repeated in the second element of each pair.

Couplet-like pairing occurs also in the opening scene, with lines 5-6:

> there were no people,
> he was all by himself.

The particular equivalence of meaning here resembles a couplet and three-step cumlative effect in a version of the "Deserted Boy" told to Sapir in Wishram Chinook by Louis Simpson a year before Sapir's work with Mrs. Johnson (Hymes 1994a:336–37):

> Now then they ran off,
> straight home they ran,
> straight across they went,
>   not a person on this side,
>   all of that side.

(The subsequent stanzas of the scene end with "no person" and "now, no people." Cf. Mrs. Johnson's "There he arrived / no people" [39–40].)

There are indeed several couplets in Simpson's text, and their recognition proves essential to grasping the form of the narrative as a whole (see Hymes 1994a:346ff).Such patterns have not been remarked in the Northwest, so far as I know. Perhaps there other examples that suggest an areal resource.

f. Expressive Role. These observations have brought out ways in which initial particles contribute to local grouping and point. If all of Mrs. Johnson's texts were studied from this standpoint, one would be able to speak with more confidence of the motivation of her choices. Let me here make general observations and note instances.

There is evidently a hierarchy among the initial particles. When *gane·hi'* occurs with other particles, it is always first. *Mi·* may occur initially, but always follows *gane·hi'*. *hono'* 'again' never occurs initially, and never precedes either of the other two. Lines 33 and 35 exhibit these relations: *gane·hi'>mi·>hono'*. The other particles that can be initial and appear to mark verses are infrequent, and are not part of this system.

[i]. Predominance of terms of time and *honò'* 'again' has been noted.

[ii-1]. Prominence of *mi·* 'now' has been pointed out.

[ii-2]. Note that the first and second pairs of verses are linked by *mi·* and *gane·hi' mi· hono'* 'Then now again' respectively. The piling up of three markers here seems especially forceful.

[ii-3]. Rhetorical questions with *Gwi·'ne di wede X* are always the second verse in a stanza (in another myth, once third).

[ii-3 A, E]. The first and last stanzas of this long act begin with the same pair of particles, *Mi· hono'/Gwi·'nè* . . . The last stanza consists solely of the pair of verses so marked. That seems a rounding out and reprise of the theme of the act as a whole.

[v D, viii A]. The use of *mi·* in all four verses of the last stanza of scene v, and initial *Mi·* in both verses of the first stanza of scene viii marks them as going together, and points up the significance of what now occurs.

[i A(b), ii-5(e)]. It seems significant that Coyote's name occurs at the beginning and end of Part One, but not between.

[vii B(a), viii B(b), D(a)]. It seems significant that Coyote's name does not mark verses again (except for his imitation of Mouse [iv C]) until the end of the narrative.

These last observations, and that regarding ii-3, reflect a tendency on Mrs. Johnson's part to link the beginning and ending of a sequence.

3. *Distinguishing Stanzas, Scenes and Acts*

The poetics of an oral tradition depends upon recognizing what counts as equivalent (Jakobson 1960). Verses can usually be recognized by explicit indications, as we have seen. It is seldom so with what count as groups of verses. With these it is a question of recognizing implicit relations.

Study of Native American narratives has shown that they make use of two kinds of implicit relations. One kind consists of relations of three and five. The other consists of relations of two and four. There is a connection with the prevailing pattern number of a culture. Over the years it has become clear that languages and traditions in and around the lower Columbia River make use of relations of three and five. This is true of all the Chinookan peoples, and true as well as of Sahaptins, lower Columbia Salish (Chehalis, Cowlitz), and the Kalapuya of the Willamette Valley. The Kwaguɬ (Kwakiutl) and Tsimshian of British Columbia make use of relations of two and four. Such soundings as have been made indicate that the Takelma do as well.

Salient indications of a pattern number are the number of siblings that form a set, the number of times an act is repeated, what number of items counts as complete. What is surprising is that the principle pervades all levels of a story. The number of verses that go together in a stanza, the number of stanzas that go together in a scene, is not random, but patterned. And the pattern is not arbitrary. A rhetorical or rhythmic relationship can be discerned.

Where the pattern is in terms of three and five, a sequence of three is likely to convey onset (initial act or condition), ongoing, outcome. An incident that might have been expressed in other ways will be said as "Coyote went, he kept on going, he got there," or, of a deserted boy, "he turned, he looked, he saw (flame)."

Sequences of five often enough show a further intricacy. Two such three step patterns are interlocked. The midpoint, the third item, will be the endpoint of the first three steps, and at the same time an onset of the last three. Nor is this is an Indian peculiarity. The same relationship has been found in Finnish traditional songs and narratives from Appalachia and Philadelphia.

Where relations are in terms of two and four, the logic of rhetorical cohesion, as it were, may have the effect of relating just onset and outcome, or, to differentiate it from the labelling just given, relations of initiation and outcome. One can discern something of this in a narrative often enough without close analysis. In "Coyote and Frog" clearly there are two sequences of the coming to the dance of uninvited guests. Coyote comes, and joins in; the Bears come, and the dance is dispersed. An attentive reader might note that there is a doubling in terms of a particular word and the trait it expresses. When Coyote runs to the dance in the first half, he is recurrently certain that the dance must be nearby (*mì·'wa*). When he runs off with Frog at the end of the second half, he twice says that she must be female, must be a woman (*mì·'wa*).

It is not always easy, however, to recognize the parts of a narrative. Small signals may make a difference to large-scale organization. (Scene vii is an example). And not just high points or salient turns are to be accounted for. The narrator is mapping, or interweaving, content and form, verse by verse, throughout. What Kenneth Burke described as "arousal and satisfaction of expectation" (1925) is found at every level, small as well as large.

The narrative itself will often indicate points of transition: change of time, change of location, change of participants, change of activity. Even these must be considered in relation to their context and place in the whole.

The *opening* scene is set off clearly enough, by internal coherence and by a change of activity that follows. Coyote sets traps for gophers four times. The second, third and fourth times are marked by "again." There are four intervals of time. Each interval is part of a pair of verses. Eight verses, four stanzas, one scene, one act. (See further discussion in section VII below.)

The *ending* of the myth is not at all clear. Sorting it out involves consideration of all the second half, the last four acts.

A. Parts Three and Four as Example. The verses about Grizzly Bear would seem an obvious unit (196–223). They seem not to be a single unit, however, on consideration of other features. The preceding scene (v) has Goose sing, Brown Bear respond, the girls sing, Brown Bear come. The act ends with his coming, and there is nothing more about Brown Bear in the story.

This four-part framework fits what follows. There is a four-step sequence of action. Three times Grizzly Bear (or a dangerous being) is said to be coming, then he comes. That outcome parallels the outcome of the preceding act about Brown Bear. Within the sequence of action there are evidently eight verses and four stanzas. (A) Some hear, now Grizzly Bear is coming; (B) don't sing, they say, but the dancing goes on; (C) don't sing, some say, but the dance continues; (D) then Grizzly Bear comes.

The eight verses are linked by details. The first and last pair (196, 197; 208–13, 214), have the same sequence of initial particles, gane·hi', mi·. I take them to be parallel, enclosing what is between. What is between consists of adjacent parallel stanzas. Each has a verse of quoted speech, introduced by a particle marked by -si' (198, 203), the warning, and a verse begun by ganga-hi' 'all the same' (207, 203). The first verse is a warning, the second says that "All the same they kept on dancing (the puberty dance)" (202, 207).[12] (Recall discussion of -hi' as possible marker in line 200).

In sum, each of these scenes (v, vi) has internal relations that indicate that each is a unit. The parallel ending of each (the bear comes to the dance) does the same. The pair indeed seem part of a pattern in the story in terms of four parts, and two halves, in which vi stands parallel to iii. At the midpoint of the first half Coyote reaches the dance (ii), then singles out Frog (iii). At the midpoint of the second half Grizzly comes to the dance (vi), then Coyote singles out Frog (vii, viii).

But two more verses involving Grizzly Bear follow. In the first (215–20), he repeats "Hàu hàu hàu hàu" (cf. 208–12). In the second he jumps among them, they fly up, he kills no one. If the continuous presence of Grizzly Bear were decisive as to form, one would have an act of five pairs of verses here, not four. We would be left with a further five pairs, to fit together into a seventh act, or to apportion among a seventh and eighth.

If one looked no further, an scene vi with five pairs of verses would be consistent. The last two pairs would show parallelism of a kind we have come to recognize as pervasive in Mrs. Johnson's narrative. In each pair the first verse has Grizzly Bear come "Hàu hàu hàu hàu," and the second states what he does—get right here (214), jump among them (221–23). (And the subordinated lines "They flew right up / he killed no one" [222–23] of the last pair complete the subordinated line "they stopped dancing suddenly" in the first verse of the first pair).

If one looks further, however, this possibility proves awkward. The second verse of the second pair (221–23) has explicit connections in what follows. It is paralleled: "Now they flew off in a bunch / Grizzly Bear scared the people all about" (226–27). And it is paired. Each mention of Grizzly Bear among the girls is followed by a mention of Coyote running off with the chief's girl (224, 228).

The picture is even more complex. Such pairs of verses (221–23, 224; 226–27, 228) should be prime candidates for going together in a stanza, were it not for two things. They say the same things. There is no advance in action. And the two pairs of verses are separated by a pair of words (225), words with the flavor of an ending (Gàhi' ganga, 'That was all').

If one attends to these two words (Sapir did not in fact translate them), they can be found to signal a moment of reflection or hesitation in performance. It is the second pair of verses about Grizzly Bear and Coyote that initiate and sustain an outcome of the story, that proceed to a full ending, with pronouncement and formal close. The first pair of verses appear to be part of an interval, perhaps of uncertainty, in which Mrs. Johnson repeats something from the preceding act (215–220), begins a finale (221–23, 224), and cuts it off (225). The four verses constitute a perhaps ad hoc scene vii. (See discussion of scene vii in section V above in connection with [12] *ganga* 'always', and of scene viii in "How this Myth Ends" in section VII below.)

The template shared by the acts about the coming of the bears stands, and the final act has its own consistent form. A brief scene vii, perhaps improvised, links them. It does, to be sure, make formal sense. It fills out a symmetrical pattern, by which there are eight acts in four pairs. Its brief *finis,* "*That* was all" matches the formal close at the end of viii, and so completes an effect of balanced pairing of the acts. And if scene vii betrays a possible improvisation as to contents, still the carrying over of Grizzly Bear's "Hàu hàu hàu hàu" from the preceding act may also be a stylistic device. Other acts are linked in such a way. The gophers of scene i are thrown away at the beginning of scene ii. Coyote's intervention in scene iv allows the act to have four stanzas, while at the same time the fourth girl told to begin, Goose, begins scene v; a word in Swan's song at the end of scene iv anticipates the song that brings Brown Bear in scene v. Repetition of Grizzly Bear's "Hàu hàu hàu hàu" at the beginning of scene vii, and of dispersal of the girls with Coyote's running into the brush with Frog at the beginning of scene viii, may draw upon a traditional resource.

So much for stanzas, scenes, and acts in the second half. What of the first half, following the opening? The grouping of verses in stanzas, scenes and acts seems evident for the singing at the dance itself (iii, iv).

(iii) A new actor, Frog, is singled out, and the act as a whole focusses on Coyote's relation to her. He sees her (described as wealthy) and says he will take her (A). He takes her hand and tells her to begin (B). She sings (C), he imitates her (D). Each stanza has a turn at speech (singing). The first two stanzas go together, with Coyote's speech the outcome of the stanza. The second two stanzas go together, being the singing itself. If Frog's stanza is elaborated internally with three successive sections, Coyote's one-verse stanza maintains a balance of four for the two as a whole.

(iv) Four actors sing, Bluejay, Mouse, Coyote, Swan. It is reasonable to take each turn as a stanza. Each stanza for a girl has two verses, one for being told to begin, the other for the singing itself. Coyote stands apart with a single stanza. That is anomalous, but also perhaps pointed: no one asks Coyote to sing. (See also section VII on song-burdens on these two acts.)

The relations among the verses that follow the opening (i) are far less clear. The difficulty is not a lack of indications, but a multiplicity of them. A variety of details are repeated, but in a variety of ways. Over the years I have revised my understanding of this part of the narrative several times. The analysis in 1979a was recast in 1980b, and that again more than once in the course of this revision. The critical step was to realize in 1992 that scene ii stood apart from the other acts, not only in length, but also in rhetorical relations.

B. Two-step Relations. Seven of the acts of the myth are shaped essentially in terms of two and multiples of two. They can be read, or heard, in terms of a rhythm of "this, then that." Or analyzed in terms of sequences of initiation and outcome. Let me point to examples in each. (To do so is in large part to summarize much that has been already discussed.)

Scene i has four stanzas. Each pair (AB, CD) begins with Coyote setting traps for gophers every day (A:C) and ends with evening (B:D).

Scene iii has four stanzas. In each of the first two Frog is first singled out (Aa, Ba), then Coyote speaks. The third pairing has the weight of half the scene, because a turn at singing seems to count always as a stanza, and there are two turns (Frog in C, Coyote in D). Frog's turn indeed contains the equivalent of three stanzas, and with Coyote's one, gives four to this half of the scene (C, D) and eight to the whole.

Scene iv has three stanzas (ABD) in which a girl is told to sing (a) and does so (b). The other stanza of four (C), like the last stanza of scene iii, has Coyote's half-right imitation.

Scene v has a stanza (A) in which a girl is told to sing (a) and does (b). There is then a response by the person sung about (B). The song is sung again (C) and the person sung about responds again (D). This time his response has four verses, not one: he speaks; he goes; he goes right to the dance; he growls, having gone right by the dance.

There is a relation of initiation and outcome at successive levels:

AB	: CD	Singing elicits Brown Bear's response :
		Further singing brings Brown Bear
A : B :: C : D		Goose sings : Brown Bear responds (twice)
Dab	: cd	Brown Bear speaks and goes : he gets to the dance
a	: b	Brown Bear speaks : he goes
c	: d	He gets to the dance : he growls at the dance.

In scene vi girls say not to keep on singing (Ba, Ca), but singing goes on (Bb, Cb).

In scene vii the first two verses (Aab) stand in a this, then that relation to the next (B). (Bb is formal; it does not develop the action.)

In scene viii Coyote entertains hope of sex with Frog in the first two stanzas (AB), and realizes he cannot in the second two (CD). The first two stanzas (AB) each end with what Coyote does for his part (b). The second two stanzas (CD) each begin with what Coyote does (Ca, Da) and end with what he says in consequence (Cb, Db).

These seven of the eight acts show that two-step relations are the norm, the unmarked relation, as it were. Often enough they show a sequence of action coming round to a parallel point or outcome.

C. Three-step Relations (scene ii). Scene ii shows sequence of action coming round to parallel points or outcomes, again and again, but not in terms of two-step relations. My earlier efforts to analyze it foundered on the assumption that two-step relations would indeed be found. The result was never entirely convincing, either for the relations internal to the act, or for the relation between it and the act that follows. It was only when I experimented with the possibility that the patterns in this act are those of three and five-step relations that a shape appeared that withstood all subsequent probing and experiment.

The general point is an important one. It is not enough to discover that a narrative tradition normally makes use of one kind of relations. Again and again one finds that a tradition, a narrator, may make use of more than one. Sometimes it seems that a narrator may carry over in a story the kind of patterning in which the story was heard. Sometimes there is an association of gender (cf. Hymes 1990c, 1991). Usually a second kind of relation is used to intensify or otherwise underscore just a part of a story. Where the unmarked kind of relation is that of three and five, sets of pairs may intensify (cf. Hymes 1985). Where the unmarked relations are those of two and four, sequences of three and five may intensify.

It now seems difficult to imagine that the first subscene of ii did not leap out at me as a sequence of five verses. It now seems so inevitably one. Now he (Coyote) hears, now he listens, then, "Where is the girl's dance being danced?" Onset, ongoing, outcome. Now he discovers the direction, "That's where I'll go." An elaboration into five steps, with the middle verse—"Where is the girl's dance being danced?"—an outcome in relation to the verses that precede it, and an onset to the verses that follow. The relation of the third and fifth verses as intermediate and final outcome is underlined by quoted speech in each (quoted speech is often an outcome in Native American narratives), and the augmentation of the initial particle from sibilant in the third verse to shibilant in the fifth.

The next lines initiate the long run to the dance. There is repetition of a number of elements: was tired, listened, rested; rushed off, ran; nearby; must be here; where; how long did he not run, and a number of ways in which they could be taken as going together. The key emerges in what proves to be the third scene.

Subscene 3 consists of five successive stanzas that begin with a three-word line in which *hono'* 'again' is constant (46, 49, 54, 60, 69). The three-word pattern is itself contant: initial temporal particle (then, now) + again + he/ran/ rushed off/went. Four of the stanzas contain the rhetorical question, "How long did he not run?" (47, 55, 61, 70).

When the three-word pattern is recognized as initiating stanzas, it emerges that each stanza but the last ends with a perception on Coyote's part that the dancing is nearby (48, 52, 59, 67). In essence, the five stanzas ring changes on the pattern, again he ran, how long did he not run, it was as if the dancing was nearby.

What precedes this sequence of verses is separate, in that it does not contain the rhetorical question, how long did he not run. What follows is separate, because it begins with a long lapse of time (71). The sequence itself is a coherent scene.

When "Now again he ran . . . / How long did he not run" occurs in lines
69–70, it might seem the start of a new scene, since the present scene begins just
this way. But the long lapse of time in line 71 (and the character of what follows
it) prevent taking it as such. One does not find two verse stanzas in the middle
of action. The parallel between these lines (69–70) and the beginning of the
scene (46, 47) is an instance of Mrs. Johnson's tendency to have the end of a
sequence parallel its beginning. In effect, the last stanza, in its two verses,
recapitulates the essence of the scene as a whole: Now again he ran, How long
did he not run?

The preceding and following scenes (ii, iv) each pose a special problem.
Subscene 2 begins with a reassertion of pairing. Two verses begin with the
same particle, one with a sequence of two actions, one with a sequence of four:

> Now he went,
>> he threw away the gophers.
> Now he ran,
>> was tired,   30
>>> stood still,
>>>> listened.

A sense of pairing is sustained in the strong and identical marking of the next
two verses, and one can take them as follows:

> Then now again he rushed off,
>> he ran.
> Then now again he rested,   35
>> still the puberty dance was danced nearby.

These two verses parallel the preceding two verses. (Especially if "listened"
and "nearby" are taken as implying each other).

The scene can be interpreted throughout in terms of this sense of pairing.
It would consist of four such pairs. The second pair would be:

> Then
>> "Ah! Must be here the puberty dance is being danced."
> There he arrived,
>> no people.   40
> "S-where *is* this dancing?"
>> he said,
>>> he spoke to himself.
> It was as if they were dancing the puberty dance right nearby.
> "It must be here upriver."   45

This interpretation of the scene is cogent enough. It suggests that the
usually unmarked pattern of pairing could be taken as intensifying if framed by
a preceding sequence of five verses. It presents the first four verses in terms of
the strong indication by their initial particles that they consist of two pairs. It

has the advantage of not raising the question as to whether the initial forms of lines 36 and 44 (*hàwi* 'still', *alí· da'ól* 'right nearby') can count as markers of verses. Its drawback, I think, has to do with those same two lines. Both have to do with location nearby. Location nearby is a chord which each of the next four stanzas will pluck, and each line containing the notion is part of a verse, marked one way or another. It seems odd to subordinate them here. In consequence, I have presented the scene as three stanzas, not four.

On this interpretation, the first two verses remain a pair, set off from what follows by its strong indication of a new stanza: "Then now *again* . . . ." The second stanza is a sequence of five verses, with a rhetorical logic like that of the first scene. There is a sequence of onset, ongoing, outcome in

> He rushed off/he ran
>> he rested
>>> still the puberty dance was danced nearby.

This verse is at once an intermediate outcome, and onset to a second triad:

>> "Ah! Must be here the puberty dance is danced."
>>> There he arrived,
>>>> no people.

In effect: Run, rest, perceive the dance nearby, say so, find out one is wrong.

The remaining three verses constitute a third stanza, one which succinctly expresses a three-step relation that recurs in this scene and the next: Where is the dancing? It seems nearby. Must be here.

This three-step relation has already occurred, distributed across scene [i] and the succeding part of scene [ii]: Where (22), listened (32) and nearby (36), must be (38). It occurs here, as said, in lines 41, 44, 45. "Nearby" and "must be" occur in that order in lines 48 and 52 of scene [iii], and "right at hand" separately in line 59 of scene [iii]. The trio itself recurs in stanza D of scene [iii], lines 63, 65, 67, if "listen" is taken as equivalent to perceiving the dance nearby. (Cf. the apparent equivalence in scene [iv], lines 73, 78, 80.)

The logic of action of stanza (B), the thematic clarity of stanza (C), and the importance of "nearby" as a recurrent element persuade me to present this scene as having three stanzas, the second and third of which have five and three verses. Perhaps the fact that the initial stanza (A) has a pair of verses is connected to the ending of scene [iii] with a stanza having just a pair of verses. Perhaps such a pair is a device for dramatizing the essence of Coyote's rushing off.

Subscene 4. Earlier it was noted that lines 74 and 75 do not appear in the published text. If these lines continued to be missing, scene [iv] would have four verses in two stanzas. There would be no apparent reason for it to differ from the three and five step relations of the preceding scenes. It completes the sequence in which Coyote comes to the dance.

If numerical consistency were the only thing to be considered, one could try to join the lines of the stanza (71ff.) with lines that follow. The four verses that one has in (71–73, 76–80) might be taken as going together with (81–93) to constitute a single longer scene. That would give the act as a whole four scenes, but this last, longer scene might be taken as having three or five units (here pairs of verses), like the rest.

To seek formal consistency in this way would be to ignore, or override, two reliable signals in Native American oral tradition of new sections, significant passage of time, and change of location and participant. The stanza begins with "Then a long time passed" (71). In lines (81ff.) Coyote arrives, sees all kinds of girls. The arrival is marked with not one, but three initial particles, "Then now again."[13]

Subscene 4, then, is set apart. Its own beginning, "a long time passed" (71), and a beginning that follows it (81), are clear. As published, its lines would show two pairs of verses (71, 72–[74–75]–76; 77, 78–80), an anomaly without motivation.

As it is, we do have lines 74 and 75, each marked as a verse ("Then . . ., Then . . ."). The scene as first written down has three pairs of verses, each a stanza. The first of the two missing lines (74) indeed maintains a pattern. In each of the three scenes of running, "nearby" and/or "right here" is indicated twice (36, 44 in subscene 2; 48, 59 in subscene 3; 73, 75 in subscene 4). Indeed, in subscene 4 the parallel between "nearby" as stanza ending point (A, B) and "listened" (C) supports other indications of mutual implication and equivalence of the two. In effect, then, each scene of running has three such indications, two with locations, as just given, and one with "listened" (32 in subscene 2, 65 in subscene 3, 80 in subscene 4).

(With one significant difference. In subscenes 2 and 3 "nearby" occurred with "as if" [44, 48], translating the inferential suffix -ki' [cf. Sapir 1922:197]. In subscene 4, it is without "as if," and without Coyote's expectant mì·wa 'must be' [lines 38, 45 in subscene 2; 52, 67 in subscene 3]. Nearness now is certain. The narrator indeed annotated Coyote's last "must be" in just that way: "And indeed the dance was being danced in the east" [68]. Coyote is no longer humorously mistaken.)

Subscene 4 is an interlude of relative quiet before the crowded stage, the singing, the dangers of the dance itself. Set off by "then a long time passed," it reiterates, briefly and less intensely, the cycle of going on. In subscenes 2 and 3, once Coyote has thrown away the gophers, the first thing said is that he ran; here it is that he is tired (72). In subscenes 2 and 3 he is tired once (30, 56), followed by resting (35, 57). Here he is tired twice (72, 79), and there is no mention of rest. Nor of rushing off. In line 74 he does not run, but start up again. (See discussion in V, Translation of Words [9].)

Subscene 5. Coyote's flagging effort, the unqualified "nearby," anticipate, prepare for the arrival, which breaks upon us as a scene in itself, a triumphal elaboration of what he wished (girls, girls, girls) concluding the story's longest act. Its five verses match the five verses with which the act began, another instance perhaps of Mrs. Johnson matching beginnings and endings. Clearly the way in which the first and last verses begin is such an instance (Then now there he arrived : Coyote now arrived). The rhetorical question and the matched lines it introduces constitute a second verse, and Coyote's initiating name (91) a third. The rhythm of the first four verses, to be sure, is one of pairings, but they are followed by a final verse whose three lines are typical of three-step patterns: onset, ongoing, outcome. (See discussion of this scene under Rhetorical Questions in the section on Distinguishing Verses in VI above.)

Is the above what Mrs. Johnson had in mind? I am prepared to say that the verses and stanzas are almost surely hers. Repetitions, internal parallelism, and recurrent rhetorical logic can be seen to underlie them, and I have experimented with alternatives. What is presented is, I think, the most attractive and persuasive possibility. To be sure, this principle of charity (accept the most attractive and persuasive possibility) is self-interested. It attributes to the narrator and reader a sense of pattern like my own. In defense, I can say that I did not begin with the sense of pattern I now have. It emerged through years of attention to stories such as these.

VII. Interpretation

1. Cultural Background

The principal actors are in character. Coyote travels in many traditions. That he travels upriver here is in keeping with other Takelma stories and aboriginal Takelma life. They lived in southwestern Oregon along the middle portion of the Rogue river. Travelling up river, or obtaining portage across it, figures prominently in the stories Mrs. Johnson told Sapir. Coyote, and the Bears, who come to the dance from elsewhere, are stereotyped as outsiders by "abnormal speech," Coyote by the exclamation s'á and the preposed s- of excited speech. Brown Bear is marked by s- as well in this story, as has been seen. In some stories Grizzly Bear actors are marked by the voiceless lateral ł preposed to words; the sound is otherwise entirely lacking in Takelma, and mocks its presence in nearby Athapaskan languages, mostly downriver.

Gophers count as undesirable food, compared to deer, salmon, berries and the like. Coyote's association with them is repeated at the end of Mrs. Johnson's telling of "Coyote and Fox," and probably was widespread in the region. It certainly is attested for the Wintu below Mount Shasta in northern California (Masson 1966, Shepherd 1989:221–22, where two duck wives leave Coyote, tired of eating gophers).

The Wintu also attest an association between puberty dance song and Frog. The word for puberty song is łuli, and the verb root łul-, łule· has the meanings 'to sing girl's puberty song; to make the noise of a frog in spring' (Shepherd 1981:136). In texts collected by Dorothy Lee there is a brief unpublished story given the title "Frog Maiden's Puberty Song." It simply says that some frogs were singing in the spring and while they were singing a frog girl started to menstruate, so the old frog women sang a puberty song for her. (There is a similar story about Coon maiden.)[14]

A girl's puberty dance would have been a major social event. The rattling associated with the attire of the chief's daughter indicates the presence of dentalia. Strings of the dentalium shell were used as ornament and as medium of exchange. They indicated wealth, but in the texts from Mrs. Johnson at least, the specious attractiveness of wealth. Such rattling occurs also in "The Otter Brothers Recover their Father's Heart," as an attribute of the father's false wife.

The girls are mostly birds. It is interesting that Mouse appears both here and in the analogous Wishram myth, where the dance is also broken up by Grizzly Bear (Hymes 1981, chs. 3, 6). (The other singers in the Wishram myth are feminine also, but roots, not birds.) This version may be indicate that the Takelma considered at least some birds foolish. The male Bluejay is typically so to the north, and there are stories of the mistakes of Swan and Goose as well. An association between Coyote and singing birds, when serious ritual is parodied, may enter here as well. In Kalapuya, Chinookan, and other traditions to the north, when Coyote presents himself as a shaman, pretending to cure a girl whose ailment is the tip of the penis he left inside here, he is aided by a chorus of birds. Their loud singing prevents people from hearing her call out that the supposed shaman is curing her by copulating again.

An audience would of course understand that one should not insult or attract attention from bears, especially grizzly bears. Where two bears appear in stories, Grizzly is always the main threat. Brown Bear, or Black Bear, may be an admirable counterpart, or at least less dangerous, and even, as here, somewhat the butt of a joke. (When it appears alone, however, not as junior partner, its generic bear character can have full scope.)

In sum, a story about a Coyote who lives on undesirable food; who is galvanized into great effort by the prospect of a woman; who repeatedly deceives himself as to the attainment of his goal; who bungles in trying to copy what someone else has done; who takes advantage of noises and confusion to get a girl; who responds to specious attractiveness, and is frustrated in the end; whose discomfiture benefits mankind, since he forthwith transforms the object of his affection into a creature that will deceive no one. This is clearly the Coyote many know and love.

2. Title

The myth was published as "Coyote Goes Courting" (1909:101–9). That title was supplied by Sapir, probably, along with the other titles in the collection. No titles are given in Takelma. Given the action of the story, "courting" does not seem the right word (unless intended ironically). I used the more specific "Coyote Ran Off with Frog at the Dance" at first (Hymes 1979a). Now just "Coyote and Frog" seems best. Antagonism between Coyote and Frog-women, sexually tinged, is expressed in various languages of the region, including Alsea, Kalapuya, and Chinookan, and the Hupa, Maidu, and Wintu have analogues of this very story, having to do with a dance, wherein Coyote chooses a partner who turns out to be the old wife he thought he had left at home

(Frog in Hupa and Maidu, Toad in Wintu). To a participant in the regional culture, the pair of names probably was enough to establish an expectation. Within Oregon country, there may have been a region in which the same expectation was involved, that Frog-women lack sexual organs. In Mrs. Johnson's Rogue River myth Coyote discovers it as a fact and turns the young woman into a frog forever. In a myth of the Alsea of the Oregon coast (near present-day Newport and Waldport) Coyote brings it about, going off with the organs of two frog-women to use whenever he wants. (See discussion under "Pronouncement" below.)

3. Headings

Acts and scenes are supplied with headings, which of course have no parallel in the original telling. They serve as an abstract of the action (as given above), and a way of keeping track. I think the headings are close to one way in which Mrs. Johnson might have provided a summary, if required to do so, except that Act II might have seemed more aptly summarized as "The girls sing, Coyote sings half-right."

4. Formal Opening

Full performances of Native American myths commonly have a conventional opening. Often the opening has three elements: a statement of location, a statement of one or two principal actors, an indication of characteristic activity. (In Chinookan myth this last is an evaluation, put into a nonnarrative future tense, best translated as "would"; it provides a clue as to the outcome, good or bad, for that actor.)

In Mrs. Johnson's narratives "There was a house" recurs as an opening, stating location generically in the abstract. The very phrase, *wíli· yowó'*, begins thirteen of the twenty texts that are properly myths (3, 4, 5, 6, 7, 8, 10, 11, 12, 13, 15, 19) and someone's house begins two others (1, 2). Three of the five that do not begin with "house" address generic conditions: the origin of death (9), no water among the people (18), the flood (20).

"Coyote would set traps for gophers all by himself every day" identifies the principal actor and a characteristic activity. A number of Mrs. Johnson's myth texts likewise identify a characteristic activity at this point.

Notice that the tense and aspect of the two translated lines are accurate. There is a tendency to translate all of a myth in the past tense, but that can be misleading. Sometimes an opening is in the present and the subsequent occurrence of past tense signals the beginning of the action proper (e.g., "Coyote and the Two Frog Women" in Frachtenberg 1917–20). Here "was" represents the aorist stem, "would" a usitative inflection (G134, para. 7).

A telling of this myth might have proceeded directly from the identification of Coyote and what he did to the action proper. Mrs. Johnson takes an interest in Coyote, gopher-hunter, and expands what he did from an opening verse to an opening scene.

Notice the play of repetition in this vignette. Coyote sets traps for gophers

(2, 4, 10 and 11, 13) in every stanza, in conjunction with the significant marker *honò'* 'again'. At the same time the first pair of stanzas is set off against the second. (A), as noted, is uniquely the opening couplet, and its picture of Coyote alone is intensified in (B): "there were no people/he was all by himself." ("There were no people" occurs again [40] and probably is part of narrative idiom throughout the region. It has a Chinookan equivalent, *k'áya idəlxam* 'no people'. Recall vi [e].)

(C) and (D) alone have a standard verse marker (*gane·hi'* 'then'); (A) and (B) do not. In that respect the common way of marking of verses and stanzas begins in this second half of [i]; all of the first half has something of the character of a differently framed opening. (C) and (D) elaborate and conclude the activity that (A) and (B) have introduced.

If the four stanzas show a sequence of pairs, with repetition within each, they also show alternation across pairs, form a proportion. (A) is to (B) as (C) is to (D). In (A) and (C) he *would* set traps for gophers *every day,* (C) an elaboration as against (A) with "set traps" in both its verses. In (B) and (D), instead of "would" and "every day," morning and the evening are set forth, (D) an elaboration as against (B): "Then/when it became evening," as against "In the evening," and "he counted gophers/how many he caught" as against "he brought them home," altogether seven words as against two.

Alternation and sequence are woven together. After the formal opening (A), each stanza uses "again" for trapping gophers, and refers to the start of the day, but (C) has "a different dawn," letting "when it became morning" in (B) and (D) mark alternation. In (D) "he counted gophers/how many he caught" elaborates its alternate in (B), "he brought them home," but at the same time gives closure to all four stanzas. What Coyote presumably did at the end of each day is noted only at the end of the scene as a whole.

The opening scene, then, is deceptively simple. It seems to tell us very little: Coyote and gophers for seventeen lines. A few lines later the gophers will be thrown away, not to be heard of again. Yet the opening conveys a great deal about Takelma verse, about the expectations to be satisfied by a well performed myth. The repeated pairing, for one thing: two lines before morning and evening are described, twofold repetition of the morning and evening, double occurrence of "every day" in corresponding places, the balanced couplet to repeat that Coyote was alone, the use of a rhetorical question to complete a pattern (Cb), anticipating its structural importance in the scenes to follow.

The care in the weaving of these relations; the timelessness of the scene, before the plot begins; the rhythm it seems possible to find, even in English, make me think that Mrs. Johnson enjoyed the picture of Coyote hunting gophers every day, and so lavished a little of her art upon it.[15]

5. Song-burdens (scenes iii, iv, v, vi)

The central acts of the myth present a frame shared with others, namely, parody of serious song performance. In the background is the practice of bringing out one's own guardian spirit song. The parodies bring on stage a series of actors whose songs express something about their character. (Cf. Chinookan parodies of guardian spirit song performance, also associated with Coyote [Hymes 1981, chs. 3 and 6].)

A humorous tone is set with the first and longest song, that of Frog, and its incompetent repetition by Coyote (scene iii). Each participant is to be understood as taking a turn by initiating a song that would be joined in by others. (Note "begin" in the instructions to a singer.) The text, sparingly and pointedly, gives as joining in only failures of Coyote to do so correctly.[16] Presumably that is to show his overreaching eagerness. (That tricksters cannot control or remember songs is a recurrent theme in the West.) Joining in by others, correctly, can be taken for granted. Coyote is a bungling guest. His singular failures do round out a four-part pattern of turns in the two scenes (iii, iv). And his error in regard to Frog can be seen to have a point (see below).

Sapir's ear and musical training enabled him to represent the measure and sometimes tune of the songs at the dance (scenes iii, iv, v). These notations are not reproduced here. But English equivalents can be added. Sapir did not translate the songs of anyone but Frog. (His translation of Frog's song does have a ring of its own, and the fine phrase, "Frog indeed," is his.) Rather, he reproduced the Takelma syllables. In footnotes, he did point out connections with other words for what is sung by Coyote, Bluejay, Mouse, Swan and Goose.[17] A combing of the Takelma vocabulary has brought to light further indications of ordinary language equivalents. Where the relation between an ordinary Takelma word and the song burden shows playful alteration, I have attempted an English analogue. (All this may be taken as a step toward a text for performance.)

The songs are apparently specific to the dance (and by implication, to the myth). In the fifth and concluding section of "VII. Interjections" (G280–81—Sapir lists verb and noun stems analytically at the end of the texts, but the other five parts of speech he distinguishes are given in the grammar), Sapir identifies two words from Frog, each of the two lines from Bluejay, and the first word from Swan, with the formula "round dance (said by X)." The second word of Swan's song and the first word of Goose is identified as "round dance; lullaby (cf. *waí·nha* put him to sleep!)" without mention of either singer.

Let me now take up the songs in turn:

Frog. Frog's dance scene (iii) has three alternations between focus on her and on Coyote. She is seen, he says he will take her (A); he seizes her hand, she is told to begin (B); she sings by far the longest song, three parts closed each by a verb of saying (111, 114–15, 122–23) (C); he takes it up with three pairs of phrases, enclosed in verbs of singing (124–31) (D). After parallel pairs of verses in the first two stanzas (with something spoken in the second of each), these last two stanzas may seem imbalanced (3:1), but they have expressive point, and balance after all. Three stretches for Frog to one for Coyote highlight her as against him, and provide four sections overall. The matching threeness of her song and his response gives the stanzas equivalent proportion.

Some of Frog's lines have been retranslated to maintain a parallel to the order of the Takelma constructions and to each other. In particular, body-part references always occur in the first part of a Takelma word as incorporated elements.

Sapir left two words untranslated. One is the first, *K'ìxinhi.* Its last syllable is probably the common emphatic element, *-hi.* No attested stem or construction answers to the first two syllables, but I have taken a hint from the construction, *kaí he'ne.* Together these two words have the sense of 'something like' (from *kaí* 'what, something' and *he'ne* 'then, at that time' [from *he'ne-* 'there, yonder' and temporal suffix *-'ne*]). There is an analogous semantic extension in Chinookan, where *aɫqi* 'a little while, later' and *dan* 'what, thing' occur together in the sense 'like, something like' (cf. the text in Hymes 1981, ch. 5). In both the Takelma and Wasco extensions there would seem to be a relation between a deictic center and a periphery. A moment that is off-center in time, "yonder" in time, or later in time, in relation to now, is analogous to something that is off-center in appearance or nature, something like, but not the thing itself.

(There is a root *xin* 'three,' and a suffix *-ki* 'belonging to, always being' that might be connected with the song word, but I have not thought of a way to think of Frog as "always being three." In any case, the order of elements in the song word is the inverse of grammatical order. There is no suggestion in the story that Frog gets words wrong, only that Coyote does.)

The song is humorous for the audience, even if sincere on the part of Frog, and she clearly begins by boasting. The notion of "something like" plus emphasis (*-hi*) suggests "Like something indeed."

The second word left untranslated is the last, twice repeated. This form, *'ošu,* seems to be attested in the vocabulary in a pertinent meaning. It is almost identical with the first element of the word for 'poor people', *osoᵘ-la·pa.* (The initial glottal stop of the song form is not distinctive [G31: "the catch as organic consonant is found only medially and finally"]). The difference between *š* and *s* is significant expressively (*š* is relatively augmentative), but not referentially. Since the second element of the expression for 'poor people', *-la·pa,* is the term for 'people' in such constructions, the first element must mean 'poor', even if Sapir does not point it out.[18]

Frog uses the word at the end of her song, having described herself as warty, blinking, skinny-rumped, and lacking fat. The likelihood that she here calls herself poor, directly or by unintentional pun, seems great. Lack of meat and fat would be a defect from an Indian standpoint, an indication that an animal would be of little use.

(One other attested word could be the basis of a pun, or song-burden distortion, and has a meaning that fits the puberty dance context. This is *hòsau* 'somewhat bigger, growing up', with plural *hòsó·u.* The phonetic differences from the song word are perhaps somewhat greater (significant initial *h-, -au,* or, less likely, plural ending -*ó·u*). Moreover, the identification with "poor" makes possible an English equivalent of the play on words detected by Sapir.)

Coyote. Sapir observes (T 104, n. 1): "Coyote evidently means to repeat the ['*ošu 'ošu*] of Frog, but perverts her burden into the verb form *ùsi*, 'give it to me'." In English, "poor me" (Frog) : "for me" (Coyote) seems analogous to the Takelma joke. The second "me: in the pair of lines by Coyote is stressed, because in Takelma the accented vowel of the second word in each pair is always held out a trifle longer than that of the first (T104, n. 1). Hence the underlining in the translation.

When Coyote imitates Frog, and later Mouse, he is said in Takelma to sing only half of it. People who have an imperfect command of a language are said to talk half of it (T104, n. 2). In the singing it is not the quantity, but quality, of Coyote's response that is meant, of course, and I translate "half-right."

Notice that on this interpretation both Frog and Coyote convey something through shibilant/sibilant alternation. If Frog is asserting her poor appearance, (perhaps with a view to being corrected) the shibilant of ['*ošu 'ošu*] augments the word for "poor" itself. In order to turn what Frog sings into "for me" (give it to me), Coyote must choose the diminutive or depreciatory sibilant often associated with himself.

Bluejay (scene iv). Bluejay sings "*Č'ai-č'i-a gwača gwača*" (twice). The repetition of the whole is matched by repetition within. The second expression (*gwača*) is repeated identically, and the first expression, playing upon Bluejay's monosyllabic name (G281, T104, n. 3), doubles its syllables. Sapir cites the name in his note to the text (as *č'ài'č* [=*č'àič'*] [cf. G220, n. 1]), that is, with the shibilant affricate (*č'*) it has in the song, but in the vocabulary (T257) and in the narrative proper (T104:5, here line 134) the name is given as *ts'ài's*. Presumably the form in the song is an expressive variant. Other instances of alternation between sibiliant and shibilant indicate that the latter is augmentative, and it fits Bluejay's character in other traditions to have him inflate his importance.

To parallel the vowel inversion in the Takelma syllables [a-i:i·-a·], I have inverted the vowels of the dipthong in English "jay" [e-i>i-e], spelling them with the equivalents "ay":"ee-ay".

The second expression, *gwača gwača,* has a rhythm of two sixteenth notes for the first occurrence, two eighth notes for the second. The form is not attested elsewhere in Takelma, being listed only as a song burden (G281). Possibly there is a connection with *gwàs* 'brush'. The language has morphological ablaut between affricate and fricative (G34). The final -*a* in *gwača* can be interpreted as from the third person pronominal possessive suffix of relationship, -*xa,* with the *x* assimilated. (Cf. the parallel analysis of four kinship terms [G234].) On this interpretation, Bluejay states a relationship to brush analogous to that of a person to kin. Such a touch fits the habits of the bird, which presumably is the Scrub Jay, or California Jay, found typically in open country, and of the character in some of the stories in the region (Who would want him as kin? He belongs to the brush). The fact that the next song clearly refers to the singer's habitat supports taking Bluejay's song as doing so as well.

Mouse. Mouse sings "be-bì-bi-ni-be·-a, be-bì-bi-ni-be·-a." Sapir notes that "the implied reference in the mind of an Indian is here to the word *bebén* 'rushes'. The mouse is often found among rushes" (T104, n. 4; G281). I have tried to match the interplay of consonant and vowel with repetitions of the consonants and vowels of the English word "rushes."[19] I have added syllables to the word to match the added syllables in Takelma. Where initial *b-* is repeated in Takelma, *r* is repeated in English. Where *n-* begins a syllable in Takelma, *sh-* does in English. The stem vowels in Takelma are parallelled by the stem vowels of "rushes," taken as [ɔ́] and [ɨ], and the first represented as "uh," the second altered to "oo" for lack of an equivalent open vowel in English. "-ah" is added parallel to the final *-a.*

In sum, *bebén* 'rushes' is $C_1V_1C_1V_1C_2$, and Mouse's song repeats $C_1V_1 C_1V_1 C_1V_2 C_2V_2 C_1V_2$-a.

Coyote. Coyote sings half-right by omitting the final *-bi·a* (C_1V_2-a), and prefixing each line with the *s-* so often associated with him.

Swan. Swan's song was in ordinary use among the Takelma, Sapir reports (T104, n. 6) as a round-dance song. Its first word, *bèlel-do* is a play upon the word for 'swan', *bel´p* (T104, n. 5, G281). The final consonant of the usual word is a repetition of the initial consonant (G220, n. 2; cf. G109, aorist type 10). Reduplication of vowel and second consonant (*-el*) in the song word fits a form of reduplication of the aorist stem (G220, n. 2).

The pattern of the play in Takelma, then, is that $C_1VC_2C_1$, *b-e-l-p,* becomes $C_1VC_2VC_2$, *b-el-el.* Taking initial sw- in English as C_1, one would have *sw-a-n-a-n,* followed by a final syllable (for which see below). This is possible in English, but a better alternative suggests itself.

The final syllable in Takelma, *-dó·,* suggests *du·* 'good, beautiful' and presumably, 'pretty'. In the play on *bel´p* 'swan' the absence of its final repeated consonant, on the one hand, and the kinds of meaning associated with the aorist, which *-elel* formally is, suggest incompleteness, and a diminutive sense. By these stretches of the imagination, *bèlel-* can be taken as 'Swanny', *-dó·* as 'pretty', and the two together as 'Pretty Swanny'.

The second word of the song, *wainha,* is literally 'put him to sleep'. Sapir thinks it "very probable that the word was originally used in its literal sense in lullabies, then transferred to other songs as a mere burden," and cites a lullaby, four quarter notes in form, the third accented (T104, n. 6):

Mo-xo wain-ha·	Buzzard, put him to sleep!
Si·m-hi wain-ha·	Sim[20]-indeed, put him to sleep!
P'el-da wain-has·	Snail, put him to sleep!

One can add that reference to putting to sleep in a song sung by a nubile girl might have sexual allusion. Such a dance was an announcement of availability for marriage. And in Takelma the person to be put to sleep need not be male, despite "him" in the translations. Gender is not marked in the third person of these verbs. The connection with lullabies would have the nubile girl invoke her own encouchment.

Alternatively, the point might be to put to sleep whoever, awake, might interfere with the dance. The song of the next act is explicitly such, and Goose and Swan can be taken as a pair. This is the more likely, if the actors singled out at the dance are taken as consisting of three sets, interwoven in the narrative sequence.

The first set are the pair, Coyote and Frog, who frame the rest. They constitute scene iii together.

The second set consist of two pairs, Bluejay and Mouse, associated perhaps in terms of reference to marginal habitat (brush and rushes), and Swan and Goose, associated through reference to putting to sleep. Bluejay, Mouse and Swan make up scene iv, together with Coyote. Goose takes up act V together with the first of the bears.

The third set consists of Brown Bear, coming in reaction to hearing Goose naming him (scene vi), and Grizzly, coming in reaction to hearing the continuation of the dance, taking up scene vii.

Coyote and Frog complete the story in scene viii.

Goose (scene vi). Nothing in Goose's song has to do with her appearance or her name. Rather, she names Brown Bear in the first of each pair of lines. Sapir comments (T106, n. 1): "Though these three words are here probably felt to be mere burdens, each of them can be translated as a regular Takelma word: "Put-him-to-sleep, brown-bear his-anus."

Sapir goes on to point out that the normal form for "his anus" would be different, *dòlkini·* or *dòlkama·.* The initial *i-* of the song form *idòlki* in the second of each pair of lines (where Brown Bear, *mèna,* is not named) must be explained, he says, either as a mere change in burden, pairing off with *mena* in the first line, or else as a demonstrative stem not ordinarily used in its bare form (cf. *ida-* 'that there', *ideme'a* 'right there'). On the latter assumption, *idòlki* would be an archaic song-form of *ìdaga dòlkini·* 'that-one his-anus'.

An archaic form in reference to Brown Bear seems quite likely, given the general Native American practice of using respectful terms to and about bears. I have adopted this interpretation in the translation of the second and fourth lines, combining the notions of a demonstrative, and a distancing phrase, in the English "that old one's."

Brown Bear, Grizzly Bear. The two bears do not sing, but their coming is epitomized in words of their own. Both express the fearsomeness of bears with the particle *hau,* but not in quite the same way. Brown Bear, the first to come, is the smaller, less dangerous bear. His coming has no effect beyond his being there, and perhaps the implicit warning that where one bear has come, another may follow. Brown Bear's *hau* has no pitch accent, while Grizzly Bear's has a grave (falling) accent: *hàu.* Thus pitch accent can distinguish words expressively as well as referentially. The difference seems an apt way to indicate the difference in aggressiveness of the two bears in the story (as in nature).

Brown Bear is like Coyote in that he comes because he has heard the singing, but unlike Coyote in that he comes only once there is explicit, insulting reference to himself (which retrospectively underscores Coyote's alertness to any sign that women are available). Still, Brown Bear is like Coyote in speaking in response to what he hears, and in how he speaks. Like Coyote, he first says *"S'à!"* This marks him as outsider and figure of amusement. The word comes, I think, from Takelma hearing of the Siuslaw of the Oregon coast, in whose language this is a third person pronoun, and the base of many words derived from it (see Hymes 1981, ch. 2). And Brown Bear's fourfold use of *hau,* associated with Bears in the Takelma texts (G280) is modulated by an initial *s-,* a characterizing prefix associated with Coyote, interloper par excellence, when excited (T56, n. 2). At the same time, the sibilant form is diminutive in contrast to the possibility of a shibilant form, as we have seen. Moreover, it has no pitch accent.

Grizzly Bear comes without prior speech, and when he comes, the threatening particle *hau* is unencumbered, but marked by a grave (falling) accent. His four part series of *hau* is repeated in the transitional act VII, which ends the dancing and leads on to the denouement of Coyote's coming and singling out of Frog. In effect, Brown Bear introduces the threatening nature of uninvited bears, but enclosed in insult and humor, continuing the tone of the preceding songs. Grizzly Bear comes silently until he is present as *hau* itself.

6. How this Myth Ends

Full performances have a patterned close. One element of such a close is often a pronouncement, or other indication that one or more of the actors is transformed. Other elements complete the story with indications that is over, and that the event of telling is over as well.

A. Pronouncement . The last action in the story is that of Coyote placing and addressing Frog:

Coyote threw Frog into the water.	(D)
"Do you think you will be a woman?	240
"You will be called 'Frog',"	
he said to Frog.	

Such a sequence, placement and pronouncement, recurs in the region. In Kathlamet Chinook Salmon enacts it a number of times in relation, first to valued plants, and then to disvalued pretenders, in Charles Cultee's "Salmon's Myth" (see Hymes 1985). Coyote tells the sisters who have kept back the salmon what and where they will be at the end of Louis Simpson's Wishram Chinook myth; so also in William Hartless's Mary's River Kalapuya analogue (cf. Hymes 1966:149–50, 1981:305–6, 1990a [Simpson], 1987 [Hartless]). In Hartless's myth, the women are Frogs. (To tell an actor its true name is to tell it its true nature.) In the Alsea myth of "Coyote and Frog-women" told by Thomas Jackson (Frachtenberg 1917–20:72–74), the culmination of the action is recognition by the women that "Yes, Coyote played this trick on us." The condition and nature of frogs, namely that they have no female organ, has already happened without pronouncement. When the two woman had "died" as a result of his trick, Coyote removed their organs and took them with him. Still, the consequence is stated by the narrator, followed by a formulaic close.

As discussed in section V (15), the verb in what Coyote says implies that he causes the stated consequence, i.e., acts indeed as a transformer. The same word is used when the transformer Daldal assigns Evening Star its place and nature.

B. Formal Close . Sapir comments on the last two sentences of this myth ("It is finished / Go gather and eat your baap seeds") on their first appearance in the published texts (T42, n. 1): "This is the conventional method of winding up a Takelma myth. The command is addressed to the children who have gathered around to listen to its recital. They are to go off and gather seeds in order to become active. Too much sitting around listening to stories makes one lazy." The intent and the form of the close can both be given a wider context.

The explanation of the purpose is no doubt from Mrs. Johnson. It is of interest because the common reason given for not telling stories in summer is that rattlesnakes would come. The thought that story-telling can interfere with necessary activity, however, is shared by at least some others in the region. According to Mrs. Alice Florendo, a Wasco of Warm Springs Reservation, myths would not be told in summer because to do so would interfere with obtaining the fresh foods which one would need to store to survive in winter. Implicit in both notions is probably a sense of complementarity between secular and sacred seasons.

The part about seeds, however, is a bit puzzling. Unfortunately, we do not know what *baap* seeds are. Inasmuch as myths were normally told at night, gathering seeds would have to wait at least until daylight. If the seeds are associated with a season other than winter, the gathering would have to wait at least until spring. In that case the Takelma command would parallel one recorded by Melville Jacobs (in unpublished notes) from the Clackamas narrator Victoria Howard. Boys and girls are instructed each to go get a kind of food (small animal for boys, plant for girls). Such an ending commands activity, to be sure, but also invokes a desire for good weather and for kinds of activity characteristic of spring, summer, and fall. Such an invocation is widespread on the Pacific Coast (some are noted in Hymes 1981:323–24).

The closing sentences described by Sapir as the conventional method of winding up a Takelma myth occur at the end of only six of the twenty-two published Takelma texts. (Texts 23 and 24 are brief reports in English.) Nor are the two sentences all of the ending of "Coyote and Frog." They are preceded by *Gè de'winìthí,* translated by Sapir as 'Proceeding just up to there (it goes).' *Gè* is the frequent adverbial element "there." *de-winit-hí* is deverbal from the root *wi·-* 'to go about, travel', with *de-/da-* 'lips, mouth' in the transferred sense of 'in front, before,' and *-hi* 'indeed'. Related forms occur in the endings of myths (3, 4): *gahi dè'winít* 'that-just going-so-far', *gè de·winìth* 'There proceeding-just-up-to (it goes)'. The notion of ending a myth as being put in front is found also with *de-/da-* and other verb roots elsewhere in the ending of (3), and in the ending of (21).

C. Formal Place. The three concluding sentences of "Coyote and Frog" cooperate in the Janus-faced role of a full ending. The first two sentences look back to the story itself, and say that it is done. The third looks ahead to the world outside the story and what is to happen there. (Cf. discussion in Hymes 1981:322–27.)

Whether the full close is part of the organization of the story proper, or an external coda, is difficult to say. It is possible to include the close by taking the last four verses of the action proper as the third stanza of the last scene (viii). The close is then the fourth. Alternatively, each pair of verses could be taken as constituting a stanza. If so, the story proper is complete in eight verses, four stanzas, and the two verses of the formal close remain. There is internal symmetry in this. The first two stanzas each end with "Coyote for his part . . .", still expecting sex. The last two stanzas each end with Coyote addressing Frog. I have opted for this interpretation.

D. Other Endings. All but one of Mrs. Johnson's myths do mark the ending, but fifteen do so in other ways. The other endings are intrinsic to the story itself, how far it goes, how much is known, how it comes out. Perhaps the command involving seeds, which turns from the story to what is outside the telling, could be added to these. If the order of publication is not the same as the order in the field notebooks, the fuller endings might be later ones.

The endings appear to be made up of six elements (abcdef), occurring alone or in combination.

(a, b) The two sentences cited by Sapir, (a) *Gweldì* 'It's finished' (cf. G 260), and (b) "Go gather and eat your baap seeds" occur together in that order in six of the twenty-two published myths (cf. 1909:[2], [5], [7], [10] [this text], [14], [15]). Each also occurs once without the other: *Gweldì* in (3), "Go gather and eat your baap seeds" in (16).

(b) The sentence that precedes this pair in "Coyote and Frog" (10)—"It goes just up to there"—also occurs once alone (21).

(b, c) Three myths combine "going so far," "that much," "to there," (b) with "know" (c):(3), (4), (12). The full ending of (3) is "Now I-have-put-it-off-in-front the-myth. That-indeed going-so-far I-for-my-part I-know-it." The full ending of (4) is "I-for-my-part there-indeed indeed I-know-it, there it-goes-indeed indeed I-know it." (For [3, 4], see also the discussion above of the ending of "Coyote and Frog.") (12) ends "Thus-it-is there-indeed indeed I-know-it."

Three endings which lack "just so far," but begin with "Thus (it is)" imply a sense of "so far" or "that much" (see 19, 17, 22 just below).

(d) The word *gana'nèx* 'Thus it is, that way, thus' (G87, 252) is sole ending in one myth (20), and first part in six others. In two cases there follow explanations or summaries of the story: (6) "Pitch would kill people" (6); a long passage with outcome and summary explanation both (11). In four cases what follows involves knowing. Two involve simply the fact of knowing: (12) "there-indeed indeed I-know-it," and (19) "I know it indeed." (12) in effect combines dbc. Two have to do with how much or how the narrator knows: (17) "for-my-part I-know-it, perchance there is much more; all did I know, I should tell it to you", and (22) "indeed my Mother told me, but she did not see it either. This for its part is a myth indeed" (22).

(e) Two myths end with returning on the river: (1) (down river), (8) (upriver). (5) ends with "Upriver finished / Go gather and eat your baap seeds" (in effect, eab).

(f) "For that reason" (*ga ga'al*) precedes an explanation ("today not people return when dead") at the end of (9). With post-position -*si'* (*gasi' ga'al* (cf. G275), it introduces the explanation of consequences with which (18) ends. In (21) it introduces the second part of a final sentence of explanation, which itself follows "There-indeed in front-it is."

"Grizzly Bear and Black Bear" (13) has no formal element of ending. It underlines its outcome: "Crane threw her into the water. But formerly Black Bear's children had escaped by just passing over Crane's leg" (13).

Perhaps naming "myth" itself counts as an element of ending. Cf. the first part of the ending of (3): "Now I-have-put-it-off-in-front the-myth," and the last sentence of (22): "A-myth-indeed this-for-its-part."

None of these elements of ending are found with texts that are not myths, except that the evidential remark at the end of (22) is paralleled at the end of "How a Bad-hearted Medicine-man Has His Guardian Spirits Driven Out of Him" (184): "My mother did tell me that account, but I did not see it." Myth endings vary among Alsea and Sahaptin narrators. Perhaps in the region generally personal preferences can hold sway. The elements of Mrs. Johnson's endings probably reflect the repertoire of her community. Those which refer back to the story itself suggest that a range of options were available. Her use of the two sentences singled out by Sapir in only six myths might reflect the sequence in which she told myths to Sapir. (I do not know if the order of publication is the same.) Victoria Howard began to use the conventional Clackamas final ending, "Story story," only well along in her work with Melville Jacobs. Mrs. Johnson's use might also reflect confidence in having told the story completely and well.

VIII. Profile (with markers)

Abbreviations and translations for markers are as follows:

	aga-si'	this (nearer of contrast [G274])
	ali	this here (G252)
	da'òl	nearby
	dalwi-si'	some (in contrast [G250])
G	Gane·-hi'	then-indeed
	ganga	always
Ge	Gè	there
Q	Gwi·'nè dì wede	How long did not . . . ? (and others)
H	honò'	again
	hawi	still (cf. -wi' 'part of a series' [G250])

M	mi·	now
S	Sgìsi	Coyote
-si'		and, but, in turn (aga-si', dalwi-si')
"-"		quoted speech

	Scene/				
Act	Subscene	Stanza	Verses	Lines	

[I] [*Coyote goes to a puberty dance*]

   [i] [Alone, he hunts gophers]

		A	ab	1, 2	Formula, S
		B	cd	3–6, 7	Time + H, time
		C	ef	8–10, 11	GH, Q
		D	gh	12–13, 14–17	Time + H, G + time

   [ii] [He hears and hurries to the dance]

     [2] [He hears the dance]

		A	abcde	18–19, 20, 21–23,	M, M, G + "-", M, "-"
				24–25, 26	

     [3] [He runs, listens]

		A	ab	27–28, 29–32	M-hi', M
		B	abcde	33–34, 35, 36,	GMH, GMH, Hawi, G + "-",
				37–38, 39–40	Ge + "-"
		C	abc	41–43, 44, 45	"-", 'alí + da'ól, "-"

     [3] [How long does he not run? (and listen)]

		A	abc	46, 47, 48	MH, Q, Da'ol
		B	abc	49–50, 51, 52-53	GH, Tga, "-"
		C	abc	54, 55–57, 58-59	GH, Q, Ganga—ali
		D	abcde	60–61, 62, 63–65,	GH, Q, "-", G + "-", Aga-si'
				66–67, 68	
		E	ab	69, 70	MH, Q

     [4] [Almost there]

		A	abc	71, 72, 73	G, M, Ge
		B	ab	74, 75–76	G, G da'o·l
		C	ab	77, 78–80	M H, G

     [5] [He arrives]

		A	ab	81, 82–88	GM, catalogue
		B	cd	89, 90	Q (Kai), Kai
		C	e	91–93	S M

[II] [*Coyote sings*]

   [iii] [Frog and Coyote sing]

		A	ab	94–97, 98–99	G, "-"
		B	ab	100–2, 103–5	G, "-"
		C	abc	106–11, 112–15,	G + "-", "-", "-"
				116–23	
		D	a	124–31	G + "-"

   [iv] [Bluejay, Mouse and Coyote, Swan sing]

		A	ab	132–34, 135–39	G + "-", G + "-"
		B	ab	140–43, 144–47	GMH + "-", GM + "-"
		C	a	148–52	S + "-"
		D	ab	153–55, 156–62	G + "-", G + "-"

[III] [*Singing brings bears*]

    [v] [Goose sings and Brown Bear comes]

A	ab	163–66, 167–72	G + "-", G + "-"
B	a	173–75	G + "-" (turn)
C	ab	176–81	GH-hi'
D	abcd	182–84, 185, 186–88, 189–95	GM, M-hi', M, M + "-"

    [vi] [Some keep singing and Grizzly comes]

A	ab	196, 197	G, M
B	ab	198–201, 202	-si' + "-", Ganga-hi'
C	ab	203–6, 207	Dalwi-si' + "-", Ganga-hi'
D	ab	208–13, 214	G + "-", M

[IV] [*Coyote finds out about Frog*]

    [vii] [Grizzly breaks up the dance]

A	ab	215–20, 221–23	G, M
B	ab	224, 225	S-si', Ga-hi' ganga

    [viii] [Coyote runs off with Frog]

A	ab	226–27, 228	M, M
B	ab	229–33, 234	G, S-'a M
C	ab	235, 236–38	G, "-"
D	ab	239, 240–42	S, "-"
Close	ab	243, 244–45	Ge, formula

Appendix I: Coyote and Fox

Mrs. Johnson uses the frame of Coyote trapping gophers, then throwing them away and rushing off, in the last (not first) act of another myth, "Coyote and Fox" (T78–79). Several of the same ingredients occur: he rushed off, he ran, how long did he not run, he rested. What is perceived is part sound (a chirping ascribable to ghosts, but made by Fox), part sight (something reddish like the glow of a fire, actually the eyes of Fox). But in this case the narrative is shaped entirely in terms of relations of two and four. There is nothing of three and five.

The differences between the two narratives, "Coyote and Frog" and "Coyote and Fox," illustrate nicely the independence and interplay of form and content. There are examples indeed within "Coyote and Fox" itself (cf. lines 16, 17–18 [one verse] to lines 24–25, 26 [two verses], and lines 27–28, 29, 30, 31 [four verses] to lines 32–33, 35, 36–37 [three verses]. The lines are numbered in terms of this act alone, not in terms of the narrative as a whole.)

Overall the act appears to have four scenes (Coyote back home, a lone time passes, Fox returns, Coyote rushes off,). The first three scenes have two stanzas of two verses each. The fourth scene has eight stanzas.

                         [VIII. How long did he not run?]

Coyote back home would set traps for gophers all by himself.   [i]   (A)
It became evening.
Then indeed he used to make the rounds of where he had set traps,   (B)
when it became evening.

Then indeed a long time passed.   [ii] (A)   5
Then indeed how long had it not been?
Now indeed again he counted gophers,   (B)
   how many he had killed he counted.
Now indeed it became evening,
   he was sitting,   10
      he counted them.

Now indeed Coyote was chirped to,   [iii] (A)
   Fox did so.
"Ah! What said that?"
   was said to him, indeed.   15
Again he was chirped to.   (B)
   He looked around:
      something just reddish like the glow of a fire.
Now he threw the gophers all away.

Now he rushed off.   [iv] (A) 20
Now he ran,
   he rested,
      he took breath.
Again indeed he was chirped to,   (B)
   he looked around.   25
again indeed it was like fire.

Now again he rushed off,   (C)
   he ran;
How long did he not run?
Now again he rested.   (D) 30
then indeed again he caught his breath.

Again indeed he was chirped to,   (E)
again he rushed off,
   he ran.
How long did he not run?   (F) 35
Now again he rested,
   he caught his breath.

Now again he was chirped to;   (G)
   he looked around,
Again, indeed, thus it was like the blaze of a fire.   40
Now he rushed off,   (H)
   he ran.
Way off to the east where the earth is set,
   where the sky is set down (to meet it),
      he bumped his head against the sky;   45
         in that place his bones just rattled.

Up river it is finished.   [Close]
Go gather and eat your baap seeds.

Appendix II: Particles and Quoted Speech

These abbreviations are used:

---	quoted speech (alone)	
G	*gane·hi'* 'then'	
H	*hono* 'again	
M	*mi·* 'now'	
-hi'	verb of saying with *-hi'*	
S	*Sgisi* 'Coyote'	
V	verb of saying (singing) without *-hi'*	
(V)	verb not of saying	

i			no quoted speech		
ii	1	22–23		G---*hi'*	
		26	---		
	2	37–38		G---	
		41–43	---*hi'*, V		
		45	---		
	3	52–53	---*hi'*		
		63–64	---*hi'*		
		66–67		G---	
	4		no quoted speech		
	5		no quoted speech		
iii		98–99	---*hi'*		
		103–5	---V		
		106–11		GV---*hi'*	
		112–15	---*hi'*, V		
		116–23	---*hi'*, V		
		124–31		GV---V	
iv		132–34		GV---V	
		135–39		GV---	
		140–43		GMH---VH	
		144–47		GMV---V	
		148–52			SV---
		153–58		G---V	
		156–62		GV---*hi'*, V	
v		163–66		G---VV	
		167–72		GV---V	
		173–75		G---*hi'*	
		176–81		GHVV---	
		182–84		GMV---*hi'*	
		189–95		M---(V)	
vi		198–99	---V		
		203–6			-*si'*---*hi'*
		208–13		G--(V)	

Notes

1. The manuscript, "Myth as Verse" (1979a) is unpublished; a copy is at the Department of Linguistics of the University of Oregon. It includes analyses of three myths: Charles Cultee's "Sun's Myth" (Kathlamet Chinook), Frances Johnson's Takelma myth, and John Rush Buffalo's "Coyote and Eagle's Daughter" (Tonkawa). The narrative text of the first, with a translation revised from Hymes (1975), appears in a volume edited by Brian Swann (Hymes 1994b). The third has been published (Hymes 1980a), and again in slightly revised form (Hymes 1987). A re-analysis is included in Hymes 1992.

2. There is a special case, scene ii, "He hears and hurries to the dance," which Mrs. Johnson amplified to the proportions of an act; it has scenes itself (five of them). (See Hymes 1985 for discussion of amplification.) The amplification shows Mrs. Johnson's interest in the part, as a dramatic tour de force at the least, and probably as portraiture of Coyote.

If the narrative is to be presented in a consistent way (and to imply a consistent model of the narrative competence behind it), there are two alternatives. One alternative is this: if one component is equivalent to an act, one can mark all the other components (seven scenes) as acts as well (I-VIII). The higher level into which these components enter can no longer be considered to consist of acts. One can take it to consist of "Parts" (ONE-FOUR).

The other alternative is this: one can treat the exception as an exception, marking its internal elaboration in a special way. The other seven components can be marked as scenes, as they normally would be, given their unity of cast and context. There are then eight scenes (i-viii), and the higher level into which they enter is that of acts (I-IV).

The second alternative seems consistent with the character of the narrative. What is unusual in the shape of the story is matched with what is unusual in presenting that shape. In "scene ii," then, its five components are distinguished by Arabic numerals (1-5). Then can be termed "subscenes."

3. See the opening of the discussion on philology for an explanation of the way in which Takelma is written here.

4. Sapir was indeed alert to the idea of phonemic patterning and contrast when he wrote the Takelma grammar, which was finished in 1909 although not published until after the First World War. An awareness is indicated by remarks such as that quoted later in this section as to the two variants of raised or rising pitch accent. The principle of minimal contrast itself is articulated in the following (1922:14): "Examples of unrelated stems and words differing only in the length of the vowel or diphthong are not rare, and serve as internal evidence of the correctness, from a native point of view, of the vowel classification made" (examples follow).

5. Sapir's phonemic orthography (Shipley 1969:227) retained a way of writing all three forms of accent, while changing the symbols to ´ (short rising), ˇ (long rising), ˆ (falling). Perhaps he felt the physical distinctiveness of long rising accent too patent not to mark.

6. So Sapir in the grammar (G) on pp. 30 and 31, identifying "voiceless media." In the phonetic key to the texts (T) (published some years earlier), he writes of "voiceless mediae," acoustically intermediate between voice (sonant) and unvoiced (surd) stops. Perhaps this is intended to address the perceptions of English speakers (cf. G31).

7. Kendall (1977, 1992) chooses an orthography equivalent to that of Shipley for stops,

representing aspiration by raised ʰ. Kendall observes that aspiration is predictable in most cases (before consonants, word-final, final vowel with falling pitch [and optionally m n l], final vowel with rising pitch). He distinguishes k^w and $k^{\prime w}$ and writes [ü] as the normal form of that vowel, and shows vowel length by repeating the vowel (aa, rather than a·).

8. Sapir considered it necessary to treat gw, kw, and k'w as single units for reasons of symmetry in distribution (permitted consonant clusters). The result is a general rule that no more than two consonants can stand at the beginning of a syllable (1922:31, 36, 37). It is not clear that a similar constraint applies at the end of syllables. Counting kw as two units, instead of one, would not change the general pattern. Notice this early attention to patterns of distribution, as also in the later, seminal, "Sound Patterns in Language" (1925).

9. The examples are labelled and numbered for ease of reference.

10. I think that in fact the first syllable of *ganga* can be taken as preceding the ubiquitous demonstrative element *ga,* and that *gan-* is cognate with Chinookan *kana-* 'all', and perhaps with the *gwana-* of *gwana-sim* 'always' (-sim occurs separately in a temporal sense). Chinookan *kana-* has cognates further afield in the Penutian family. The example shows that verse analysis contributes to descriptive and comparative linguistics. Questions posed by analysis of form and meaning in terms of line and verse force reconsideration of local and underlying meanings. A *ganga* labelled 'only' does not seem connected with the Chinookan form and Penutian series just mentioned. A *ganga* with a sense of 'always' does.

11. What Sapir calls "periphrastic phrases in na(g)- DO, ACT" (G186–89).

12. These two verses have line 213 as outcome, "They stopped dancing suddenly," but it is formally subordinated. The line might have been marked as a verse (by initial *gane·hi'* or *mi·*), and thus have been the eighth and last verse of the stanza. That would have made the sequence of action that runs through the stanza focus on the dancing of the girls. Mrs. Johnson evidently chose to focus on the coming and arrival of Grizzly Bear. To do otherwise would have required omitting the present last verse about Grizzly Bear altogether, or subordinating it instead:

> "Now the girls stopped dancing suddenly,
>   Grizzly Bear had gotten right here."

13. These three particles occur together in this way four times in the text (lines 33, 35; 81, 140, 144; 182). Line 81 introduces a culmination, Coyote's arrival in the last subscene of scene ii. Line 182 also introduces a culmination, the last stanza of scene v, in which Brown Bear hears what the girls have been singing about him. The other occurrences are not culminations. Being paired, they appear to foreground in other ways. One pair introduces two repeated elements of Coyote's running to the dance, "he rushed off," "he rested" (lines 33 [subscene 2], 49, 54, 61 [subscene 3, stanzas B, C, D] for "rushed off," and lines 36, 57 [subscene 2, subscene 3 stanza C] for resting.) The other pair frames the call to Mouse to sing, and her response (140, 144). Mouse is the third singer, not even the first of those that follow Frog, so what is marked cannot be introduction. The scene *is* significant, evidently, because it entails the only other report of Coyote's attempting to imitate a singer. Mouse sings about rushes, and perhaps that can be heard as an allusion to the brush in which Coyote will end up with Frog. But that is speculation.

14. I am grateful to Alice Schlichter Shepherd for this information. Pitkin (1985:312) gives the meanings "sing winter dream songs; sing girls' puberty songs; croak, of frogs."

15. See the appendix for a related sequence.

16. When Black Bear hears what Goose sings, repetition by them all is conveyed by the English translation "just that they said," and Black Bear's remark, "Where are they talking about my anus?" "They" does seem the most natural English translation, but the Takelma verb form is the third person impersonal in the first case, and the third person passive aorist

READING TAKELMA TEXTS 157

in the second. The third person is not overtly marked, and there is no indication of number, singular or plural. It may well be that the second time the song is heard, others have taken it up, but that is not said. Again, when Grizzly Bear comes, girls speak to one another in warning, "Don't sing." What is said to be continuing, and heard by Grizzly Bear, however, is not singing, as such, but dancing. With the bears, individual singing fades into the background. Coyote is the only figure foregrounded as joining someone's song.

17. In his grammar (G280–81), Sapir lists these song-burdens as "round dance" (indicating the singer [except for Goose]), and then the name or other word on which there is a play.

18. Two other words suggest a preference for back rounded vowel and [s] in expressions having to do with being small or having little: *tosò·* 'small, a little', and *al-t'uí's-ít* 'little-eyed' (epithet of squirrel, where *al-* indicates 'eye').

19. The stem itself would seem to be a "complete duplication of the radical element" (G220), but Sapir lists *bebé-n,* not as duplication, but with instances of a repeated initial consonant (G219–20). Reduplicated nouns are far less frequent than verbs, and many of the nouns correspond to verbal types, where the reduplication is almost never identical. None of the examples of 'complete duplication' have a derivational ending. All that may have been enough to let *bebé-n* slip by as if it were *beb-én* (it is followed in its column by *bu·b-án* 'arm').

20. *Si·m* is an unknown animal.

References

Bright, William, ed.
    1990 *Wishram Texts and Ethnography.* The Collected Works of Edward Sapir, vol.
        7. Berlin and New York: Mouton de Gruyter.
Burke, Kenneth
    1925 Psychology and Form. *The Dial* 79 (July):34–46. Reprinted in *Counter-Statement.*
        New York: Harcourt, Brace, 1931. Third edition, Berkeley and Los Angeles:
        Univ. of California Press, 1968.
Frachtenberg, Leo J.
    1917–20 Myths of the Alsea Indians of Northwest Oregon. *International Journal of
        American Linguistics* 1:64–75.
G See Sapir 1912.
Golla, Victor, ed.
    1990 *Takelma Texts and Grammar.* The Collected Works of Edward Sapir, vol. 8.
        Berlin and New York: Mouton de Gruyter.
Hymes, Dell
    1966 Two Types of Linguistic Relativity (with Examples from Amerindian Ethno-
        graphy). In *Sociolinguistics.* Ed. William Bright. The Hague: Mouton. Pp.
        114–67.
    1972 Introduction. In *Functions of Language in the Classroom.* Eds. Courtney B.
        Cazden, Vera P. John, and Dell Hymes. New York: Teachers College Press.
        Pp. xi–lvii.
    1974 *Foundations in Sociolinguistics.* Philadelphia: Univ. of Pennsylvania Press.
    1979a Myth as Verse. Ms.
    1979b How to Talk Like a Bear in Takelma. *International Journal of American
        Linguistics* 45(2):101–6. Revised in 1981.
    1980a Tonkawa Poetics: John Rush Buffalo's "Coyote and Eagle's daughter." In *On
        Linguistic Anthropology: Essays in Honor of Harry Hoijer 1979.* Eds. Joseph

Greenberg, Dell Hymes, and Paul Friedrich. Other Realities, vol. 2. Malibu: California: Undena Publications. Pp. 33–87.

1980b Particle, Pause and Pattern in American Indian Narrative Verse. *American Indian Culture and Research Journal* 4:7–51.

1981   *"In Vain I Tried to Tell You."* Philadelphia: Univ. of Pennsylvania Press.

1984   *Vers la compétence de communication.* Paris: Hatier-Credif. Based on a Working Paper in Sociolinguistics of 1971.

1985   Language, Memory, and Selective Performance: Charles Cultee's "Salmon's Myth" as Twice-Told to Boas. *Journal of American Folklore* 98: 391–434.

1987   Tonkawa Poetics: John Rush Buffalo's "Coyote and Eagle's daughter." In *Native American Discourse: Poetics and Rhetoric.* Eds. Joel Sherzer and Anthony C. Woodbridge. Cambridge and New York: Cambridge Univ. Press.

1990a The Discourse Patterning of a Wishram Text. In *Wishram Texts and Ethnography.* Ed. W. Bright. Collected Works of Edward Sapir, vol. 7. Berlin: Moutin de Gruyter. Pp. 343–54.

1990b The Discourse Patterning of a Takelma Text, "Coyote and His Rock Grandson." In *Takelma Texts and Grammar.* Ed. V. Golla. Collected Works of Edward Sapir, vol. 8. Berlin: Mouton de Gruyter. Pp. 583–98.

1990c Verse Retranslation of "Split-his-own-head." Appendix in *Nehalem Tillamook Tales.* Told by Clara Pearson, recorded by Elizabeth Derr Jacobs, and edited by Melville Jacobs. Northwest Reprints. Corvallis: Oregon State Univ. Press. Pp. 220–28.

1991   Clara Pearson's "Split-his-own-head": A Thrice-Told Tillamook Narrative. *International Conference on Salish and Neighboring Languages* 26. See Hymes 1993.

1992   Use All There Is to Use. In *On the Translation of Native American Literatures.* Ed. Brian Swann. Washington: Smithsonian Institution Press. Pp. 83–124.

1993   In Need of a Wife: Clara Pearson's "Split-His-(Own)-Head." In *American Indian Linguistics and Ethnography in Honor of Laurence C. Thompson.* Ed. Anthony Mattina and Timothy Montler. University of Montana Occasional Publications in Linguistics, vol. 10. Missoula: Univ. of Montana. Pp. 127–62.

1994a Ethnopoetics, Oral-formulaic Theory, and Editing Texts. *Oral Tradition* 9:330–70.

1994b The Sun's Myth. *In Coming to Light.* Ed. Brian Swann. New York: Random House. Pp. 273–85.

Jakobson, Roman.

1960   Concluding Statement: Linguistics and Poetics. In *Style in Language.* Ed. Thomas A. Sebeok. Cambridge, Mass.: MIT Press. Pp. 350–73.

Kendall, Daythal L.

1977a A Syntactic Analysis of Takelma Texts. Ph. D. diss. Univ. of Pennsylvania.

1990   Takelma. In *Northwest Coast.* Ed. Wayne Suttles. Handbook of North American Indians, vol. 7. Washington, D. C.: Smithsonian Institution. Pp. 589–92.

1992   Coyote and Pitch and Coyote Goes Courting. Ms.

Pitkin, Harvey

1985   *Wintu Dictionary.* Univ. of California Publications, Linguistics, 95. Berkley: Univ. of California Press.

Sapir, Edward

1909a *Takelma Texts.* Univ. of Pennsylvania, The Museum, Anthropological Publications 2(1). Philadelphia. See Golla 1990. Cited as T.

1909b *Wishram Texts* American Ethnological Society Publications 2. Leiden: E. J. Brill. See Bright 1990.

1912 The Takelma Language of Southwestern Oregon. In *Handbook of American Indian Languages, Part 2.* Ed. Franz Boas. Bureau of American Ethnology Bulletin 40. Washington: Government Printing Office. Pp. 1–296. Issued separately; the complete Part 2 appeared in 1922. See Golla 1990. Cited as G.

1925 Sound Patterns in Language. *Language* 1:37–51.

Schlichter, Alice

1981a *Wintu Dictionary.* Survey of California and Other Indian Languages, Report no. 2. Berkeley: Department of Linguistics, Univ. of California.

1981b Personal communication, June 25.

Shepherd, Alice [Schlichter]

1989 *Wintu Texts.* Univ. of California Publications, Linguistics, 117. Berkeley: Univ. of California Press.

Shipley, W. F.

1969 Proto-Takelman. *International Journal of American Linguistics* 35:226–30.

T See Sapir 1909.

EXPERIMENTAL FOLKLORE REVISITED

Virginia Hymes

In 1967 Kenneth Goldstein published an article, "Experimental Folklore: Laboratory vs. Field" (1967), in which he told of having had the opportunity, on separate occasions, to hear two sisters, Lucy Stewart and Margaret McKay of Aberdeenshire, Scotland, tell the same story that both had learned from their mother but had never heard the other tell. Finding that the second telling, by the older sister Margaret McKay, had elements not present in Lucy's version, he hit upon the idea for his experiment. He decided first to tape the story from Lucy Stewart and then to arrange with their niece Elizabeth Stewart to start a storytelling session at a family gathering and, if this particular story was not told, to ask her Aunt Margaret to tell it. The family had tape recorders they used often on such occasions so taping was no problem. Goldstein then managed to tape two more tellings of the story by Lucy Stewart. The first was three weeks and the second seven months after her having heard her sister tell it. In the article, Goldstein comments on the changes that take place in the content of Lucy's tellings as a result of hearing her sister's telling.

During the early eighties, when I was teaching a course called "Ways of Speaking" at the University of Pennsylvania, Kenny brought this article to my attention and suggested that I might want to try doing verse analyses of the four versions transcribed as prose in the article, and have the students try their hand at it also.[1] In what follows, I present my verse analyses of the four tellings, three by Lucy Stewart and one by her sister, and make a few comments on their structure. The texts will follow the numbering of Goldstein's article, so the first will be text 3. (Texts one and two in Goldstein's article are given only in outline from field notes.) In presenting my analysis, I have used a convention of indicating the grouping of lines into verses by capitalizing the first word of a verse and having it at the left margin with successive lines indented. Groups of verses (stanzas) are indicated by extra spacing between them. Because some stanzas in these texts have internal organization that also is indicated by spacing (e.g., between pairs of verses in a stanza that has three such pairs), I

have used an asterisk (*) at the left margin above the first line of a stanza to
indicate all stanzas after the first in each text.

Text 3. Lucy Stewart. *Recorded by K. Goldstein on December 28, 1959, before
Lucy had heard her sister tell the story.*[2]

The Brewer and the Devil

Noo this is the story of a brewer who had a four-wheeled lorry
    and went around til his customers.
Sometimes he arrived home very late at night.

*

So there wis one night in partic'lar he wis very late
    and it was dark.
So he was comin on home
    singin til hissel'
        and in a minute he seed a man sittin at the roadside.

So he says to this man, he says,
    "Are ye tired?"
So the man he never spoke.

He says,
    "jump in ower aside me," he says,
        "and I'll give ye a lift."
So just as he says the word,
    the man jumpit fae the roadside
        but when he lookit at the man he had a tail.

*

So the man he was in an awful state.
He seed it was something unearthly.

So he's drivin along
    and tryin to get intae a conversation with him
        but this man never spoke.
And he sat by his side for a couple or three miles
    and yet not a word did he speak.

And the brewer, he was terrified.
He aye lookit doon at the tail.

*

So they came til a bridge.
And when they come to this bridge

the man, he jumpit out of the cart and over the bridge
        and disappeared in a light.
So he saw that he was drivin the Devil.

*

So the man went home
        and he was in a terrible state
            and terrible ill afterwards.

In this analysis the story has a two-verse introduction and a one-verse conclusion with three major stanzas between. The first two of these stanzas have three pairs of verses each, and each ends with the man looking down and seeing that his passenger has a tail. The third main stanza has three verses in which they come to a bridge, the passenger jumps out and disappears in a light, and the brewer sees that he has been driving the devil (who can't cross water). Thus each of the stanzas that constitute the three major parts of the story ends with a hint and finally (in the third) a certainty that the stranger was the devil.

Text 4: Margaret McKay. *Transcribed by K. Goldstein from a tape recording he made on January 3, 1960.*

The Carrier and the Devil

It was once we was out on holidays,
        out at Hatton o' Fintray
            and of course we were there for a week or two.

*

The carrier was comin home at night.
He was goin up to Kinmuck
        at Inverurie
            and he was comin home
                and he was pretty loaded up.
And he was goin on
    and he lookit around to his side and there was a man standin.
He says,
        "Ye'll be tired," he says
        "Come in ower and rest your feet."
He never got no answer,

*

He walkit a bit on
        and he jumpit in on the side of the lorry.
And the two horses stopped.
They couldn't pull.
And he lookit roond tae his side

and he says,
    "You're a queer lad."
He says,
   "Foo are ye?"
      and got no answer.

*

Well, it took that horses aboot two hours tae gang
    about a quarter o' a mile.
The sweat was breakin aff them.

And when he lookit round
    he had a big cloven fit.
And when he come to the top of the water bridge,
    he jumpit off.

The man went home and he never rised.
He dies
    with shock.

After a one-verse introduction, this telling of the story has two five-verse stanzas, each ending with the carrier getting no answer from the stranger. The second of the two stanzas introduces the element of the slowing down of the horses once the stranger is on board. In the third and final stanza, which is composed of three pairs of verses, the first pair enlarges on the slow struggle of the horses, the second gives two more clues that the stranger is the devil: cloven foot and jumping off to avoid crossing water. The final pair of verses describes the carrier's fate: illness and death.

    Now a look at the two tellings by Lucy Stewart after her hearing her sister's version of the story:

Text 5: Lucy Stewart. *Transcribed by K. Goldstein from a tape recording he made on January 27, 1960.*

The Carrier and the Devil

Now this wis a carrier fit went tae Aberdeen every day from this place that ye call Kinmuck
    beside Hatton O' Fintray
        not far fae Hatton O' Fintray and Inverurie.
And one night he'd been comin home terrible late
    and when he wis drivin he lookit at the roadside
        and he saw a man sittin.
And it was very late
    and he thocht the man wis tired

and wid offer him a hirl.
So he says tae the man, he says,
    "are ye wantin a lift?"
So the man he just rose and jumpit up beside him in the front seat.

*

But he noticed when he started to drive the horses
    the horses refused to go.
They widna pull.

So he tried the horses and tried them
    but they wid go a bittie and stoppit.
So he wondered what was a-dee
    and he lookit doon tae the man
        and he seed the man had a cloven fit.

And he spoke a lot tae the man
    but the man never made no answer.
But again he seed he'd a cloven fit.

*

So he tried to get the horses tae go for along the road for about a mile
    and it took him about two hours to get that mile.
So when they come to a bridge not far fae his home,
    the man he got up
        and he disappeared across the bridge in a light.
And when he got up
    he seed he'd also a tail.

*

So he took feart of this
    and when he got home to his wife he was just about fite.
So the wife she says to him,
    "Oh," she says,
        "John, what's ado?"
So he told her like what he'd saw
    and he said he felt very ill and wis wantin his bed.
So the woman she helpit him to lowse the horses and stabilt them,
    put him to bed,
        and she went to make him a cup of tea.
And when she went to give him the cup of tea,
    he wis dead.

This retelling by Lucy Stewart shows the effects of her sister's version in both its length and its structure. The first stanza of five verses gives a lot of details and gets the stranger into the seat beside the carrier. It is followed by a stanza consisting of three pairs of verses, each of which builds up new evidence of the stranger's problematic nature: 1) the horses refuse to start up again after the stranger has jumped in; 2) the horses stop and start, and the man sees the stranger has a cloven foot; and 3) the man can get no response to his talk to the stranger, and again he notices a cloven foot. Now follows a three-verse stanza describing the slow journey to the bridge where the stranger jumps off in a light; almost as an afterthought, the fact that the stranger also has a tail is mentioned in the final verse of this stanza. (Recall how central this had been to Lucy Stewart's text 3.)

The final stanza of this retelling of the story by Lucy—after she heard it told by her sister and was reminded, as she told Goldstein, of things her mother had included in it—has grown both in relation to her own earlier single-verse mention that the carrier went home in a terrible state and was terribly ill afterwards and to her sister's terse two-verse stanza saying he went home, never rose, and died, with shock. It has become five verses (totalling thirteen lines) in which are introduced the carrier's wife, his conversation with her, her offering and bringing him tea, and her finding him dead.

Finally, I present my verse analysis of Goldstein's transcription of his recording of Lucy Stewart's telling of the story seven months later:

Text 6: Lucy Stewart. *Transcribed by K. Goldstein from a tape recording he made on July 19, 1960.*

The Carrier and the Devil

Well,
    once there wis a carrier lived in Aberdeenshire in a place ye call Kinmuck
        a place between Fintray and Aberdeen.
And he went every day to Aberdeen.
He was a carrier and took home his oats every night.

*

So one night he was comin home very late
    about twelve o'clock
        and it was a very bright, moonlight night.
So he wis comin along and singin til hissel'.
He wis comin on a piece o' a steep brae
    and he seed a man sittin at the roadside.

So he thocht til hissel'
    "Oh,
        here is a puir man.
        He wid think it nae harm in giein him a lift."
So,
    when he comes along just across from the man,
        he says,
            "Wid ye like a lift?"

*

So the moment he said that, the man rose from the roadside
    and come toward the lorry
        and jumpit in ower.
So the man he seated hissel' beside the carrier.
But when he seated hissel' beside the carrier,
    the horses refused to go on.

So he thocht this was very funny that the horsed wid nae go on.
That wis never their usual way . . . .
    they never stoppit up for anything before.

*

So he tried and tried but the horses refused to pull.
So he gaed doon
    and he worked aboot a while with the horses til he gae them tae start,
        but they went very, very slow.
They jist went a bit and stoppit aye.

So he lookit doon at the man
    and he seed that the man had a funny shapit foot . . .
        a cloven foot.
So he thocht til hissel'
    "Oh, this is something funny.
     This is something unearthly."

*

So he travelled on an' it took him aboot a oor tae go two mile,
An' when he come to a bridge,
    this man he jumpit doon.
An' when he jumpit doon
    he seed he'd a tail.

So he jumpit doon til the bridge
    and he went up in a blue light and disappeared.
So the man he turned very unwell goin on the road . . .
    he wis just shakin with fear.

*

So when he got home tae the wife,
    the wife she wis oot lookin for him
        and she wondered what kept him so late.
So he said,
    "Oh," he says,
        "ye might lowse the horses."
He says,
    "I gotten a terrible fear."

So he went intae the hoose
    and the woman she lowsed the horses
        and made him some hot tea.
But when she gaed tae the bed
    he wis dead.

After an introductory stanza of three verses, this telling has five stanzas each with five verses. It seems to me, however, that in the first four of these five stanzas there is a pattern of three verses followed by a pair of verses that always includes the carrier's reaction to what precedes in the stanza. In stanzas two, three, and four, this pattern is clearly marked in that the final pair of verses includes one that starts, "So he thocht . . ." ("he" being the carrier). In stanza four, the reaction is one of feeling unwell and shaking with fear, as described in the final verse. The final stanza of five verses can be seen as a full elaboration of the carrier's ultimate reaction to the encounter with the stranger: his death.

    Whether one agrees with this analysis of the first four stanzas of the five main ones, it is clear that this last telling is one in which all the signs of the stranger's unconventionality, and finally his identification as the devil, have been integrated into a well-formed narrative with a consistent pattern of five verses in each stanza after the introductory one. The narrative incorporates all the elements of Lucy's original telling of the story, those she heard from her sister, and the new elements she introduced in the final stanza in Text 5. No element hangs as an afterthought, in the way the stranger's having a tail does in Text 5.

    What verse analysis has done for me in understanding how the two sisters' original tellings differed and how Margaret McKay's version affected her sister Lucy's later tellings is to pinpoint the differences in both content and structure. Working with the texts in this way helped me to see how Lucy Stewart worked her way toward the well-integrated form of the final telling after her earlier, briefer, but also well-formed, narrative had been jarred by the new elements she heard from her sister.

Notes

I want to thank Kenny for all the help and support he gave me in my work on narratives in English in the years at Penn, and to promise him that he'll see more of the results of that help in the near future.

    1. At around the same time, Kenny generously offered me a copy of a tape with four stories by people whom he described as the best Irish, American, British, and Scottish storytellers he had recorded. Those stories, by Joe Heaney, Sarah Cleveland, Ruth Tongue, and Belle Stewart have been worked and reworked over the years and will be used in a volume of verse analyses from a wide variety of narrative traditions that my husband, Dell Hymes, and I are working on. The analyses have the advantage of my being able to listen to the tape and use intonation contours in addition to all the other levels of language and content to arrive at the rhetorical structure of the performance. In the case of the stories from "Experimental Folklore" I have had to work entirely from the prose transcriptions in the article, using

Kenny's punctuation as one guide to how the lines and verses were realized.

2. This verse anaslysis, and the three that follow, are my reworkings of Goldstein's prose transcriptions.

Reference

Goldstein, Kenneth A.
   1967   Experimental Folklore: Laboratory vs. Field. In *Folklore International: Essays in Traditional Literature, Belief and Custom in Honor of Wayland Debs Hand*. Ed. D. K. Wilgus. Hatboro, Pa.: Folklore Associates. Pp. 71–82.

TIMES SQUARE
A Pedestrian Perspective

Barbara Kirshenblatt-Gimblett

WHEN THE Times Building was dedicated on December 31, 1904, it established the building, the location, and the activities that would occur there as a media event. The tallest building in the city at the time and focal point for the ritual of bringing in the new year, the twenty-five-story Times Building was to become a gigantic front page, with an illuminated headline for all to see. The area achieved supreme imageability precisely through the combination of the intersection of Broadway, 7th Avenue, and 42nd Street, which interrupted the regularity of the city's grid and created an open space in an area of heavy traffic, the prominence of the Times Building, the liveliness of activity in the streets, and the highly visible ritual events staged in the area.

This essay explores Times Square as a total environment, shaped in large measure by the occupational subcultures, largely theatrical, whose enterprises Brooks McNamara (1991) has described, and experienced most vividly by walkers in the city. Michel de Certeau (1984), in his discussion of poetic geography, suggests three symbolic mechanisms that relate spatial practices and signifying practices: the believable, the memorable, and the primitive. These practices yield in turn the major topoi of urban discourse in the vernacular—legend, recollection, and dream. These practices and topoi are everywhere evident in the guidebooks, journalistic accounts, and reportage of tourists who have visited Times Square.

Toponomy, Geography, Itinerary

Guidebooks, touristic accounts, and journalistic treatments, even those published during the same period, do not agree on the area designated by Times Square. They disagree on terminology, boundaries, orientation, focal point, itinerary, key sites, and root metaphors. While differences in accounts published during different periods generally reflect actual changes in the area, there is also evidence that even at one point in time Times Square is more than one place, or on occasion, that Times Square is no place. Some accounts of the area where Broadway, 42nd Street, and 7th Avenue intersect do not even mention Times Square by name.[1]

Notions of Times Square are shaped by six fundamental spatial orientations: 42nd Street as the main east-west artery across the center of Manhattan; Broadway as the main north-south artery of Manhattan; the Midtown or the West Side as regions; the X-shaped intersection where Broadway traverses 42nd Street and 7th Avenues; the triangular plaza formed by the northern half of the intersection; and a composite of microregions. These orientations are expressed in the organization of guidebooks, which either devote a separate chapter and map to Times Square or absorb the area into chapters devoted to 42nd Street, Broadway, Midtown, or the West Side.

These orientations are also expressed in root metaphors, literal definitions of the area, and toponymy, as evidenced by the following excerpts from guidebooks and reportage from 1899 to the present dealing with the area in and around the intersection of Broadway, 7th Avenue, and 42nd Street:

Broadway orientation: "Broadway from Thirty-fourth to Forty-seventh Street," "the very heart of the 'Great White Way' [across 42nd Street]" (Jenkins 1911:256, 262); "modern Appian Way," "a savage street," "wickedest street" in America (McIntyre 1924:25, 227, 222); "wicked Broadway" (Josephy and McBride 1931:12); "Gay Gulch," "Glittering Gash," "street of a million lights," "crest of the White Way," "the Stem" (Lait and Mortimer 1948:19, 20, 27); "Times Square occupies a small section of Broadway" (Chiang 1953:48); "in tracing the course of Broadway to the point where it creates Times Square" (Laas 1965:25); "a pinched strip" (Dunford and Holland 1987:113).

42nd Street orientation: "[Forty-Second Street,] considered by New Yorkers as the center of the city and, at its intersection with Broadway, the center of the world," "Sin Street [42nd Street between Seventh and Eighth Avenues]" (Wolfe 1988:276).[2]

Intersection orientation: "the angle formed by the junction of Seventh Avenue and Broadway" (Jenkins 1911:259); "corner of Broadway and 42nd Street . . . center of the hotel district" (Brown 1920:283); "the crossroads carnival" (Lait and Mortimer 1948:28); "Crossroads of the World" (Laas 1965; Wright 1983:248); an "X-shaped intersection" (Shepard and Drechsler-Marx 1988:71; see also Zeisloft 1899:490).

Midtown or West Side region orientation: "region of theaters, and hotels and restaurants of the best class," "Uptown Rialto" (Zeisloft 1899:487, 628); "theatre district," "hotel district" (Brown 1920:283); "White Light District" (Worden 1932:34); "Times Square District," "Times Square Theatre District" (Guild Committee [*WPA Guide*] 1982 [1939]:167, 168); "the theatrical and hotel area" (Burpee 1939:3); "Rialto of the western world" (Lait and Mortimer 1948:26); "theatrical district" (Nagel 1954:30).

Plaza orientation: "wide plaza formed [by X-shaped intersection] is known by the name of Longacre Square" (Zeisloft 1899:490); "triangular block between Broadway and Seventh Avenue" (Jenkins 1911:262); "a sort of town commons," "in its prime, a plaza [where different classes met]" (Shepard and Drechsler-Marx 1988:73). The very name Times *Square* suggests the plaza orientation, even though the area is actually triangular in shape.

Composite of microregions: Tenderloin, Furious or Roaring or Upper Forties, the Canyon, Dream Street, Duffy Square, Tin Pan Alley, Swing Alley, Hell's Kitchen, Little Athens, Paddy's Market, Shubert Alley, cafeland, West 42nd Street (between 7th and 8th Avenues), Garment District, automobile row, Chelsea.

Various combinations of these microregions form various larger wholes—Midtown, West Side, the Times Square District, the theatre district, and so on. The issue is not simply a matter of "internal differentiation," which suggests both the prior existence of a larger whole and an analytic rather than pedestrian perspective. There is also the juxtaposition, agglomeration, or coalescence of microregions that exist in relation to each other but may or may not be perceived by city inhabitants as subsets of a larger urban district. Itineraries, not just mass transit but also pedestrian, are crucial in shaping these perceptions, for walkers are, in their way, cartographers. Their paths define areas.

So too does toponymy. The name of a street may be strongly associated with a relatively small segment of its totality, the case with both 42nd Street and Broadway (less so with 7th Avenue). As Henry Miller writes in *Tropic of Capricorn:*

> It's only a stretch of a few blocks from Times Square to Fiftieth Street, and when one says Broadway that's all that's really meant and it's really nothing, just a chicken run and a lousy one at that, but even at seven in the evening when everyone's rushing for a table there's a sort of electric crackle in the air and your hair stands on end like an antennae and if you're receptive you not only get every bash and flicker but you get the statistical itch, the quid pro quo of the interactive, interstitial, ectoplasmic quantum of bodies jostling in space like the stars which compose the Milky Way, only this is the Gay White Way, the top of the world with no roof and not even a crack or a hole under your feet to fall through and say it's a lie. The absolute impersonality of it brings you to a pitch of warm human delirium which makes you run forward like a blind nag and wag your delirious ears. (Cited by Dunford and Holland 1987:114)

As the meaning of a street name narrows to refer to a small section of its entirety, the application of the name—Broadway, for example—may also expand to designate a larger region or a set of activities, no matter where they are found.[3] This obviously is also the case with the designation Times Square itself, as numerous guide books explain. There also arises an elision of terms:

Cohan's shows and songs were to help make "Broadway" synonymous with Times Square. There would be no question which quarter-mile he had in mind in *Forty Five Minutes from Broadway,* "The Man Who Owns Broadway," "Too Many Miles from Old Broadway," or in "I Long for the Hustle-Bustle of Hurly-Burly Lane, Where Midnight Is as Noisy as Midday." (Laas 1965:41)

Even as theatre in the area atrophied, the Times Square area continued to be presented as the "theatrical center of America" (Guild Committee [*WPA Guide*] 1982 [1939]:167) and "the Rialto of the western world" (Lait and Mortimer 1948:26). By 1964, long after the decline of legitimate theatre, Frances Diane Robotti asked: "So what is there to keep the Times Square area from being just Coney Island without an ocean? The theater." (Robotti 1964:42)

Guidebooks from 1899 to the present use spatial metaphors such as river and tributaries, stem, trunk, buds, offshoots, branches, feeders, tentacles, heart, hub, and outposts, all of which suggest a walker's way of thinking about the Times Square/Broadway area. These terms suggest paths through space, experienced on the ground as a series of partialities, rather than as the outer boundaries of a region visually apprehended in its totality from the air. In contrast, the 1939 *WPA Guide to New York City* characterized Times Square as "an outer shell of bars and restaurants, electric signs, movie palaces, taxi dance halls, cabarets, chop suey palaces, and side shows of every description [that] covers [sic] the central streets" (1982:167). The image of "outer shell" signals a significant shift in how the environment is experienced. Building facades in earlier accounts are generally characterized as enticements and entrances into interior spaces, often a regressive series of public spaces from the street to the lobby, vestibule, corridor, dining room or theatre, and the activities within them. The "outer shell" image makes ambiguous the location of the interior: is it inside the buildings or inside the square? In contrast with the many centrifugal metaphors of paths through a space or of itineraries with specified sites of interest, "outer shell" is an image of centripetal containment. It captures vividly the extent to which Times Square as an outdoor environment had coalesced as an experience in its own right, possibly even superseding its indoor commercial entertainments as an attraction.[4] It also anticipates the recent proposal for a 24-hour, six-level mall that would "recreate Times Square where Times Square once stood." Times Square itself would be brought indoors as a "distillate" of itself, through a process that converts a district into a thematic environment under the banner of urban redevelopment (Dullap 1989).

Accounts also vary in their identification of where the "center," "hub," or "heart" of the area is: Broadway north of 42nd Street (Jenkins 1911:262), corner of 42nd and Broadway (Brown 1920:283), Times Square proper (Guild Committee [*WPA Guide*] 1982 [1939]:170; Chiang 1953:48ff), Duffy Square (Robotti 1964:41), Shubert Alley (Nagel 1954:30), Roaring Forties (Laas 1965:42).[5] Such variations are consequential for they suggest different conceptions of the region. These difference are in part a function of the various occupational subcultures in the area.

With firsthand knowledge as a professional journalist, William Laas writes in 1965:

> Today, by extension, the Times Square district or "Broadway beat" of the columnists embraces a rectangle with the crossroads at its center. It ranges from about 40th Street to 56th Street, south to north, and to a little beyond Sixth and Eighth Avenues east to west. That is, from the Metropolitan Opera to Carnegie Hall, and from Rockefeller Center to Madison Square Garden. But Times Square itself is the trunk of the tree from where the lifesap flows, the heart of the heartland. Its buds and offshoots may not reach beyond a brisk walk or a quick whisk by taxi. (Laas 1965:42)

This account delineates but one of multiple "maps" of the area that could be drawn, according to occupational subculture: the boundaries of the area are defined by institutions significant to the reporter's beat. Indeed, the "fly-beat" is itself a tourist attraction in unorthodox guides to the city: Helen Worden's *The Real New York: A Guide for the Adventurous Shopper, the Exploratory Eater, and the Know-It-All Sightseer Who Ain't Seen Nothin' Yet,* in a chapter entitled "After Midnight," features "the fly-beat" and "the tenderloin station-house" (1932:53–54). The intrepid adventurer is encouraged to visit the hide-away headquarters of reporters covering the midtown area, which was located in the basement of a brownstone tenement at 342 West 47th Street. Right across the road was the 47th Street Police-Station:

> At one time it had the busiest blotter in town. If you are lucky, you may strike a crowded hour. Tell the sergeant that you would like to take a look at some of the old cells and have your finger-prints made, just to see how it is done. All of the policemen assigned to this station know the history of it. Get them to tell you some of the stories. (Worden 1932:53–54)

Just as the reporters delineate their beat, so too do the police precinct and the post office: the zip code area designated Times Square extends from Fifth Avenue to the Hudson River, and from 41st to 48th Streets (or from 42nd Street between 5th and 6th Avenues).

Within each of these "precincts," there are highly charged sites that take on the quality of microworlds unto themselves, with their own lingo, customs, and legends. One of the most famous examples is the Algonquin Hotel in the twenties, scene of the social gatherings of theatrical and literary celebrities who exchanged witticisms and played poker. Their coteries, which came to be known as the Round Table and the Thanatopsis Literary and Inside Straight Club, developed distinctive practices: "Various traditions, customs, and observances grew up around the [poker] table, one of the most popular being the practice of signalizing a flagrantly misplayed hand by all rising and intoning to the strains of the 'Englishman' song from *Pinafore:* 'He remains a god-dam fool'" (Adams 1945:126). In an example of what might be termed urban narcissism, such microworlds were both inhabited and reported on by journalists and writers. In the columns of the city's newspapers, journalists reported on each others' witticisms at the Algonquin; the reporter Alexander Woollcott even wrote a Sunday special on the gatherings.

To convey the completeness and power of this world, some used the idiom of monarchy: "In its days of richest glory, Broadway's crown jewels were its masters of stage production; their thrones were its theatres where their works reigned" (Lait and Mortimer 1948:16). Others spoke in terms of religion, pilgrimage, and mecca: "The crowded hagiology of Times Square is a unique one. To be held in sacred memory on Broadway two requirements must be filled: one must be a great success, and the act of the success must be known to all people, everywhere (well, almost everywhere) . . . . Here are just a few of the saints and shrines of bygone Broadway." (Robotti 1964:42). There follows a list of impresarios, talent, writers, songwriters, shows, institutions, places and things, and scandals. Such accounts contribute to the canonization of Times Square.

As metaphors of monarchy and enshrinement suggest, a major attraction of the area, even as a theatre district, has long been the occupational subcultures of the entertainment industry itself, the chance to see celebrities and the places they habituated—bars and restaurants, residential hotels, and the sidewalks. By night, the crowds flowing out of the theatres after the curtain came down and the places they and theatre people frequented after the show were one attraction. By day, some of the earliest accounts note that members of the theatrical profession thronged the streets—"The best and the worst of it is to be met here—stars, supers, soubrettes, specialists, and managers alike," and their presence on the streets was an attraction in itself (Zeisloft 1899:487). A decade later, Stephen Jenkins, a member of the Westchester Historical Society, reported that "in the 'off' season, the sidewalks are crowded with actors and actresses seeking engagements" (Jenkins 1911:256). Astute observers mapped out their exact locations and the sequence of their appearance in what Oscar Odd McIntyre (1924:218) called the "White Way's passing pageant" and the *WPA Guide* (Guild Committee 1982 [1939]:167) "a permanent moralizing tableau."

There developed a language specific to the occupational subcultures themselves. According to *New York: Confidential!*, billed as an off-the-record, unorthodox guide to New York based on the authors' observation and experience:

> Tin Pan Alley has its own glossary. All songs are "numbers." Love songs, mother songs, anything romantic, are "ballads"—a remote adaptation of the original word. All songs of regret and revenge and love's bitter grief are "torches." All crazy songs, which make no sense, are "freaks." All crazy songs which make some sense are "novelties." War songs are "flag wavers." All songs about the south are "Dixies." (Lait and Mortimer 1948:31)

There also developed a distinctive language for talking about this world, a language that changed over time. In McIntyre's 1924 account, *White Light Nights,* there are gold diggers, known as Dumb Doras by the "hardened habitue's of that half-world of the Tenderloin" and as "O.M.D's—Old Men's Darlings" farther uptown. There are sugar papas, stage door Johns, square shooters, saps, and dupes of various kinds, including "a group of illuminati known colloquially as 'The Poor Fish Club'. . . . The members are those who have been hooked through the gills" (McIntyre 1924:183–87).

Theatrical metaphors, an old and well established topos for social life, abound in descriptions of Times Square, Broadway, and the theatre district more generally, which are variously characterized as a comedy or tragedy, the "White Way's passing pageant" (McIntyre 1924:218), a "permanent moralizing tableau" (Guild Committee [*WPA Guide*] 1982 [1939]:167), and "the greatest free show on earth" (Laas 1965:72). The richness of public behavior, the ebb and flow of thronging crowds, the sheer variety of people, the highly distinctive local characters and types, glamorous celebrities and notorious criminals, were the protagonists in the drama of the streets.[6] Tragedy and comedy were visible in the district's occupational subculture, in "the extremes of success and failure characteristic of Broadway's spectacular professions: gangsters and racketeers, panhandlers and derelicts, youthful stage stars and aging burlesque comedians, world heavyweight champions and one-acclaimed beggars" (Guild Committee [*WPA Guide*] 1982 [1939]:167). The volatility of the theatre professions was exacerbated by the Depression. Numerous accounts of the area, particularly from the twenties on, consist of melodramatic vignettes of the rise and fall of the district's characters. Duplicitousness, seduction, blackmail, and con games brought acting into everyday life. Broadway, anthropomorphized, is also the protagonist in a grand drama: after the death of Bert Savoy, a popular female impersonator in vaudeville, the *New York Times* reported that "Broadway heard and went home early to bed" (McIntyre 1924:231).

Such accounts created moral landscapes and itineraries of the Times Square area. Writing about aspiring theatre people, McIntyre notes the volatility of the industry: "The pauper of today is the prince of tomorrow. And the prince of today may be the pauper of tomorrow. Tin Pan Alley sings truly of this modern Appian Way as a lane of smiles and tears, a highball and a headache, a rose with thorny stems" (McIntyre 1924:25). Ladies of the evening, many of whom once aspired to a stage career, "swing off into the primrose path, the path Tin Pan Alley lyricizes as leading to Potter's Field," while others plunge into the "whirlpool—the cafes, the night life and dawn parties," only to end up "flushed with the life that glows like a dead, rotting phosphorescent fish along the White Way" (McIntyre 1924:185, 226) Others were undone by drugs, a story that is also mapped onto the street:

It was the ancient story along the Phosphorescent Path—youth, beauty and joyous health, the triple combination upon which Broadway feeds. First the cocktail. Then the champagne and wild nights of revelry.
In the end—a twitching, hollow-eyed wreck. Cocaine. But she came back!

Her regeneration was complete and today she is Broadway's "Little White Sister"—to whom the bruised and the beaten go for comfort. . . . Her past is a Broadway symbol of hope. What other street would so elevate its fallen? (McIntyre 1924:250)

New York: Confidential!, which characterizes the area as a place where "the Lord and the Devil work side by side," maps the accomplishments of each, specifying the precise locations of speakeasies, gangland killings, dope peddlers, reefer kiosks, and hookers—block by block, corner by corner (Lait and Mortimer 1948:16).

Such accounts also created memory maps, itineraries of what no longer existed but was remembered: "you feel the grandness of the 1890s meeting the already dated glitter of the 1980s. . . . Here, the new is a brash overlay on the old heart of the theatre district, and only a sentimentalist could despise it" (Dunford and Holland 1987:113). The imminence of change, and the possible disappearance of Times Square, and for that matter Manhattan, as one knows and loves it, is a theme that appears quite early. Stephen Jenkins's 1911 account of Broadway, *The Greatest Street in the World: The Story of Broadway, Old and New, from the Bowling Green to Albany,* describes the dismay of store-keepers and theatres on Broadway above 23rd Street during the first decade of this century, when the Rialto moved north. He remarks of the "very heart of the 'Great White Way'," which he locates on the north side of the intersection of Broadway and 42nd Street, that "Hotels, theatres, and restaurants abound, and the owners and purchasers of property seem to be imbued with a perfect mania for tearing down and rebuilding" (Jenkins 1911:262). He then forecasts the future location of the Great White Way during our own time:

Perhaps, at the end of this century, the "Great White Way" will be as quiet and colorless as is now the section of Broadway below Fourteenth Street, while the gay populace of that future time will find its pleasures in the neighborhood of Kingsbridge. This seems to be the law of the street. When that day comes, Manhattan Island will have lost the greater part of its population and will be devoted almost entirely to business; while the enormous mass of people will live in the suburbs of Westchester County, of New Jersey, and of Long Island, carried daily to and from their occupations at rates of speed now undreamed of, and by means of transit which exist at present only in the dreams of visionaries. (Jenkins 1911:256–58)

Jenkins is not the only one to express the fear that Manhattan would be depopulated, or that the rapid transit system would have this effect. Published for the Bowman Hotels, *The Sidewalks of New York* (1923) extolls the well-dressed throngs of Wall Street and Times Square as the place for "amusements," the "vivid presentation of the immigration problem" to be seen on the Lower East Side and the chance to observe "vividly those dangerous elements that make for crime . . . in the notorious Gas House District" or a "real" Hungarian wedding on East Houston or Italian saint's feast on Mulberry Street. The book then expresses the fear that all this is about to vanish:

It is not inconceivable that the time is coming, when New York will lose this flavor. There may be a time, not many generations hence, when Manhattan Island, the stage of all the city's romantic history, may be just a commercial center,—a business island to which her peoples commute. The ever increasing network of underground tunnels, layers upon layers of tubes, subways, vehicular tunnels,—as well as additional bridges and elevated lines, may ultimately unpeople the island! Business rents are so enormous that apartment seekers can not bear the competition. (Kielty 1923:12–13)

Providing statistics to document the decline in Manhattan's population, Kielty exhorts the reader: "So the time is ripe now to see the drama of New York! It is in transition; it is full of variety and contrasts" (Kielty 1923:13). This is a classic touristic (and ethnographic) trope, the need to see and inscribe a site on the threshold of its disappearance, thereby producing an anticipatory memory map. Predictions as to what will change determine what must therefore be experienced now and banked for future memories.

Changes specifically in the Times Square area in the twenties were detailed by McIntyre, who noted that when he returned to Broadway after being away only two months, "there is almost a different Broadway"—Chinese eateries have opened near the Winter Garden, four tiny shops have sprouted near the Automat, three revues have appeared in cellars on 47th Street, Freeman's cafe, near the Palace Theatre, changed its name to Gertner's; Nat Lewis's haberdashery and Benny and Ma's tailoring place expanded; and Eddie and Jimmie's cafe was doing a brisk trade after only one month in business (McIntyre 1924:222–23). Citing Prohibition as the cause, he declares that "The map of cafeland is entirely changed," and notes the disappearance of fancy restaurants and appearance of "rapid-fire lunches, chain coffee-shops and pastry parlors" along upper Broadway (McIntyre 1924:191). McIntyre concludes: "There are a hundred and one other changes along the rollicking old street. They are symbolic of Broadway's shifting modes. Even the newsies have changed their pace. They used to cry their morning editions and racing forms at ten o'clock; they now cry them lustily at eight" (McIntyre 1924:23).

These accounts of change and the apprehension they precipitated indicate that mass transit not only brought people to the area, they also took them away. Nor were these the same people, for it was the suburbanite and excursionist who came to visit and the local resident who left for good. Subways are described as "disgorging" their passengers at Times Square (Lait and Mortimer 1948:34), an image that reaches an apotheosis of sorts in the *AIA Guide to New York*'s characterization of the Port Authority Bus Terminal as "the city's vomitory for commuter and long-distance buses" (White and Willensky 1978:138).

The Times Square area, particularly in terms of Broadway and the theatre district, thus became an "overdetermined sign," one that carried a multitude of meanings, amplified over time by the accumulation of memories, images, and metaphors. While the area was compared favorably with

Paris—the "grand orgy" of New Year's eve in Times Square rivals "the wildest capers of the Moulin Rouge, Maxim's, and other notorious places in Paris" (Jenkins 1911:269), others argued that Broadway's uniqueness precluded comparison (McIntyre 1924:217). Imperialized, 42nd Street is "considered by New Yorkers as the center of the city and, at its intersection with Broadway, the center of the world" (Wolfe 1988:273)—in other words, as a point of orientation. Etherialized, "Broadway is a "state of mind" (Lait and Mortimer 1948:16), "a definite part of the national consciousness" (McIntyre 1924:25), "not a street but a condition" (Lait and Mortimer 1948:25). That condition is further specified as insomnia ("The Square Never Sleeps" [Laas 1965:7]), "a private dream publicly shared" (Laas 1965:17), intoxication, delirium, and a "form of dementia" (McIntyre 1924:227; Miller, quoted by Dunford and Holland 1987:114; Lait and Mortimer 1948:16)—in other words, as a point of *dis*orientation.

There is an iconographic reciprocity between the part and the whole: the Times Square area is the quintessence of New York—"Eventually Broadway runs into TIMES SQUARE, a pinched strip that in its excess and brashness is a distillation of the city itself" (Dunford and Holland 1987:113), while the entire city is sometimes characterized as Times Square writ large. In some accounts, New York is even defined by Broadway. If not for Broadway, New York would be indistinguishable from any other city with factories, a seaport, and railroad: "The difference is still Broadway. There is only one!" (Lait and Mortimer 1948:16).

McNamara (1991) argues that by the thirties Times Square had been transformed from a "theatre district" to an "entertainment environment." "Theatre district" implies not only the presence of actual theatres, but also their supporting institutions—costume houses, clubs and professional organizations, trade papers, boarding houses, hotels, and restaurants. McNamara carefully documents the decline of legitimate theatre by the thirties, arguing that though theatre was no longer the primary form of entertainment in the Times Square area, it remained its "signature activity." This transformation, which brought cheaper amusements and amenities, tarnished the area's former gentility while creating a lively and more diversified entertainment environment akin to an amusement park. Statements from the thirties characterize Times Square as a Coney Island without the Ferris wheel, noting many of the same kinds of barkers, hawkers, fortune tellers, refreshments, amusements, and ambiance. Several factors are implicated in this transformation, including Prohibition and the Depression.

The theatre thus helped to define the Times Square area, not only by virtue of its prominent physical presence and the vividness of its subculture, but also though the memory of that presence long after the area had changed. What distinguished Times Square, even after it lost many of the legitimate theatres, from Coney Island, to which it was compared, was the presence and memory of the theatre. That memory was strongly shaped by representations of Broadway as a theatrical district on the stage and in song, as well as in journalism, tourism, literature, and film.[7]

Time, Space, and Ritual

Times Square is also defined in terms of time, as a place that is awake twenty-four hours a day and particularly lively at night. At the turn of the century, E. Idell Zeisloft explained: "The life of the street is as active at midnight as at noon, for the theaters create a constant patronage for the restaurants, which are crowded up to the early hours of the morning" (Zeisloft 1899:487). This was to change during the twenties, as places to go after the theatre closed earlier and the tone of the area declined. Referring to the grand displays of electrical lighting, commentators on the area noted that the night was more brightly illuminated than the day. In the neighborhood that never slept, life proceeded in shifts. Various Times Squares were on a rotation around the clock as the crowd and its activities moved through an established cycle.

The continuous twenty-four-hour round, inversion of night and day over-rode circadian rhythms set in other parts of the city by sun and moon. The sensory overload of milling crowds, dazzling light, rushing traffic, myriad enticements, spontaneity and surprise, sharp contrasts, the thrill of celebrity, scandal, and danger, and the quick pace of life created a vertiginous, intoxicating, disorienting effect.[8] Describing his experience of Times Square after World War II, Chiang Yee notes:

> The many restaurants and eating stores appear always to be full, and there seem to be no definite times for meals; one eats when one feels like it. I found this had its advantages but disturbed my sense of the time of the day.... I looked up and down and round about, and peeped through windows and round corners. My eyes were never still.... To Americans, street phenomena are commonplace. To me they were like things out of Baron Munchausen.... Sometimes, after dusk, Times Square reminded me of some big exhibition such as I had seen at Olympia in London before the war, the stands of the exhibition vying with each other in the brilliance of their illumination.... I became quite blind after watching them for a while and would find myself bumping into people. I saw this happening to others too, but the crowds were good-natured and no one seemed to mind. (Chiang 1953:50, 53–55)

Comparisons of Times Square to a carnival, shifting kaleidoscope, amusement park, exposition, Coney Island, frontier town, and midway all suggest the dizzying effects of the stimulus saturated environment. The language of chaos, bedlam, orgy, wild capers, a form of dementia, and allusions to Rabelais, Boccaccio, and Baron Munchausen evoke the prodigious, grotesque, wondrous, and incomprehensible qualities of the Times Square experience. They also invoke moral ambiguity of transgression, the danger of disorder, the blurred line between carnival and crime.

The area was characterized in terms of carnival as early as 1899 by Zeisloft, who wrote of Broadway in his day as holding "its farewell carnival at Forty-second Street," the blocks to the north being "humdrum" (Zeisloft

1899:490). Elsewhere, he characterizes the midtown area as showing "the life and carnival of New York" in contrast with the characterlessness of modest residential blocks, dismal and dreary poor areas, and streets that display nothing but a "commercial aspect" (1899:628). By noting the areas that "do not lend themselves to description" and sometimes noting why, Zeisloft suggests the contours of an urban picturesque, one that requires "enough action and elegance to make them [streets] celebrated in the annals of the town," "color in the streets to attract the eye," "novelty," movement of crowds and vehicles, "fashionable traffic," distinctive characteristics, architectural interest, and strange contrasts (1899:628ff). Despite the many changes in the area by 1939, the *WPA Guide to New York City* still compared Times Square to large town carnivals, and characterized the area more specifically in terms of the midway of amusement parks.

The carnivalesque potential of the area is realized most dramatically when large crowds gather for events such as New Year's eve, the announcement of election results, the announcement of the end of a war, and the inauguration of a marathon race. The first New Year's eve celebration at the Times Building was marked with flares that spelled out 1905, extravagant fireworks, music specially composed for the occasion, and noisemaking. By the time 1908 was welcomed in, the fireworks, now illegal, had been supplanted by an electrically illuminated ball, five feet in diameter:

> At ten minutes to midnight, the whistles on every boiler in Manhattan, the Bronx, Brooklyn, and the waters thereof began to screech. Tens of thousands stood watching the electric ball. And then—it fell. The great shout that went up drowned out the whistles for a minute. (*New York Times* January 1, 1908)

The whistles continued to screech until they finally ran out of steam by a quarter past one. Visible throughout the city and boroughs, the Times Building established itself as the timekeeper of the city, outshining the church bells that served that function, and because it was visible over so great a distance, the Times Square festivities coordinated people and their celebrations on a scale and with a precision unprecedented in New York. By the 1930s, the Times Building had been overshadowed by its neighbors.

With the advent of television in the fifties, the event again achieved even greater visibility, making the Times Building the timekeeper and town square for the nation. While more and more people celebrated New Year's eve by watching the festivities in Times Square on television in their homes and local bars, Californians had the bizarre experience of seeing the ball drop in New York before the new year had arrived in California. The *New York Times* (January 10, 1981) reported that Californians were demoralized by the televising of this pre-emptive event. They had been dislocated both spatially and temporally (see Becker 1983).

Time and space are organized in Times Square to produce a zone of perpetual carnival—first as a theatre district, then as an entertainment region. With the hard realities of the area's continued decline exacerbated by a series of economic recessions in New York City during the 1970s and 1980s, the enshrinement of Times Square in memory is propelling its redevelopment in practice. The area's eventual demise was anticipated during the early years of this century, when the advent of rapid transit and surburbanization fueled fears that Manhattan itself would be depopulated. What might be called anticipatory memory, a sense of what would be lost and ought to be enshrined, has helped to ensure than an image of Times Square, fashioned in the course of this century, will continue to figure in the definition of New York. If Times Square during its heyday served as a distillation of the city (Dunford and Holland 1987:113), a concern in today's redevelopment of the area is somehow to distill Times Square itself—in a facade, a mall, an exhibition of what it was—for the memory of what was is preferable to the sight of what is. A new Times Square is rising like a phoenix from the ashes of the old one. Walkers of the city have their work cut out for them.

Notes

This paper was first presented on the panel "The Life of a Place: Performance and Pleasure" at the conference "Inventing Times Square: Commerce and Culture at the Crossroads of the World, 1880-1990," organized by the New York Institute for the Humanities at New York University on February 3, 1989. I would like to thank Minda Novak, who located most of the guidebooks that served as the basis for this paper.

1. McIntyre (1924) writes about Longacre Square, not Times Square. Burpee's *The Book of Trips* (1939:3) states: "From Forty-second to Fifty-third Street is the theatrical and hotel area, with Hell's Kitchen to the west. That name comes from the tough gangs which made the section their hangout in the olden days," but neglects to mention either Times Square or Broadway. *Flashmaps!*, first published in 1969 and appearing in revised forms ever since, omits Times Square from its map of Manhattan neighborhoods, though it does include Theater District, Midtown, Garment District, Lower West Side, and Chelsea (Lasker 1982). Times Square per se does not figure prominently in Botkin's *New York City Folklore* (1956), though many selections deal with places and events that occurred in the district.

2. Wolfe includes Times Square as part of a walking tour of 42nd Street.

3. "Those portions of the New York scene which, not physically on the street known as Broadway [in the Times Square area], are so intimately connected with it that in the idiom of the city they are referred to as 'Broadway'" (Lait and Mortimer 1948:36). Other examples include enterprises such as 47th Street Photo, which retains its name no matter where it is located.

4. The ground-level perspective of verbal accounts contrast sharply with visual iconography—the bird's-eye view of maps and panoramic views of picture postcards.

5. "To a sailor, the Roaring Forties are the latitudes in the Atlantic Ocean where the winds howl and the waves get rough. But to a New Yorker, the Forties are the numbered streets from 40th to 49th and their 'roaring' is the pulsebeat of Times Square." (Laas 1965:42)

6. In years to come, behind-the-scenes tours of theatres would also become popular.

7. Times Square is not only a tourist attraction in its own right, but has long been the departure point for bus tours of the city.

8. Discussing tourism in the Times Square area, Gilbert Millstein quotes a sociologist who was running a night club for a living: "New Yorkers are perpetually drunk—not with whisky, but with motion—with subways, buses, cabs" (Millstein 1956:57).

References

Adams, Samuel Hopkins
  1945   *A. Woollcott, His Life and His World.* New York: Reynal and Hitchcock.
Becker, Bonnie L.
  1983   *Days of Auld Lang Syne: A Look at Times Square on New Year's Eve.* Unpublished paper, New York University.
Botkin, B. A., ed.
  1956   *New York City Folklore: Legends, Tall Tales, Anecdotes, Stories, Sagas, Heroes and Characters, Customs, Traditions, and Sayings.* New York: Random House.
Brown, Henry Collins
  1920   *Valentine's City of New York: A Guide Book.* New York: Valentine's Manual.
Burpee, Royal H.
  1939   *The Book of Trips.* New York: Association Press.
Certeau, Michel de
  1984   *The Practice of Everyday Life.* Trans. by Steven F. Rendall. Berkeley: Univ. of California Press.
Chiang, Yee
  1953   *The Silent Traveller in New York.* New York: John Day.
Dunford, Martin and Jack Holland
  1987   *The Rough Guide to New York.* London: Routledge and Kegan Paul.
Dunlap, David W.
  1989   Mall to Evoke Memories of Times Square. *New York Times,* February 24. B3.
Guild's Committee for Federal Writer's Publications, Inc.
  1982 [1939]   *The WPA Guide to New York City.* Rpt. ed. New York: Pantheon Books.
Hotel Association of New York City
  1919   *Official Metropolitan Guide.* New York: Hotel Association of New York. May 4, 1919.
Jenkins, Stephen
  1911   *The Greatest Street in the World: The Story of Broadway, Old and New, from the Bowling Green to Albany.* New York and London: G. P. Putnam's Sons.
Josephy, Helen and Mary Margaret McBride
  1931   *New York is Everybody's Town.* New York and London: G. P. Putnam's Sons.
Kielty, Bernardine
  1923   *The Sidewalks of New York.* New York: Little Leather Company, published by the Bowman Hotels.
Laas, William
  1965   *Crossroads of the World: The Story of Times Square.* New York: Popular Library.
Lait, Jack and Lee Mortimer
  1948   *New York: Confidential!* Chicago: Ziff-Davis Publishing Co.
Lasker, Tony
  1982   *Flashmaps! Instant Guide to New York.* Rev. ed. Chappaqua, N.Y.: Flashmaps Publications.
Lynch, Kevin
  1960   *The Image of the City.* Cambridge, Mass.: M.I.T. Press.
MacCannell, Dean
  1976   *The Tourist: A New Theory of the Leisure Class.* New York: Schocken.

McIntyre, Oscar Odd
1924   *White Night Lights.* New York: Cosmopolitan Book Corp.

McNamera, Brooks
1991   The Entertainment District at the End of the 1930s. In *Inventing Times Square: Commerce and Culture at the Crossroads of the World.* Ed. William R. Taylor. New York: Russell Sage Foundation. Pp. 178–90.

Miller, Henry
1961   *Tropic of Capricorn.* New York: Grove Press.

Millstein, Gilbert
1956   Night Life: Brash, Bubbly and Boppy, Out-of-Towners are Known to Night Clubs by Their Recklessness and Their Teeth. *New York Times Magazine,* April 29. Section 6, Part 2: 56–57, 69.

Nagel Publishers
1954   *Nagel's Travel Guide to New York.* Paris: Nagel.

Robotti, Frances Diane
1964   *Key to New York: Empire City.* New York: Fountainhead.

Shepard, Richard F. and Carin Drechsler-Marx
1988   *Broadway from the Battery to the Bronx.* New York: Harry N. Abrams.

White, Norval and Elliot Willensky
1978   *AIA Guide to New York City.* Rev. ed. New York: Collier.

Wolfe, Gerard R.
1988   *New York: A Guide to the Metropolis, Walking Tours of Architecture and History.* Rev. ed. New York: McGraw-Hill.

Worden, Helen
1932   *The Real New York: A Guide for the Adventurous Shopper, the Exploratory Easter, and the Know-It-All Sightseer Who Ain't Seen Nothin' Yet.* Indianapolis: Bobbs-Merrill.

Wright, Carol von Pressentin
1983   *Blue Guide New York.* London: A and C Black.

Zeisloft, E. Idell, ed.
[1899] *The New Metropolis: 1600-Memorable Events of Three Centuries; 1900— From the Island of Mana-hat-ta to Greater New York at the Close of the Nineteenth Century.* New York: Appleton.

IT'S ABOUT TIME—OR IS IT?

Four Stories of/in Transformation

Margaret A. Mills

THE RECYCLING of theoretical and methodological concerns in folklore studies, as in other disciplines, is, we hope, not circular but helical. In recent years, the comparatist impulse has not been very prominent in American folklore studies, somewhat cast in the shade by the often more particularistic or localistic interests of performance-centered studies. The broad-ranging collecting efforts that best support comparatism may also have seemed to lack an immediate goal beyond their own obvious joys. Thus Dundes (1989:57–82) could bewail the lack of substantive findings in purely taxonomic motif- and type-indices. If text-comparatism is inevitably to reassert itself (Finnegan 1992:31), however, we can hope that it will do so by incorporating contributions of performance-oriented studies toward the understanding of text production. Dundes (1989:63) calls us to account for any failure to consider possible comparative dimensions cross-culturally: "It is always an error to analyze a folktale (or any other folkloristic item) as if it were unique to a given cultural context, when it is obviously not so." Conversely, however, one ought not to ignore cultural particularities that help make individual texts, in Lévi-Strauss's now-legendary phrase, "good to think with" in particular situations. Indeed, some basic theoretical schemata for pursuing the integration of taxonomic and contextual studies have been in place for some time (Ben-Amos 1972, 1976).

Yet the new dimensions of the comparatist task, however elegantly schematized, are not easily realized, mainly because performance-based studies have demonstrated to us the necessity of including in taxonomies information on appropriate use: what a "text" "is" depends on its contexts of generation, use (whether "performance" or not), and interpretation. Likewise, indigenous interpretations can be seen to have micro or macro effects on the morphology of a narrative (Hymes 1981:Ch. 3, 8; Mills 1981, 1991). The recognition of emic genres challenges us to integrate comparative *generics* and comparative (emic) *interpretation* into our cross-cultural studies of any given array of material, however we select it. It is in this light that one might seek to answer Dundes's basic question (1989:57), "What is the nature of the unit being compared?" In the discussion of stories that follows, the "nature of the unit" is one of the things that varies across cultures: a small assemblage of very similar narratives surveyed across cultures operates across oral and literary channels, and across genres that might be designated "myth," "parable," "legend," or "lie," as well. Three of the four examples discussed below are literary retellings, which to varying extent come prepackaged with interpretations that shed light on critical components of each telling, at least in the eyes of those responsible for the present entextualizations. Ultimately debatable are the "boundaries of the text" (Flueckiger and Sears 1991), even when the comparative task chosen appears to beg the question of the comparability of the "unit."

The foregoing is all by way of excuse for juxtaposing here four narrative texts from diverse sources, closely related by the typological standards of the historical-geographical method, but of very diverse provenance and application.[1] All are stories worth telling on their own, but perhaps still more so in the reflective light of a comparative exercise. I have used this particular cluster of stories for some time in my undergraduate courses on myth, to try to open up for students the basic questions of what myth "is" and what narrative might be "for." The array of stories also challenges any categorical polarization of "literary" and "oral" genres. The point concerning genres is a basic one, here presented for a general audience, but the particulars of possible comparison, combining issues of morphology and interpretation, continue to open up to me in complicated ways.

Possibly the oldest of the written versions of these stories, and most exotic to a European audience in its interpretive dimensions, is actually two, both of which are attributed to the Sanskrit Puranas, verse treatises on Hindu myth, ritual, and cosmology that are variously dated from the 4th to the 16th centuries C.E. The Puranas, of which there are eighteen, are extensive collections of narratives, descriptive and prescriptive texts, meant for reading aloud and study by religious devotees, and cast as conversations between a *rishi* (enlightened teacher) and one or more disciples, within which other conversations, especially ones between deities or enlightened beings and human seekers, are also reported. The literary mode thus invokes oral dialogue. One of the stories, which Zimmer (1946:27) attributes to the *Matsya Purana,* goes like this:[2]

> A group of holy men had gathered around the venerable hermit, Vyāsa, in his forest-solitude. "You understand the divine eternal order," they had said to him, "therefore, unveil to us the secret of Vishnu's Māyā."
>
> "Who can comprehend the Māyā of the Highest God, except himself? Vishnu's Māyā lays its spell on us all. Vishnu's Māyā is our collective dream. I can only recite to you a tale, coming down from the

days of yore, of how this Māyā in a specific, singularly instructive instance worked its effect."

The visitors were eager to hear. Vyāsa began:

"Once upon a time, there lived a young prince, Kāmadamana, 'Tamer of Desires,' who, conducting himself in accordance with the spirit of his name, spent his life practicing the sternest of ascetic austerities. But his father, wishing him to marry, addressed him on a certain occasion in the following words: 'Kāmadamana, my son, what is the matter with you? Why do you not take to yourself a wife? Marriage brings the fulfillment of all of a man's desires and the attainment of perfect happiness. Women are the very root of happiness and well-being. Therefore, go, my dear son, and marry.'

"The youth remained silent, out of respect for his father. But when the king then insisted and repeatedly urged him, Kāmadamana replied, 'Dear father, I adhere to the line of conduct designated by my name. The divine power of Vishnu, which sustains and holds enmeshed both ourselves and everything in the world, has been revealed to me.'

"The royal father paused only a moment to reconsider the case, and then adroitly shifted his argument from the appeal of personal pleasure to that of duty. A man should marry, he declared, to beget offspring—so that his ancestral spirits in the realm of the fathers should not lack the food-offerings of descendants and decline into indescribable misery and despair.

"'My dear parent,' said the youth, 'I have passed through lives by the thousand. I have suffered death and old age many hundreds of times. I have known union with wives, and bereavement. I have existed as grass and as shrubs, as creepers and as trees. I have moved among cattle and the beasts of prey. Many hundreds of times have I been a brahmin, a woman, a man. I have shared in the bliss of Shiva's celestial mansions; I have lived among the immortals. Indeed there is no variety even of superhuman being whose form I have not more than once assumed: I have been a demon, a goblin, a guardian of the earthly treasures; I have been a spirit of the river-waters; I have been a celestial damsel; I have been also a king among the demon-serpents. Every time the cosmos dissolved to be re-absorbed in the formless essence of the Divine, I vanished, too; and when the universe then evolved again, I too reentered into existence, to live through another series of rebirths. Again and again have I fallen victim to the delusion of existence—and ever through the taking of a wife.

"'Let me recount to you,' the youth continued, 'something that occurred to me during my next to last incarnation. My name during that existence was Sutapas, "Whose Austerities Are Good"; I was an ascetic. And my fervent devotion to Vishnu, the Lord of the Universe, won for me his grace. Delighted by my fulfillment of many vows, he appeared before my bodily eyes, seated on Garuda, the celestial bird. "I grant you a boon," he said. "Whatever you wish, it shall be yours."

"'To the Lord of the Universe I made reply: "If you are pleased with me, let me comprehend your Māyā."

"'"What should you do with a comprehension of my Māyā?" the god responded, "I will grant, rather, abundance of life, fulfillment of your social duties and tasks, all riches, health, and pleasure, and heroic sons."

"'"That," said I, "and precisely that, is what I desire to be rid of and to pass beyond."

"'The God went on: "No one can comprehend my Māyā. No one has ever comprehended it. There will never be anyone capable of penetrating its secret. Long, long ago, there lived a godlike holy seer, Nārada by name, and he was a direct son of the god Br_hma himself, full of fervent devotion to me. Like you, he merited my grace, and I appeared before him, just as I am appearing now to you. I granted him a boon, and he uttered the wish that you have uttered. Then, though I warned him not to inquire further into the secret of my Māyā, he insisted, just like you. And I said to him: 'Plunge into yonder water, and you shall experience the secret of my Māyā.' Nārada dived into the pond. He emerged again—in the shape of a girl.

"'"Nārada stepped out of the water as Sushilā, 'The Virtuous One,' the daughter of the king of Benares. And presently, when she was in the prime of her youth, her father bestowed her in marriage on the son of the neighboring king of Vidarbha. The holy seer and ascetic, in the form of a girl, fully experienced the delights of love. In due time, then, the old king Vidarbha died, and Sushilā's husband succeeded to the throne. The beautiful queen had many sons and grandsons, and was incomparably happy.

"'"However, in the long course of time, a feud broke out between Sushilā's husband and her father, and this developed presently into a furious war. In a single mighty battle many of her sons and grandsons, her father and her husband all were slain. And when she learned of the holocaust she proceeded in sorrow from the capital to the battlefield, there to lift a solemn lament. And she ordered a gigantic funeral pyre and placed upon it the dead bodies of her relatives, her brothers, sons, nephews, and grandsons, and then, side by side, the bodies of her husband and her father. With her own hand she laid torch to the pyre, and when the flames were mounting cried aloud, 'My son, my son!' and when the flames were roaring, threw herself into the conflagration. The blaze became immediately cool and clear; the pyre became a pond. And amidst the waters Sushilā found herself—but again as the holy Nārada. And the God Vishnu, holding the saint by the hand, was leading him out of the crystal pool.

"'"After the god and the saint had come to the shore, Vishnu asked with an equivocal smile: 'Who is this son whose death you are bewailing?' Nārada stood confounded and ashamed. The god continued: 'This is the semblance of my Māyā, woeful, somber, accursed. Not the lotus-born Brāhma, nor any other of the gods, Indra, nor even Shiva, can fathom its depthless depth. Why or how should you know this inscrutable?'

""""Nārada prayed that he should be granted perfect faith and devotion, and the grace to remember this experience for all time to come. Furthermore, he asked that the pond into which he had entered, as into a source of initiation, should become a holy place of pilgrimage, its water—thanks to the everlasting secret presence therein of the god who had entered to lead forth the saint from the magic depth—endowed with the power to wash away all sin. Vishnu granted the pious wishes and forthwith, on the instant, disappeared, withdrawing to his cosmic abode in the Milky Ocean."

""""I have told you this tale," concluded Vishnu, before he withdrew likewise from the ascetic, Sutapas, "in order to teach you that the secret of my Māyā is inscrutable and not to be known. If you so desire, you too may plunge into the water, and you will know why this is so."

"Whereupon Sutapas (or Prince Kāmadamana in his next to last incarnation) dived into the water of the pond. Like Nārada he emerged as a girl, and was thus enwrapped in the fabric of another life."

We can note here that the language is clearly Zimmer's, not that of a Purana, judging from the inclusion of numerous explanatory and descriptive details that would be superfluous to a Hindu audience, and indeed seem foreign in comparison to the language of various Puranas, even in translation. The tone of this telling is extensively explanatory and somewhat novelistic, in the way that it is, in order to accommodate non-Hindu European readers toward an understanding of what Zimmer believes to be essential Hindu concepts. It would be most appropriate to see this text, even as we acknowledge the antiquity of its sources, as a twentieth-century literary performance by a European scholar for an audience not part of the community of believers for which the story was framed in the Puranas. By that token, it carries with it a good deal of interpretive baggage, of which we will shortly make some use.

In the meantime, however, let us look at the next version of the story, also from a Hindu context, this time from the published *Sayings of Sri Ramakrishna,* a well-known Bengali saint and religious teacher of the nineteenth century. His teaching technique was entirely non-literate, sometimes even non-verbal; the written *Sayings* were compiled and organized from transcriptions by his disciples. The introduction to the volume cautions that the actual stories and observations were occasioned by all sorts of situations, written down in bits and pieces, and have been stripped of their immediate contexts of utterance in an effort to organize them somewhat according to topic. The story in question is taken from the standard English translation, in the 6th revised edition (Madras 1943), Book 4, Ch. 22, "Parables," No. 1110 (p. 384):

Maya is unknowable. Once Narada besought the Lord of the universe, "Lord, show me that Maya of Thine which can make the impossible possible." The Lord nodded assent. Subsequently the Lord one day set out on a travel with Narada. After going some distance, He felt very thirsty and fatigued. So He sat down and told Narada, "Narada, I feel much thirsty [sic]; please get me a little water from somewhere." Narada at once ran in search of water.

Finding no water nearby, he went far from the place and saw a river at a great distance. When he approached the river, he saw a most charming young lady sitting there, and was at once captivated by her beauty. As soon as Narada went near her, she began to address him in sweet words, and ere long, both fell in love with each other. Narada then married her, and settled down as a householder. In course of time he had a number of children by her. And while he was thus living happily with his wife and children, there came a pestilence in the country. Death began to collect its toll from every place. Then Narada proposed to abandon the place and go away somewhere else. His wife acceded to it, and they both came out of their house leading their children by the hand. But no sooner did they come to the bridge to cross the river than there came a terrible flood, and in the rush of water, all their children were swept away one after another, and at last the wife too was drowned. Overwhelmed with grief at his bereavement, Narada sat down on the bank and began to weep piteously. Just then the Lord appeared before him, saying, "O Narada, where is the water? and why are you weeping?" The sight of the Lord startled the sage, and then he understood everything. He exclaimed, "Lord, my obeisance to Thee and my obeisance also to Thy wonderful Maya!"[3]

While Narayan (1990) gives us an extended portrait of another Hindu guru's actual use of narrative in the give-and-take of ashram teaching, by which we can partly infer the contextual dynamics which might have conditioned the telling of a story such as this by Sri Ramakrishna, its presentation in the collected *Sayings* provides a minimal exegetical context: It is set in a section called "Parables," and begins, "Maya is unknowable"; we are left to infer that someone has asked, or that one may, perhaps should, ask such a question as, "How can we know Maya?" even if the answer can only be indirect. Zimmer's Purana story, indeed, offers a more elaborate framing of exactly the same question and answer, arranged in a Chinese-box of nested narratives. The very nesting of these personal-experience narratives, these lives, one inside the other, in fact adds a rhetorical dimension to the attempt to convey the illimitable, transcendent Reality through limited life experience. (I am assuming here that while Zimmer has probably tinkered considerably with the texture of a text he found in the Puranas, he has not in fact supplied the gross structure of this multiple narrative.)

A short discussion of the concept of *Māyā*, for present purposes, develops out of our interest in variant tellings of this story. *Māyā*, a female noun, may be translated as "illusion" and indeed refers to a female conceptualization of the experienced world as illusory, because transitory. The *Māyā* of a god is that divine power by which a god can create things which seem to humans to be absolutely real, but are, from the point of view of the god, dreams or illusions.

Vishnu, the High God who sustains the created universe, is the supreme purveyor of *Māyā;* in the deepest sense, his dreams are our realities. Thus the ascetics in these stories, Narada and Sutapas, are asking to see the world of which they are created component parts, from the point of view of the Creator. One might say, the mirror wants to see itself.

Nor is the particularity of gender roles in these Hindu narratives incidental or subconscious. *Māyā* in some religious discussions is personified as a female character. From the point of view of the (male) ascetic, who is struggling to transcend the emotional snares of daily life in order to assimilate his own consciousness with that of the Divine, emotional attachment to the world is the greatest threat to that effort, and its most seductive form is female. (Anger and greed run close behind lust in screwing up the chances of would-be renouncers.) Sri Ramakrishna's biographers emphasize that it was at the point that he offered *puja* (worship) to his own (virgin) wife as the incarnation of the Mother Goddess, perfect in loving devotion but devoid of all carnality, that he arrived definitively at the status of spiritual guide to others (Sri Ramakrishna 1943:9-10).

By the same token, becoming a female, becoming engrossed in conjugal love as a male, or becoming a householder (i.e. a husband and father, a clearly defined spiritual category, prior and inferior to that of ascetic world-renouncer in Hindu thought) are transformations of equivalent significance; in either case, the specificity of gender is a radical impediment to spiritual transcendence. When one tries, from the vantage point of a particular, conditional existence, to understand the whole of Reality, the closest one can get is to understand (a) the conditional, particular nature of (b) predicaments that seem absolutely real and tragic, while they are going on, especially the aftermath of love and procreation. Hence Vishnu tries to accommodate the ascetics' search for unconditional Knowledge by radically manipulating their immediate conditions, to show them the nature of attachment by first-hand experience of disjunction. The direct experience of finite time and mortality is essential to the power of this message. One can generalize, cautiously, about Hindu time concepts (a huge topic) by saying that time as we experience it in the world, as a commodity whose passing matters, is the quintessential experience of *Māyā* (illusion). God's time is eternally out of our reach; the crucial moments of our lives disappear into the hugeness of cosmic time.

Eliade (1969:70), drawing in part on these same stories as purveyed by Zimmer, discusses in some detail the "terror of time" as he sees it in its particular Hindu form, in deriving a general model of the nature of time in myth. For Eliade, these narratives are mythic because of the way they address the problem of time. More generally, these stories are of sacred matters: Nārada himself is regarded as semi-divine by Hindus, and the Purana narratives in general are stories of avatars, of gods manifesting themselves in bodily form, complete with particular qualities (such as Vishnu's thirst in Sri Ramakrishna's story: gods can get thirsty when they are being avatars). As to the genre of these stories, truth value may be considered to distinguish parables from myths (as allegories from historical reports), but the ascription of such value may have to be left to specific audiences' interpretations. Truth value might best be conceived as not either/or, true or false, but as a series of options within each culture and/or rhetoric, investigatable within and across traditions, but not ascribable without such investigation. Interpretation thus affects typology, and interpretation is an emic affair of different audiences, especially different communities of believers whose very notions of the nature of reality may be at odds with one another. (In *Māyā*, perhaps all narrative is fiction just as all experience is illusion.)

With the issue of communities of believers and qualities of belief in mind, let us look at the next version of this story, which I ran across in an eighteenth-century C.E. Chinese version of the life of Muhammad (Liu 1921), written by Liu Chai-Lien, "the most noted author among the Moslems of China," as he is described by his translator, the early twentieth-century Christian missionary Isaac Mason. Mason in his introduction points out that many elements of the Chinese biography of the Prophet do not appear in the canonical *Sirat Rasulullah* (*Biography of the Prophet*) by his Arabic-language biographers, Ibn Ishaq and Ibn Hisham.[4] The story under discussion is one such added element. It reads as follows (Liu 1921:124–26):

> **Ascent to Heaven.**—In the twelfth year of the Prophetship, as the Prophet was one night staying at the home of his paternal aunt, in the middle of the night he heard sounds in space, and supposing that a revelation was coming he quickly arose and sat in fear while Gabriel, with innumerable angels, came at the command of God bringing a precious vase of water of the immortals, and garments, headcovering and shoes which were put on the Prophet; then an immortal steed came and the Prophet was called to mount and ascend to heaven, which he did from the mount Merwa, Gabriel leading and all the spirits following; he ascended to the ninth heaven and on the way saw many wonderful things and met all the former prophets and worthies and kings; then he passed on into the absolute sphere to the presence of God and there heard His wonderful instruction, and then all the mysteries of all time, and all principles and all matters, were made known to him. On his return he told his disciples about this experience, and at the time there was a Jew sitting there who did not believe that in such a short space of time he had travelled so far and seen so many things; this man had a strange experience on going home where he told his wife to cook some fish while he went to get water from the stream, and there he was transformed into a beautiful *woman* [emphasis in original], and the grandson of a king came there hunting and took the pretty woman to his home where she remained seven years and bore sons and daughters; then she remembered her previous state and was changed back into the original form of a man and was by the side of the stream with the water-carrying utensil, and on returning to the house his wife was still cooking the fish which was not yet sufficiently done; he marvelled at this and went to tell the Prophet who was still in the mosque

telling of his ascent, and who called out saying: "Here is so and so who has been away and has returned, let him tell us his experiences in order to satisfy any doubt." The Jew was very much alarmed that the Prophet should know that he had cherished doubts, so he confessed before all what he had seen, and repented of his sin of doubts and entered the Faith. It is one thousand years since the ascent, but there still remains a suspended stone from which the Prophet mounted the horse, as a proof of the event.

Besides the topic of a reversible sex change mediated by God for the enlightenment of a human, one can see correspondences of other themes and elements between the Muslim and the Hindu tellings of this tale. Divine Time and the human experience of time are central in all three tales. Water is also a basic element in all three transformations. While Zimmer (1946:34–52) develops an extended discussion of the cosmic ocean, and Vishnu's place upon it, in connection with this story, tracing the symbolic elaboration of water in transformative events in Hindu tales, water is such a common feature in transformations, especially transformations from one life or world to another, in narrative traditions world-wide, that one must see the particularly extensive development of the concept of the ocean in Hindu cosmology as enlarging philosophically and cosmologically upon an extremely widely shared concept. In this Muslim variant, two kinds of water are present: the "water of the immortals" supplied, presumably, for the Prophet to make ablutions before he puts on the divinely provided clothing for his ascent to heaven, and of course the water source at which the skeptic experiences his transformations. They are not explicitly connected, and need not be: water is ritually transformative in Muslim ablutions in general, and in this miraculous case, physically transformative as well.

Time, while it is central to the revelation purveyed, seems also somewhat off to the side in this Muslim tale, compared to its central significance in the Hindu stories. The skeptic, hearing the Prophet's narrative of the Night Journey (an extremely important and famous revelation, comprising Surah 17 of the Qur'an), is said to doubt specifically "that in such a short space of time he could have travelled so far and seen so many things." The skeptic's subsequent transformation demonstrates to him that God can, at will, fit seven years of human time, together with all its personal attachments, into less than the time it takes to cook some fish for lunch.[5] Thus the point here seems to be that Divine intervention can expand human time to accommodate revelation: compare the Hindu case where the revelation itself consists in seeing human time shrink to the vanishing point in the eyes of God.

Similarly, while Islam lacks an explicit ideological construction of femaleness as the embodiment of illusion in the manner of Hinduism (the Prophet specifically excluded celibacy from appropriate spiritual behavior, saying "No monkery in Islam!"), yet women are legally defined as less reliable witnesses than men, such that two female witnesses are required for every male witness at law. In the story, the Jew's credibility as a witness is established by his stepping in and out of female status; had he appeared at the mosque in female form, claiming to be the Jew that everyone knew, one wonders about the rhetorical effect. A transcendence of particular temporal states is certainly implied by the Muslim legend, but the messages about human time and Divine time are quite different in the finite, linear world of revealed, millennial religion (Judeo-Christian-Islamic) from those of the Hindu world of infinite return, of eternal, unimaginably huge cycles.

As to the question of genre, the Chinese Muslim narrative has been fitted out with a *sine qua non* of sacred legend, the token: at the end of the story, Liu cites the continuing existence of the Suspended Stone "one thousand years [after] the ascent," as evidence of its truth. Nārada's sacred pool, consecrated as a pilgrimage site (in Zimmer's Purana story), may similarly serve believing listeners as a physical token (experienced or reported) that ties the story's events firmly to this concrete world, moves it from parable-truth-value to legend- or myth-truth-value.[6]

And so onward to our final example, resisting the temptation for voluminous further commentary. As authority for this last text I can only claim my own memory, both as to its form and setting. I heard this story performed by a Scots-language storyteller at a concert performance at the August 1979 meeting of the International Society for Folk Narrative Research, in Edinburgh, Scotland. Unfortunately her name is lost to me, and what I have to offer is my own retelling from memory of a story she entitled "The Biggest Lie." To wit:

> There was a laird who used to entertain his crofters every year at a banquet at Christmas time, and one year, by way of variety, he announced that everyone who came would have to tell a story for their dinner, with a prize for the best story. That was all fine and good except for one poor, simple soul, who showed up but protested that he didn't know a single tale to tell. The laird, in exasperation, said to him, "Well, then, let's see you make yourself a little useful at least—go down to the shore and bail my boat that's lying there full of water."
>
> The poor man went down to the boat, and finding a bailing can in it, got in and started to bail. No sooner had he got into the boat, though, than it began sliding down the shore at great speed and launched itself, with him in it, and headed out to sea. It drifted into the night, and eventually he fell asleep exhausted, only to be awakened by the sound of the boat grounding on a strange beach in the early light of morning.
>
> He got out of the boat, and found to his amazement that he had been transformed into a young woman. (S)he hadn't been sitting there long, wondering what to do, when along came the laird of that country, riding along the beach on his horse, and he took pity on the stranded woman and took her home to look after. In due time, seeing that she was an attractive woman and modest, and he was single, he married her and they lived together happily for some years, having children.
>
> One day the two of them happened to be riding again on the shore, and the wife saw the little boat, now lying half ruined and full of water, and

said, "I owe all my happiness and good fortune to that little boat. Let me just get down and bail it a little to keep it from rotting away."

As soon as she got in the boat and began to bail, the boat took off again down the beach, and drifted out to sea again, and next morning, the man found himself once again on his old laird's beach, transformed back into his old crofter self. Astounded, he ran up to the great house, where all the lights were lit and the Christmas feast was still in progress. He shouted at the top of his voice, "You'll never believe what has happened to me—the most amazing thing!" and quickly told about the boat and his transformation and his years' absence. When he had finished, the laird said, "Congratulations! That's the biggest lie that's been told here tonight!" and handed him a purse of gold as his prize.

Despite the obvious secularization of the tale, I think it is clear enough that the core event of transformation and revelation is still in place. But now the revelation, the "lack to be supplied" (in Propp's terms), is not of knowledge of transcendent truth, but of a story, of "The Biggest Lie." I suppose it would be fair, on a general level, to point out that there are agenda differences among Hindu mystics, Muslim missionaries, and Scots Protestant storytellers, but I think too one can go a little further, here, and consider how the "poetics of context," if one can use that phrase, push the secularization of this tale or make its secularism particularly appropriate. The illusion/reality riddle in this story is played out as a joke about would-be virtuoso performers and their supposedly aficionado audiences: the performance was framed as entertainment by someone who was a professional fiction-monger, a storyteller, for an audience of professional skeptics, if you will, academic folklorists. What a joke on us if the "best lie" is actually a miraculous truth! It seems particularly delicious in this performance context that the crofter's audience could only see his extraordinary experience, real enough to him, as a virtuoso fictional performance, as "The Biggest Lie." This is *Māyā* of a particularly Presbyterian sort, perhaps, that excludes miraculous experience from the "real world" but permits and celebrates it as a particularly human form of illusion-making—or does it? After all, we are asked to take the story from the viewpoint of the crofter.

Yet the absence of the element of Divine instruction does make the suffering of the crofter different in implication from that of the other heroes. In the Hindu stories, suffering is very centrally part of the point: the hero's sense of bereavement when deprived of his (her) newly-acquired family demonstrates the entangling effects of *Māyā* and is to be resisted and transcended. In the Muslim story, we get no indication of how the returned skeptic felt about the royal family (s)he bore only to leave behind: perhaps this was just an illusion sent by God, to demonstrate the power of revelation, and not a "real" family at all. The skeptic's reported feelings are of shame for having doubted the reality not of his own experience, but of the Prophet's. In the Scottish tale, perhaps there is a thinly-veiled message about class: the poor crofter feels him(her)self to be better off female, as the beloved wife of a wealthy laird, and is in the process of celebrating that happiness when rudely transported back to his regular life. One can compare here the conditionality and relative untrustworthiness of female experience (even elite female experience, as in the other two sex-change stories) in the Hindu and Muslim tales, respectively: knowing the other two stories perhaps causes one to hear of the crofter's delight in his (elite) female status with a more ironic ear, but this may well be importing extraneous interpretation to this performance, obscuring for us the possibility of a statement about class as a more significant differentiator than gender.

Once returned, the crofter is rewarded but not believed. The audience is left to decide which condition was preferable, as well as what was real. The openness of this question in the Scots tale among other things perhaps serves the sensibilities of a female narrator; I cannot speak for my (female) source, but it certainly appeals to me. No doubt a Hindu ascetic would say that my preference for openness and uncertainty concerning illusions has to do with the fact that I am female and relatively unenlightened.

Without belaboring these four texts unduly, I think a short consideration of their sources, their didactic purposes (insofar as their textual settings reveal that), and the contexts of their dissemination considerably enriches any study of their morphology. Present evidence is far too thin to try to argue lines of transmission, though it seems somewhat likely that the sex-change legend was added to the biography of Muhammad under some kind of Indian influence. According to Annemarie Schimmel (personal communication), the earliest appearance of this tale of the Prophet in Muslim writings may be in the poetry of Amir Khusrau of Delhi (b. 651 H./1253 C.E., d. 725 H./1325 C.E.), an extremely important figure in the Chishti Sufi mystical order, which itself was a major force in Islamic missionary efforts in North India and in the rise of vernacular Muslim poetry on the subcontinent (Schimmel 1975:350). This was a time when whole literary collections of Indian stories were being done into Persian and recast according to Indo-Muslim sensibilities (Schimmel 1988:410). It seems reasonable that the story could have found its way into the Muslim writings of western China from the Subcontinent.

The oral history of the tale is, however, a huge blank. It is important to remember that transmission in writing, from one authoritative source to another, may give added credence to such a story, but oral tradition alone is more than enough to give it currency. And didactic literature in both Hindu and Muslim contexts is intended for oral propagation, in any case: literacy remained (as it did in Europe down to early modern times) for centuries the province of the few, who took it on themselves to interpret for the many through reading aloud in settings that we have yet to research fully. Oral materials were also freely taken up by the literate, for didactic or other purposes. Thus any attempt to differentiate between oral and literary paths of transmission, before mass literacy, seems quite misguided. While the literary antiquity of this tale in Europe would be very interesting to know, our ignorance of it does not render the modern, secular tale irrelevant for comparison to the Hindu and Muslim religious entextualizations. What we have in these examples are not four points establishing a line, but four configurations which, in good dialectic fashion, allow us to consider in part what they are not (formally and interpretively), and what they are, in the light they reflect on one another, as well as whatever light their contexts of performance and/or entextualized framing may supply. In conclusion, it hardly seems necessary that "cultural relativism" must "ultimately insist that each separate and distinct culture is a noncomparable monad" (Dundes 1989:71). Comparatism with a not-too-prescriptive focus (e.g., neither Freudian nor nationalist nor classical Marxist) can aspire to a reasonably relativist scope and leave its participants with open rather than closed texts, as well.

Notes

1. As clearly as these texts seem to be related tales, they do not receive the status of "tale type" in any of the several type indices I have consulted. They do so consistently cluster a similar array of recognized motifs, however, that I think they deserve that status.

2. Zimmer's text does not appear in the English translation of the *Matsya Purana* available to me *(Matsya Puranam* 1916, 2 vol.). Either this translation is incomplete, or Zimmer was working with another variant of the Sanskrit text (there is variation in different editions from this complex manuscript tradition) or his reference to this Purana, which is not specific, was in error.

3. A comparison of this 1943 text to Zimmer's quotation of it (Zimmer 1946:32–34) from the 1938 Madras edition (not presently at my disposal), reveals two variants with systematically different detail, perhaps an indication of the Sri Ramakrishna Math's editorial activities, but more likely establishing both this and Zimmer's *Matsya Purana* quotation, above, as free retellings.

4. Ibn Ishaq's original formulation of the official biography, dating from the early second century of the Muslim era (9th C. C.E.), survives in Ibn Hisham's edition, completed at the end of that century. I worked from a standard English translation by Guillaume (Ibn Ishaq 1955).

5. The fact that it is fish on the menu also connects in various possibly subconscious ways with the transformative power of water; fish are life symbols both in Hinduism and in Judeo-Christian-Muslim tradition, in quite different formulations. The Islamic legend of the close brush with the waters of immortality experienced by Alexander the Great and/or the Prophet Khidr, prominently features cooked fish that come to life, but is beyond the scope of the present discussion.

6. Muslims themselves make a clear distinction between scripture as the direct word of God (the Qur'an) and trustworthy human documents, such as the Prophet's collected sayings and doings (the *Hadith* and *Sunna* respectively) or his canonical biography, for which editorial standards matter. Whether those Chinese Muslim clergy who were fluent in Arabic might have been able to compare Liu's narrative with that of Ibn Ishaq, and what might have been their procedures for reconciling or interpreting the differences between them, is a topic for research rather than speculation.

References

Aarne, Antti, and Stith Thompson
    1961 *The Types of the Folktale.* 2nd rev. ed. Helsinki: Suomalainen Tiedeakatemi.

Ben-Amos, Dan
  1972   Toward a Definition of Folklore in Context. In *Toward New Perspectives in Folklore*. Eds. Americo Paredes and Richard Bauman. Austin: Univ. of Texas Press. Pp. 3–15.
  1976   Analytic Categories and Ethnic Genres. In *Folklore Genres*. Ed. Dan Ben-Amos. Austin: Univ. of Texas Press.
Dundes, Alan
  1989   The Anthropologist and the Comparative Method in Folklore. In *Folklore Matters*. Knoxville: Univ. of Tennessee Press.
Eliade, Mircea
  1969   *Images and Symbols*. Trans. P. Mairet. New York: Sheed and Ward.
Finnegan, Ruth
  1992   *Oral Traditions and the Verbal Arts*. London and New York: Routledge.
Flueckiger, Joyce B., and Laurie Sears, eds.
  1991   *Boundaries of the Text*. Ann Arbor: Michigan Center for South and Southeast Asia.
Hymes, Dell
  1981   *"In Vain I Tried to Tell You."* Philadelphia: Univ. of Pennsylvania Press.
Ibn Ishaq
  1955   *The Life of Mohammed* (Sirat Rasulullah). Translated by A. Guillaume. New York: Oxford Univ. Press.
Liu Chai-Lien
  1921   *The Arabian Prophet*. Trans. Isaac Mason. Shanghai: Swarthmore Press/Fleming H. Revell Co.
Matsya Puranam
  1916   The translation by "A Taluqdar of Oudh." 2 vols. Allahabad, India: Sudhindra Natha Vasu/Indian Press.
Mills, Margaret A.
  1981   The Lion and the Leopard. In *ARV: Scandinavian Yearbook of Folk-lore*. Pp. 53–60.
  1991   *Rhetorics and Politics in Afghan Traditional Storytelling*. Philadelphia: Univ. of Pennsylvania Press.
Narayan, Kirin
  1990   *Storytellers, Saints and Scoundrels*. Philadelphia: Univ. of Pennsylvania Press.
Pickthall, M. M.
  n.d.   *The Meaning of the Glorious Qur'an*. Karachi: Taj Co. Ltd.
Ramakrishna, Sri
  1943   *Sayings of Sri Ramakrishna*. Mylapore, Madras, India: Sri Ramakrishna Math.
Schimmel, Annemarie
  1975   *Mystical Dimensions of Islam*. Chapel Hill: Univ. of North Carolina Press.
  1982   *As Through a Veil: Mystical Poetry in Islam*. New York: Columbia Univ. Press.
  1988   Persian Poetry in the Indo-Pakistani Subcontinent. In *Persian Literature*. Ed. E. Yarshater. New York: Persian Heritage Foundation. Pp. 405–21.
Thompson, Stith, and Warren E. Roberts
  1960   *The Types of Indic Oral Tales*. Helsinki: Suomalainen Tiedeakatemi.
Zimmer, Heinrich
  1946   *Myths and Symbols in Indian Art*. New York: Pantheon.

INCREASE MATHER'S
ILLUSTRIOUS PROVIDENCES

The First American Folklore Collection

Peter Narváez

INCREASE MATHER'S *An Essay for the Recording of Illustrious Providences*, an assemblage of personal experience narratives and local legends initially printed in 1684, should be considered the first published American folklore collection.[1] One might question whether the texts presented in Mather's collection constitute authentic "American folklore" rather than "folklore in America" (see Dorson 1978; Stern and Bronner 1980), especially since, as John Demos has noted, most seventeenth century New England residents thought of themselves as "transplanted Englishmen, as carriers of *the* culture to a distant land" (1972:1). It may be argued, however, that the narratives displayed in *Illustrious Providences* are early forms of "American folklore" for they represent not only cultural transplantation but the unique *experiences* of immigrants in a strange place (see Jones 1982). While these expressions exhibit a continuity of European traditions, they also communicate the ideas, concerns, and anxieties of colonists coping with the American environment. In producing this work, Mather (1639–1723), one of the leading Puritan theocrats of his time, proceeded as would a folklorist of today: he employed a conceptual approach for his collecting project; he faithfully garnered accurate texts from living informants as well as from other fieldworkers who also strove for truthfulness in transcribing their informants' oral accounts; and he carefully prepared a typology and analysis of his collected materials.

Illustrious Providences has not always received sympathetic treatment from the pens of American historians and literary critics, however. In keeping with the view first set forth by Robert Calef in his scathing criticism of Increase Mather and his son Cotton for the part they allegedly played in reviving fears of witchcraft, many scholars have viewed *Illustrious Providences* as the spark that ignited the Salem witchcraft conflagration of 1691–92 (Calef 1823). Accordingly, Edward Eggleston portrayed it as "a store-house of those dragons' teeth that bore such ample fruit in 1692" (1959:30). Vernon Louis Parrington wrote, "the emphasis laid upon witchcraft was an unfortunate if unconsidered influence in preparing the psychology of New England for the Salem outbreak" (1927:107). Harvey Wish claimed that the essay was an "incendiary" influence that lit "fires of fear" (1950:42). One work has claimed that *Illustrious Providences* "read with wide-eyed interest throughout New England . . . planted the seeds of later hysteria" (Gaer and Siegel 1964:90). Notwithstanding his knowledge of the superb work of George Lyman Kittredge in illuminating the pervasiveness of witchcraft belief in England and America in the seventeenth century, Samuel Eliot Morison asserted that *Illustrious Providences* "begins the history of the Salem witchcraft delusion" (Kittredge 1929; Morison 1956:256). Carol F. Karlsen has similarly emphasized the witchcraft connection, characterizing Mather's book as a "lengthy defense of the existence of apparitions, witches, diabolical possessions, and other 'Remarkable judgments upon noted sinners'" (1987:33).

On the positive side, Demos has maintained that "for evident human interest, for richness of detail, for all they reveal about the intersection of character and culture," accounts of providences such as those published in *Illustrious Providences* "are unsurpassed among extant materials from the seventeenth century" (1982:99). With regard to folkloristics, the significance of the publication for the discipline was noted in 1925 by Mather's biographer, Kenneth B. Murdock: "Few of its pages can be dull to the . . . student of folklore. There is, moreover, much good story telling, and always a certain sharpness and directness in the recital of facts" (1925:176).

With the important exceptions of Richard M. Dorson and Deborah D. Carey, American folklorists have largely ignored Murdock's cue (Dorson 1959a; Dorson 1959b; Dorson 1966; Dorson 1973; Carey 1963). This discussion will bolster Dorson's and Carey's endeavors through assessing Mather's *Illustrious Providences* as a scholarly folklore publication. Moreover, in evaluating the work as the first American folklore collection, it will be demonstrated that criticisms such as those of Eggleston and Wish are unfounded in that Mather's selective presentation of oral traditions stresses the godly in New England life and de-emphasizes the diabolical.

The Doctrinal Basis

As is the case with all first-rate collectors of folklore, Increase Mather had a clear purpose in mind before he began gathering and classifying oral materials. In the broadest sense his intent was to apply in a positive and practical manner the Puritan doctrine of "special providences." First developed in the publications of Puritan divines in England, notably William Perkins and John Preston (Miller 1961:228), this doctrine found American expression in Urian Oakes's *The Sovereign Efficacy of Divine Providence* (1682) and in Increase Mather's

The Doctrine of Divine Providence Opened and Applyed (1684) (Oakes 1963; Mather 1684). The basic premise of the doctrine was the Calvinistic conception of the complete omnipotence of the deity, that "the God of Heaven has an over-ruling hand of providence in whatever cometh to Pass in this world" (Mather 1684:1). God predetermined terrestrial affairs along customary patterns or "second causes" which made it possible for men through observation to foretell what was "rationally to be expected" (e.g., the order of the seasons) (Oakes 1963:353). The "law and cause of Nature" in supporting the earthly order was itself a reflection of such "ordinary" providence, for "the frame of nature would be dissolved the next moment, if there were not an hand of Providence to uphold and govern all" (Mather 1684:21). This aspect of Puritan worldview was an inheritance from sixteenth century Elizabethans who feared mutability and chaos as "the cosmic anarchy before creation and the wholesale dissolution that would result if the pressure of Providence relaxed and allowed the law of nature to cease functioning" (Tillyard 1942:16). Beyond "ordinary" providences," however, Puritan divines believed that there were some "events of providence in which there is a special hand of Heaven ordering of them . . . *Magnalia Dei*, things wherein the glorious finger of God is eminently to be seen" (e.g., preservations, mercies, deliverances, judgements, signs, and prodigies) (Mather 1684:12). These providences were referred to with a variety of adjectives including "special," "extraordinary," "illustrious," and most commonly "remarkable." Like the "exemplum" (see Mosher 1911), "illustrious providence" conveys the idea of a narrative which serves to illustrate the power of God, an apt description of particular utility to clergymen. But from a folkloristic perspective, "remarkable providence" is especially poignant since it stresses orality in signifying a striking event that circulated through talk. While such remarkable providences were often seemingly "above and beyond the constituted order of nature," they did not contradict nature (Mather 1684:46–47). Since God's hand was eminently revealed in all these proceedings, it behooved the Puritan regenerate "saint" to apply this doctrine by being on the alert for the slightest deviations in the course of everyday affairs.

> It is our wisdom, to look for change and chances, some occurrents and emergencies that may blast our undertakings, that faith and prayers may be kept agoing, and lest if such frustrations befall us unexpectedly, we either flyout against God, or faint and sink in discouragements. (Oakes 1963:366)

The publication of the results of such religious observations, therefore, was an extension of this everyday practice. Thus, Mather possessed many published collections of divine providences in his library such as those of Samuel Clark, *Mirrour or Looking-Glass both for Saints and Sinners* and *Looking-Glass for Persecutors; Containing Multitudes of Examples of God's Severe, but Righteous Judgements*. In addition, Mather was familiar with Thomas Beard and Thomas Taylor's *The Theatre of God's Judgements* and

Stephen Henrie's *A World of Wonders* (see Wright 1920:130–31). These collections, however, were unlike Mather's *Illustrious Providences* in that they were culled totally from published works.

The Collection Project

Mather first got the idea of gathering orally transmitted materials from contemporary informants when it came to his notice that in 1658 a "design for the recording of illustrious providences" had been considered by some "eminent ministers in England and Ireland" (Mather 1977:xxi), the principal personality being Rev. Matthew Poole (Thomas 1971:110–11). Although this plan was never carried out in England, an anonymous manuscript was drawn up there which contained examples of some special providences and guidelines for their collection. This manuscript somehow was obtained by John Davenport, who apparently never took much interest in the idea. Mather discovered the proposal among Davenport's papers sometime after his death in 1670 and "communicated it to other ministers, who highly approved of the noble design aimed at therein" (Mather 1977:xxvi). On the basis of this document, Mather, with or without the help of his colleagues it is not clear, formulated a group of suggestions which were submitted to a general meeting of Massachusetts ministers on May 12, 1681. All the clergymen were urged

> diligently [to] enquire into and record such illustrious providences as have hapned, or from time to time shall happen, in the places whereunto they do belong; and that the witnesses of such notable occurrents be likewise set down in writing. (Mather 1977:xxvii)

Notices were to be mailed to elders in neighbouring colonies that the Massachusetts divines might "enjoy their concurrence and assistance" (Mather 1977:xxviii).

In *The Doctrine of Divine Providences Opened and Applyed*, Mather clearly distinguished divine providences (godly acts through natural means) from "preternatural" things (satanical acts against the natural order). One might suppose that the project of collecting "illustrious providences" would have excluded preternatural things, but such was not the case. In actual practice and in the final publication of *Illustrious Providences*, a Calvinistic divine omnipotence subsumed even the satanic. The categories on what today would be called the "prompting list" or "interview schedule," which was to be used by ministers in eliciting narratives from informants, therefore, indicated that both types of material were to be collected:

> Such Divine judgements, tempests, floods, earthquakes, thunders as are unusual, strange apparitions, or whatever else shall happen that is prodigious, witchcrafts, diabolical possessions, remarkable judgements upon noted sinners, eminent deliverances, and answers of prayer, are to be reckoned among illustrious providences. (Mather 1977:xxvi–xxvii)

These believed, orally transmitted events, i.e. personal experience narratives and legends, were to be recorded with the "utmost care" and sent to Mather, who would prepare a collection for publication within one or two years, that "posterity may be encouraged to go on therewith" (Mather 1977:xxvii). At the time of its proposal, therefore, *Illustrious Providences* was considered part of a grander scheme. This is further verified by the fact that clerics continued to send Mather remarkable providences after they were aware that *Illustrious Providences* had been published (see Massachusetts Historical Society [hereafter MHS] 1869:367–68, 475). That the formal collection of providences was to be an ongoing affair implies, firstly, that the collection of remarkable providences was considered a form of religious practice and as such an end in itself; and secondly, that through the amassing of such texts over a prolonged period Mather and his colleagues hoped to compile an accurate historical account as to the number and specifics of unusual earthly activities of God and Satan in New England.

The Publication

Three years later when *Illustrious Providences* was finally published, approximately half of the bulk of the book contained fifty-nine narratives concerning remarkable providences in New England while the rest of the work was devoted to commentary, analysis, and the presentation of comparative texts from published sources. On receiving his copy, the Rev. James Fitch of Norwich wrote Mather expressing surprise at the brevity of the collection: "I am sorry that your book of Remarkable Providences was no larger, seeing God hath given us many occasions of enlargement" (MHS 1869:475). There are two possible reasons why *Illustrious Providences* did not contain more special providences from New England. On the one hand, Mather probably did not receive as many texts in the post as he had hoped. Thus at one point in *Illustrious Providences* after quoting an exemplary report he reprimands, "had all others been as diligent in observing the works of God, as this worthy person has, the account of New Englands Remarkables would have been more full and compleat" (Mather 1977:260).

On the other hand, Mather may have deemed unacceptable much of the material he received or had knowledge of. That he was aware of similar material is clear. His brother Nathaniel Mather wrote from England, August 12, 1685:

> Why did you not put in the story of Mrs. Hibbons witchcrafts, & the discovery there of, as also of H. Lake's wife, of Dorchester whom, as I have heard, the devill drew in by appearing to her in the likenes, & acting the part of a child of hers then lately dead, on whom her heart was much set: as also another of a girl in Connecticut who was judged to dye a reall convert, tho she dyed for the same crime? Storyes, as I have heard them, as remarkable for some circumstances as most I have read. Mrs. Dyer's & Mrs. Hutchenson's monstrous births, & the remarkable death of the latter, with Mr. Wilson's prediction or threatening thereof which I remember, I heard in New England would have done well to bee put in. (MHS 1869:58–59)

A possible reason for these omissions was that Mather assessed that he did not possess sufficient corroborative evidence. As he admits, "other remarkables, besides those already mentioned, have hapned in this country, many of which I cannot insert, as not having received a full and clear account concerning them" (Mather 1977:220). Thus, Rev. Joshua Moody of Portsmouth submitted a report concerning a monstrous birth "by the wife of one William Plaisted." The infant was described as follows:

> Above the waste all defective or misplaced. The Head extraordinary large & no skull or bone in it. The face as big as a womans face. It had no right Arm, but somewhat like a Teat, some say like a finger where the Arm should have come out. The left arm extraordinary long, the hand reaching down to the knee. No nose, but somewhat nosethrills, & those in the forehead. The two eies upon the two cheeks. No mouth, but a little Hole & (if I mistake not) misplaced also. The eares, one under the chin, the other at the top or near the top of the head. A very short neck. Somewhat on the Breast like a kidney. The Belly seemed as if it had been ript open, & the Bowells were out, & eithr by one side, or on the Back. (MHS 1869:362; see Halpert 1958)

Moody, however, did not actually see the child himself, and he cautioned that "tho I doe not at all question the substance of what I have written, yet one would be exact in such a thing to ev[ery] circumstance" (MHS 1869:362). It was perhaps because of the lack of certainty on the part of the collector that Mather decided not to publish this account.

Another possible cause for not including the episodes his brother mentioned is that Increase Mather did not want to overburden his account with satanical items. While Perry Miller is correct in noting the propagandistic side of the special providence doctrine, as a "strategic device for arousing the emotions of a sluggish generation" (Miller 1961:229), a quantitative analysis of narratives having to do with New England in *Illustrious Providences* suggests that Mather did not want to instill fear so much as to arouse faith. It is a god of love who dominates the New England proceedings described in Mather's collection. Twenty-six independent incidents display God in a merciful role (i.e. sea deliverances, preservations, the deaf and dumb being saved and the providences at Norwich), eight concern the more wrathful side of the deity (i.e., remarkable judgments), nineteen describe natural phenomena (i.e., thunder and lightening, tempests) and only six focus on the activities of the Devil (i.e., things preternatural).

If Mather's editing of the Rev. Samuel Willard's manuscript, "Account of the Strange Case of Elizabeth Knapp of Groton," is any indication of the attitude that the former had toward narratives clearly displaying cases of diabolical possession, it is quite possible that he dismissed many more texts of a similar nature. In this particular instance Mather took a narrative that could have filled sixteen pages of his collection and reduced it to an eighth of its former length. More importantly, whereas the original account ends with the victim Elizabeth Knapp still in a sad state "speechlesse in this instant" (MHS 1869:569), the truncated version which Mather presents terminates on an incident from an earlier part of Willard's text, giving the impression that all ended well. After Mather describes Elizabeth Knapp's confession, that Satan had deluded her into thinking a neighbor was the cause of her ills, he paraphrases the original text, indicating that Elizabeth Knapp did not afterward "complain of any apparition or disturbance from such an one" (Mather 1977:101). The very next words in the Willard text read "these fits continuing" (MHS 1869:555)!

Similarly, the endings of the other five preternatural texts, on the subject of possession by evil spirits, lead the reader to believe that at the time *Illustrious Providences* was published, New England was relatively free of such pernicious influences. Such is the case with Ann Cole in Hartford:

> After the suspected witches were either executed or fled, Ann Cole was restored to health, and has continued well for many years, approving herself a serious Christian. (Mather 1977:101)

And with the demon that molested William Morse's household in Newberry:

> And they being well terrified with it, called upon God: the issue of which was, that suddenly, with a mournful note, there were six times over uttered such expressions as "Alas! me Knock no more! me Knock no more! me Knock no more!" And now all ceased. (Mather 1977:109)

And with the diabolical injuries inflicted on Nicholas Desborough of Hartford:

> This molestation began soon after a controversie arose between Desborough and another person [John Androsse], about a chest of clothes which the other said that Desborough did unrighteously retain. . . . Not long after some [one Major Talcott and a Captain John Allyn] to whom the matter was referred, ordered Desborough to restore the clothes to the person who complained of wrong; since which he hath not been troubled as before. (Mather 1977:113; see MHS 1869:86–88)

Mather omits an additional fact from the original account: the day after the chest of clothes was returned "two or three small stones or pieces of d[irt] fell upon the hatt of the said Desborough" (MHS 1869:87). Notice that while Mather's published wording de-emphasizes Desborough's diabolical troubles ("he hath not been troubled as before"), the author does not lie; Desborough had not previously experienced this particular difficulty with his hat.

And concerning the mysterious activities of a demon in the home of George Walton in Portsmouth, Mather comments that since "this last summer he has not made such disturbances as formerly" (1977:116). Lastly, the case of Mary Hortado ends with "Mary has been freed from those satanical molestations" (1977:118), although exactly how such freedom was achieved is not made explicit.

Related to the relatively small number of reports about preternatural occurrences in *Illustrious Providences* and Mather's propagandistic stress on godly events in New England is the campaign he wages against practices which attempt to force a preternatural, devilish effect, i.e. magic, or what the author specifically designates as "superstition." From the tone of the chapter "Cases of Conscience," one can gather that Mather was unnerved at the large number of unchristian practices apparent in the reports he received. Clearly, his irritation with "superstitions" in New England was not because he thought them wasteful and ineffectual practices, the manner in which the term is colloquially used today. Quite the contrary, his blast against superstitions was grounded on a firm belief in their efficacy. Men were quite likely to fall into the trap of superstition because of the Devil's ability to take "bodily possession of men," therefore making it at times "very hard to discern between natural disease and satanical possessions" (1977:120). Circumstances were even made more complicated since "Satan who has the power of death, Heb. ii, 14, has also (by Divine permission) power to inflict, and consequently to remove diseases from the bodies of men" (1977:192). Magic, then, was a tool used by Satan to ensnare unsuspecting souls through the relief of illness: "The devil heals the body that he may wound the soul; he will heal them with all his heart provided that he may entangle many souls with superstition!" (1977:191). Mather argued that the Roman Catholic Church was a living example of how well this diabolical tactic worked: "What strange things have been done, and how have diseases been healed, by the sign of the cross many times, by which means Satan's design in advancing staurolatry to the destruction of thousands of souls, has too success-fully taken place!" (1977:192).

Mather similarly dismissed preventative magic. One of the narratives Mather received described the following practice:

Some (who should have been wiser) advised the poor woman to stick the house round with bayes, as an effectual preservative against the power of evil spirits. This counsel was followed; and as long as the bayes continued green, she had quiet; but when they began to wither, they were all by an unseen hand carried away, and the woman again tormented. (1977:118)

Mather explains that since spirits "are by nature incorporeal substances . . . it is not possible that herbs or any sensible objects should have a natural influence upon them as they have upon elementary bodies" (1977:177). That is, the efficacy of such substances is accomplished against the natural order through the volition of diabolical spirits. Though the victim of such superstitions might suppose a cause and effect relation, he or she is being deceived since the effect is willed by the Devil and is not induced by simple formula alone.

With the same reasoning Mather condemns the magical use of words and incantations, music, putting urine into a bottle, nailing a horseshoe over a door, and drawing blood from one who is suspected to be a witch (1977:177,

181). Mather also questions the virtue of using various forms of homeo-pathic magic:

> Whether a bewitched person may carefully cause any of the devils sym-bols to be removed, in order to gaining health? As, suppose an image of wax, in which needles are fixed, whereby the devil doth, at the instigation of his servants, torment the diseased person, whether this, being discov-ered, may be taken away, that so the devils power of operation may cease, and that the sick person may in that way obtain health again? (1977:188)

All such practices are "impious follies," Mather asserts, and "they that obtain health in this way have it from the devil" (1977:188). Similarly, all practitioners of such positive magic such as "white" witches (1977:190) and the notorious Indian *powaws* are denounced since "God in his Holy Word, has forbidden his people to imitate the heathen nations" (1977:179).

Of course, divinatory customs in New England are hardly less sinful. Mather angrily attacks

> the foolish sorcery of those women that put the white of an egg into a glass of water, that so they may be able to divine of what occupation their future husbands shall be. It were much better to remain ignorant than thus to consult with the devil. (1977:204)

While Mather's arguments in this short chapter are cogent and persuasive, such sermonizing hardly seems necessary when one recognizes the sparsity of diabolical activities contained in *Illustrious Providences*. As Mather explicitly states, preternatural phenomena "rarely happen" in New England (1977:96). From the vantage of the twentieth century, Mather's polemics against supersti-tion seem to betray a basic insecurity for New England. This anxiety, which he shared with many other New England authors of his time, situates his collection in a category that Perry Miller has accurately described as the "literature of self-condemnation" (1956:15).

In another vein, the sections of Mather's book which are descriptive of natural phenomena, i.e. tempests, earthquakes, and floods, do little in the way of stressing either the providential or the preternatural and constitute the most detached and objective portions of the work. Whereas in *Kometographia or a Discourse Concerning Comets* Mather attempted to prove that comets were "forerunners of some great and commonly miserable hastening upon the world" (1683:131–32), through an individual case-by-case historical cause and effect analysis, in *Illustrious Providences* that didactic method is replaced by a simple chronological narration of the events themselves so far as Mather has "received credible information concerning them" (1977:51). The most slanted commen-tary in these chapters is revealed in Mather's introduction to narratives con-cerning "thunder and lightning":

> There are who affirm, that although terrible lightnings with thunders have ever been frequent in this land, yet none were hurt thereby

(neither man nor beast) for many years after the English did first settle in these American desarts, but that of later years fatal and fearful slaughters have in that way been made amongst us is most certain; and there are many who have in this respect been as brands plucked out of the burning, when the Lord hath over thrown others as God overthrew Sodom and Gomorrah. (1977:51)

It is questionable, however, whether these natural phenomena accounts could have prompted the kind of fear that would serve as a catalyst for a witchhunt seven years later at Salem. Even in the few citations of persons killed by lightning, several are depicted in pious situations. Hence, in 1664 Matthew Cole in North Hampton was "struck stone dead as he was leaning over a table, and joining with the rest in prayer" (1977:53). Similarly, in 1673 one Richard Goldsmith of Wenham, who had just recently become "a very conscientious and lively Christian" was hit by lightning with the words "Blessed be the Lord" on his lips (1977:58). When coupled with the sections of the book discussed earlier, such narratives hardly bear out Parrington's claims that the "emphasis" of *Illustrious Providences* is "laid upon witchcraft" (1927:107).

Accuracy of the Texts

Another way in which Mather's folklore collection has been misunderstood is reflected in the many criticisms it has received concerning its "scientific" character. Again Parrington is typical in deprecating the work as being the antithesis of science.

In one chapter only does Mather suggest the spirit of scientific inquiry; four out of the twelve deal with witchcraft and kindred topics; and the rest are made up of such instances of divine providence as great fish jumping out of the sea into boats, of starving sailors adrift, of the freaks played by lightning and tornadoes and of God's punishments on wicked Quakers. (1927:107)

Not only does Parrington exhibit a bad case of "chronocentricity" (judging cultures of the past on the basis of one's own contemporary cultural values), but he fallaciously attacks *Illustrious Providences* as being unscientific because of its subject matter rather than drawing his attention to the method whereby such materials were gathered. On the criterion of their content alone, a great number of American folklore collections would have to be judged as unscientific, supernatural publications.

Folkloristics is a social science only to the extent that the discipline employs scientific methods for amassing accurate research data. The aims of *Illustrious Providences* were scientific in that it was the intention of the author to present precise empirical information. Hence, Mather urged his theocratic collecting staff to provide him with accurate reports on the basis of personal interviews. He believed that much of the data he received came verbatim, directly from the lips of the informants. Consider the following introductions to letters sent to Mather:

> The enclosed . . . I transcribed from Mr. Tho Broughton [a Boston merchant], who read to me what he took from the mouth of the woman & her husband, & judge it credible. (MHS 1869:360)

> A brief Narrative of sundry Apparitions of Satan unto, an Assaults at sundry times and places upon, the person of Mary, the wife of Antonio Hortado, dwelling next Salmon Falls, Taken from her own mouth, Aug. 13, 1683. (Mather 1977:116)

In nearly a third of the published narratives Mather indicates that he is quoting from primary sources. Although he makes editorial alterations in punctuation and wording, usually for the sake of brevity, in general his transcriptions are faithful to the original manuscripts he received. As an illustration, compare a special providence as it was mailed to Mather with the form in which it finally appeared in *Illustrious Providences:*

Original	*Published Version*
We have had of late, great storms of rain & wind, & sometimes of thunder & lightning, whereby some execucon hath been done by the Lord's holy hand, though with sparing mercy to mankind. Mr. Jones in his house at N.H. broken into & strange work made in one room thereof especially wherein one of his daughters had been but a little before; and no hurt to any of the family, but the house only. This was about the middle of the 4th month last. (MHS 1869:310)	We have had of late great storms of rain and wind, and some of thunder and lightning, whereby execution has been done, though with sparing mercy to men. Mr. Jones his house in New-Haven was broken into by the lightning and strange work made in one room especially in which one of his children had been but a little before. This was done June 8, 1682. (1977:61)

It should be noted in regard to this text that Mather's insertion of a specific date was a result of his writing directly to the informant, William Jones, who responded with the exact day of the occurrence (MHS 1869:612).

In cases where Mather does not quote, as with the Willard text mentioned earlier, his wording is often copied directly from the account in his possession (see Wright 1920). Note how closely Mather reproduces this report concerning a hailstorm, sent to him from Edward Taylor in Westfield:

Original	*Published Version*
But at Springfield, in the upper end of the long meadow, it was most dreadful where the Haile were, a great deale of it, pieces of ice, some 7 some 9 inches about, falling with such violence as they struck the shingles off of some houses, & holes in the ground that one might put ones hand in, beating down & destroying severall Acres of Wheat Indian, Morning Grass, & laying all down as if timber had been rowled over them. (MHS 1869:629)	But at Springfield it was most dreadful, where great pieces of ice, some seven, some nine inches about, fell down from the clouds with such violence that the shingles upon some houses were broken thereby, and holes beaten into the ground that a man might put his hand in. Several acres of corn (both Wheat and Indian) were beat down and destroyed by the hail. (1977:225)

For the most part, then, Mather as an editor might be questioned for what he omitted rather than for what he distorted or included. In the last regard it is only on rare occasions that he interlarded a secularly worded text with religious evaluations of his own. One such providence is that concerning the judgment of the Indian Simon. After discussing the facts as to how Simon, who was wounded by one of his own warriors and died an agonizing death after two years of going to *powaws*, Mather cannot resist saying "thus was the wickedness of that murtherer at least returned upon his own head" (1977:254).

Conclusion

Illustrious Providences provides us with a host of reliable oral expressions which circulated amongst the rank-and-file population of Puritan New England during the latter seventeeth century. More than just reflecting widespread belief in the supernatural, these texts offer specific insights into the traditions, experiences, and worldview of these residents as well as a sampling of their attitudes on a multitude of subjects including Quakers, Indians, medicine, personal conduct, and cosmology. In short they must be considered significant documents for American social and cultural history as well as for the study of American folklore and vernacular religion.

American historians and culture critics who erroneously link the Salem witch trials with the publication of *Illustrious Providences* tacitly accept a "trickle-down," *gesunkenes Kulturgut* theory of cultural history. They assume that over a period of time the ideas contained in the publications of elites are eventually accepted by inarticulate substrata. While top-down history is often a reality, there is no basis for believing that such a causal link existed between Mather's book and the Salem witch hysteria. Clearly, like the majority of his contemporaries, Mather was a believer in witchcraft. Moreover, as a committed Puritan divine, he constructed *Illustrious Providences*, like so many other folkloristic works, with an ideological perspective (see Green 1983). Had the book accomplished the effect which its author intended, however, it would have strengthened religious faith by illustrating that the oral accounts of extraordinary but concrete events from the lives of ordinary people, stories known as "remarkable providences," reified the supernatural power of the deity. As Demos has observed, Mather's published providences exhibited a further purpose: "to reduce the Devil's influence by holding him up to public scrutiny" (1982:99). Some scholars fail to recognize these designs because, as Kittredge noted long ago, they naturally tend "to find some notable personage to whom their propositions, commendatory or damaging, may be attached" (1929:359).

Table of Motifs

The motif numbers here refer to Stith Thompson (1955–58) and Ernest W. Baughman (1966). They only represent those narrations pertaining to New England in Increase Mather's *An Essay for the Recording of Illustrious Providences* (1977).

Pages	*Motifs*
10	S262.3, sacrificial victim chosen by lot.
11	B147.2.1, bird of good omen.
24	F668, skillful surgeon.
42	N126, lots cast to determine fate.
52–55	F797, fire from heaven kills people.
94–95	A1142.1, creator's voice makes the thunder.
96–99	G263.4.2, witch causes fits.
98	D102, devil transformed to animal.
98	G303.3.3.2.8, devil in the form of a deer.
98	G243.3, witches have sexual intercourse with devil or his minions.
98	G211.4.1, witches in form of crow.
99	H222.5, ordeal by water to test suspect of witchcraft.
101	G303.3.1, the devil in human form.
101	F473.5, poltergeist makes noises.
101, 114	F473.1, poltergeist throwing objects.
103–9, 113, 117	F473.3, poltergeist mistreats people.
109	E279.3, ghost pulls bed clothes from sleeper.
109	D1766.7.1.1, evil spirits conjured away in name of deity.
110	D1385.9, magic horseshoe keeps off witches.
113	G269.15, witch scratches person.

115	B147.1.2.2, cat as beast of ill-omen.
115	F552.4, hand without wrist.
117–18	E422.4.4, revenant in female dress.
118	G272.2.4, bay leaves protect against witches.
185	D1241, magic medicine.
243	E231, return from dead to reveal murder.
252	Q263.1, death as punishment for perjury.
252	Q559.2, punishment: man stricken blind.

Notes

I dedicate this essay about an old book of folklore texts to my friend and colleague Dr. Kenneth Goldstein, a lover of old books and folklore texts. Colorful, provocative, wise, and never dull, "Kenny" has been an inspiration.

1. Increase Mather, *An Essay for the Recording of Illustrious Providences* (Boston: Samuel Green for Joseph Browning, 1684). This edition was reprinted by the same printer in a different format in the same year and it was simultaneously printed in London by George Calvert. The volume was again reprinted in London in 1687 by "Tho. Parkhurst." There were two subsequent London reprints in the nineteenth century, printed by John Russell Smith (1856) and Reeves and Turner (1890), both with the changed title *Remarkable Providences Illustrative of the Earlier Days of American Colonisation*. George Offer wrote an introductory preface for these editions (see Holmes 1931). In 1977, Arno Press, New York, reprinted the 1856 edition in its entirety. The latter will be the edition cited here. Quotations are reproduced verbatim from original sources and original spellings are preserved.

References

Baughman, Ernest W.
  1966 *Type and Motif Index of the Folktales of England and North America*. The Hague: Mouton.
Calef, Robert
  1823 *More Wonders of the Invisible World Displayed*. Salem: John D. and T. C. Cushing, Jr., for Cushing and Appleton.
Carey, Deborah D.
  1963 The Divine Providence: Its Nature and Tradition in Seventeenth Century New England. Master's thesis, Indiana University, Bloomington.
Demos, John, ed.
  1972 *Remarkable Providences, 1600–1760*. New York: George Braziller.
  1982 *Entertaining Satan: Witchcraft and the Culture of Early New England*. Toronto: Oxford Univ. Press.
Dorson, Richard M.
  1959a *American Folklore*. Chicago: Univ. of Chicago Press.
  1959b A Theory for American Folklore. *Journal of American Folklore* 72:197–215.
  1973 *America in Legend*. New York: Pantheon.
  1978 American Folklore vs. Folklore in America. *Journal of the Folklore Institute* 15: 97–111.

Dorson, Richard M., ed.
  1966 *America Begins.* Greenwich, Conn.: Fawcett.
Eggleston, Edward
  1959 *The Transit of Civilization from England to American in the Seventeenth Century.* Boston: Beacon Hill.
Gaer, Joseph and Ben Siegel
  1964 *The Puritan Heritage: America's Roots in the Bible.* New York: New American Library.
Green, Archie
  1983 Interpreting Folklore Ideologically. In *Handbook of American Folklore.* Ed. R. M. Dorson. Bloomington: Indiana Univ. Press. Pp. 351–58.
Halpert, Herbert
  1958 Legends of the Cursed Child. *New York Folklore Quarterly* 14:233–41.
Holmes, Thomas J.
  1931 *Increase Mather: A Bibliography of His Works.* 2 vols. Cleveland: Cleveland Public Library.
Jones, Michael Owen
  1982 Another America: Toward a Behavioral History Based on Folkloristics. *Western Folklore* 41(1): 43–51.
Karlsen, Carol F.
  1987 *The Devil in the Shape of a Woman: Witchcraft in Colonial New England.* New York: W. W. Norton and Co.
Kittredge, George Lyman
  1929 *Witchcraft in Old and New England.* Cambridge: Harvard Univ. Press.
Mather, Increase
  1683 *Kometographia or a Discourse Concerning Comets.* Boston: S. Green for S. Sewall.
  1684 *The Doctrine of Divine Providence Opened and Applyed.* Boston: Richard Pierce.
  1977 *Remarkable Providences Illustrative of the Earlier Days of American Colonisation.* New York: Arno Press.
Miller, Perry
  1956 *Errand into the Wilderness.* New York: Harper and Row.
  1961 *The New England Mind: The Seventeenth Century.* Boston: Beacon Press.
Morison, Samuel Eliot
  1956 *The Intellectual Life of Colonial New England.* Ithaca: Cornell Univ. Press.
Mosher, Joseph Albert
  1911 *The Exemplum in the Early Religious and Didactic Literature of England.* New York: Columbia Univ. Press.
Murdock, Kenneth B.
  1925 *Increase Mather, the Foremost American Puritan.* Cambridge: Harvard Univ. Press.
Oakes, Urian
  1963 The Soveraign Efficacy of Divine Providence. In *The Puritans.* Ed. P. Miller and T. H. Johnson. New York: Harper and Row. Pp. 350–67.
Parrington, Vernon Louis
  1927 *Main Currents in American Thought: The Colonial Mind, 1620–1800.* New York: Harcourt, Brace and World.

Massachusetts Historical Society (MHS)
  1869   *The Mather Papers. Massachusetts Historical Society Collections. Volume 8, 4th Series.* Boston: Wiggin and Lunt.
Stern, Stephen and Simon J. Bronner
  1980   American Folklore vs. Folklore in America: A Fixed Fight? *Journal of the Folklore Institute* 17(1): 76–84.
Thomas, Keith
  1971   *Religion and the Decline of Magic: Studies in Popular Beliefs in Sixteenth and Seventeenth-Century England.* Harmondsworth: Penguin.
Thompson, Stith
  1955-58   *Motif-Index of Folk-Literature.* 6 vols. Bloomington: Indiana Univ. Press.
Tillyard, E. M. W.
  1942   *The Elizabethan World Picture.* New York: Random House.
Wish, Harvey
  1950   *Society and Thought in Early America.* New York: Longmans, Green and Co.
Wright, Thomas
  1920   *Literary Culture in Early New England 1620–1730.* New Haven: Yale Univ. Press.

AFRICAN AMERICAN DIVERSITY AND THE STUDY OF FOLKLORE

John W. Roberts

RECENTLY, SCHOLARS in various disciplines concerned with the fair and accurate representation of African American creative cultural traditions have begun to challenge simplistic notions of black culture and creativity by insisting that African American cultural diversity become a conscious dimension of praxis (Awkward 1988; Christian 1985; Hull, Scott, and Christian 1982; Rose 1989; and Wall 1989). In this regard, the concern is one not only of representation but also of the representativeness of what is produced for academic and public consumption. The task is complicated for students of the African American experience by the knowledge that much of the work in this area of cultural study continues to be educational in the broadest sense of the term. That is, despite over four hundreds years of African presence in the New World, knowledge of the accomplishments of people of African descent remains limited in both academic and public circles. Therefore, representations of the creative cultural traditions that African people claim, the cultural innovations that they inspire, and the creative power that they continue to wield all too often serve as introductions rather than as confirmation of a vital African cultural presence in the New World. While this knowledge confronts all scholars of the African American cultural experience with an important responsibility to make representations of African American creative traditions scrupulously fair and accurate, it presents a particular challenge to American folklorists. The simple truth is that American folklorists have historically struggled with diversity both as a practical reality in American life and as an influence on theoretical development within the discipline (Stern 1991). Therefore, if we are to create an African American folkloristics sensitive to African American cultural diversity, we might begin with a recognition that we are heirs to and continue to participate in a disciplinary discourse that historically has made it extremely difficult to recognize intra-group diversity as an influence on vernacular creativity.

However, if we are to confound this discursive tradition, we must become sensitive to and knowledgeable about the ways in which the discipline structures a discourse that renders virtually impossible a recognition of the influence of diversity not only on cultural-specific creative traditions but also between diverse cultural traditions. That is, folklore is a discipline that has historically envisioned the folk as the focus of attention. The "folk" in folklore has traditionally been conceptualized as a homogeneous category of cultural producers. As a result, folklorists have historically embraced methodologies and created theories to illuminate the nature of vernacular creativity among the "folk" but not within or between specific cultural groups. This is not to suggest that folklorists have not historically studied diverse cultural traditions, especially within the American context. In fact, the focus of American folklore study has always been the vernacular traditions of diverse groups within the society (Newell 1888:3; Dundes 1980:6–7). However, in approaching these traditions, folkness rather than creative cultural tradition of origin has historically served as the basis on which vernacular creativity is evaluated regardless of where it is found. In this context, "folkness" can be conceptualized as a mode of ideation based on a perceived ontological and epistemological distinction between "folk" and "nonfolk" that traditionally has served as the basis of folkloristic theorizing.

By the time of the inauguration of an American folkloristics in the late nineteenth century, "folkness" had already acquired the status of a discourse replete with a vocabulary and ideas that could be used impersonally by anyone who wanted to speak or write about the "folk." In a discourse of folkness, the important distinction has always been between the folk, that is, those individuals in the society who have been perceived as participating in processes of vernacular creativity, and the nonfolk or those individuals whose creative energies have been seen as leading to other modes of creative cultural production in the society. From its inception, a discourse of folkness envisioned these categories as oppositional and created definitive boundaries between "folk" and "nonfolk" as well as the modes of creative cultural production associated with them. Moreover, these categories have been treated as if they re-presented natural cultural and social processes whey they, in fact, inscribe a we/they division that is not only oppositional but ethnocentric. In addition, they allow for the perpetuation of an essentially static conception of the "folk" and folklore. That is, in a discourse of folkness, "folk" has become a reified category of cultural production that characterizes both creative and mental processes.

As a discourse, folkness is Eurocentric in its origins and applications. From the beginning, folkness sought to develop knowledge of the "folk" not merely out of intellectual curiosity but rather as a sign of the prerogative and power of elite classes in Europe to define their Other. As such, folkness has always maintained an inherent ideological and political dimension. The political dimension of folkness as a discourse is most evident in the fact that the term "folk" originally referred exclusively to European peasants—a definition of the folk made possible by a hierarchical and evolutionary view of society (Dundes

1980:2–4). In the European context, a discourse of folkness allowed folklorists early on to envision a cultural and historical continuity between the folk and nonfolk within perceived culturally homogeneous societal contexts in that vernacular forms came to be seen as survivals of more developed forms found among the nonfolk. In addition, to be "folk" was to be European in this initial formulation. The equation between folkness and European-ness was particularly evident in the treatment of so-call primitives in early folklore study. So-called primitives in a discourse of folkness were situated not only temporally, that is, as living in the past of European folk, but also spatially outside of European societies and were constituted in the discourse as the Other of European folk and, by extension, of whole European societies (Dundes 1980:2–4; Mudimbe 1988:28). That is, the initial concept of the "folk" embraced by folklorists could not register non-European-ness as a subject of discussion.

Not surprisingly, in the more culturally pluralistic context of American society, a Eurocentric discourse of folkness has always been problematic--a problematic that has been recognized and addressed at various times in the history of American folklore study (Redfield 1947; Dundes 1966, 1980, 1989; Bauman 1971). In fact, at the inception of American folkloristics, this problematic arose with the attempt to include Native American creative traditions in a discourse of folkness—a decision that was greeted with controversy. While this controversy has been dismissed by some historians of the discipline as a definitional dispute (Bell 1973:7–22; Zumwalt 1988:16–21), it was in reality an early barometer of the difficulty that folklorists faced in their efforts to institute a Eurocentric discourse of folkness within the culturally pluralistic context of American society. In other words, this controversy, when viewed from the perspective of a discourse of folkness, reveals the extent to which folkness had become a discourse on European-ness by the time it reached America. That is, folkness could not register Native American-ness as a subject for discussion. Despite this early perception of a problematic inherent in the European concept of the "folk" in the American context—a problematic that denied Native Americans the status of "folk" because of their non-European-ness--American folklorists have attempted historically to maintain continuity with a Eurocentric discourse of folkness in which the folk are seen as a homogeneous category of cultural producers. In order to do so, they have embraced an affiliative process in which groups whose traditions of vernacular creativity are related neither historically nor culturally are simply inserted into a Eurocentric discourse of folkness without regard for their unique historical or cultural heritages. In so doing, American folklorists perpetuate a discursive tradition in which the European folk are still seen as the original folk and all other folk are mere imitators.

The consequences of a Eurocentric discourse of folkness for the study of African American vernacular creativity have been in almost all respects devastating. In an important sense, it has led to the development of paradigms for its study that attempt to explain the difference in African American vernacular creativity as a deviation from supposed original forms. That is, in the study of

African American vernacular creativity, this discursive model has historically led to controversy revolving primarily around questions of origins (Herskovitz 1941; Wilgus 1959; Roberts 1989). In more recent times, it has caused African American folklore to be envisioned as occupying a pathological space within the discipline. The source of a perception of pathology associated with African American vernacular creativity derives from the fact that, within a Eurocentric discourse of folkness, the European folk are not only seen as the original folk but European folklore defines folklore. Therefore, the discovery of new forms of vernacular creativity among African Americans comes to be seen as a sign of pathology rather than of vital creative energy within African American communities (Weldon 1959; Abrahams 1970 and Jackson 1974). In addition, American folklorists have traditionally studied African American folklore as a source for generating statements about the black character and/or experience in the United States. The black character and/or experience within these paradigms have been conceptualized as products of either biological inferiority and/or the pathological results of black exposure to a devastating slave experience and continuing oppression within the society (Lanier Seward 1983:48–49).

The point is that by inserting and attempting to contain African American vernacular creativity within a discourse of folkness, folklorists from the very inception of an American folkloristics problematized the most important source of difference claimed by African Americans—an African cultural heritage. This cultural heritage, which served as the foundation for the development of African American culture, continues to be the tradition-rich source of black vernacular creativity in the United States. In a general sense, the history of African American folklore study can be characterized as an extended and extensive discourse designed to deny African American difference as a viable and vital sign of African cultural presence in the United States. The negation of an African cultural presence in folklore study was overdetermined at the inception of an American folkloristics by the social and political climate in which the discipline sought to define itself. That is, in the late nineteenth century, political debate raged about the nature of the black character, especially its indebtedness to an African past. This debate concerning the importance of the African heritage to an understanding of the contemporary African American character was fueled both by social Darwinism and the continuing conflict between the North and South concerning the fate of recently freed African people. In both cases, the extent to which black freedpeople retained elements of their African past were seen as important to their future role and place in the society. On the one hand, social Darwinists debated the possibility of evolution versus devolution for people of African decent in that some held out the possibility of inevitable progress of newly freed Africans without the corruptive effect of slavery while others maintained that "reversion to type," that is, a return to savagery, was inevitable without the discipline of slavery (Frederickson 1971:231–32). On the other hand, Southerners and Northerners debated the need for paternalistic approaches in dealing with the black population versus social and political equality for enfranchised African Americans

(Frederickson 1971: 58–60, 104–7). The scientific debate carried on by social Darwinists and the political debate carried on by activists in the South and North were often interrelated and intertwined in important ways. In addition, they shared an intimate concern with the importance of the African heritage to an understanding of the contemporary African American character.

Inasmuch as the institution of slavery had been justified on the basis of African difference—a difference that enslavement was supposed to eradicate—it is not surprising that the African heritage would figure prominently in post Civil War debates concerning the fate of former enslaved Africans. Interestingly, in the political debates of the late nineteenth century, both Southerners and Northerners eventually found it advantageous to minimize the possibility that Africans in Americans retained significant elements of their African heritage, though for very different reasons. Southerners who had maintained throughout the period of black chattel slavery that slavery had a civilizing effect on Africans pointed to what they frequently characterized as a docile and childlike character for Africans as ample proof that containment represented the most effective approach in dealing with Africans. In so doing they argued that Africans needed paternalistic care and guidance to protect and continued their stride toward civilization. On the other hand, Northerners, especially abolitionists, had during the period of black chattel slavery promoted the view that Africans were a gentle and charitable people who were being morally corrupted by the institution of slavery. In the aftermath of the Civil War, they maintained that Africans did not constitute a dangerous Other and, indeed, were fully capable of acculturation to Euro-American norms with the advent of full equality in the society.

These debates had a profound influence on the emerging field of folklore. Though politics or even the political leanings of collectors were seldom mentioned during the early years of African American folklore study, politics had a profound influence on the development of a discourse on this tradition of vernacular creativity. For example, northerners who collected and studied African American folklore tended to focus almost exclusively on religious folk forms such as the spirituals that supported their position concerning the natural Christian, or civilized, state of Africans in America. Southern collectors, on the other hand, tended to focus their efforts on the collection of animal tales and folk beliefs that supported their position that Africans constituted a potentially dangerous and unpredictable Other on the American landscape. In addition, the impact of politics is reflected most clearly in the early development of approaches to African American folklore that envisioned it primarily as a gauge for charting African American acculturation to Euro-American cultural norms. A consequence of acculturative models in the study of African American folklore has been not only the denial of the very basis on which African Americans claim difference within the society but also a tendency to envision the black experience as a categorical experience, one undifferentiated by such social constructions as class, gender, and sexuality or even by geographical distinctions as salient as region.

Therefore, if we are to inaugurate a discourse on African American vernacular creativity reflexive of the diversity of the African American population, we must, first of all, embrace paradigms for its study that recognize the African American vernacular difference as the product of an African cultural heritage. In so doing, we are able to approach African American vernacular creativity as a filiative process of creativity that has it roots in diverse African cultures. As such, the most appropriate paradigms for its study are those that recognize African American vernacular creativity as a cultural-specific process intimately related to processes of identity and institution formation and maintenance peculiar to African people in the United States. Of equal importance, we must accept it as a dynamic creative cultural process reflexive not only of an African cultural heritage but also one influenced historically by economic, political, and social conditions as well as creative traditions encountered by African people in the New World context.

When we accept African American folklore as a dynamic tradition of creativity within an African American cultural context, we are then able to initiate a discourse that illuminates its difference from other vernacular traditions. That is, we come to realize that African American vernacular creativity is a process intimately related to black culture-building—a dynamic process of identity formation and maintenance. Of equal importance, we are able to inaugurate a discourse that addresses the diverse intra-group influences on African American vernacular creativity. However, we should not loose sight of the fact that many of the differences that have and continue to influence African American cultural diversity and, by extension, the maintenance of a tradition of vernacular creativity influenced by diverse intra-group factors reflect the continuation of an African cultural heritage in the United States. That is, African people arrived in the New World already very diverse not only in terms of different cultural backgrounds but also in their perceptions of what constituted appropriate roles defined by gender, social position, and other factors. While Euro-American cultural hegemony had and continues to have a profound influence on the ways in which African people evaluate and respond to their own internal groups differences, I would argue that it does not now nor has it ever been the sole determining factor.

Although African Americans as a cultural groups have historically been subject to similar economic, political, and social conditions within American society, they have experienced and evaluated the consequences of these conditions in very different ways. As a result, their expressive responses to both external and internal conditions encountered in New World contexts have been different. Whether these conditions have impacted on African Americans from outside of their communities or from within, their responses have been mediated by such factors as gender, class, sexual orientation, region, education, and group affiliation. That is, while vernacular creativity has historically served as a way for African Americans to express their sense of difference from other cultural groups within the society, it has simultaneously serves as a way for African American to express their sense of diversity as a cultural group. In most instances, however, it would extremely difficult to separate the internal and external factors that influence African American diversity. Therefore, our analysis of issues related to African American cultural diversity must recognize the complex and interrelated factors always influencing its expression in vernacular traditions.

Our failure to consider the influence of diversity on vernacular creativity within black communities means that we have at present a very limited vision of African American vernacular resources and a distorted view of the intra-group dynamics that animate this tradition of vernacular expression. Of the distortions plaguing this tradition, none are more glaring than those resulting from the absence of a gendered perspective in African American folklore study. While African American males have certainly received more attentions as performers of folklore than females, the study of African American male traditions have for the most part not sought to reveal the ways in they reflect a gendered discourse in black vernacular culture. In fact, these studies have most often been used to generate statements about the nature of the black experience in a holistic fashion. Even when traditions performed by males have been used to generate statements about black manhood, they have been most often conceptualized within paradigms that envision black maleness as an essentially pathological condition (Eddington 1965; Liebow 1967; Hannerz 1969; Abrahams 1970; Jackson 1974; and Wepman et al. 1976). While these tendencies reflect in many ways the continuing influence of a discourse of folkness on the study of African American folklore, they also reveal the limited view of the ways in which African American males use vernacular creativity as resource in their efforts to create and express a sense of identity as males in a racist society and in the unique cultural environment of black communities.

On the other hand, the participation of African American women in vernacular creativity has hardly been noted by folklorists. In most respects, the study of African American folklore has been structured in ways that either minimize the participation of women in African American vernacular creativity and performance or ignore it altogether. When women have surfaced in discussions of African American folklore, they have most often emerged as objects of the black male gaze in such genres as the blues, toasts, and the dozens. Or they have been associated with domestic space in which they either quilt or cook. However, in the few glimpses of African American women as public performers of vernacular traditions that we have, we learn that they have been historically not only powerful and influential performers of African American folklore but that they have used their performances as ways of expressing their sense of identity as black women in the society and in their own communities. Of equal importance they have historically used their performances to express what it means to be black and female in a society which oppresses both.

The absence of a gendered discourse in African American folkloristics means that we have little sense of how the construction of gender and gender relations in African Americans communities influence vernacular creativity. As such we have not explored important dialogical relationships between

African American male and female genres and/or participation in the produc- tion of any single genre. That such exploration can be productive of new understandings of African American creative processes and traditions is re- vealed rather poignantly in recent works on African American female blues performances by Daphne Harrison (1989) and Hazel Carby (1986) and the ongoing work of Tricia Rose (1989 and 1990) with female rappers and Adrienne Lanier Seward's present work with women preachers, which will culminate in a film. The work of these scholars serve not only as an important corrective to the male-dominated scholarship on African American musical traditions but it also reveals how African American men and women find in these genres ways of expressing a gendered sense of identity through a single expressive form. Additionally, these studies illuminate issues of social and sexual politics within the African American community.

The influence of sexuality on African American vernacular creativity is closely related to gender but should be seen as a separate issue. "Sexuality", according to Evelyn Brooks-Higginbotham, is defined "not in terms of biologi- cal essentials or as a universal truth detached and transcendent from other aspects of human life and society. Rather, it is an evolving conception applied to the body but given meaning and identity by economic, cultural, and historical context" (Brooks-Higginbotham 1992:254). Racialized constructions of black male and female sexuality have figured prominently in American history and folklore. Often associated with violence against both, its expression in vernacular traditions is in need of serious critique. By the same token, African American constructions of male and female sexuality as represented in folklore also needs investigation. We certainly need to move beyond rather simplistic and pathological views of black male and female sexuality generated in studies of the blues and other genres that seem to offer extended conceptions. In fact, we need in-depth and focused studies of images of black sexuality that illuminate the ways in which African American conceptions of sexuality influence and are represented in vernacular forms and performances and reflect culture specific conceptions.

This need seems particularly appropriate in the representation of sexuality as it relates to sexual orientation. As a creating community in black culture, gay and lesbian contributions to African American vernacular resources have been all but ignored. The invisibility of gays and lesbians in the black community and the society has historically led to their traditions been appropriated by the general population without acknowledgment of source or meaning. For ex- ample, we are presently witnessing a continuation of this process with the popular television show, *In Living Color*. That is, we find individuals of various sexual orientation giving "three snaps and a circle" without apparent knowl- edge or acknowledgment of its origin and meaning in the gay community. Given the history of oppression of gays and lesbians in the society and in the black community, we should expect to find a tradition of vernacular creativity reflexive of what it means to be black and gay. In fact, we need to pay more careful attention to the ways that blackness constructs sexuality in the broadest sense, and, of equal importance, for what purpose.

Class has historically been a missing dimension of African American cultural study. Because folklorists have tended to conceptualize African Americans as an undifferentiated mass whose folkness results naturally from their otherness on the American landscape, the possible influence of class on vernacular creativity has hardly been considered. However, African American culture has always been characterized by class or, at the least, social distinctions reflective of different intra-group statuses based on perceptions of privilege. For example, if we turn to the period of black chattel slavery, we find ample evidence of social distinctions such as free versus the enslaved, house versus field workers, and so on. The recognition of these distinctions in plantation societies undoubtedly influenced vernacular creativity in ways yet to be explored. In the post emancipation era, social distinctions based on skin color as well as economics have been well documented (Powdermaker 1939 and Johnson 1934). While literary scholars have devoted a good deal of attention to textual representations of the lore and language associated with skin color both in terms of its social and political ramifications, especially as it relates to the practice of passing, folklorists have barely noted its frequent expression in such vernacular forms and rituals as the blues and the brown paper bag test.

Among contemporary African Americans, enhanced economic opportunities have meant that a strong perception of class distinctions based on economics has emerged in recent years. Political rhetoric suggests that members of the new black middle-class have simply lost touch with the masses of African Americans. The perception of cultural detachment on the part of the black middle-class derives in large part from an increasing tendency of economically successful African Americans to live outside of the physical environment of traditional black neighborhoods thereby complicating traditional definitions of community and paradigms of black identification. This contention fails, however, to consider the myriad ways in which middle class African Americans retain strong cultural ties to and envision themselves as part of something called the black community. In many instances, the abilities of many African Americans to survive and prosper in high profile professional positions mean that they must mute their expressions of cultural identity in the workplace. At the same time, most continue to believe that if they are to survive psychically and socially in racist institutions and the society they must continue to maintain strong ties to their families and communities. Therefore, most African Americans turn frequently to black neighborhoods for familial, religious, and social activities. In other instances, they try as best they can to re-create and express their cultural heritage in the context of neighborhoods as well as occupational settings in which the expression of their culture is often neither valued nor wanted. In other words, black middle-class-ness as well as class in general constructs black folkness in unique ways. The need at this point is careful research into the ways and means by which middle-class African Americans express their sense of African American-ness in vernacular forms.

My intention is not to offer an exhaustive discussion of the manifestations of diversity that influence African American vernacular creativity. Rather I simply want to suggest that diversity is a fact of African American life that undoubtedly influences black vernacular creativity. In addition to the differences already noted as particular needed, I would add region as a factor that we need to consider in far more complex terms than the South (rural) and North (urban) dichotomy generally envisioned. While the tendency to use a South/ North or even rural/urban dichotomy has always been problematic, it has become increasingly so in recent years due to mass technology as well as increased mobility among African Americans. However, any model designed to address regional differences among African Americans must be sensitive to the differences in the historical, economic, and even cultural factors that have influenced the development of black culture in different parts of the country. In a more limited sense, I would note the need to consider the influence of different group affiliations within specific African Americans communities on vernacular creativity. For instance, African American affiliations with social organizations such as lodges, fraternities, sororities, clubs, and even different religious denominations have led to the development of various forms of vernacular expression often overlooked in the effort to imagine an African American folk in a traditional sense. In the process, the rituals, narratives, songs, and various other expressions of African American-ness to be found in social organizations have been overlooked. While these forms of expression need to be examined in terms of how they express a sense of group affiliation, they can and should also be examined in terms of how they contribute to an understanding of black vernacular forms and processes of creativity in the United States.

In exploring African American culture diversity as an influence on black folklore, I could create an almost endless list of differences that animate African American culture and influence the dynamism of the African American tradition of vernacular creativity. Certainly, if we accept the contemporary perspective that all of us are the folk, that we all indulge in processes of vernacular creativity, an extensive list of differences that animate the African American folk tradition can be easily justified. However, my point is that various differences influence the ways in which African Americans participate in processes of vernacular creativity as well as give both general and specific meanings to these efforts. While it is probably impossible to take into consideration all of the differences that animate any given vernacular performance let alone an entire tradition of vernacular creativity, our analytical efforts must at least attempt to consider the most salient ones. In my view, we can no longer live with approaches and paradigms that envision African American vernacular creativity as a process reflective of what it means to be folk or even as a simple one-dimensional reflection of something called the black experience. The experiences of African Americans have always been diverse, and the ways in which they have represented these experiences in creative cultural traditions have always reflected this diversity. The simple truth is that our analytical tools have not been capable of capturing the complex nature of African American creative traditions. Culture is always a site of contestation, and we contest on the basis of difference, not similarity. The prize—or, at least, *a* prize—in the contest is identity conceived of as a fluid and ever-changing sense of who we are in relation to others.

Note

A version of this article was published in a special issue of *Western Folklore* entitled *Theorizing Folklore: Toward New Perspectives on the Politics of Culture,* edited by Charles Briggs and Amy Shuman (1993).

References

Abrahams, Roger
    1970 *Deep Down In the Jungle: Negro Narrative Folklore from the Streets of Philadelphia.* Chicago: Aldine Press.
Awkward, Michael
    1988 Race, Gender, and the Politics of Reading. *Black American Literature Forum* 22:5–27.
Bauman, Richard
    1971 Differential Identity and the Social Base of Folklore. *Journal of American Folklore* 84:31–41.
Bell, Michael J.
    1973 William Wells Newell and the Foundation of American Folklore Scholarship. *Journal of the Folklore Institute* 10:7–21.
Briggs, Charles, and Amy Shuman, eds.
    1993 *Theorizing Folklore: Toward New Perspectives on the Politics of Culture.* Special issue of *Western Folklore* 52:109–400.
Brooks Higginbothan, Evelyn
    1992 African American Women's History and the Metalanguage of Race. *Signs* 17:251–74.
Carby, Hazel
    1986 It Jus Be's Dat Way Sometime: The Sexual Politics of Women's Blues. *Radical America* 20:9–24.
Christian, Barbara
    1985 The Dynamics of Difference: Book Review of Audre Lorde's *Sister Outsider.* In *Black Feminist Criticism: Perspectives in Black Women Writers.* New York: Pergamon Press. Pp. 187-204.
Dundes, Alan
    1966 The American Concept of Folklore. *Journal of American Folklore* 3:226–49.
    1980 *Interpreting Folklore.* Bloomington: Indiana Univ. Press.
    1989 *Folklore Matters.* Knoxville: Univ. of Tennessee Press.
Eddington, Neil A.
    1965 Genital Superiority in Oakland Negro Folklore: A Theme. *Papers of the Kroeber Anthropological Society* 33:99–105.
Fabian, Johannes
    1983 *Time and the Other: How Anthropology Makes Its Object.* New York: Columbia Univ. Press.
Frederickson, George
    1971 *The Black Image in the White Mind.* New York: Harper Torchbooks.

Hannerz, Ulf
  1969 *Soulside: Inquiries into Ghetto Culture and Community.* New York: New York Univ. Press.
Harrison, Daphne
  1989 *Black Pearls: Blues Queens of the 1920s.* New Brunswick: Rutgers Univ. Press.
Herskovitz, Meville
  1941 *Myth of the Negro Past.* New York: Harper.
Hull, Gloria, Patricia Bell Scott, and Barbara Smith, eds.
  1982 *All the Women are White, All the Blacks Are Men, But Some of Us Are Brave.* Old Westbury, N.Y.: Feminist Press.
Jackson, Bruce
  1974 *Get Your Ass in the Water and Swim Like Me: Narrative Poetry from Black Oral Tradition.* Cambridge: Harvard Univ. Press.
Johnson, Charles S.
  1934 *Shadow of the Plantation.* Chicago: Univ. of Chicago Press.
Lanier Seward, Adrienne.
  1983 The Legacy of Early Afro-American Folklore Scholarship. In *Handbook of American Folklore.* Ed. Richard M. Dorson. Bloomington: Indiana Univ. Press. Pp. 48–56.
Liebow, Elliot
  1967 *Tally's Corner: A Study of Negro Streetcorner Men.* New York: Little Brown and Company.
Mudimbe, Y. V.
  1988 *The Invention of Africa.* Bloomington: Indiana Univ. Press.
Newell, William Wells
  1888 On the Field and Work of a Journal of American Folk-lore. *Journal of American Folklore 1:3–7.*
Powdermaker, Hortense
  1939 *After Freedom.* New York: Viking Press.
Redfield, Robert
  1947 The Folk Society. *American Journal of Sociology* 52:293–308.
Roberts, John W.
  1989 *From Trickster to Badman: The Black Folk Hero in Slavery and Freedom.* Philadelphia: Univ. of Pennsylvania Press.
Rose, Tricia
  1989 Orality and Technology: Rap Music and Afro-American Cultural Theory and Practice. *Popular Music and Society* 13:35–44.
  1990 Never Trust A Big Butt and a Smile. *Camera Obscura* 23:109–31.
Stern, Stephen
  1991 The Influence of Diversity on Folklore Studies in the 1980s and 1990s. *Western Folklore* 50:21–40.
Wall, Cheryl A., ed.
  1989 *Changing Our Own Words: Essays on Criticism, Theory, and Writing by Black Women.* New Brunswick: Rutgers Univ. Press.
Weldon, Fred O.
  1959 Negro Folktale Heroes. *Publication of the Texas Folklore Society* 29:170–89.
Wepman, Dennis, Ronald B. Newman, and Murray B. Binderman
  1976 *The Life: The Lore and Folk Poetry of the Black Hustler.* Philadelphia: Univ. of Pennsylvania Press.

Wilgus, D. K.
  1959   *Anglo-American Folksong Scholarship since 1898.* New Brunswick: Rutgers Univ. Press.
Zumwalt, Rosemary L.
  1988   *American Folklore Scholarship: A Dialogue of Dissent.* Bloomington: Indiana Univ. Press.

ETHNOGRAPHY AND POETIC THOUGHT

Reflections of a Native Ethnographer

Dan Rose

IT IS fortunate when ethnographers such as Kenneth Goldstein have ready access to field sites and can return again and again over the course of a lifetime. Friendships become possible and the cultivated distinction between fieldworker and informant can blur within the entanglement of lives. As a native ethnographer, I have not been able to leave where I work except for foreign travel and brief stays abroad. Entanglement has become a way of life and so has assimilation, for as one studies aspects of one's culture that were not part of growing up, one tends rather easily toward developing a closer, professionalized resemblance to what one studies. At times there has not been enough distance, and much valuable access, so it seems, has been lost to knowledge because I could not present it freshly and from a unique perspective. The poetic pieces included here represent a strange complement to continuous fieldwork, in part because they are not about native peoples or persons from the British Isles marginalized by the metropolis. By studying, arguably, the most advanced market culture, in a world whose sensibilities are increasingly dominated by a system of global exchange, the topics touched upon in the poetic are topics that frame inquiry, and inquiry is profoundly informed by the objects of inquiry.

These poetic pieces, as I've called them, are not poems per se, though they have been informed by a poetic imagination. They tend toward prose, do not have the intent to be made as poems, do not conform consistently to the metric demands of a poetic line, even blank verse, and treat topics that seem remote from the stuff of most poetry, such as the market or machines. They also avoid the directly personal, which has been a significant mark of much poetry in the modern project.

There are five thematic elements woven at times together: experimentation, anthropology and the disjunction of past and future, the arts, the market, and a philosophy of the place of humans in the physical universe, also an anthropological subject, but ordinarily a physical rather than metaphysical one.

Experimentation

The idea here is to play as close as possible to the edge of sense and nonsense, in a mode of great abstraction. This probably amounts to an American version of European surrealism where language experiments always sought to tap into what was thought to be the pure stream of the unconscious. In any given composition, I have tried to preserve the unconscious quality of spontaneity and present a string of nonsequiturs in order to evoke rather than present. "Desire," "Einstein," "Epiklesis," and "Poem Bisected by a Line" come as close to that as anything I've written.

Anthropology and the Disjunction of Past and Present

One reality of contemporary commercial civilization is its discontinuous quality, the breach with the past as well as the desire to reinvent it, the crisis for achieving, finding, or making identity, and the breaks and fissures attending the infinite replacement of nearly everything foisted on us by the market. Even the larger questions of humanity are being raised in ways that once received somewhat firmer and more controllable answers in the great religions. In "Island," I use the great energy unleashed by parody to poke fun with a Yoruba myth, probably bent out of recognizable shape even for Africanists. But "Blueprints," "Fire," "Landscape," and "Remarks" all touch on the intermission in temporality, the old versus the new.

The Arts

The arts respond to and are wholly caught up within the contemporary commodification procedure, and they represent in the poetic the eruption of the new, just as markets offer new objects and processes as substitutes for, and seek to make obsolete, what is now at hand. Architecture, sculpture, and urban design make appearances as standing in for the notion of pure making. At a deeper level, artistic making is very different than the scientific inquiry of classical ethnographic practice. Ethnographers describe and explain. Artists make art. These two are not comfortable cohabitants if artificially mated. Artists are not ethnographers, ethnographers not artists—routinely. The tension between art and science is embodied in such writing as "Designer" and "Architect." For me, being caught up in my own culture means celebrating it as well as critiquing it, and art is a form simultaneously of making and celebrating. Despite its, at times, overwhelming faults and failures, this is a magnificent moment to be living, and it is an energized and exciting place. Righteous heir to the Enlightenment, the United States is in many respects a microcosm of the global marketplace, a cultural R & D laboratory for the rest of the world, much of which attempts to emulate our successes and learn from our failures.

The Market

The market is now the defining reality for a humanity linked together by it. This seems too true to be insightful, but I have attempted to capture some aspects of its pervasiveness in "Epiklesis," "Jacob," and "NIKE." Are the twin towers of "NIKE" those of the World Trade Center in Manhattan?

Philosophy

In "Before Dawn," the idea was to give voice to a conclusion I had reached from reading in the physical sciences for a number of years: that humans have evolved on this planet as wholly interior outcomes of physical processes. Since humans now intervene in evolutionary processes through the manipulation of DNA, the making of materials from first principles, and the detonation of nuclear devices using isotopes that would not occur naturally without human intervention, I assume that we have evolved in order to speed up the evolution of the universe. Rather than just learning to learn, we have evolved to accelerate evolution. The side-effects, one must quickly point out, are themselves deadly and devastating. Take human-induced extinctions, for example. Are humans more deadly than giant meteors or sunspots? Will we create more disorder than order, thus inducing the most entropy imaginable, our own extinction and the ruination of the planet? Such questions, embodied in the poetic, move beyond the confines of scientific anthropology—or science—as they are meant to.

Island
> *from the Yoruba*

I.

This afternoon I stood on the quay drinking
a Coca-Cola when my ship came in

The hold was loaded with mouths
and I called to the longshoremen and drivers
"Take them up to the warehouse"
                    LATER THAT NIGHT

the mouths were connected to voices and
there rose a mighty jangling
at first sounding like all the telephone
bells of the continent

II.

I opened the venetian blinds
and saw the sun had turned the world
into a yellow fruit

For as far as I could see, the mouths had become
leaves on all the tropical trees
and were a fluttering townspeople--
voices chattering to one another in the marketplace

III.

I stood on the quay this afternoon
drinking a Coca-Cola while waiting for my
ship to come in,
expecting necks or heads

Remarks to a Fashion Model on St. John the Divine

Before breakfast this morning he shared his feeling with her that they must rethink St. John the Divine living in Judeo-Christian exile on the Isle of Patmos.

In these latter days, he told her, "I once revisited the island, jogged nude on the beach, grew darker, consumed cocoa butter lotions, and the advertised secretions of aloe. My skin tanned the hue of Nigerian soils and I smiled like advertising in every magazine of the world.

"Rethink St. John the Divine and the molting religious shell of humans. After school your child and mine will engineer another star machine.

"Let me finish just by saying that in my revery I saw St. John stagger his way through a field
of laser gyroscopes that keep the present world on course.

"He was seeing visions and dreaming dreams and he witnessed the new heaven and new earth. The plans were smuggled away in the pocket of a cellulose man who hitchhiked distraught and alone the Florida Keys looking for a motel."

The Poem Bisected by a Line

She told me she thought the surfaces of her
friends—some in particular—enclosed a
primal secrecy within themselves akin to
darkness.

Their surfaces she said, are finely
toothed but I am not attracted beneath;
I have no idea what goes on with them,
who they are.

I know that architects, masters of surface and light, hide
behind their works and Armageddon
for them lies in a remote human future,
just before the universe collapses to iron.

Earlier today I discovered that salt had
turned to rain and there was bitterness in the air--falling with precision
along surveyor's sight lines--hitting in our region it ran into
long strings composed of blue crystals.

We could use the crystals for markers in a game
where the opponents try to surround one
another and capture the most fortified
positions.
Was this the local displacement of warfare?

Architect

As he began to design the house, he realized it was not the first or last house but was to be a dwelling inserted into the river of time—
a mathematical river that barely held to its banks, broke far inland, and looped finally upon itself.
This river, he told the client, inspires the designer. At flood stage it brings the annual source of irrigation for the region.

As we stood there I felt that we were not on a riverbank but really on the edge of the sea. Cold air shot inland above our heads. The summer house, constructed to resist the encroaching dunes, was where the architect came to escape from city life.
"The distances between houses," he remarked ironically, "must resemble, but not exactly, the distances between ourselves."

In the magnificent pink and gold veneer of the late afternoon sky—a sheet of scenery forever unrolling overhead into space—the architect considered the number of houses appropriate to this view and their rooms

Designer

In this house the author drafted differing versions of reality

Less density

For example,
a lamp that opens like flowers, sheds a space of light that resembles a
white circle painted on a black stage.

The actors recite their parts taking turns in the klieg circle

The flower opens into yellow
and yellow upon brighter yellow

The set of all points of light
the set of all possible words

He rehearses in front of the mirror
in front of the window
in front of the other architects

he rehearses before the critics
he rehearses within the new words
drawn from the set of all possible sentences.

The First Bird's Eye View:
From the Lost Poems of Leonardo da Vinci

From this altitude directly above the bay,
over the sea wall,
just outside the curved port,
I look down upon the city which is fortified by a ring of perfect stones.
I draw the axonometric houses that seem to rise behind one another,
street after narrow street. The subtle lines of this time of day fall
exactly in the shadows between apartments.

I can imagine what I see; am sitting on a chaise at the end of the quay,
sketching angles on the picture plane. I imagine I am that gull out
there, hung in aerial space, poised to glance back over the city for a
moment, fixed high in the mind's eye.

NIKE Leaving the Roof of the Building   Between
the Twin   Towers

It is not a spirit rising but the right wing can be discerned, it appears
slightly torn though lifted up; the torso twisted, and a single leg partly
obscured as she emerges.

In the distance, seemingly much more remote than the figure itself, we
hear the sound of a pair of slow incessant beating wings, perhaps a
futile wanging of the air
unmodulated
and repetitious

Sculpture

Atomic brains

The maroon shoulders of a merrillynch bull

The thorax of a goose neck lamp

Chrome vagina

Reticular knees

and

Feet shaped like the blades

of a speed

skater

Blueprints

The architect knelt on one knee and spread the coil of drawings for his clients. The older man bent his head over the blue page and remembered the thin, exquisite lines.

A third person, little more than a child, perhaps the granddaughter, faced us, as if we were the camera and talked directly in a flat tone as even as if she were reading her memoirs to herself half aloud.

She told us that it was either the beginning or the end of time. Her tone remained uninflected and we began to think of Eden, in the fall of the year, when the angels have sealed the garden with swords of fire.

The structure took shape behind your face. You imagined yourself at the drafting table, felt as if for the first time the pencils, the trace, the hard line between the imagination and the clear measures of the orbits, the number of your days—the twenty thousand nights in this bedroom.

Landscape

I remembered the scream of the children and the molten metal that first had popped and twisted, the child's sharply exhaled breath on sudden impact, the gargle in the throat, the winged monkeys' final flight through the broken fuselage, as they darkened the air, flapping and whirring.

I staggered onto a new landscape, alien trees, brown and green gave way to violet trunks and magenta leaves, distorted distances through which the old ways of seeing were now impossible.

Fearful views opened on the medieval map I held, orange at the border, the fractal edges of the continents, and the scrawled place-names backed by cartographic theory: a map that could erase the separation of life and death, or establish the fictional location of Zion, home for the heart's dread wandering. It was here beneath the faintly inscribed X that marked the spot that I read for the first time how human lives are tied to the remotest acceleration of the stars.

Epiklesis from the Marketplace

God of simulacra, our heavenly alter ego we do pray that
the noctilucent clouds shall fall from our children's eyes
And the cigarette boats speed close to the Milky Way
And radio galaxies shall tune to our exploded neurons

That dreams shall invade computers
And the sky fill with the affluent
wearing Mercedes Benz in their hair

And the children of parents shall be born to
the rapture of machines
And the fires of their imaginations shall rage across the planet
And they shall hold moon rockets in sensitive hands
And shock diamonds appear inside their crystal brains

A Version of Einstein's Dream

Last night I dreamed a version of Einstein's dream.
In the dream Einstein and his friends travel at the speed of light.

Are they light?

In the darkness they imagine what they are doing,
and whisper to one another their equations.
They are projected onto a mirror surface,
their images bound in 2 dimensions like a photograph.

The flat plane of their imagery collapses, sucked into a tiny capsule. A
man swallows the medicine.
A chemical key unlocks the pill. From the center of being rays of light
beam through every muscle of his body.

Muscles turn to liquid aluminum and when he tries to walk, he wobbles
erratically in space.
A thin film of silver water washes over his face.

Einstein bends over like a physician and listens near the face to the
running water music that reveals the voices of his friends. They walk
beside him inside the other frames of time.

Desire

I want to feel that feeling.

Inside it's spaceless
engulfed on all sides

desire without coordinates

Our skin:
two warm sheets of pliant plastic film
touching ten to the one hundredth power
perpendicular worlds to this one

they scatter into the quantum foam of being
Now we're everywhere
moving together   we kick toward god.

Fire

We discovered the dancing surfaces of fire long before you suspected it. One night we sat around listening to the combustion of the wood, and above our heads in the cone of darkness a lens formed. Through it we could see far into the future and vague figures of the future looked back into their past toward us squatting there. We barely discerned the faces, perfectly formed in birth and transformed by longing or desire; and faces broken by fire and healed in a shaman's pharmacy. There were experiments with freezing human time and the obvious failures, and the thinning of the legends of the gods of earth. We began to learn that knowing about it all, in some deep way, was within ourselves in the magical molecules of becoming. We were shaken by the rush of sound that fell upon us. Then sonic detonations, the drumming of voices, voices that gave way to just the drums, electronic sounds amplified beyond the terror of pure revelations, and sounds from the apocrypha that resembled an ocean storm plunging its floating objects to the orchard of wreckage among the coral grasses at the bottom of the sea. We saw our children's children's children riding the arrow of time away from us and we discovered within ourselves a fear of the blinding speeds of the worlds.

Jacob

Yesterday afternoon I lay down for a nap and there was a presence in
the room like plastic film preventing sleep:
An angel of god.

I stood up and wrestled with the winged beast and as it threw me to the
floor I grabbed its bronze foot and grunted out,

"...the poetic cannot compete with the language of the world
market..."

And I added, " I shall not release thee unless thou bless me."

Then I put the thing in a hammer lock but it twisted away and elbowed
me hard in the stomach. Gasping for breath I heaved the words at it,

" . . . cultural formation more rapid than the words of poets to
possess it . . . " and it flew away.

Before Dawn

I walked downstairs feeling by memory through the utter darkness
with my hands in front. It seemed that Chinese singers wearing blue
pants poured abstract songs into my heart. The music made me think of
human time and the story of the universe that evolved itself into this
planetary motion and the soundless touring of the nebulae. Each moment, I knew, the universe grew more complex, the stars drilled
photons at the earth--and back there the distant origins of life.

There was a whispering in the house meant for me. I could hear my
voice in my throat.
—the universe sends us to itself
—it is given to us to know ourselves
—it is given to us to make it over, to suffer and triumph in our smart
machines
—and we accelerate this universe of time by constructing matter with
pure theory

I glanced through the kitchen window and saw the lights of space
hurtle toward me through white curtains at the speed of light. Time
spread below me like a void, like looking through a mailing tube, into
an abyss reflective like my darkening cup of tea. I was wearing a
winged rocket suit, navigational instruments, and scientific labs of
health and astral vision.

My children woke up then. They rolled into the future; it was a
morning in which they exploded time backward and forward in unfold-
ing strata like a tier of fountains shaped outwardly by thought and
shaped inwardly, enclosing the hidden universe itself.

THE DEVIL IN THE BACK SEAT

Neil V. Rosenberg

Preface

THE FOLLOWING TEXT is a reprinting of my presidential address to the Folklore Studies Association of Canada, originally read at the Association's annual meeting in Montreal, Québec, on June 5, 1980, before an audience the majority of which was francophone Quebequois (advocates of *séparatisme* for the most part) in a Japanese community center hall (a gesture to the idea of multiculturalism then dominant in national politics). Addressing political, social, and philosophical issues that emerge in the fieldwork experience, it seems an appropriate presentation for this volume. Recently I re-read my field notes and was struck by how much I had to leave out. Today I would write differently about some aspects of this experience, for I'm now convinced that we have an obligation to participate in the dialogue of cultural nationalism to ensure that the insights of our research can contribute to progressive social democracy. Still, this is what I thought back then, and it remains, for me, a vivid reminder of the existential character of our primary research.

The Original Text

In planning my talk for this evening I reviewed past presidential addresses to the Association. Each is quite unique, but they have one common aspect—the assumption that folklore is something which the professional can recognize and gather with relative ease. Indeed it is this assumption which makes it sometimes difficult for us to define our area of study succinctly to outsiders; we know intuitively what it is but cannot always put this into a brief definition.

An experience I had during my field research several years ago remains in my consciousness because it cast doubt upon this assumption. It began simply enough when I heard what I thought to be a legend. At the time I was not looking for legends; I was studying musical traditions in central New Brunswick. It was Thanksgiving weekend and I had come to a lumbering, mining, and manufacturing town where one of my informants, a fiddler in his forties named Frank (this like all the other names is a pseudonym), had offered to introduce me to musicians I was interested in meeting. I had a choice—a pair of brothers who sang country gospel music, or a man in his seventies who knew the old lumberwoods ballads.

It soon became apparent that I would not be able to meet the gospel singers, for a faith healer had just come to town for his yearly two-week stand at the local Pentecostal church and one of the brothers was helping with the music. There was much interest in Frank's home about the faith healer. Frank, his family, and his friends all had some comments to make on the subject. Was his a "real" power or one of suggestion? How could he possibly cure people of things which doctors couldn't cure? Was it ethical for him to tell a certain woman to throw away her heart pills? From here conversation turned to *Chariots of the Gods* (von Daniken 1970), UFOs, and parapsychology. Debate and discussion about the overlapping realms of rational science and religious faith occupied much of the conversation as plans were laid for me to meet the singer of lumberwoods ballads. As a professor I was expected to have an opinion, and I entered the discussion from the position of one who knew little about faith healers but found the literature on UFOs fascinating and sometimes even believable.

On the evening of our planned trip outside of town to meet the singer, it was discovered that he was not at home, having gone to a wedding anniversary celebration at the home of an Acadian woodsman well known for his parties. It was suggested that I go to this party, for I could meet the singer there and maybe even record him. To this day I suspect that we ended up at the party not by chance but by design. My entrée with Frank was as a fellow musician and I had been asked to bring my banjo along, "just in case." I think that Frank had been asked to provide music and that in this instance my research interests were not as important to him as my ability to help out with his obligations as an entertainer.

I travelled to the party by car with Frank and two others, a younger guitarist named Pete and an older man named Walt who was a step-dancer and played just enough fiddle to keep the music going when Frank took a break. En route a bottle of rum was produced from under the front seat and passed around. Conversation developed into a story-telling session as each man related earlier experiences along the same road: sighting a panther, a confrontation with an angry moose, driving off the road on a high school graduation night. I made a mental note of these personal experience narratives.

When we reached the party, it was already in full swing. The old singer I had hoped to record was there, but he was quite drunk and would sing no more than one or two verses of any song. He performed that way all night long, even though his only audience was another old man, also quite drunk, seated next to him. This type of ballad performance, which we might call the "inebriated-fragmentary," is probably more common than we realize. Perhaps it is the musical equivalent of the local legend, so familiar that a part may stand for the whole. Obviously this folksong phenomenon deserves further study (and sober reflection). But I was not able to document it here because as a musician I was obligated to help provide music for the entire evening's worth of singing and dancing, while the rest of the party became increasingly jovial. Such was the uproar that even if I had been free and the singer able to perform coherently I could not have made a recording.

I didn't really mind that the evening's music required me to spend virtually all of my participant-observer time as a participant. Our obligations to the people we study often must be met by providing useful services for individuals upon demand. Such services are usually worth the trouble; in this case when I returned to record the singer the next day he greeted me cordially and commented on the previous night's music. I recorded a substantial number of his songs. But I am getting ahead of my story, for what happened directly after the party proved most interesting.

We left around one o'clock in the morning, returning toward town along the same country road. Once again conversation developed into storytelling about experiences on this road. For no apparent reason, talk turned to the supernatural. Frank, at the wheel, noted first that we were passing a place where a ghostly hitch-hiker was once encountered.[1] For the next part of this storytelling event, I quote from my field notes, written two days later:

> Then Frank described an experience he said had happened to his wife's cousin Stan. This chap, he said, was a soft-spoken chap who would never pull your leg or tell a lie, which was why the story had made such an impression on everyone who had heard it. Stan and another fellow were driving along a road (may have been this one, but my impression was that it was a road such as this one) at night and all of a sudden looked back in the rear view mirror and there was the Devil, sitting in the back seat! The only way they could get rid of him was to speed up to ninety miles an hour, but each time they slowed down, there he was again. Sitting in the back seat with a cynical look on his face. They realized that this was his trick—trying to make them speed up so they'd have an accident. Eventually, Frank said, they just stopped the car, abandoned it, and came back for it the next day. And Stan swears this really happened, and he had no reason to make up the story, either.

Following this brief narrative, which the other two men had apparently not heard before, Walt launched into a story about something that happened to his father many years ago when he was working in a lumbercamp in the American West. It was a version of the well-known tale of the mysterious card player who is discovered to be the Devil when another player, retrieving a dropped card from the floor, sees a cloven hoof.[2] When he'd finished Pete said, "I bet that was the end of that game," and Walt replied, "I guess so." Then conversation moved to other topics.

To me this was one kind of typical legend-telling session, in which accounts of allegedly true happenings were swapped in a conversational context. As a folklorist I recognized two of the three stories that had been told. I wanted to record them all, especially the story not familiar to me, the one about the Devil in the back seat.[3] Next morning as we were heading out on the same road to record the old singer, I asked Frank if he would tell the story to me again so I could record it. Frank responded cautiously, saying we would be going past cousin Stan's home, and why didn't I get it from him first-hand? Frank's response surprised me. Here he was going out of his way to help me record one informant, but he didn't want me to record him telling the narrative he had told the night before. He felt strongly that I should go directly to his source. Unfortunately, though, no one was home at Stan's that morning.

A month later, at the annual meeting of the American Folklore Society, I told the story to legend specialist Linda Dégh. She asked me how did they know it was the Devil—was he dressed in some distinctive way? I realized that I didn't recall such details being mentioned. When I next visited Frank I asked him how Stan knew it was the Devil and what the Devil was wearing. Frank said he figured that it was the Devil because of his behaviour and the look on his face. Again Frank told me he would take me by to talk with Stan so I could get the full story.

I continued my attempts to record this legend. Early in the new year I visited Frank and his family. My purpose was to record his son telling about the ghosts he had seen in the home of his grandmother, which was said to be haunted. Before starting the interview, I had supper with the family. Conversation turned to the haunted house, and I discovered there was strong difference of opinion about it. As the son spoke of his experiences, Frank kept interrupting to say that only mentally retarded people had these experiences, that they were seeing things, and so forth. His son and wife opposed this view, basing the argument upon their own experiences in the haunted house. They told Frank, who for some reason had never spent a night there, that he would be a believer if he had seen these ghosts. The son pointed out that Frank had not seen UFOs either, yet he believed that they existed. Frank responded to this accusation of inconsistency by saying "Why even policemen have seen UFOs," and glancing toward me for affirmation.

The arguing was done in good humor with Frank and his son taking diametrically opposed positions and the rest of the family falling between them, sometimes siding with one, sometimes with the other. Although the debate was obviously a kind of ritual within a family that had long ago agreed to disagree about supernatural matters, Frank felt strongly enough about this issue to try in subtle ways to postpone my recording of his son's account about the haunted house. But we proceeded, recording in the living room while the rest of the family sat in the kitchen where they talked casually and monitored my interview. Eventually I learned that the house was on land that had been cursed, but the son would not divulge the terms of the curse beyond saying that in his opinion Satan was behind it all.

Although I did not record the legend of the Devil in the back seat at this time, it was here that I began to understand Frank's reluctance to record it for me. Both he and his family made a clear distinction between first-person and third-person accounts of experiences with the supernatural. Using the analytic terminology of von Sydow, I would call the first "memorate" and the second "legend."[4] Neither was considered a "story"; they were simply descriptions of real happenings. A first-hand report was, obviously, better than a second-hand one. Because the son was telling his own experiences in the haunted house, it was proper for me to interview him. But during the interview, comments flew between the son and the rest of the family whenever he touched upon elements of the haunting which were not his own experience. In this overlapping territory between memorate and legend, communal knowledge was tempered by the family debate about the reality of the situation. Frank hesitated to record his story of Stan's experience because he took a negative position in this family debate. It is significant that he did tell the story outside of the family context, when we were in the car. In that context, he did not have to take a position in the continuing debate about such matters—it was just a good story. And in the car we were not seriously discussing the supernatural, just talking.

Frank's acceptance of UFOs, which are described in books and verified by such important secular authorities as policeman and professors, contrasts with his son's belief in the existence of Satan. Behind this contrast lies the basic differences between father, a religious sceptic, and son, a faithful Christian fundamentalist. Eventually I began to suspect that Frank's reticence about telling the story of the Devil might be a result of his lingering fear that Satan really did lurk in the back seat. And I sensed that Frank was much more comfortable as my go-between than as my informant. He didn't see himself as a folk, but felt he could help me find folk.

I made a number of attempts to interview cousin Stan, culminating in an evening spent at Frank's during which we spoke with Stan over the phone and apparently convinced him to come over to Frank's house. After a wait of several hours, Stan's wife phoned to check on him. He was not yet there, and it was surmised that he had taken advantage of our invitation to sneak out to the Legion for a drink, something his wife did not permit. It was at this point that I finally prevailed upon Frank to tell his story for me on tape.

He was obviously uncomfortable. Sitting tensely in front of the microphone, he grabbed the stand, drawing the microphone to within a few inches of his face, and began narrating as if he were a CBC announcer:

> This is the story of Stan Smith and a chum, Rex Ryan, who were out driving one evening in Brewster, New Brunswick. They'd had some liquor but not an overly amount, they were—

Here I interrupted to ask "were they driving right here in town?"

> Mmm-hmm, like within five miles on each side of it. So they happened to glance in the rear view mirror and there was a gentlemen of a cynical

expression on his face and, I think, a little peaked cap; sitting behind in the back seat. And, which frightened them nearly to death and they didn't know quite what to do. But anyway they stepped on the gas and went as fast as they could and the faster they went, he would disappear. But then as soon as they slowed down he would come again, he would appear again. They gathered from this that the man, that the person wished them to go to their death at a high speed. So, then therefore they slowed the car right down to a stop or nearly a stop and got right out and run and hid in behind the Bijou Theater here in Brewster. So I don't know quite what happened after that. We saw 'em the next day, and he was telling us about it, and still pretty worked up about it. That's about all I'd, I can say about it.[5]

Further questioning revealed the fact that this incident had occurred soon after Stan's brother had died tragically through drinking a substance sold as an air freshener, a kind of drug-abuse overdose quite common at that time and place. This death was still a topic of conversation in the community, even though it had occurred fifteen years earlier. I tried to establish some relationship between Stan's encounter with Satan and his brother's death in a similar sinful context, but neither Frank nor his wife saw any connection between the two incidents.

The two texts of the story which Frank told me, one from my notes, the other from his recording, differ only in one significant fact: in the second telling Frank adds that he thinks the Devil was wearing a little peaked cap. I am pretty certain that he added that detail in response to my question at Christmas about what the Devil wore.

I learned a good many things from this attempt to document a legend. I discovered in probing for the text that even though my informant had told it as a story in one context he was unwilling to consider it a story worth recording as such. Only because I created a sense of obligation for him by performing as a musician at his house parties was he eventually willing, with great reluctance, to tell the story to my tape recorder. Here, then, is a fine example of a situation in which context is considerably more important than text, and in which the field worker and the informant did not agree about what constituted an appropriate performance.

I also discovered in my quest to get this Devil legend that by questioning my informant I had prompted him to add some details to the story that I do not believe were present in the original. In a sense I had forced him to give the Devil a silly-looking cap he probably was not wearing.

And in my search for this narrative I discovered that what I had supposed to be a homogeneous group was divided in many ways: constant debate arose whenever I ventured into the realm of the supernatural. Discussion about the faith healer, the haunted house and cursed property, UFOs, the Devil: these were manifestations of the same attitudes, beliefs, personality conflicts, and family roles. Maybe these things are real, maybe they aren't. Credible trustworthy people have had such experiences, but others do not have the faith to accept them. When I described these debates in my field notes, I said that "the various components of the active legend debate as outlined by Dégh and Vázsonyi (1973) in *The Dialectics of the Legend* unfolded before me." But I could only explain my difficulties in recording Frank's account by adding another dimension to this theory—that as context changed, so the same individual might take differing positions or abstain from debate. Frank was willing to use Stan's experience as a story in the context of the male peer group in the car, but was reluctant to tell it as such within the family context. The legend as related in the car was "extinct" (I'm using Dégh's and Vázsonyi's terminology here) and was thus not subject to serious debate. But it was "active" and therefore open to debate in the family setting. Because Frank took a negative position in the family debate, he attempted to steer me to the source of the legend, Cousin Stan. Cousin Stan's reluctance to speak to me of this experience gives rise to further uncertainty about the nature of the phenomenon—was his a true memorate or a legend in disguise? This is the fertile soil in which belief, memorate, and legend flourish. As I discovered, it can be difficult to harvest such growths.

I think the difficulty goes beyond any particular folklore genre. Time and time again I found that my contacts were much more comfortable when I was dealing with older individuals performing well-defined genres. Knowing I was a folklorist, they eagerly led me to seventy- and eighty-year-old men who sang ballads or recited poems about life in the lumberwoods. When I started to dissect the active traditions, I met with less enthusiasm. I never really got to the bottom of the story behind the haunted house, for instance. The family clearly knew more than they were willing to tell, especially when the tape recorder was running. And I am sure there was more to the story of the Devil in the back seat than I was told. Similar reticence was evident when I sought to examine the repertoires of the two gospel singers, and of two fiddlers. In varying circumstances certain songs and tunes were acceptable to one, and not to the other. The reasons lay in personality, family, class, religion; hence what I saw as simple matters of repertoire involved the entire social fabric.

What is to be learned from all of this? For one thing, it underscores the fact that folklore is certainly not dying out, at least not in New Brunswick; but that we often do not find out about it until it is safely interred. Perhaps this is not a bad thing, for we do not always realize how deeply we are probing when we seek folklore. What was to me an interesting story text was to my informant the tip of a dangerous iceberg, part of a complex issue which was approached with considerable care because of the emotional issues it engendered.

It is on this intense personal level that folklore most often functions. Perhaps some day I will see my way clear to speak about folklore as the symbolic baggage of a culture or a community. But when one family—or even single individuals—can be so uncertain about the meaning and relevance of their own traditions, how are we to speak with certainty about a community? This doesn't bother me so much as you might think, for I believe that fieldwork experiences such as the one I have described lead us to realize that the Devil is with us all, and that in studying folklore we are indeed dealing with something that is intrinsically important for an understanding of humanity, whether or not it has political or cultural relevance. How many of us, after all, have looked apprehensively in the rear view mirror while driving at night down a lonely road?

Notes

It is my pleasure to present to Kenny Goldstein this reprinting of my presidential address to the Folklore Studies Association of Canada. The research reported in this paper was made possible through a Canada Council Leave Fellowship (W74-0346). Thanks also to David Buchan, Martin Laba, Monica Morrison, and Ann Milovsoroff Rosenberg. The article was originally published in the *Bulletin of the Folklore Studies Association of Canada* 4:3/4 (Nov. 1980):13–19.

1. This was a variant of motif E332.2.2.2, "The Vanishing Hitchhiker."
2. A variant of motif G303.4.5.3.1, "Devil detected by his hoofs." See also C12.5.12*, "Man swears he can beat the Devil in card playing."
3. For a somewhat similar tale, see Louis C. Jones, "The Devil in New York State" (1952). In Jones's story, the Devil pursues a "hard-drinking man" who is driving a wagon with a team of horses. He escapes and vows to stop drinking.
4. The use of these terms varies considerably. See Pentikainen 1973.
5. The recording from which this is transcribed is on deposit at the Memorial University of Newfoundland Folklore and Language Archive under accession number 80-127, tape C4770.

References

von Daniken, Erich
    1970 *Chariot of the Gods?* Trans. Michael Heron. New York: G. P. Putnam's Sons.
Dégh, Linda, and Andrew Vázonyi
    1973 *The Dialectics of the Legend.* Folklore Forum Reprint Series [1:3]. Bloomington, Ind.: Folklore Publications Group.
Jones, Louis C.
    1952 The Devil in New York State. *New York Folklore Quarterly* 8:12–13.
Pentikäinen, Juha
    1973 Belief, Memorate and Legend. *Folklore Forum* 6:217–241.

RITUAL HOUSE ASSAULTS
IN EARLY NEW ENGLAND

Robert Blair St. George

SHORTLY AFTER daybreak on August 14, 1765, residents of Boston made a startling discovery. "This morning," Deacon John Tudor confided to his diary later that day, "was discovered hanging on the great Trees at the South end of Boston the Effiges of And[rew] Oliver Esqr. as Stamp Master & a Large Boot with the Divel coming oute of the top. . . . The effiges hung all Day," he continued, "and towards evening a number of people assembled, took down the effiges carr[i]ed them throw the Town as far as the Townhouse, then March'd down King Street, and then proceeded to Oliver's dock, pulled down a New Brick Building caled the Stamp Office, belonging to the s[ai]d Oliver & carried the Wooden part of it up to Fort Hill and with Shouting made a Bonfire of it with s[ai]d Oliver's Fence which stood near s[ai]d Hill." If this were not sufficient mayhem for a summer's evening, these violent episodes climaxed in a vicious attack on Oliver's brick house, an impressive Georgian structure near the wharves at the south end of town. The "mob" wrecked his office and tore up his prim fence. Then, according to Tudor, the mob "surrounded Mr Olivers House, Broke his Windows & entred the House & destroyed [a] great part of the Furniture & c" (Tudor 1896:17–18).

Tudor's short reference to this strange occurrence raises many questions. As one of a series of house attacks in the stormy Stamp Act months of 1765, the attack on Oliver's property seems to have been a well-planned strike at an individual associated with the "corrupt" imperial policies of George III and his court circle. While many American historians have noticed the differences between "riots" in pre-Revolutionary America and the "mobbings" held on English soil—the frequent participation in the colonies of "middle class" people, for instance, or the relative lack in the colonies of needless violence or death—it was not until Gordon S. Wood called attention in 1966 to George Rudé's work on English popular violence that the Stamp Act riots offered an opportunity of systematically exploring early American popular *mentalité*. In particular, Rudé's *The Crowd in History* suggested to Wood that crowds may not have been witless or passive instruments of elites or outside agitators (Wood 1966:635–42).[1] Their actions instead were rational and directed to morally logical ends. But if so, what purposes had Boston's Stamp Act rioters in mind as they attacked the house of Andrew Oliver? In fact, Oliver was only one in a series of assault victims in such urban centers as Boston and Newport, the large towns this essay explores, although other skirmishes occurred in many smaller places as well. A gap remains in our knowledge of what transpired at street level, and how the performance of key cultural metaphors in public spaces helped both to reveal popular unrest and to focus its symbolic meanings.

Deacon Tudor's diary account provides a place to begin. One question it raises concerns *context* and demands a brief description of the social connections, political intrigue, and moral judgments made apparent in the "mobbings" of the Boston houses of Andrew Oliver, Charles Paxton, William Storey, Benjamin Hallowell, and Thomas Hutchinson, and the Newport houses of Martin Howard, Thomas Moffatt, and Augustus Johnston. Another problem centers on issues of *form* and *participation*. Why did these episodes of ritual violence take the particular shape that emerged? Why stage effigy hangings, burnings, and mock funerals? And why vent such rage on material possession? Doors were smashed with axes, partitions were split, important documents were scattered to the winds. A final set of questions explores *metaphors* and *meanings*. Was such pillaging a type of symbolic performance that made immediate sense to its participants? If so, what did they mean?

Context and causation warrant our attention first. Boston and Newport were beset by a host of difficulties during the decades leading up to the 1760s, and historians agree that a steady economic decline spanned the years between 1690 and 1760 (Nash 1979:16–17, 63–64, 114–23; Warden 1976: 593; Henretta 1965:81–87). This depression had diverse causes: a lull in maritime trade and building following the Treaty of Utrecht, a marked rise in the number of new arrivals to these ports, and a desparate lack of silver specie all contributed to the picture. So did the arrival of a new cohort of petty political bureaucrats, whose monied interests and quick alliances with wealthy local merchants raised prompt cries of distrust and apprehension. In Boston the sanctioned control of property by leading families had grown top heavy by 1770, as the town's wealthiest five percent controlled almost one–half of all capital (Henretta 1965:87). Essentially, the rich were getting richer, and the poor and middling classes either dug in or left town. House assaults in eighteenth–century New England were thus grounded in a society undergoing traumatic separations in economic and social order. House assaults targeted individuals who had used public, political, and economic influence for private ends. Like the *charivari* (Alford 1959; Thompson 1972), the house attack was a strategy of moral outrage and correction.

The attacks themselves were a complex blend of inherited customs, distinct forms, and participants with different reasons for joining in the festivities. Like many pre–Revolutionary events, it made recognizable references to the English Civil War, a powerful emblem in Puritan New England of republican virtue and popular political will. In August, 1642, for example, angered parliamentarians attacked the dwelling house of royalist John Lucas in Colchester, Essex. The assault demonstrated the ardor of Puritan reform and the efficiency with which they dismantled the mansion itself:

> they now spend their rage upon the house, they batter down the doores and walls, beat down the windowes, teare his Evidences, deface his Walks and Gardens, doe any thing that may doe mischiefe. From thence they goe to his Park, pull downe his Pales, kill his Deere, drive away his Cattle. And to shew that their rage will know no bounds, and that nothing is so sacred and venerable which they dare not to violate, they breake into Saint Giles his Church, open theVault where his Ancestours were buryed, and with Pistols, Swords, and Halberts, transfix the Coffins of the dead. ([Ryves] 1646:95–96)

The attack on Lucas, along with other widely published instances of ritual pillaging, set a forceful example in early modern English popular culture. A proper attack was precisely planned and designed to dishonor the victim's family lineage by literally laying waste to their estate. But such historical referent provided only one point of reference for the mobs in Boston and Newport. They could have also read about an episode attack in July 1765 in which a London mob "of upwards of a thousand men and women" gathered to "destroy the windows of a certain house" (*Newport Mercury* July 22, 1765:2). As these references suggest, the house assault was a form of popular protest in Anglo-American culture that was familiar to and recognized by "elites" and "plebs" alike.

The actual form and meaning of these assaults varied. They commonly started with a rumor, a bonfire, a gathering at a prominent location near the center of town. Early in the evening of August 26, 1765, "there was some small Rumour that Mischeif would be done that Night; but it was in general discarded. Towards Evening Some Boys began to light a bonfire before the Town house, which is an usual Signal for a Mob: before it was quite dark a great Company of People gathered together crying Liberty and Property, which is the usual Notice of their Intention to plunder & pull down an House." Effigies, however,were the focus of the universal opening act in the drama. "The surprize and joy of the public" greeted the stuffed figure of Andrew Oliver when it was discovered hanging in Boston's South End. Accompanied by a boot (symbolizing John Stuart, Earl of Bute, one of George III's most despised cronies) painted with a "Greenville" sole (mocking George Grenville, Chancellor of the Exchequer), the mock-theatrical scene was termed "a spectacle," and "continued the whole day without the least opposition, tho' visited by multitudes" (*Newport Mercury* September 9, 1765:2).

In eighteenth-century society, effigies of course carried meanings deeper than the immediate resemblance to the specific persons they imitated. Visitors to Westminster Abbey will recall the types of people often effigiated: members of the royalty, military heroes whose sacrifices and heroism had protected the English constitution, and ecclesiastical leaders who wrapped political might in divine mandate. The tradition of using effigies to honor courageous leaders was well known to seventeenth—and eighteenth—century New Englanders, and their use of effigies to mock—rather than honor—their leading citizens represents an inversion of convention. In an engraving for Samuel Butler's *Hudibras* emphasizing the popular festivities that ushered in England's return to a free Parliament in 1660, William Hogarth showed a stuffed effigy making just such a mockery (Fig. 1): "Some on the Sign Post of an Ale house / Hang in Effigie on the Gallows, / Made up of Rags to personate / Respective *Officers* of *State* (Trusler n.d.:166–68; Harris 1987:49, 213–22).[2]

Unfortunately, few contemporary images show what effigies looked like as they swung in the breeze blowing through Boston's south end. They seem to have been of two basic types. The first was a full-body example, similar to Hogarth's, that was hanged, paraded, and cremated. An engraving from the *Boston Gazette* in 1766 (Fig. 2) shows the full-body effigies of Lord Bute and George Grenville hanging from a gallows, chained to a devil who extends a copy of the Stamp Act for their mutual inspection and approval. Bute is dressed in the tartan and kilts of a highland Scots chieftain, apparent references to his Celtic political "savagery." Grenville has been dressed in the clerical garb of an Anglican priest, a sure sign for New England's Puritans of his imperial and Satanic leanings.

The second type of effigy consisted of a grimacing wooden head supported on a stick or pole. An engraving of 1770 (Fig. 3) shows the use in Boston of a pole-and-head effigy figure. A crowd has posted it in front of merchant Theophilus Lillie's retail shop, calling attention to Lillie's refusal to comply with the anti-importation agreement designed to boycott British goods. Lillie's face is grotesque, and his powdered wig is severely drawn back. This type of effigy certainly relied on an exaggerated scale to make its victim terrifying and terrified, but it also referenced the vernacular custom of posting the head of an executed leader on a pike (or gateway, or bridge) for all to see, something New Englanders could easily remember from the decapitation of Charles I in 1649 and from their own bloody exhibition of King Philip's head on the road leading into Plymouth in 1676. Effigies used in the house attacks also invoke the laughable costumes worn by participants in Pope's Day contests and antic garb of mummers. Loose motley dress and a minister's hat adorn an effigy in Portsmouth, New Hampshire (Fig. 4). Effigy-makers in Windham, Connecticut, employed a similar stylistic opposition in 1765: "on the morning of the 26th instant, a certain ever memorable and most respectable gentleman, made his appearance in effigy, suspended between the heavens and the earth, (as an emblem of his being fit for neither) he was cloathed in white and black, with a view to represent the great contrast of his character" (*Newport Mercury* September 2, 1765:2).

Figure 1. William Hogarth, "Burning ye Rumps at Temple Barr," from the series for Samuel Butler's Hudibras, 1726. (Photo, The Colonial Williamsburg Foundation)

Figure 2. Effigies of Lord Bute (John Stuart), in kilt at left, and George Grenville in "ministerial" garb at right. Emerging from a boot, the Devil holds out a peice of paper to be stamped. From the *Boston Gazette,* February 24, 1766. (Photo, New York Public Library)

Figure 3. Head of merchant Theophilus Lillie held aloft on a pole, outside his shop in Boston. From *The Life, and Humble Confession of Richardson, the Informer* (broadside) 1770. (Photo, The Historical Society of Pennsylvania)

Figure 4. Effigy of stamp-master being paraded and stoned by crowd, Portsmouth, New Hampshire, 1765. From John Warner Barber, *Interesting Events in the History of the United States* (New Haven, 1829). (Photo, Metropolitan Museum of Art)

The performative effects of effigial costume and style were intensified by intertextual allusions to aspects of related festive forms. In Skimmingtons, humbled transgressors rode in carts through the streets to mock gallows, a motif encountered as the effigies of Howard, Moffatt, and Johnston "amidst the Acclamations of the people . . . were paraded through the streets [of Newport] in a cart with halters about their necks, and then hung on a gallows in front of the Colony House on the Parade" (quoted in Stevens 1927:25). An effective effigy brought into symbolic congruence and compressed the meanings of these diverse traditions—the doubling of masks, the levelling lampooning of leading citizens, and sympathetic magic—into a multivalent sign that attached them to a specific individual. The effigy's strange power lay in the terror these compressed meanings at once struck in onlooker's souls. In Durham, Connecticut, in September 1765, just such an effigy was created when a small group of people did "begin a Procession with an Image . . . representing [BenjaminGilliam] . . . figured and fashioned in the Likeness of a Man and habited in dolefull frightfull & dismall Hue" (*Gillam v. Dimmock et al.* 1768).

The representational power of an effigy increased as written messages attached to its body addressed spectators. Pinned to the breast of Andrew Oliver's effigy were the words "in praise of liberty" and "denouncing vengeance on the subvertors of it." His right arm reportedly bore the betraying initials "A.O.," while its left arm announced *"What greater pleasure can there be, / Then to see a Stamp-Man hanging on a Tree."* Beneath the effigy final missives appeared: "HE THAT TAKES THIS DOWN IS AN ENEMY TO HIS COUNTRY," and an admonitory verse:

> *Fair Freedom's glorious Cause I've meanly quitted,*
> _____ *For the Sake of Self,*
> *But ah! the Devil has me outwitted,*
> *And instead of* stamping *others, have* hang'd *myself.*
> *P.S. Whoever takes this down, is an Enemy to*
> *his Country.* (*Newport Mercury* August 19–26, 1765:2)

Usually effigies were left to swing ominously for a day and were then cut down. They were then pronounced "dead" for festive purposes. Mock funerals for the deceased effigies drew spectators who turned into participants as the parades moved raucously through the streets. In Boston, the procession escorted the dead body of Andrew Oliver's effigy through the winding streets, making sure to pass by the sites of official culture and political control:

> About evening a number of reputable people assembled, cut down the said effigies, placed it on a bier, and covering it with a sheet, they proceded in a regular and solemn manner, amidst the acclamations of the populace through the town, till they arrived at the courthouse, which after a short pause they passed, proceeding down King-street soon reached a certain edifice then building for the reception of stamps, which they quickly levelled with the ground it stood on and with the wooden remains

thereof marched to Fort-hill, where kindling a noble fire therewith, they made a burnt-offering of the effigies for those sins of the people which had caused such heavy judgments as the STAMP Act &c. to be laid upon them. (*Newport Mercury* August 26, 1765:3)

Other mock processions traced a similar and more complete rectangular route that took them past the courthouse, past the large houses of Cornhill merchants, past the third meetinghouse, up to the burial ground, and, finally, back to where they started after passing by the Anglican churchyard. By retracing a geometric square in the middle of a town plan dominated by linear thoroughfares, the mob was intentionally transforming a "linear merchant city" shaped for the efficient communication of goods and services into an archetypal "orthogonal" city whose gridded geometry recalled for Puritans biblical visions of heaven's perfect order. They were thus inscribing a layer of consecrated, popular meanings on an avowedly secular and heirarchic landscape; the purpose of the inversive mockery was not to overturn social order alone, but also to demonstrate the perfectability of the social order they envisioned (Moholy-Nagy 1968:198–240; Archer 1975:140–49).[3]

After the effigies were hanged and burned, what came next? Sometimes nothing. Occasionally, attacks stopped at this point, as mob members must have been sure that their display of symbolic cruelty had been effective. Through "killing" the effigy by tearing out its eyes, tongue, guts, and either hanging or beheading it, they had "murdered" the intended victim of their discontent. But in some instances at this point energies focussed and the violence escalated dramatically, as the mob actually assaulted the houses of their victims. On August 14, 1765, Andrew Oliver's house met the mob's fury. The day itself was an auspicious choice, since it was the anniversary of the birth of Sir Robert Walpole, a figure widely portrayed as epitomizing the image of the machivellian court minister bent on consolidating his own interests at colonial expense. First the mob levelled a small brick structure Oliver used as his office. Next fell his stable, coach house, even his prized chaise—an emblem par excellence of wealth and aristocratic posturing. Then the house itself beckoned. The mob careened through his front door, splintered his furniture, smashed his windows, drained his wine cellar, and laid waste to his ornamental shrubbery. A quick study, Oliver promised immediately to resign his post (Almy to Story 1765).

The crowd flexed its muscles next on August 26, scheduling a series of homes for demolition. At first, a fast-talking landlord told the mob that Paxton was not at home and succeeded in buying off the crowd with a round of drinks at a local tavern. From the tavern, as provincial Governor Francis Bernard later explained it, the mob went to the house of William Storey, deputy registrar of the Vice-Admiralty Court, and "broke the Windows of the House and Office, destroy'd & burnt part of the Goods scattered & burnt most of the papers in a Bonfire they made in King Street near the House." Their level of confidence was rising. Benjamin Hallowell, the comptroller of the Custom House, was the next target. The mob "Broke down the Fence & Windows of his Dwelling house, & then entered the House, Broke the Wainscot and great part of the Furniture & c. and carried of[f] 30£ Sterling in money & c." Three houses down, one to go. The mob wheeled, and headed for its final prize: the stately mansion of Thomas Hutchinson, the Lieutenant Governor of the Province, whose commitment to the Stamp Act was by no means certain. Francis Bernard's narrative reveals the basic details:

> This brought it to the dusk of the evening, tho' it was a moonlight Night near the full Moon. Then the monsters being enflam'd with Rum and Wine which they got in s[ai]d Hallowells Celler proceeded with Shouts to the Dwelling House of the Honl. Thos. Hutchinson Esqr. Lieut Governor & enter'd in a Voyalent manner, broke the Wainscot, partitions, Glasses, & c.; broke & distroy'd every Window, Broke, tore or carr[i]ed of[f] all the Family's Apparel, Jewels, Books & c. and Carr[i]ed off about £900 Sterling in Cash, they worked hard from 8 O'Clock on the House, Fences & c. till about 12 or one O'Clock; when they got on top of the House and cut down a large Cupola, or Lanthorn which took up their Time till near Daylight, leaving the house a mear Shell. (Bernard to Halifax 1765)

Figure 5. Thomas Hutchinson's house in Boston, built by his grandfather, merchant John Foster, ca. 1686, attacked in 1765, and finally taken down in 1834. (Photo, Society for the Preservation of New England Antiquities)

The next morning, as gawkers gathered to inspect the damage, money and mahogany lay scattered in the narrow lanes of Boston's North End. His house, a fine Georgian structure built in the mid-1680s by his grandfather, merchant John Foster, was ruined (Fig. 5). Hutchinson himself described the assault in dramatic terms, positioning himself as the benevolent father figure besieged by undeserved anger:

> In the evening while I was at supper & my children round me somebody ran in & said the mob were coming. I directed my children to fly to a secure place & shut up my house as I had done before intending not to quit it but my eldest daughter repented her leaving me & hastened back & protested she would not quit the house unless I did. I could not stand against this and withdrew w[i]th her to a neighbouring house where I had been but a few minutes before the hellish crew fell upon my house with the rage of devils & in a moment with axes split down the door & entred my son being in the great entry heard them cry damn him he is upstairs we'll have him. Some ran immediately as high as the top of the house others filled the rooms below and cellars & others remained without the house to be employed there. . . . Not contented with tearing off all the wainscot & hangings & splitting the doors to pieces they beat down the Partition walls & altho that alone cost them near two hours they cut down the cupola or lanthern & they began to take the plate and boards from the roof & were prevented only by the approaching daylight from a total destruction of the building. . . . Such ruins were never seen in America. (Quoted in Anderson 1924–26:32–33)

These house-attack narratives are remarkable summaries of the violence that characterized house assaults. But who, precisely, was being violent? Who did Hutchinson mean when he said "they"? The answer to this question is complicated. Gary Nash argues that some protesters (merchants who had profited as smugglers) found the Stamp Act damaging, while poorer individuals viewed the Act as a convenient occasion to present a list of complaints they had been compiling for years (Nash 1978:297–98). The ostentatious consumption and accumulation of property that had turned some of Boston's streets into theaters of pomp and puffery no doubt touched a popular nerve. By the 1710s in Boston and the 1730s in Newport, expensive mansions lined certain streets, while in back alleyways and among wharves laboring people lived in ramshackle, overcrowded wooden structures.

The "mob" consisted of educated, wealthy Whigs striving to protect self-interest, as well as radical artisans eager to ease economic burdens. It was a group that with one voice concealed divergent interests, a point Governor Bernard perceived in precise terms. After Andrew Oliver's property had been levelled, Bernard attributed the violence to the fact that "Everything that for years past had been the Cause of any popular discontent was revived; & private resentments against Persons in Office work'd themselves in & endeavoured to execute themselves under the Mask of Public Cause" (Bernard to Halifax 1765).

Given the complicated, "mixed" nature of the mob's membership, a second question remains: Why houses? Perhaps houses of the wealthy provided fitting targets for people who could never hope to live in such stylish surrounds. This is the "material" argument: the standard of living of "the rabble" was much starker than the material comfort enjoyed by Thomas Hutchinson, whose fine mansion, in Bernard's words, "from its structure & inside finishing seemed to be from a Design of Inigo Jones or his Successor" (Bernard to Halifax 1765). From this perspective, the mob may have felt it had a vernacular right to level distinctions after enduring without complaint times "when good Honest, Industrious, Modest People, are driven to such streights, as to Sell their Pewter and Brass out of their Houses." Perhaps they were offering systematic pillage for systematic pillage, since English customs officials had already rifled private homes with impunity. "Our houses," Bostonians argued, "and even our bedchambers, are exposed to be ransacked, our boxes chests & trunks broke open ravaged and plundered by wretches, whom no prudent man would venture to employ even as menial servants; whenever they are pleased to say they suspect there are in the house wares & c for which the dutys have not been paid." Because of these invasions, they claimed, "we are cut off from that domestick security which renders the lives of the most unhappy in some measure agreeable" (quoted in Bailyn 1967:117).

At Hutchinson's, the mob "emptied the house of every thing whatsoever except a part of the kitchin furniture"—that is, they had plundered the house to the point that what remained resembled the very things they had in their own tenements. But house assaults had an additional symbolic meaning that complemented the magical power of effigies and words to afflict a real person. To reveal this level of significance we need to explore in brief the symbolic connections that tied architecture to the human body in early New England culture. The language of contemporary building manuals shows that people in early modern English culture viewed buildings as metaphoric transformations of the body. In his *City and Countrey Purchaser* of 1703, for example, Richard Neve claimed that the first step in evaluating a house "is to pass a running Examination over the whole Edifice, according to the Properties of a well shapen Man; as whether the Walls stand upright, upon a good Foundation; whether the Fabric be of a comely Stature, . . . whether the principal Entrance be in the middle of the Front, like our Mouths; [and] whether the Windows, as our Eyes, be set in equal Number, and distance on both sides [of] the Entrance" (Neve 1703:84).

On the other hand, the writings of poets and ministers in New England offer many analogies between buildings and bodies that support the arguments of architectural theorists. Anne Bradstreet described her aging body as "my Clay house mouldring away," while Edward Taylor allowed that "I but an Earthen Vessell bee," "a Mudwall tent, whose Matters are / Dead Elements, which mixt make dirty trade." Cotton Mather urged widows to view their deceased husband's corpse as "the forsaken Mansion of the Soul which was dearer to her than the World." The human body was thought of in terms of building and had a distinctly architectural identity. When seeking help through prayer, for instance, Taylor beseeched God to "Sill, Plate, Ridge, Rib, and Rafter me with Grace" (Miller and Johnston 1963:579; Taylor 1977:46, 218–19; Mather 1692:110).

Analogies employed by clergyman and carpenters were much more precise—and more useful to our present problem. Edward Taylor referred to the windows of a house as "the Chrystall Casements of the Eyes." The cupola or "lanthorn" of a house—like that torn from Hutchinson's building in the early morning—he equated with a "brain pan turrit." In England, John Donne sketched in additional parts of the house-body: "The rafters of my body, bone / Being still with you, the Muscle, Sinew, and Veine, / Which tile this house, will come again." Robert Herrick added his version: "The body is the Soules poore house, or home / Whose Ribs the Laths are, and whose Flesh the Loame." The loam or plaster that Herrick describes was the flesh that covered up the "carcass" of the house, which Neve described as "TheTimber-work (as it were the Skeleton) of a House, before it is Lathed or Plaister'd" (Taylor 1977:48, 72; Donne 1967:111; Herrick 1968:367). Taken together, the house-body references made in seventeenth- and early eighteenth-century Anglo-American literature yield a remarkably complete inventory. A brief sample: the roof is the head of the house, the laths are its ribs, the clapboards its skin, the door its mouth, the windows its eyes, the doorjambs its lips, the chimney its breast, the hearth its heart, the flame its soul, and the gutters its veins. This house-body relationship helps to explain why crowds attacked houses the way they did, and it also suggests that millenial zeal, grounded in typological thought, was crucial to successful mob violence. To destroy a house was to destroy symbolically the body of its owner by tearing out its eyes, its tongue, opening its head, exposing its brain (just as the mob worked on the windows, door, roof, and cupola of Hutchinson's house) and, in tearing down interior partitions and throwing broken furniture and mangled household possessions out onto the streets, to publicly disembowell his corpse in front of his own eyes. The trope is Rabelaisian: by turns gruesome, grotesque, and surprising to find in a Puritan society so deeply committed to the disciplined regulation of the human body.

The combination of Gothic horror and melodramatic morality play recalls another Hogarth image—his 1751 engraving of Tom Nero's body being eviscerated as the "Reward for Cruelty" (Fig. 6). Nero began life by torturing small animals with no remorse. His downhill slide continued, and soon he had senselessly beaten a young woman to death. Nero was apprehended, convicted of murder, and hanged at Tyburn. As frequently happened to those turned off at Tyburn, Nero was promptly stretched on a stone table. There his body greeted the gaze of spectators in the anatomy theater: "Behold and shudder at the ghastly sight! See his tongue pulled from the root, his eye-balls wrung from their sockets, and his heart torn from his body, which the dog is gnawing beneath the table!" Elsewhere, verses commented on "Those eye-balls from their sockets wring, / That glow'd with *lawless lust.*" Symbolic disembowelment through the destruction of their human house-bodies and the evisceration of their inner, "consumed" contents was a just form of symbolic punishment for

Figure 6. William Hogarth, "The Reward of Cruelty," from his series on *Cruelty* (no. 4), 1751. (Photo, The Colonial Williamsburg Foundation)

Hutchinson and the others, characters repeatedly denounced in the penny press as willing agents of a distant tyrant, and "cruel" and "merciless" "oppressors of the weak" (Trusler n.d.:191–92).

Unwarranted cruelty, even when couched in political language and political debates, violated the moral boundaries of the body social, the established Christian model of proper social order. Thomas Hooker had even equated society and a house frame when he warned that "if the parts be neither morticed nor braced, as there will be little beauty so there can be no strength. Its so in setting up the frames of societies among men, when their mindes and hearts arre not mortified by mutuall consent of subjection to one another, there is no expectation of any succeseful proceeding with the advantage of the publicke" (Hooker 1648:188). With this in mind, we can see that the significance of house assaults derived in part from the parallelism of effigy as body, house as body, society as body—a cognitive paradigm in which virtue and property must be defended from curruption just as a house's fortitude must depend on the sturdiness of its frame. The parallelism was affirmed in Durham, Connecticut, when a local mob caused the "Image or Effigy to be beheaded & within also a Small Distance of the Persons Dwelling House to be burnt," thus establishing an crucial symbolic connection between the destruction of the effigy, the mock destruction of the person, and then the "transference" of "personness" to the impending destruction of their house (*Gillam v. Dimmock et al.* 1768). The metaphoric connections became clear when furnishings in Martin Howard's Newport house were themselves effigied on the parade ground just as if they were the dishevelled components of a body. "And first they went to Martin Howards," a newspaper report revealed, "And Broke Every Window in his house Frames & all, Likewise Chairs Tables, Pictures & every thing which Stood before his door & Bro[ugh]t them & *stuck them up on two Great Guns which have been fix'd at the Bottom of the Parade Some Years as Posts* (*Newport Mercury* September 2, 1765:2).

With wise leaders at its head and obedient followers at its extremities, the body social was an organism that resembled the model of the early Christian covenanted community outlined by St. Paul in 1 Corinthians, chapter 12, verses 12–27. Like many educated Puritans, John Winthrop revealed the influence of Pauline interpretation when he described "our community as members of the same body." And the belief continued, nurtured by the covenant theology so vehemently defended in the eighteenth century by preachers like the outspoken Jonathan Mayhew. For John Adams, the analogy had lost none of its force. Writing during the heat of the Stamp Act riots, seeing houses in which he had been entertained disembowelled before his eyes, he considered that a political constitution is like "the constitution of the human body," some of whose "contextures of the nerves, fibres, and muscles, or certain qualities of the blood and juices . . . may properly be called *stamina vitae,* or essentials and fundamentals of the constitution; parts without which life itself cannot be preserved a moment" (quoted in Bailyn 1967:68, n.12).

The body social lived at the symbolic center of Adams's Puritan social inheritance, and resonated deeply with his nostalgic invocation of the same concept in a neo-Harringtonian defence of the English constitution. Yet what seems equally significant is the fact that almost without exception the houses that were attacked were not traditional, "organic" New England salt-box houses, but Palladian-style mansions whose closed, controlled, and symmetrical facades concealed the inner workings of affective family life, while their central hallways moved people through private rooms with precise, mechanical efficiency and predictability. People did not have to get in each other's way in the course of a day's work or a night's relaxation. A Georgian house like Thomas Hutchinson's was not a projection of the owner's being, but a mask, a planned image that was separable from his true persona, or the inner self that lay hidden behind the well-managed veneer of a public persona for whom self-control—in business, politics, and family life—was essential.

In attacking these architectural masks, the mob was trying to peel away the mystifying mask of mechanical control and expose the face of the hidden householder, the exalted patriarch, to public ridicule. A key to exposing the person behind the facade to public shame, and a clue that no one was really after a "real" murder of the homeowner, is that all of the targeted individuals received adequate warning to vacate before the mob's arrival; the mob's organizers must have sent runners in advance to ensure that only symbolic murder would ensue. When the mob reached Oliver's house, its doors had been barricaded. Hutchinson had plenty of warning; using language curiously reminiscent of witchcraft narratives, Bernard explained that he "had been apprized that there was an evil Spirit gone forth against him" (Bernard to Halifax 1765). As Hutchinson himself admitted, "messages soon came one after another . . . to inform me the mob were coming in pursuit of me" (quoted in Anderson 1924–26:32–33). But he remained in the house, knowing that trouble was on the way.

Why? Perhaps he was being falsely heroic, living out the characters traced to life by Alexander Pope. More likely, however, is Hutchinson's realization that both he and the mob were interdependent players in Anglo-American popular culture, and that his only hope of retaining authority depended on a voluntary subjection to the "collective will" of the mob. Despite his lofty position and august breeding, he had to undergo the inversive process of ritual shaming and publicly atone before the "rabble" for their "cruelty." Again using the skimmington as a model, the house assault stripped a transgressor of his separable facade and forced him to atone for his sins through voluntary self-effeminization and mendicancy.

Hutchinson's narrative of the attack suggests his adoption of a feminine demeanor. He admits that when the mob arrived, "I had undressed me & slipt on a thin camlet surtout over my wastcoat." Waiting for the mob, he was in fact dressed in an overgarment defined at once by its loose, flowing qualities and by its evocation of the equally protective "surtout"—meaning a hooded mantle—worn by genteel women during the period.[4] Hutchinson stayed in the house long enough to be saved by his daughter—certainly a reversal—and then flee, "obliged to retire thro yards & gardens to a house more remote," embarassed in his "undressed" state. The next day, still in rags of retreat, he reported that "I had not cloaths enough in my posession to defend me from the cold & was obliged to borrow from my friends" (quoted in Anderson 1924–26:32). Having experienced the forced entry of the "mob" into his house-body, with all its implications of political rape, Hutchinson's feminized shaming was complete.

As he looked around his estate the next morning, Hutchinson felt the loss of certain possessions more than others. As the most serious student of New England's history since Thomas Prince, Hutchinson bemoaned the loss of rare manuscripts and records he had been collecting during his researches; he discovered that the mob had left not "a single book or paper in it & [had] scattered or destroyed all the manuscript & other papers I had been collecting for 30 years together besides agreat number of publick papers in my custody" (quoted in Anderson 1924–26:33). Bernard, in his official report to the Earl of Halifax on the attack on Hutchinson's house, confirmed the extent of the loss of precious historical records:

> They went to work with a Rage scarce to be exemplified by the Most Savage People. Everything Moveable was destroyed in the most minute manner, except such Things of Value as were worth carrying off, among which was near 1000 Pounds sterling in Specie, besodes a great quantity of family plate & c. But the loss to be most lamented is, that there was in one Room kept for that purpose a large & valuable Collection of Manuscripts & Original Papers which he had been gathering all his Lifetime, & to which all Persons who had been in Possession of Valuable Papers of a Publick Kind, had been contributing as to a publick Museum. As those related to the History & policy of the Country from the Time of its settlement to the present & was the only Collection, the loss to the publick is great & irretrievable, as it is to himself the Loss of the Papers of a family, which had made a figure in this Province for 130 Years. (Bernard to Halifax, 1765)

But a report the next day from Providence suggested that Hutchinson's house had been attacked because people did not like *his* version of *their* history. Not only did they shred rare written documents, but they destroyed the "museum" he had been assembling of New England rarities and then, in a move designed to destroy Hutchinson's personal history of family "effigies," slashed—literally "de-faced"—the ancestral portraits hanging in the formal parlors next to the street. The destruction of Hutchinson's family archives was also a redressive strategy intended to point out the gross inequality of property relations, an inequality that laboring people felt with a special intensity. As Bernard himself noticed, the documents they destroyed were ones specifically "relating to the claims and titles of this province; all dispersed, stolen and defaced, so that the damage in its consequences may be esteemed publickly as well as privately injurious" (Bernard to Halifax 1765).

In summary, attacking a house was not an act of frenzied vandalism. It was undertaken by mobs once they or their leader(s) had selected an appropriate target for legitimate redress, and was a form of planned symbolic violence that pointed out a failure on the part of leading citizens to act in a morally responsible way. Attacks on houses were frontal assaults on moral transgression. The metaphoric invocation of the body—that prime emblem of the nation state, political order, and Christ's perfect symmetry—and the successful ritual shaming of victims argues that the "mixed" members of mobs—even in their most "radical" moments—did not have in mind the erasure of social distinctions, as Bernard intimated when he worried that the Boston house assaults represented a *"generall levelling & taking away [of] the Distinction of rich and poor"* (Bernard to Halifax 1765).

Members of the Boston and Newport mobs did not want to do away with deference and the linkages between wealth, power, knowledge, and property it appropriately subsumed. To do so would have contradicted the ethical tradition that bound them together as inheritors of Harringtonian republicanism and that motivated their protest. What they wanted to accomplish through these symbolic murders was to reassert their complementary vision of an organic, covenanted society and their concept of a moral political economy that acknowledged the perfectability of society. They were not urging a "return" to a lost world, but rather aspiring for the benefits of a political structure they had never in fact experienced. They wanted to warn against the dangers of accumulating too much money, which, according to William Petty, "is but the fat of the Body-politick, whereof too much doth as often hinder its Agility as too little makes it sick" (quoted in Braudel 1973:327). Finally, they sought to villify the attempt by some of those in control of money and power to define society, economy, and the body per se, as machines, running according to their own inner laws, protected like Georgian houses by separable facades and detached from providential revelation by slipping gears of form and language. Ritual house assaults in early New England were about the conflicting metaphors that shaped society and culture in eighteenth-century New England.

Notes

1. Specifically, Wood called attention to Rudé (1964); see also Rudé (1959) and the essays gathered in Kaye (1988). Wood stated that what Rudé's work "requires at the very least, it seems, is a new look at American mob violence during the American Revolution focussing on the structure of the society which prompts popular demonstrations and on the nature of the institutions which are compelled to deal with them" (1966:641). For a recent summary essay see Slaughter (1991). My concern in this essay is to extend analysis to include the cultural significances and aesthetic meanings of symbolic violence and approach it not as "reflective" of social or institutional structure, but as constitutive of feeling and symbolic force.

2. Effigies remain an essential but largely misunderstood aspect of popular violence in many cultures. The best single work on effigies in western European culture is Brückner (1966). For the meanings of effigies in New England, see also the local English studies in Rogers (1877), Hope (1907), Laurence and Routh (1924), Ropes (1931), and Drury (1931).

3. On funerals and public ceremony in early Boston, see the 1687 procession for Lady Andros in Samuel Sewall (1973:1, 16). In the eighteenth century, Boston shopkeeper Benjamin Walker confirmed this street pattern for the funeral processions of Penn Townsend in August 1727 and Mary Belcher, the wife of the provincial governor, on October 8, 1736. Of the Townsend procession, Walker noted: "August 24. Saint Bartholomew's Day Townsend buried, a very large funeral Came from his house down Queen Street & Down King Street round ye Town house & so up to ye New burying ground." Of the Belcher funeral: "she was buried, bro[ugh]tt fro[m] ye Province house thro Cornhill Street went down fro[m] our front into Kingstreet went as far as Colo[ne]l Fitche['s] house turn'd up street on South side off Town house to burying Ground" (Walker n.d., vol. 1 [August 21, 1727], and vol. 2 [October 17, 1736]).

4. On the femininization of male costume discussed here, see *OED,* "surtout," and Montgomery (1984:188, plate D-9) for a sample of camlet used by Mary Alexander to order garter material in 1736 in New York. See also the description of men's costume in Parker and Wheeler (1938:43) describing the garb of merchant Nicholas Boylston in 1767: "His loose blue-green banyan of flowered silk is worn over a yellow & cream waistcoat. His shirt and hose are white. On his shaved head he wears a crimson turban"; for his 1773 portrait (p. 44): "He wears a blue banyan, buff waistcoat, and crimson turban. His slippers are red and his hose grey."

References

Alford, Violet
    1959   Rough Music. *Folklore* 70:505–18.
Almy, William, to Elisha Story
    1765   *Miscellaneous Bound, 1761–1765.* Massachusetts Historical Society.
Anderson, George P.
    1924–26   Ebenezer Mackintosh, Stamp Act Rioter and Patriot. *Publications of the Colonial Society of Massachusetts* 26:32–33.
Archer, John
    1975   Puritan Town Planning in New Haven. *Journal of the Society of Architectural Historians* 34:140–49.
Bailyn, Bernard
    1967   *The Ideological Origins of the American Revolution.* Cambridge, Mass.: The Belknap Press of Harvard Univ. Press.
Bernard, Francis, to the Earl of Halifax
    1765   Francis Bernard Papers, "Governor Bernard's Official Paper" (Sparks Mss. 4, Letter Books 1765–66), 13 vols., Houghton Library, Harvard University, 4:150–52 (August 31).
Braudel, Fernand
    1973   *Capitalism and Material Life 1400–1800.* Trans. Miriam Kochan. New York: Harper and Row.
Brückner, Wolfgang
    1966   *Bildnis und Brauch: Studien zur Bildfunktion der Effigies.* Berlin: E. Schmidt Verlag.
Donne, John
    1967   *The Complete Poetry of John Donne.* Ed. John T. Shawcrosse. Garden City, N. Y.: Anchor Books.

Drury, G. Dru
    1931   Early Ecclesiastical Effigies in Dorset. *Proceedings of the Dorset Natural History and Archaeological Society* 53:250–64.

Gillam, Benjamin v. Daniel Dimmock et al.
    1768   Durham, Connecticut, in New Haven County Court, Records, Book 7:100, and New Haven County Court, Files: Drawer 40 (April).

Harris, Tim
    1987   *London Crowds in the Reign of Charles II: Propaganda and Politics from the Restoration until the Exclusion Crisis.* New York: Cambridge Univ. Press.

Henretta, James
    1965   Economic Development and Social Structure in Colonial Boston. *William and Mary Quarterly* 3rd ser., 22:81–87.

Herrick, Robert
    1968   *The Complete Poetry of Robert Herrick.* Ed. J. Max Patrick. New York: W. W. Norton.

Hooker, Thomas
    1648   *A Survey of the Summe of Church-Discipline.* London: n.p.

Hope, W. St. John
    1907   On the Funeral Effigies of the Kings and Queens of England. *Archaeologia* 60:517–23.

Ingram, Martin
    1984   Ridings, Rough Music and the "Reform of Popular Culture" in Early Modern England. *Past & Present* 105:79–113.

Kaye, Harvey J., ed.
    1988   *The Face of the Crowd: Studies in Revolution, Ideology and Popular Protest. Selected Essays of George Rudé.* Atlantic Highlands, N.J.: Humanities Press International.

Laurence, R. H. and T. E. Routh
    1924   Military Effigies in Nottinghamshire Before the Black Death. *Transactions of the Thoroton Society* 28:114–28.

Mather, Cotton
    1692   *Ornaments for the Daughters of Zion, Or, the Character and Happiness of a Virtuous Woman.* Boston: n.p.

Miller, Perry, and Thomas Johnston, eds.
    1963   *The Puritans: A Sourcebook of Their Writings.* 2 vols. New York: Harper and Row.

Moholy-Nagy, Sybil
    1968   *Matrix of Man: An Illustrated History of Urban Environment.* New York: Praeger.

Montgomery, Florence M.
    1984   *Textiles in America, 1650–1870.* New York: W. W. Norton.

Nash, Gary
    1979   *The Urban Crucible: Social Change, Political Consciousness, and the Origins of the American Revolution.* Cambridge: Harvard Univ. Press.

Neve, Richard
    1703   *The City and Countrey Purchaser, and Builder's Dictionary.* London: n.p.

Parker, Barbara Neville, and Anne Bolling Wheeler
    1938   *John Singleton Copley: American Portraits in Oil, Pastel, and Miniature with Biographical Sketches.* Boston: Museum of Fine Arts.

Rogers, W. H. H.
   1877   *The Ancient Sepulchral Effigies and Monumental and Memorial Sculpture of Devon.* Exeter: W. Pollard.
Ropes, Ida
   1931   *The Monumental Effigies of Gloucestershire and Bristol.* Gloucester: H. Osborne.
Rudé, George
   1964   *The Crowd in History: A Study of Popular Disturbances in France and England, 1730–1748.* New York: John Wiley and Sons.
   1959   The London 'Mob' of the Eighteenth Century. *The Historical Journal* 2:1–18.
[Ryves, Bruno]
   1646   *Mercurius Rusticus: Or, the Countries Complaint of the barbarous Out-rages Committed by the Sectaries of this late flourishing Kingdome.* Oxford: n.p.
Sewall, Samuel
   1973   *The Diary of Samuel Sewall.* Ed. M. Halsey Thomas. 2 vols. New York: Farrar, Straus and Giroux.
Slaughter, Thomas P.
   1991   Crowds in Eighteenth-Century America: Reflections and New Directions. *Pennsylvania Magazine of History and Biography* 115:3–34.
Stevens, Maud Lyman
   1927   The Wanton-Lyman-Hazard House, Newport, Rhode Island. *Old-Time New England* 18:25.
Taylor, Edward
   1977   *The Poems of Edward Taylor.* Ed. Donald E. Stanford. New Haven: Yale Univ. Press.
Thompson, E. P.
   1972   "Rough Music": Le Charivari Anglais. *Annales E.S.C.* 27:285–315.
Trusler, John
   n.d.   *The Works of William Hogarth in a Series of Engravings.* 2 vols. London: Jones and Co.
Tudor, John
   1896   *Deacon Tudor's Diary, Or Memorandums From 1709, & c. By John Tudor, To 1775 & 1778, 1780 And to '93.* Ed. William Tudor. Boston: Wallace Spooner.
Walker, Benjamin
   n.d.   Diary of Benjamin Walker. Mss., Massachusetts Historical Society, Boston, Mass.
Warden, G. B.
   1976   Inequality and Instability in Eighteenth-Century Boston: A Reappraisal. *Journal of Interdisciplinary History* 6:593.
Wood, Gordon S.
   1966   A Note on Mobs in the American Revolution. *William and Mary Quarterly* 3rd ser., 23:635–42.

THE RADICAL CHILD IN CHILDREN'S FOLKLORE

Brian Sutton-Smith

Childhood and the Rhetoric of Progress

WHAT HAS happened to the science of childhood, in particular in child psychology, is that it, more than any other scholarly discipline, has become a legatee both of the Enlightenment and of evolutionary theory, which is to say, it is a legatee of the belief that rational progress and development is what childhood is centrally about. This assumption is so deep in social science that it hardly ever reaches the level of awareness. A cynic might say that modern child psychology is in part a residual legatee of the colonial notion of the romantic primitive whose naivety requires control and management, and that the concern with the child's developmental stages, and the ways in which to accelerate these, have mirrored our nineteenth-century attempts to goad the so-called Third World into civilization. It can be argued that these progress-oriented views of childhood continue to deny to children the kind of cultural relativity that has long been acknowledged as relevant to the UNESCO of modern world adult cultures. Instead we increasingly colonize children's fantasies with our adult kind of imperial Disney-park puerility and dark play that satisfies ourselves about our own earnest child-oriented social character while effectively containing the potential manifestation of the children's neotenous and heteroglossic differentiation. There is no adequate dialogue between us and them.

Children's Folklore

Children's folklorists have unwittingly and often naively accumulated over the years a colligation of accounts on childhood that, while seldom theorized adequately or theorized in any fashion at all, serve the purpose insofar as they stick in the conventional throat of our conceptions of childhood. They just don't fit our expectations. In the nineteenth century, it could be argued by Herbert Spencer, Stanley Hall, and others that these were just remnants of cultural primitivism. With Freud, they became remnants of personal primitivism. In children's literary scholarship, after heavy bowdlerism, they often are said to be delights of children's fancy. But none of these alternatives are sufficient to explain the body of subversion and nonsense accumulated by William Newell, Alice B. Gomme, Norman Douglas, Dorothy Howard, Paul Brewster, Iona and Peter Opie, Herbert and Mary Knapp, Andy Slukin, Diana Kelly-Byrne, Simon Bronner, and all the contributors to *Children's Folklore: A Source Book* (1995).

What are we to make of child subcultures that include as a part of their way of life, regardless of adult requirements, such phenomena as ghosts, verbal duelling, games, play, graffiti, levitations, pranks, autolore, puns, parodies, argots, rituals, legends, urinal and excrement play, panty raids, toiletlore, fire play, food fights, obscene jokes, sex play, skits, camp songs, scofflore, hazing, oral legislation and repartee, guile, riddles, nicknames, epithets, telephone pranks, torments, fartlore, kissing games, calendrical customs, and playground culture?

The Source Book as Sample

As there is no generally accepted authority on children's folklore, and as most of the data is, as suggested, a colligation of relatively diverse kinds of scholarship, the procedure to be followed here will be to put the question of how we should interpret the childhood that is revealed in children's folklore to the authors in the aforementioned, and first of its kind, *Children's Folklore: A Source Book* (Sutton-Smith *et al.* 1995). How do they position their subject matter?

Sylvia Ann Grider sees the special focus as documentation and analysis of traditional child materials of all kinds. The key word for her is *tradition*, though contemporary work on nostalgia, identity, and innovation make the concept itself less obvious than it once seemed. Still, children do have their own group traditions, and children's folklore is about the only scholarship that focuses on that fact even if Newall's paradox of the character of the dialectic between the two, tradition and innovation, still remains.

Rosemary Levy Zumwalt advocates putting aside these historically based foci and viewing childhood instead in terms of the various structural functional analyses now available in psychology, sociology, and linguistics. More importantly, she focuses on the way in which folklore allows the modern girl to express her ambivalence about being an ideal female as well as a less than ideal female, a real female. She says that in her own earlier scholarship she typically attended only to the "ideal" version, but now she says that what is particular to folklore is the fluid interrelationship between the ideal and the real. The separateness is in our adult cultural categories not in theirs.

John McDowell likewise struggles with the same dialectic, and he finds resolution in the child as a performer who is constantly generating his play materials as an emergent function of his own limitations, perceptions, and strengths, his ambivalences, subversions, and parodies and as a function of the immediate utility and aesthetic value of the material to that performer as well as a function of his response to the group and its situated activity. He talks of performance as contingent activation and gives fine examples of the way children playfully transcend their own antitheses of seriousness and fun—one moment riddling and a moment later tarradiddling. But we see also in McDowell a romantic attachment to the generating power of the young performers that the Opies found in their traditional historical continuities. They sought the universal and the constant whereas McDowell seeks the specific and the emergent.

Ann Richman Beresin, with her modern video and audio recording techniques, brings a richness to her children's playground analyses that methodologically lift children's folklore to an entirely new level of "thick" data. One is no longer dealing just with the "games" of the playground but instead with the way in which children of different ethnic and gender cultures create an interactive fabric of activity out of their own emotions and hierarchies as well as out of the school requirements, and the urban and media influences that surround them.

What Beresin does on the macro level Linda Hughes does on the micro level, showing that what is going on among the girls in her study is not the game alone but the way in which it is used as a medium for their real social life in general. They use it to fashion and express their etiquettes of sociability at the same time as they often manage deceptively to use the game to subvert those very etiquettes. The complexity of the girls' game activity is at the meta-social level rather than within the formal structure of the game itself.

It is clear that most earlier focuses on children's games have been hopelessly simplistic, clear also that the major historical play theorist, Johan Huizinga of *Homo Ludens* (1949), has been simplistic. What he sees as immutable—play as free, not ordinary, not serious, absorbing, nonproductive, boundaried, orderly, secret—is upset again and again by the data of Beresin and Hughes. One could even say that all the prior theories of games and play and children's folklore have sought to view them as a kind of containment of childhood, a logical category of impotence, an asylum but not Roger Abrahams's free marketplace, whereas in Beresin and Hughes we have a much more open field, a deconstruction of such static adult-serving images.

Gary Fine discusses the methodological problems of dealing with children's folklore given that the children in our Rhetorics of Progress are not supposed to be bestial in any way, and with honesty and ingenuity he invents and compromises for the sake of information in a way that many of my undergraduates readers of his chapter were simply unable to tolerate. It is true that informed consent, credit to informants, lack of deception, and lack of harm to subjects are essential to a humane modern view. But if one is dealing with lore that is often arcane, antithetical, racist, obscene, cruel, and sexist, the investigators are themselves at risk as are their informants. It is not surprising that the sacral view of Western Childhood is likely to claim that much of what a child folklorist tries to find out is a kind of molestation. Seeing that children themselves are not supposed to be sexual and subversive, discovering that they are sexual and subversive is, it follows, a molestation.

When we arrive at the content section of this sourcebook, that which is about songs, poems, and rhymes (C. W. Sullivan III), riddles (Danielle Roemer), tales and legends (Elizabeth Tucker), teases and pranks (Marilyn Jorgensen), we find again that this material is like the working content of a real antithetical culture. Sullivan, for example, categorizes children's rhymes in terms of the functions they fill for children's groups: for legislating outcomes, as an expression of power relationships between children, for making judgments about each other and for humor's sake. In all of this material, the formative role of the verse in the establishment and maintenance of the peer group and its antithetical relationship to adult conventions, in particular the use of phonology for the political purposes of childhood subversion, rings out loud and clear. The subculture of childhood moves against its adult overlords with a phonological armamentarium.

Danielle Roemer's analysis of riddles profits from the sociolinguistic tradition of analysis, and like Linda Hughes she shows how each riddling session is an ongoing achievement and not merely a reflex of tradition. What is clear again here is that when folklore analyzes only textual collections, tradition is the central concern, but when players themselves are analyzed while riddling, then their social construction of reality is at stake. Newall's paradox becomes in part a text *vs.* context methodological problem, a problem of the investigation rather than of childhood play.

Elizabeth Tucker reminds us that we children's folklorists often become somewhat intoxicated with the enjoyment of our informants and that we are probably self-selected for this kind of work. Not everyone enjoys children's stories, nonsense, or subversion. In the meantime, however, we will spare ourselves from any investigator reflexivity or psychological analysis. There is simply not enough of the former enthusiasm to go around. It is not yet a plague.

Marilyn Jorgensen shows that whereas most of the prior contents deal with the "hidden transcripts" (Scott 1990) of the child subculture, pranks overflow into adult culture in an intentionally disruptive fashion. Her chapter brings to the forefront some of the less pleasant aspects of the culture of childhood. There is often nothing very romantic about the politics of childhood. It is a paradox that studying children's folklore is often a romanticist undertaking, and yet if studied honestly might itself be something of a cure for such an obsession. Perhaps that's why almost everyone has bowdlerized its content as Norman Douglas argued so forcefully in *London Street Games* (1916) more than eighty years ago.

The next section of *Children's Folklore* is on settings and activities, and features Bernard Mergen on playground lore, Simon Bronner on material culture, and Jay Mechling on children's folklore in total institutions. There is perhaps a male emphasis here as compared with the female emphasis in the articles by Rosemary Zumwalt, Ann Beresin, and Linda Hughes. The focus is now on macro not micro environments and is mostly about males, not about females who are not found in these places and with these objects so frequently, or at least not analyzed so frequently. The treatments by Bernard Mergen and Simon Bronner are fairly Arcadian descriptions of the way in which children make do with what is available and transform it in their own myriad ways— their "traditional creative encounter with physical things," as Simon Bronner puts it. Jay Mechling samples more captive environments such as summer camps, boarding schools, hospital wards, and orphanages and speaks of the "vibrant resisting folk culture" to be found in these institutions. He suggests that these are not special environments because in modern society we are all prisoners. Nevertheless they seem special enough to the reader whatever his local form of incarceration. But what we would like to concede is that relative to us adults, children are indeed a kind of prisoner of the larger normative adult society, and much of what we call children's folklore reflects that predicament.

In a final chapter, Faye McMahon takes up the issue of theoretical directions for the future of children's folklore. She considers the alternatives for children's folklore as being thought of as:

(a) a collection of texts and focussed on tradition,

(b) an account of child performances, and

(c) a manifestation of power relationships.

Not surprisingly from what has gone before, most of her attention is given to children's relative disempowerment and the various forms that it takes both as to content and to the disguises adopted (following James Scott [1990], Joan Radner and Susan Lanser [1993], and others). Finally, she questions whether the "triviality barrier" of children's folklore is perhaps a reaction formation by adults against the dangers of recognizing that the world of children would seem very different to us if we attended to the neoteny of their struggles for power. Children's folklore as the struggle for power certainly has a different ring to it, doesn't it? If we studied children's folklore as an account of disempowerment and, at the same time, as an ecstasy of performance, then children's folklore, as contrasted with all the other scholarships of childhood, would indeed be dealing with a most radical concept of childhood.

A Personal Note

It is with considerable pleasure that I contribute to this very deserved festschrift for Kenny Goldstein. He was a major reason for my going to the University of Pennsylvania in 1977, and along with Dell Hymes, Henry Glassie, and Barbara Kirshenblatt-Gimblett, he allowed me to combine children's folklore and the psychology of childlore into my two courses: (a) Children's Folklore and (b) Play, Games, Toys and Sports, which I taught in both the Department of Folklore and Folklife and the Graduate School of Education for the next fifteen years. I was honored by the department with a professorship in folklore (which I hardly deserved), and I was greatly helped by Kenny's gift lectures on such topics as the early chapbooks for children and the obscenities of childhood. The latter was particularly poignant for me as I had collected this kind of material in New Zealand (it was a natural part of the reporting of their play and games by the children) but was forced by my advisor to extirpate that chapter from my dissertation, delaying my graduation by two years in the process. Although I sent it on to Gershon Legman, then in Paris (1954), that was not quite as satisfying as seeing Kenny being appropriately forthright about legitimate folk material in my own classroom. He was there for us also when later Barbara Kirshenblatt-Gimblett, Tom Burns, and I launched the Children's Folklore Section of the American folklore Society, and when Jay Mechling, Tom Johnson, and I launched the "Handbook of Children's Folklore," which because of his prodding became in due course, and with additional editorial support from Faye McMahon, *Children's Folklore: A Source Book* (1995). Throughout all of this and lots more, I felt a support and commitment from Kenny (and, importantly, from Kenny's wife, Rochelle). Although my heavy role in the Graduate School of Education kept me very busy, it was a pleasure to be a part of and observe a department that treasured the character of its own collegiality no matter how difficult that was, unlike most other academic departments where typically there is difficulty in rising above the minimal communality of the professor and his or her chosen students. It follows that my own conceptions of childhood, which were radically different from the orthodox social science literature, found no barrier within this folklore context. I trust that Kenny will enjoy the lusty account of children's folklore that the *Children's Folklore* occasions, that is, if I have indeed summarized it faithfully here.

References

Abrahams, Roger D.
  1987   An American Vocabulary of Celebrations. In *Time out of Time*. Ed. Alessandro Falassi. Albuquerque: Univ. of New Mexico Press. Pp. 173–83.
Douglas, Norman
  1916   *London Street Games*. London: St. Catherine's Press.
Huizinga, Johan
  1949   *Homo Ludens: A Study of the Play-Element in Culture*. London: Routledge and Kegan Paul.
Radner, Joan N., and Susan S. Lanser
  1993   Strategies of Coding in Women's Cultures. In *Feminist Messages*. Ed. Joan N. Radner. Urbana and Chicago: Univ. of Illinois Press. Pp. 1–30.
Scott, James C.
  1990   *Domination and the Arts of Resistance: Hidden Transcripts*. New Haven: Yale Univ. Press.
Sutton-Smith, Brian, Jay Mechling, Thomas W. Johnson, and Felicia McMahon, eds.
  1995   *Children's Folklore: A Source Book*. New York: Garland.

ALL THAT BEEF, AND SYMBOLIC ACTION, TOO!

Notes on the Occasion of the Banning of 2 Live Crew's *As Nasty As They Wanna Be*

John F. Szwed

> If I feel physically as if the top of my head were taken off, I know that it is poetry.
> —Emily Dickinson

> And is it art just because folklorists can analyze it?
> —"The Importance of Being Nasty," *Newsweek*

BAWDINESS, LASCIVIOUSNESS, smut, trash, lewdness, pornography, obscenity, ribaldry, the erotic, the risqué, the salacious, the prurient, whatever you want to call it (I prefer *blue* myself), the sheer variety of terms points to a long cultural obsession. We have more words for blue texts than the Eskimos have for *snow*: surely this tells us something profound about ourselves, and about our past. Now, with the culture police moving on many fronts (and the real police right behind them), with rap music under assault and 2 Live Crew's record *As Nasty as They Wanna Be* the first recording to be banned in many years, and several of the group's members accused of violations of the Racketeer Influenced and Corrupt Organizations (RICO) Act and under arrest for performing the record live in the adults-only Futura Club in Broward County, Florida, a brief meditation on the blue seems timely, if not exactly asked for.

Blue literature is not a recent development, nor is it an exclusive product of a single culture, of the lower classes, of people of color, or of men. Although ingenuously ignored by guardians of tradition, blue comedy has been part of English literature at least since the origins of Middle English and is perpetuated today as part of the canon as taught to high school and college students.[1] Bawdy laughter is at the heart of the work of such writers as Shakespeare and Chaucer, who are deified as representing the greatest ideals of the Western humanistic tradition; the same humor also resonates in the writings of such local colorists and regional writers as Robert Burns and Mark Twain. The point seems to be that if it's funny, it's not obscene. "Ornery," maybe, or "cute," but not obscene.[2] In their pornography decisions the courts have in effect been ruling on what is funny and what is not.

Whether all cultures have blue literature remains a question, since the comparative study of pornography has yet to begin. But oral literature of the world—being freer from the constraints of judges, publishers, and other arbiters of taste—suggests that the blue may well be universal. Records such as 2 Live Crew's are themselves inheritors of a variety of spoken-word traditions which include the Jody ("the Grinder") cadence-counts of the military; the routines of burlesque and standup comics; "party" records; the epic toasts of prisons and work camps; American boasting and tall-tales; the songs and verse of fraternities and sororities[3]; and Euro- and African-American children's taunts, jump rope rhymes, and Mother Goose parodies. (Just how bawdy Euro-American children can be has been massively documented for English speakers by Wendy Lowenstein [1974], Sandra McCosh [1979], and Ian Turner [1969]; for German-speaking children by Ernest Borneman [1973–76]; and for the French by Claude Gaignebet [1977]. Judging by these scholars' evidence, it is not kids who need protection from pornography; it's adults who need protection from children).

Because of this tangle of cultural sources, our efforts at understanding blue material have usually been superficial or wrong. Take for example, the dozens, the game in which young black males insult each other with sexual remarks about each other's mother. In the 1960s, social scientists glibly diagnosed this contest as a consequence of slaveholders' breeding practices, matrifocal families, or a reaction to racial stereotyping; or again, as proof of sexual ambivalence, arrested development, whatever. But how differently reads this 164-year-old African account, which may be the earliest written reference to such 'playing': "We must distinguish the respect, obedience and affection which they always show toward their mothers. The greatest insult one can utter is the all too familiar *sahr sa ndci* (by the genitalia of your mother). This oath has frequently been drowned in blood" (Roger 1828). Needless to say, the cultural pathologists never bother to look for historical antecedents. If they did, they would have seen that blue rapping is neither recent nor especially black. To name only one case close to home, Vance Randolph's "Ribaldry at Ozark Dances" transcribes blue square dance calls from country parties in the early 1900s, where drunkenness, gang wars, gun play, and sexual assaults were also common. From Columbia, Missouri, circa 1918, here is a call for "Turkey in the Straw":

> Grab her by the right leg, swing her half around,
> Grab her by the left leg, throw her on the ground,
> Stick it in the middle and a bobble up and down,
> When you come to her ass-hole, go on around.
> (Randolph 1989:17)

Or from Washington County, Arkansas, circa early 1900s:

> The more you fuck her, the louder she'll squeal,
> The louder she hollers, the better you'll feel
>
> ***
>
> Log-chain your sweetie, log-tie your honey,
> Stick it up her ass, get the worth of your money
> (Randolph 1989:14–15)

It would truly be an academic exercise to attempt to determine whether these "traditional" Anglo-American texts are more or less violent and misogynous than those of contemporary Afro-American youth.

Nor is the blue domain occupied by men alone. The relative scarcity of women's bawdy texts in print is more a matter of who controls publication than it is evidence of a lack of interest. At least we know that when sound recordings became possible, gross themes flourished among many women performers: Victoria Spivey's "Handy Man" (1928), Lucille Bogan's "Shave 'Em Dry" (1935), Lizzie Miles's "My Man 'o War" (1930), and Lil Johnson's "Hottest Gal in Town" (1936) are classic blues of their kind (see Oliver 1968). By the 1940s it was possible for a woman to build a commercial career on blue material. (Julia Lee, for example, had hits with "Snatch and Grab It," "My Man Stands Out," "Don't Come Too Soon," and "All This Beef and Big Ripe Tomatoes.") Nor is verbal sexual abuse exclusively male: Millie Jackson's recordings and performances of the '70s seethe with caustic suggestion and censure,[4] and in more recent times Roxanne Shanté's live appearances are strewn with male-baiting and trashing.

Censorious law-makers fatuously talk about community standards, but in practice it is hard to know who is going to find what offensive. Even pornographers can be offended: Bessie Smith's "Empty Bed Blues," a favorite of Freida von Richthofen, so enraged her lover, D. H. Lawrence, that he furiously broke the record against the wall in Harry Crosby's Paris apartment. And we are continually surprised to find out who's been working on the blue production line. Tampa Red's Hokum Jug Band 1929 recording of "How Long, How Long Blues" (a record admittedly without a single offensive word, but with such moaning, puffing, and double-entendres that its meaning is all too clear) included Georgia Tom Dorsey, the same Thomas A. Dorsey who was one of the inventors of gospel music. And Jimmie Davis—twice a fundamentalist, segregationist Governor of Louisiana—had in a former life recorded such songs as "High Behind Blues"(1932) and "Tom Cat and Pussy Blues" (1932), accompanied by black guitarist Oscar Woods.

By the same token, the line usually drawn between the acceptable and the obscene is outrageously hypocritical. When the Hollywood Argyles sang "I'm a mean motorscooter and a bad go-getter" in their 1960 hit "Alley Oop," their sly bowdlerization rested on their audience's familiarity with rough street talk.[5] In fact, all of the "cute" and "ornery" double-entendres of TV, movies, and

Vegas clubs depend on an underlying community of shared deeper blue meanings. And today no one raises an eyebrow over the mainstreaming (and franchising) of corporate names such as that of the Mother Truckers, or the restaurant chain, Fuddruckers.[6]

Rock and *roll* are themselves words whose sexual meanings are barely concealed.[7] But these same terms also have their place in black religious discourse, as do words like the *house, daddy, baby,* being *taken higher,* and all those words of ecstasy and possession. The aesthetic of vernacular music always draws at least part of its strength from this criss-crossing of semantic domains and the teasing ambiguity that results. From its origins in burlesque, vaudeville, and the tent show, rock 'n roll is built on a hierarchy of tease that implies that lipsyncing is singing, that the body is doing something other than dancing, that white may be black, that male may be female, and that something other than music may be about to happen—revolution, violence, spiritual revelation, sex. But when on the rare occasion that something else does actually happen, the show is over, the spell shattered. (The final phase of the decline of The Doors can be marked in 1969, when Jim Morrison exposed himself on stage in Miami.)

But what of the case in point, 2 Live Crew's *As Nasty as They Wanna Be?* Recorded by a group of young men who think of themselves as comedians and perform in the Rudy Ray Moore tradition, the record—which in another age would have been found in the "comedy" bins of stores that cater to Afro-Americans—somehow found its way under the broad category of popular music of America.[8] The record itself is a catalog of rude bumper sticker slogans, schoolyard catches, and taunts; selections of toasts; conventional male boasts and student fantasies about teachers; received sexual wisdom of the streets; perverse pillow talk; sampled disco moans and lines from *Full Metal Jacket;* advertising slogans; Latin music struts; reggae allusions; metal riffs; parodies of various ethnic dialects; and songs whose melodies are built from the speech tones and rhythms of insults and expletives. Throughout it all runs a selection of what in Anglo-American folklore is known as monstrous tools, awed maidens, lethal bitches, much mechanico-surreal sexual posturing and verbal cod pieces, and not a little bit of anxiety and distrust of women.[9] Gritty stuff, disrespectful, and only occasionally funny, but very little that couldn't also be found spread among the writings of Norman Mailer, *Finnegans Wake,* and the documented outbursts of ex-President George Bush. (And nothing, for that matter, that couldn't be heard in the many X-rated records of Blowfly, an artist-producer who has been churning out blue rap unmolested in Miami for at least the last 15 years.[10])

Offensive, yes, and especially offensive to women, but is *As Nasty as They Wanna Be* legally obscene? Does it appeal to prurient interests? Less so, I would think, than the TV soaps (where *bitch,* incidentally, is apparently an acceptable word), even among the pathologically suggestible. Does it contain patently offensive conduct? Yes, but compared to what one routinely sees in the movies? More to the point, no judge seems willing to locate both arousal and disgust within the same text or audience (and certainly not within themselves). So, as legal scholar Kathleen M. Sullivan has argued, to make *Miller v. California* work as a standard, the community must be segregated, and arousal attributed to a sexual or ethnic minority, while disgust is located within the majority (Sullivan 1990).

Yet the Court may still ask if there is any literary, artistic, political, or scientific value to these songs and chants. Suffice it to say that this is not very deep stuff (that Judge José Gonzalez, Jr., could get a sixty-two-page decision out of it means nothing other than someone was paying him more per word than they are me). But at least this much about it is of value: it serves to remind us that in an age when no other forms of literature are believed to have any social force (even sedition is no longer taken seriously, and cop-killer songs seem protected by the First Amendment), obscenity is still believed to have social consequences. If that were really true we ought to be devoting ourselves to its study in order to understand its verbal magic. Yet I suspect that on the contrary, the hatred of obscenity is part of a sentimental and desperate attempt to cling to an imagined past where some form of literature mattered. But it's too late even for porn. Left to itself, it has little demonstrable effect overall, except as part of the deadening semiotic barrage that we respectfully still speak of as our culture.

I suppose the cynic will say that if 2 Live Crew or other rappers ever do time in the slammer they will at least find new ideas there for future recordings. But I would say that they could also find fresh material at less public expense in that other dwelling place of the incorrigible and the recidivistic, the library.

Addendum: 1993

After the foregoing was written 2 Live Crew went to court and was acquitted.[11] Central to the defense argument were the testimonies of John Leland, pop music critic for *Newsday*, who argued that the defendants' material was well within the rap tradition, and that of professor Louis Henry Gates, Jr., of Harvard, who extended Leland's point by arguing that routines such as 2 Live Crew's were part of the black folk aesthetic and were examples of literary art. In hindsight we know that the jurors claimed that the literary and cultural arguments played no part in the decision, and indeed did not even consider race in their discussions. Instead, 2 Live Crew was acquitted in part because the police could not accurately transcribe what they claimed was obscene, much less decode what they had transcribed, so that the jury and the witnesses could not agree on what they were hearing. (A similar conclusion was reached by the FBI, when it gave up after two years of trying to find the obscene meaning of the Kingsmen's 1963 recording of "Louie Louie."[12]) But in spite of this, the jury had no difficulty in recognizing that the material was funny, and even asked the judge for permission to laugh. In the end the jury foreman said that they felt it wasn't obscene because it was funny (*New York Times,* Oct. 21, 1990, p. 30).

In his recent *Black Studies, Rap and the Academy*, Houston A. Baker, Jr., struggles mightily to locate the 2 Live Crew affair outside of a strict context of race and to find a middle ground between George Will's association of rap music with the Central Park jogger rape and Gates's and Leland's literary and cultural defense of what many consider antiwomanist poetry (Baker 1993). In fact, Baker's criticism of Gates's testimony would regard my "defense" of 2 Live Crew as being what he calls the "others do it, so why persecute we?" argument, and answers that the "widespread existence of male sexual brutality does not mean that any given appearance of it should be regarded by scholars as simply another speeding vehicle on the highway of popular culture's dark underbelly" (Baker 1993:72). He goes on to say that 2 Live Crew was "understandably banned" and to imply that they should have been because "common sense alone suggests a correlation" between the existence of such verbal material and the incidence of violence against women in the United States, and that such violence should not be protected by free speech (Baker 1993:73–74). Granting Baker the correlation (though not necessarily the significance of the correlation), one might also correlate much of Western art and literature with such violence.

I am sympathetic with Baker's plea for treating such a case in a larger framework than race. In fact, my previous comments were meant to call attention to a cultural complex that goes far beyond the American mythology of color. And I agree with his resentment of the law and the media for handing us the choice of having to defend *this* kind of verbal behavior. But we do not get much choice as to where our battles will be fought—even the trial of *Lady Chatterley's Lover* left literary critics uneasy. Leland and Gates were given a case in which still more young black men were going to jail and it was not clear what their crime was. Were they guilty of saying nasty, even violent, things about women in an unfunny way? Or of allowing a culturally specific text to be recontextualized, both in terms of audience and medium?[13] Whatever it was, they were made scapegoats of race, in long unresolved cultural matters, as part of the current demoralization of young black men. And on that point, I believe Baker would agree with me.

Notes

1. Some of the most important blue folkloric texts are kept in print by university presses (Vance Randolph's *Pissing in the Snow, and Other Ozark Folktales* (1976), for example, is published by the University of Illinois Press), and the most erotic of Jelly Roll Morton's songs are preserved in the Library of Congress.

2. For an early discussion of this distinction, see Ralph Bass's account of his dispute over Hank Ballard and the Midnighters' 1954 hit, "Work With Me Annie," on the Jack Parr TV show (in Lydon and Mandel 1974:84).

3. Nasty's "Fraternity Record," a song of intragreek insults, suggests that 2 Live Crew is the latest in a long series of Southern college gross-out house party bands such as the semi-legendary Doug Clark and the Hot Nuts.

4. See, for example, Millie Jackson, *Feelin' Bitchy*. Spring Records, 1977.

5. Kenneth Goldstein's ground-breaking "Bowdlerization and Expurgation: Academic and Folk" (1967) is an obvious inspiration for this paper.

6. See, for example, older blues song/dozens euphemisms like *fudderrucker* and *feathermucker*.

7. In an interview published in the *Village Voice* during the 1988 presidential campaign, then-candidate and warning-label advocate Al Gore laughed when it was pointed out to him that his generation had their own form of objectionable pop songs such as Little Richard's "Good Golly Miss Molly" ("she sure likes to ball"); he allowed that the difference was that you weren't supposed to know such things then.

8. For 2 Live Crew's claim to being comedians, see Martha Frankel (1990:62, quoting their interview from *Hitmakers*). For a survey of Rudy Ray Moore's career, see Charles Kilgore 1990:24–25. Not only was *As Nasty* self-labeled as potentially offensive, but it also was issued in a sanitized version, *As Clean as You Wanna Be*.

9. To many, it seems, "bitch" is the most offensive word in the rap vocabulary, yet response to it appears to be distributed along cultural lines not yet fully understood. In the Afro- American domain, at least, its use sometimes appears to be more literal, as in "Men are dogs; women are bitches." For some women rappers' views of the word, see Kim France, "5 Slammin' Women Rappers Bitch, Cuss, Sound Off, Get Down, Let Loose, and Get Nasty as They Wanna Be and You've Never Heard Dis Like This" (1991).

10. For an interview with Blowfly that surveys his career, see "The Weird World of Blowfly," (1992).

11. For accounts of the record banning, arrests, and trial see Jones 1990a and 1990b; Loren 1991; Campbell and Miller 1992; and *2 Live Crew Comics*, No. 1 (June 1991).

12. See Marsh 1993. Other commentators claimed to have no problems in understanding the 2 Live Crew text and transcribing it. Cf. George Will 1990.

13. To my knowledge, *As Nasty as They Wanna Be* was never played on the radio or television. Nor was it turned into print until George Will followed the lead of religious and political journals (and in doing so, I believe, reprinted erroneous transcriptions).

References

Baker, Houston A. Jr.
1993   *Black Studies, Rap and the Academy*. Urbana and Chicago: Univ. of Chicago Press.

Borneman, Ernest
1973–76   *Studien zur Befreiung des Kindes, Unser Kinder im Spiegel ihrer Lieder: Die Umwelt des Kindes*. 4 vols. Often, Switzerland: Walter-Verlag.

Campbell, Luther, and John R. Miller
1992   *As Nasty as They Wanna Be: The Uncensored Story of Luther Campbell of the 2 Live Crew*. Fort Lee: Barricade Books.

France, Kim
1991   5 Slammin' Women Rappers Bitch, Cuss, Sound Off, Get Down, Let Loose, and Get Nasty as They Wanna Be and You've Never Heard Dis Like This. *Egg* (March):64–69.

Frankel, Martha
1990   2 Live Doo-Doo. *Spin* (October):62.

Gaignebet, Claude
1977   *Le folklore obscene des Enfants*. Paris: Maisonneuve and Larose.

Goldstein, Kenneth S.
1967   Bowdlerization and Expurgation: Academic and Folk. *Journal of American Folklore* 80:374–86.

Jones, Lisa
   1990a 2 Live For You. *Village Voice*, October 12.
   1990b The Signifying Monkees. *Village Voice*, November 6.
Kilgore, Charles
   1990   Rudy Ray Moore: The Life and the Laughter. *Uncut Funk* (Winter):24–25.
Loren, Todd
   1991   2 Live Crew: 1 Bad Mother. *Rock 'n' Roll Comics*, April.
Lowenstein, Wendy
   1974   *Shocking, Shocking, Shocking: The Improper Play-Rhymes of Australian Children*. Melbourne: Fish and Chips Press.
Lydon, Michael, and Ellen Mandel
   1974   *Boogie Lightning: How Music Became Electric*. New York: Dial Press.
Marsh, Dave
   1993   *Louie Louie*. New York: Hyperion Press.
McCosh, Sandra
   1979   *Children's Humour: A Joke For Every Occasion*. London: Panther/Granada.
Oliver, Paul
   1968   *Screening the Blues: Aspects of the Blues Tradition*. London: Cassell.
Randolph, Vance
   1989   Ribaldry at Ozark Dances. *Mid-America Folklore* 17:17.
Roger, Jacques-François
   1828   *Fables Senegalaises recueilles de l'Ouolof*. Paris: Nepveu.
Sullivan, Kathleen M.
   1990   2 Live Crew and the Cultural Contradictions of *Miller*. *Reconstruction* 1:19–20.
Turner, Ian
   1969   *Cinderella Dressed in Yella*. Melbourne: Heinemann.
"Weird World of Blowfly, The"
   1992   *Ungawa!* n.d.; c. 1992.
Will, George
   1990   America's Slide into the Sewer. *Newsweek*, July 30.

A LIFE'S WORK

Women Writing From the Kitchen

Janet Theophano

SEVERAL YEARS ago, while browsing in an antique shop, I found an old book with a broken binding. When I opened it, I realized that I had discovered a manuscript. The text, however, was visually more like poetry than a story. Looking closely, I discovered that what I had was not a manuscript of a story but a book of receipts for the kitchen: receipts for Lady Cake and Parker House Rolls, folk remedies for flushing the colon and dyeing hair. Inserted between the pages were newspaper clippings of other recipes as well as a letter and a poem. The letter was addressed "My dear" and signed "Kiss the babies for me. John." It was dated August 3, 1894. I'll return to the poem later.

I bought the book for a dollar because the dealer didn't think it was worth much more, and I hoped that the pages would not fall apart during the hours I spent reading the recipes and the single poem. Nowhere could I find the author's name.

The book of recipes and the poem, especially, intrigued me, but I was somehow not satisfied to consider this a mere collection of recipes. It seemed no accident that poetry and letters were insertions between the texts. I had stumbled across the fragments of writing of a woman's life, and I wanted to understand the role of such writing in women's lives.

The restrictions on women's intellectual life in the nineteenth century were numerous, and the consequences upon their creativity were harsh (Draine 1989).[1] I speculate that within this context, the writing, reading, and sharing of recipes became a significant source for women's imaginative life.

To examine the issue of women's writings about domestic life in general and about food, specifically, I turned to several sources of nineteenth-century literature available to women, largely from the middle classes: published cook books, household guides, and books of etiquette. In so doing, other problems were raised such as the shift from oral to written forms and the difficulties encountered by these women in rendering or transforming the physical world into the realm of language.

While I looked originally only at the writing of the recipes, the form, the words—the language itself—it struck me that the organization of many recipe collections and the uses of them by their creators were as provocative as the writing itself. Further I was curious about the relationship of the receipt books of my nineteenth-century anonymous author (and others who lived in that period) to the recipe collections of the women I knew, both of my generation and that of my mother. Surely, similar creative energy was at work, albeit differently, in the diverse forms of culinary invention, imagination, and writing that guide the selection and organization of such documents, collections and manuscript receipt books.

What were the models for and sources of these women's food writings? Can we assume that other published cookery books served as models for their own writings? Or were formulas for writing recipes exchanged privately as were the recipes themselves? What were the processes by which these writers translated their culinary idiosyncrasies into a standardized format? How did they make the commonplace uniquely their own?

Though I was unable to find a guide to the proper art of recipe writing in this period, questions of language usage or phraseology, replicability, and reliability were, however, sometimes discussed and commented upon in the cookery books and manuals published for the purpose of instructing women in the domestic arts. If not the conventions and the style of recipe writing, the search for wholesome and proper foods was of interest to women, according to the domestic arts manuals published in the mid- to late nineteenth century. An 1887 edition of *The Hearthstone; or, Life At Home, A Household Manual* authored by Laura C. Holloway precedes its presentation of cookery recipes with the following caution:

> Cookery books are numerous; they multiply continually, yet practical recipes are scarce, and true and tried ones are a commodity much in demand. . . . Whatever may have been said on the subject to the contrary, it is a fact that women desire to cook well, and they are ever on the lookout for reliable information on the subject. (1887:403)

In an earlier discussion of the uses of recipes, Holloway points out:

> Cookery books are too often like guidebooks, which take you by a round-about way to where you did not want to go. The best teacher in the kitchen is experience, and experience is learned by experiment. If one begins right, "practice makes perfect" in the kitchen as everywhere else. (1887:402)

What was sought then were recipes that had been successful in the past and were based on the experience of reliable sources. The reliability of the recipes was derived in two ways: 1) knowing the cook; 2) being able to render or transform the recipe accurately.

The difficulty of these acts of writing for many women whose recipes had not been widely disseminated or ever written, the shift from orality to literacy, is framed by the apology that prefaces the *Presbyterian Cook Book* compiled by the Ladies of the First Presbyterian Church, Dayton, Ohio, and published in 1873. The cook book purports to avoid venturing "into the mystical realm of fancy cookery; but is a collection of safe and reliable recipes for the preparation of plain food" (1873:7). It is here the compilers apologize for the unsophisticated writing of the book's contributors:

> The matter of the book, we claim, is all right; for the manner of it we beg indulgence. The phraseology is often peculiar, and may provoke a smile; but it must be remembered that the recipes were written by ladies unaccustomed to writing for publication; and in most cases, they have been inserted precisely as written, and, whenever no objection was made, the name of the author has been given. (1873:7–8)

The following recipe for Strawberry Shortcake may have been one such recipe.[2] It is attributed to Mrs. W. R. S. Ayres.

> In one quart of flour mix one tablespoonful of baking powder and one teacupful of butter, roll, and cut out with a bucket-lid the size of a breakfast plate. Bake in a quick oven. Sugar the berries well, and mash them; spread between the cakes, and over the outside, after they are put together. (1873:67)

Though the literary construction is awkward, the writing follows precisely the chronological sequencing of actions required to construct the cake.

Despite the claims of tolerance for the oddities of language and the claim to have included the recipes "precisely as written," there is still a standardized format or formula for recipe-writing evident. The most frequent presentation, especially in the section on meats, begins with a verb: "Parboil sweetbreads," "Take some cold roasted veal," "Allow a beef's liver to remain in corn brine for ten days," "Season," "Stuff," "Cut-up," "Pare," "Singe," "Put," "Truss," etc.

The other most frequently used model begins with the ingredients themselves, such as "Three quarters of a cup of bread crumbs," "Eight eggs," "Three or four teaspoonsful of sugar," "Twelve apples." These listings of ingredients seem to be the most common format for cakes and pastries. Despite the standardization, there are abundant examples of individuality and variation in writing represented in this text.

Not as many writing styles are apparent in a third variety of published cook books, that represented by *The Carolina Housewife by a Lady of Charleston*. It consists of a collection of recipes from family and friends, but it was edited by a sole editor. First published in 1847 and reprinted several times thereafter, it was, as were many such documents, published anonymously. "For until about 1920-odd, the name of a Charleston woman appeared in print but thrice—when born, when married and when buried—the legal necessities" (Rutledge 1979:vii). Anna Wells Rutledge, the descendant of the Lady of Charleston, tells us that these cookery books were compiled by women for the purpose of raising money for worthy causes. They solicited recipes from one another and, in turn, sold the printed work to each other. Despite the volume of its contributions (there were 550 recipes), the standardization of the format is striking, even more so than is evident in the style of the Dayton, Ohio, regional collection. The writing is more formal, less colloquial. In the edited *Carolina Housewife*, the units of measurement used were more consistent, whereas in the Presbyterian cook book, household cutlery, dishes, and other objects (such as a bucket lid) were used to describe the amounts of ingredients. However, the format of recipes in the Carolina book is comparable to those of the Dayton book.

From the simplicity of the instructions or the lack thereof, I speculate that the women shared a common repertoire and set of understandings about food preparation. It is understood that in face-to-face interaction, what is known between the interlocutors can be implied. In writing, what was implicit may become more explicit. It is not apparent in these texts that the distance between writer and reader/audience has been marked. As is the case with many written forms, ellipsis in recipe writing assumes a shared base of knowledge (Camitta, personal communication). One could call them, according to Riffaterre, "a code" of the language and a kind of poetic text (Riffaterre 1983:200–201). Carrying the poetic metaphor further, let me draw on the work of Barbara Herrnstein Smith, who quotes Paul Valéry:

> A poem like a piece of music, offers merely a text, which, strictly speaking, is only a kind of recipe; the cook who follows it plays an essential part. To speak of a poem in itself, to judge of a poem in itself, has no real or precise meaning. It is to speak of a potentiality. The poem is an abstraction, a piece of writing that stands waiting, that lives only in some human mouth, and that mouth is simply a mouth. . . . Or to put it another way, the text of a poem and the score of a piece of music each provide minimum directions for the performance of the work in question. (Herrnstein Smith 1968:9)

Let's return to our anonymous nineteenth-century author. She varied her style only slightly from recipe to recipe. Each "text" was largely a list of ingredients, carefully written, with some editing. Occasionally, directions for preparation were included. In some cases, words that had been chosen to articulate the process were changed to represent her techniques more accurately or what the product should feel or look like. In her Caramel Cake recipe, she altered the description of her blanc mange from a "thick cream" to a "very thick cream." Several recipes were modified (at some point) as to ingredients:

"FRENCH LOAF CAKE"
10 cups flour
6 cups sugar
4 cups butter (here she adds the comment "not quite a pound is better")

Several of the recipes were modified or altered either to suit her own tastes or because she had forgotten to include all of the information in the first copying. However, I discovered a distinction between the format of the recipes that she had written in the book and those that were written on loose pages or scraps of paper. For the most part the recipes in the book essentially only list the ingredients of the dish. This is, of course, in keeping with the style of many recipes found in cookery books. Those written on scraps of paper inserted between the pages of the bound text are quite specific in their directions for the combination of ingredients and heat application. These explicit instructions were more detailed than any I was able to find in the cook books I surveyed. For example, the recipe for ginger snaps written in her book merely lists the ingredients ("half pound butter, half pound sugar . . ."). Another recipe for ginger snaps written on a scrap of paper includes, in addition to the list of ingredients, a detailed set of instructions for combining them, rolling the dough, and baking. ("Put all in together. Let come to a boil then teaspoon soda dissolved in hot water. . . . Roll out thin, very thin and bake in a quick oven.")

I suspect that these were the recipes with which she was unfamiliar, while those in her book and written in her own hand had been appropriated by her as part of her repertoire (from whatever sources); that is, recipes she used repeatedly and with which she was familiar because of long use. We can conjecture that the novelty of detailed and refined cooking instructions was introduced through the private circulation of recipes, which were more than likely written in the context of social interaction.

Not surprisingly, there was a disproportionate number of recipes for cookies, cakes, pies, and puddings, as well as folk remedies in her book; these culinary achievements and medicinal cures require at least several ingredients or more, and precision in measurement is essential. For these dishes and brews, the recipes act as mnemonic devices. Assuredly also, these recipes reflect important occasions and memories as well as the flavors and tastes preferred by her family and friends. Encoded in these recipes are the stories of her life. M. F. K. Fisher, among others, alludes to the autobiographical quality of recipe writing in all of her work.

Few of the recipes in the anonymous nineteenth-century manuscript receipt book were attributed to others: Mrs. Rossiter and Aunt Caddy's mother were the source of a Peach Cobbler and a Dutch Cake.[3] One recipe is attributed and dated; this one may have been written for her by its author, for it ended with the editorial and personal "You may strain through a cloth if you wish, but I prefer the spices left in." This recipe for Blackberry Cordial was signed Mrs. Ed. B. Eckman, Black Bairen, 1890. In her own book, there were no attributions with one exception: two recipes were labeled "mama's" and one "mine." The issue of attribution, in this case, may not revolve around authorship but rather signal a relationship between a teacher and student (Camitta, personal communication). Or perhaps it reminds her of her preferred version. This sharing and borrowing of recipes contributed to the establishment of a common form and a common fund of knowledge with the freedom to pass it on. "To share a recipe—both to request one and to give one—. . . is an act of trust between women" (Leonardi 1989:346). In the view of Susan J. Leonardi, recipe writing is "an embedded discourse"; it "implies an exchange, a giver and a receiver. Like a story, a recipe needs a recommendation, a context, a point, a reason to be" (1989:340).

Recipes for well-known and popular dishes were in circulation, orally and in written form. Women may have modified the variant they received; each modification reflected the preferences of its author and made the dish uniquely her own. In fact, far from being upset by changes, alterations were invited:

> Take this liberty with whatever receipt you think you can improve. If I chance to find in your work-basket, or upon the kitchen dresser, a well-thumbed copy of my beloved *Common Sense* with copious annotations in the margin, I shall, so far from feeling wounded, be flattered in having so diligent a student, and with your permission, shall engraft the most happy suggestions upon the second edition. (Harland 1876:25)

Thus we can speak of a collaborative enterprise characterized by a shared code. Our anonymous author's receipt book boasts an entire second section of printed recipes and written commentary in the margins indicating later emendations or its passage to another hand, perhaps a daughter. The book, which speaks of years of long use, seems an excellent example of such collaboration.

The recipe book is akin to the song books kept by women in Newfoundland (Kodish 1983) and the scrap books described by Katriel and Farrell (1991), genres of vernacular writing and collectanea. The recipes are not only spotted with grease and flecks of food but interspersed with rhymes and readings, suggesting that more than food was thought about while browsing or writing in these pages. Following a recipe for washing blankets from Aunt Mary that ended with "hang out to dry" was the following verse:

> Suppose life doesn't please you
>   Nor the way some people do
> Do you think the whole creation
>   Will be altered just for you.
>   Dieu-donnee

Concluding a recipe for Soft Ginger Cakes, which were to be "rolled out in the morning and cut in large cakes they puff up" [sic] was the following list:

> "A Book of Nonsense Edward Lear 1846–1888
> Nonsense Songs, Stories Botany and Alphabets. 1871–1888
> More Nonsense, Pictures, Rhymes, Botany ect. [sic] 1872–1888
> Laughable Lyrics ect [sic] (Music) 1877–1888."

On the back of a recipe for Roasted Oysters she wrote about the "Spread of Gospel in the Cities, Jerusalem, Antioch, Ephesus, Corinth and Rome. St. Paul was beheaded. Peter crucified. A.D. 68."

Since the author of these writings no longer lives, I cannot ask her questions about her recipes or the verses and the scraps of information that reveal aspects of her life, on the pages of her book; I can only speculate about their presence there among her recipes.

In *The Hearthstone*, the same household manual that describes appropriate feminine conduct and activities, the claim is made that

> the place of poetry in the home must be ranked with the story as an educator of the imagination. . . . The guiding principle of all readers should be to read such books as give them power, not such as weaken them. The analogy of the body and food holds good of the mind and reading . . . . Where are the milk and eggs for the mind? . . . It is not possible to overrate the influence of the imagination upon every phase of human life. . . . A quick, vivid and reason-tempered imagination is the most powerful weapon for success in life. A warped, perverted, feeble, irresolute imagination will never get from the shadow to the substance. Hence, so many lives are spent in dreaming and nothing else. That only is true imagination which sets the will in motion and leads to definite results. Poetry comes in as proper food for this divine gift. (Holloway 1887:127)

The analogy between poetry and food, imagination and production made explicit here merges the realms of imagination and poetry with food as long as these lead to useful cultural productions. Time spent in reverie which leads to nothing of substance is time wasted, lost and misguided. For women who participated in the "Cult of True Womanhood," the most important responsibility was the nurturance of husband and children. In all the acts of their now solitary and isolated days, cleaning, cooking and making a pleasant and safe haven for family, all without complaint, women spent their newly invented lives as "hostages in the home" (Welter 1978:313). At least one of these tasks offered women the potential for reverie, reading, and writing—imagining the untried and unknown and translating their own experience into suitable language and form. The very substance of their reverie and their art was the concrete realities of their day-to-day lives. (Though the artistry involved in culinary achievements or haute cuisine is self-evident and has been recognized within particular domains, i.e. male chefs, ice sculptures, medieval banquets; when associated with women's work, quotidian cooking has been trivialized.)

A long history of recipe writing in verse form may have facilitated the nineteenth-century elevation of ordinary and extraordinary cooking responsibilities to an art form, now relegated to women's sphere (and obscuring the restrictions on women's intellectualism) while it was simultaneously manipulated by women as an expressive form.[4] This vernacular form of writing confounds or constructs an association between poetry and domestic writing, writing activity safe for pious women to use as an outlet for their creative energies and in keeping with their primary responsibilities as wives and mothers. The relationship between poetry and recipes finds expression in the *Presbyterian Cookbook* referred to earlier. Printed in the section on vegetables was the following recipe-poem titled "Cooking Beans." Its source is "From Moore's 'Rural New Yorker.'"

> If, my dear Rural, you should ever wish
> For breakfast or dinner a tempting dish
> Of the beans so famous in Boston town,
> You must read the rules I here lay down.
> When the sun has set in golden light,
> And around you fall the shades of night,
> A large, deep dish you first prepare;
> A quart of beans select with care;
> And pick them over, until you find
> Not a speck or a mote is left behind.
> A lot of cold water on them pour
> Till every bean is covered o'er,
> And they seem to your poetic eye
> Like pearls in the depth of the sea to lie;
> Here, if you please, you may let them stay
> Till just after breakfast the very next day,
> When a parboiling process must be gone through
> (I mean for the beans, and not for you);
> Then if, in the pantry, there still should be
> That bean-pot, so famous in history,
> With all due deference bring it out,
> And, if there's a skimmer lying about,
> Skim half of the beans from the boiling pan
> Into the bean pot as fast as you can;
> Then turn to Biddy and calmly tell her
> To take a huge knife and go to the cellar,
> For you must have, like Shylock of old,
> "A pound of flesh," ere your beans grow cold;
> But, very unlike that ancient Jew,
> Nothing but pork will do for you.
> Then tell once more your maiden fair,
> In the choice of the piece to take great care,
> For a streak of fat and a streak of lean
> Will give the right flavor to every bean!
> This you must wash, and rinse, and score,
> Put into the pot, and round it pour
> The rest, till the view presented seems

Like an island of pork in an ocean of beans;
Pour on boiling hot water enough to cover
The tops of the beans completely over,
Shove into the oven and bake till done,
And the triumph of Yankee cookery's won! (1873:53–54)

Here again the relationship between poetry and recipes is made explicit both in the form of the recipe and its reference to the cook as poet.[5]

The written forms of recipes evoke an exquisite convergence of human sensory experience which in turn evokes—through reverie—place, time, and identity. The "recollection of recipes . . . is a memory of how things were; it is a time and a place and people remembered. . . . And we fix the scene, like a photograph, like a perfume, in the distillate memory of what we ate. Recipes become subtle mnemonics" (Schmidt 1974:194).

Rather than "the assertion of self implied by the written text" (Camitta, personal communication), a bold act uncharacteristic of proper ladies of the nineteenth century, the format of the recipe texts and their compilation suggests that some women chose a condoned form of creativity, that which contributes to the making of a home—a friendly, warm, aesthetic, private place for a family's retreat from the world.[6] Nowhere in the text of my nineteenth-century receipt scribe is to be found the personal pronoun "I" with one exception. The poem mentioned earlier, entitled "One of Three" describes a mother's grief and self-consolation at the death of one of her children.

"'I am not quite alone,' she said;
  'I have fair daughters three:
And one is dead, and one is wed,
  And one remains with me.

"'Awhile I watch, with tenderest care,
  Her growth from child to maid,
And plait her fair and shining hair
  A long and golden braid—

"'(Ah! sweet the bloom upon the grape
  Before it leaves the vine)—
And deck and drape her dainty shape
  With garments soft and fine,

"'And keep her sacred and apart
  Until some stranger's plea,
With flattering art, shall win her heart
  Away from home and me.

"'Leaving her childhood's home and me
  Forgotten and bereft;
Then there will be, of all my three,

Only the dead one left.
   "'Why count the dead as lost? Ah me!
   I keep my dead alive;
  For only she, of all the three,
   Will always be my own.

  "' She will not slight, at morn or eve,
   The old love for the new;
  The living leave our hearts to grieve—
   The dead are always true.'"[7]

This poem inserted between recipes is not devalued or trivialized by this placement. What it suggests is that in the context of the kitchen, poetic verse about food and other facets of life is appropriate, perhaps even acceptable only there. It should not be surprising that the themes of life and death are reflected upon in the familiar and intimate context of the kitchen; that this homely location engenders acts of writing about "mortality and immortality, upon perfection and disaster" (Schmidt 1974:180), among them, this poem. Women whose lives were devoted to the nurturance of others, nonetheless, found opportunities for self-expression. In describing the work of nearly half a lifetime, the words of an eloquent quiltmaker reflect upon a woman's world:

> It took me more than twenty-five years, nearly twenty-five, I reckon, in the evenings after supper when children were all put to bed. My whole life is in that quilt. It scares me sometimes when I look at it. They are all in that quilt, my hopes and fears, my joys and sorrows, my loves and hates. I tremble sometimes when I remember what that quilt knows about me. (Stewart 1974:28)

For many women in the nineteenth century, the keeping of a receipt book was a life's work, a book of memories, an evocation of sensory experience and imagination, an account of friendships, exchanges and relationships to others, a testament of devotion, nurturance, skills, and knowledge acquired over a lifetime—a written legacy of their art and of their lives.

Notes

1. Support for the restrictiveness of nineteenth-century women's intellectual development can be found in Welter 1978; Homans 1986; Kelley 1984. However, Carroll Smith-Rosenberg has pointed out that despite this repression, there was a range of reading materials from novels, magazines, and health manuals to advice literature of all sorts available to women (personal communication). For this point of view, see Baym 1978, Stevenson 1991, Douglas 1977.

2. The recipe is reproduced exactly as it appeared in the book, lacking mention of any liquid needed to roll dough. Margaret Mills has suggested that this oversight may be an error in copying. My hunch is that this omission represents a set of common understandings about what is required to roll a shortcake dough.

3. As William Woys Weaver has lamented, many cook book writers have failed to acknowledge their sources (1982). A similar complaint was made in the introduction to *Pepys At Table* by Christopher Driver and Michelle Berriedale-Johnson. I would like to suggest that in the tradition of recipe exchange, attribution may not be required, especially since modifications by each cook were most likely commonplace.

4. Manuscript cookery books are extant as early as the fourteenth century or earlier although "it is likely that peripatetic courts, strong tradition, apprenticeship, efficient oral transmission and remarkably retentive memories normally eliminated the need for written guides in the kitchen of the late medieval Europe, even in the seigneurial ones" (Scully 1986:xxv). The written recipe collections were often given as gifts from one King's court to another throughout Europe (Lorna Sass, personal communication). The tradition continued through men's and women's domestic writings up to and through the nineteenth century. See for example: *Stere Htt Well, A Book of Medieval Refinements, Recipes and Remedies* from a manuscript in Samuel Pepys's Library (1972); *An Ordinance of Pottage*, edited by Constance B. Hieatt, (1988); *Pepys at Table* (1984); *The Larder Invaded*, W. W. Weaver (1986). In the second chapter of *A Jane Austen Household Book*, Peggy Hickman refers to the custom that women of the period had of keeping "commonplace or household books" (1977:37).

5. The disturbing anti-Semitic lines suggest another avenue of exploration for this literature and its audience. This paper does not, unfortunately, attempt to deal with these issues though they are revealing of the anti-ethnic and anti-immigrant sentiments of the late nineteenth century.

6. For a discussion of eighteenth-century women's autobiographical writings see, among others, Felicity Nussbaum, "Eighteenth-Century Women's Autobiographical Commonplaces" (in Benstock 1988).

7. It is not clear that the anonymous writer of the nineteenth-century receipt book authored this poem. It may as likely have been copied from another source. It is, however, written in her own script.

References

Anonymous
  Undated. Family receipt book. Unpublished manuscript.
Baym, Nina
  1978 *Woman's Fiction: A Guide to Novels By and About Women in America, 1820–1870*. Ithaca: Cornell Univ. Press.
Benstock, Shari, ed.
  1988 *The Private Self: Theory and Practice of Women's Autobiographical Writings*. Chapel Hill: Univ. of North Carolina Press.
Douglas, Ann
  1988 *The Feminization of American Culture*. New York: Anchor Press/Doubleday.
Draine, Betsy
  1989 Refusing the Wisdom of Solomon: Some Recent Feminist Literary Theory. *Signs* 15:144–70.
Driver, Christopher and Michelle Berriedale-Johnson
  1984 *Pepys at Table*. Berkeley: Univ. of California Press.
Herrnstein Smith, Barbara
  1968 *Poetic Closure: A Study of How Poems End*. Chicago: Univ. of Chicago Press.

Hickman, Peggy
 1977   *A Jane Austen Household Book.* Newton Abbot: David and Charles.
Hieatt, Constance B.
 1988   *An Ordinance of Pottage.* London: Prospect Books.
Hodgett, Gerald A. J.
 1972   *Stere Htt Well: A Book of Medieval Refinements, Recipes and Remedies.* From
     a manuscript in Samuel Pepys Library. London: Cornmarket Reprints.
Holloway, Laura C.
 1887   *The Hearthstone; or, Life at Home: A Household Manual.* Chicago: L. P.
     Miller and Company.
Homans, Margaret
 1986   *Bearing the Word: Language and Female Experience in Nineteenth Century
     Women's Writing.* Chicago: Univ. of Chicago Press.
Katriel, Tamar and Thomas Farrell
 1991   Scrapbooks as Cultural Texts: An American Art of Memory. *Text and Perfor-
     mance Quarterly* 11:1–17.
Kelley, Mary
 1984   *Private Woman, Public Stage: Literary Domesticity in Nineteenth-Century
     America.* Oxford: Oxford Univ. Press.
Kodish, Debora
 1983   Fair Young Ladies and Bonny Irish Boys: Pattern in Vernacular Poetics.
     Journal of American Folklore 96:131–50.
Ladies of the First Presbyterian Church, Dayton, Ohio
 1873   *Presbyterian Cook Book.* Dayton, Ohio: Historical Publishing Company.
Leonardi, Susan J.
 1989   Recipes for Reading: Summer Pasta, Lobster a la Riseholme, and Key Lime
     Pie. *PMLA* 104:340–47.
Riffaterre, Michael
 1983   *Text Production.* New York: Columbia Univ. Press.
Rutledge, Sarah
 1979   *The Carolina Housewife.* Columbia, South Carolina: Univ. of South Carolina
     Press.
Schmidt, Paul
 1974   As If a Cookbook Had Anything To Do With Writing. *Prose* 8:179–203.
Scully, Terrence, ed. and trans.
 1986   *Chiquart's "On Cookery": A Fifteenth-Century Savoyard Culinary Treatise.*
     New York: Peter Lang.
Stevenson, Louise L.
 1991   *The Victorian Homefront, American Thought and Culture, 1860-1880.* New
     York: Twayne.
Stewart, Susan
 1974   Sociological Aspects of Quilting in Three Brethren Churches in Southeastern
     Pennsylvania. *Pennsylvania Folklife* 23:15–29.
Weaver, William
 1982   *A Quaker Woman's Cookbook: The Domestic Cookery of Elizabeth Ellicott
     Lea.* Philadelphia: Univ. of Pennsylvania Press.
 1986   *Thirty-Five Receipts From "The Larder Invaded."* Philadelphia: The Library
     Company of Philadelphia, The Historical Society of Pennsylvania.

Welter, Barbara
 1978 The Cult of True Womanhood: 1820–1860. In *The American Family in Social-Historical Perspective*. Ed. Michael Gordon. New York: St. Martin's Press. Pp. 372–92.

NOEL, LA CHANDELEUR, MARDI GRAS

Begging Rituals in French Newfoundland

Gerald Thomas

THIS PAPER will examine three classic customs ostensibly associated with the Christian calendar and its rituals, as they exist or existed in the enclavic francophone culture of Newfoundland's Port-au-Port Peninsula, which, to a greater or lesser degree, involve a traditionally sanctioned form of begging. And insofar as one of the main conceptual *points de départ* will be that of acculturation, some attention will also be focussed on a fourth custom, also ostensibly associated with the Christian calendar and also a now traditionally sanctioned form of begging, though not traditionally French in its origins. I am referring in the first instance to Christmas, Candlemas, and Shrove Tuesday, and in the second instance to All Hallows Eve, or Hallowe'en. I will endeavour to demonstrate that these constituents of contemporary Franco-Newfoundland culture illustrate variable chronological polymerous acculturational evolution; in English, this means that each custom has common elements, but each has been influenced primarily by distinctive external factors operating at different times in history. Acculturation can thus be seen as part of the dynamic process of change.

To begin at the beginning, however, I must outline briefly the origins of the contemporary francophone enclave, which is one of the smallest in Canada, for on the Port-au-Port Peninsula today there are probably no more than 2,000 French speakers, and some would argue that my estimate is exaggerated.[1] There were in fact two distinct waves of French settlement to wash up on Newfoundland's West Coast, both during the same period, the nineteenth century, but from different immediate geographical origins. France had been making extensive use of the Newfoundland coastline for purposes of the fishery from the sixteenth century on, to the point of having established a colony at

Plaisance, or Placentia as it is today.[2] But this colony was lost, as was the colony of *Acadie*, with the signing of the Treaty of Utrecht in 1713. France did retain the monopoly of use of most of the coast of Newfoundland, with the exception of the eastern shores occupied by English fishermen and merchants, but the wars of the eighteenth century between France and Britain, which strictly speaking came to an end in 1815, saw the extent of French coastal rights constantly shrinking; after 1815, the so-called 'French Shore' extended from Cape Ray in the extreme southwest, north and east to Cape St. John. Rights to this stretch of coast disappeared with the 1904 *Entente cordiale*, but anglophone settlement had been spreading into the area well before 1904.

It was in the period 1815–1904 that the seeds of contemporary French settlements were planted. One segment of French settlement derived from the control of the southern half of the French Shore by French merchants based in or operating from the islands of St. Pierre and Miquelon, off Newfoundland's Burin Peninsula. The northern and northeastern section of the French Shore was dominated by the St. Malo-based fishery, and it had a much less durable impact on settlement than did the St. Pierre fishery, whose season was longer and whose shore bases lasted longer than those of St. Malo. Embryonic settlements, as will shortly be noted, were made on the Port-au-Port Peninsula.

A little farther south, along the shores of the interior of Bay St. George and down into the Codroy Valley, other French communities were coming into existence, but they were of Acadian, rather than continental French origin. These settlers represented one of the last out-migrations of Acadians following the *Grand dérangement* of 1755 when British interests, whose deeds were justified by pseudo-geopolitical fears on the one hand and economic jealousies on the other, attempted the mass deportation of the population of what was by then a thriving 150-year-old former colony of France.[3] The Acadians were of course widely dispersed, from Louisiana in the south to Québec in the north; many of those who escaped the British round-up moved to other parts of today's Maritime Provinces; some of these subsequently left Cape Breton Island and the Magdaleine Islands to move to the then largely uninhabited and totally unpoliced west coast of Newfoundland, to start a new life as farmers. Not as fishermen, which would have put them in illegal competition with the French, but as farmers, as they had been in *Acadie*; indeed, there is evidence of reciprocal support between the two French groups. The chief difference between the Acadians and the French of the Port-au-Port Peninsula was that the former were descendants of settlers from the centre west provinces of France who, by the mid-nineteenth century, had been established in Canada for some two hundred and fifty years, and out of direct contact with France for about one hundred and fifty years—who had developed a farming culture and whose language and traditions had been following their own evolution since the early seventeenth century. The latter, on the other hand, the Port-au-Port French, arrived in the first instance as deserters from the French Shore fishery. They were from Normandy, Brittany, Poitou, St. Pierre, and Miquelon—from a slightly different linguistic and cultural background geographically, but also

removed in time—arriving from nineteenth-century France rather than seventeenth-century France as was the case for the Acadians. Further, such work
experience as the French had acquired was in the fishery, farming and garden-
ing being no more than secondary to the fishery. Finally, whereas the Acadians
coming to Newfoundland did so frequently in family units complete with
livestock and equipment, the metropolitan French brought next to nothing,
materially speaking, with them, and only in the rarest cases did the deserters
arrive with wife and family.

Until 1904, moreover, French authorities were known to undertake sweeps
of the coastline looking for deserters. One informant of mine remembered such
a case as late as 1902. The contemporary francophone communities of L'Anse-
à-Canards/Black Duck Brook, Maisons-d'Hiver/Winterhouses, La Grand'Terre/
Mainland and Cap-St-Georges/Cape St. George were settled by young men
who, for the most part, eventually found wives amongst the stable Acadian
communities, or amongst those Acadian families that moved into the Peninsula,
or amongst the very few French families allowed to reside year round on the
Peninsula to take care of fishing facilities. Thus, there was a gradual melding of
Acadian and metropolitan French cultures, though to varying degrees, Acadian
influence being greatest at Cape St. George and least at Mainland. Even today,
however, those of metropolitan ancestry are quick to distinguish themselves
from their Acadian cousins; and there are many linguistic features permitting
differentiation between their respective types of spoken French.

Today, close to the end of the twentieth century, French language and culture
are most lively on the Port-au-Port Peninsula, whereas the Acadian culture of Bay
St. George and the Codroy Valley has been very nearly assimilated, linguistically at
least, to the now dominant anglophone culture of the region.

Such cultural integrity as both francophone groups were able to maintain
between their foundation in the early nineteenth century and the present is marked
by major acculturation pressures, the most significant of which began in 1940. Prior
to 1940, the evolving French communities of fishermen on the peninsula and of
farmers further inland had remained in relative isolation, despite the arrival of
anglophones of English, Irish, and Scottish origins during the latter half of the
nineteenth century; assimilative pressure—to learn English—came from the Catholic
Church and the schools it eventually opened, schools in which French was forbidden. But schools were late in arriving in the French peninsular communities, and
attendance was never good until well into the twentieth century. English was also
required for dealings with fish merchants, but there are numerous jokes and
anecdotes still extant, amongst both French and English speakers, poking fun at the
poor command of English amongst the French.

All this began to change quickly and radically with the creation in 1940 of
an American Air Force base at the present town of Stephenville. Many French
speakers found work there in construction, maintenance, and services, but the
inducement of cash payments, as opposed to the barter that characterised their
dealings with merchants, and the material goods made available through the
Post Exchange, also served as a powerful inducement to learn English. While

the peninsular French remained geographically isolated, with only the roughest of roads linking them to the burgeoning town of Stephenville, and cultural depredations, chiefly those of dislocation of traditions brought about by absentee husbands and a concomitant reduction of family involvement in community activities, Acadian tradition suffered doubly: first because a great deal of prime farming land was taken over for the base, displacing Acadian families, and second, because anglophones from all over Newfoundland descended on the region seeking work, and soon constituted a linguistic majority. Thereafter, the demise of a viable Acadian culture was only a question of time.

The peninsular French, being geographically more isolated, some forty miles from Stephenville, maintained for a time a tenuous grasp of their language, with many families deliberately shunning the use of French with their children on the grounds that English alone would provide the means to personal betterment. Matters did not change with Confederation in 1949—indeed assimilation was, if anything, buttressed—but the closure of the base in 1966, followed by new bilingual-bicultural policies from the federal government in Ottawa, contributed to a reaction which, by the end of the sixties, signaled a generalised renaissance of interest in their French heritage. Today there are more francophones than ever before, and there are French language schooling, French radio and television, and community groups strongly supportive of their ethnocultural identity, based in part on the efforts of a small but growing number of university-trained individuals, the nucleus of an eventual élite.

So what then of their French cultural heritage, and what then of their begging rituals? It is a sad fact, from the point of view of the folklorist interested in the traditionally studied genres, that in-depth and extensive fieldwork only began on the Port-au-Port Peninsula in 1970, at a time when many of the time-honoured modes of customary behaviour had disappeared or been displaced by alternate forms. Thus the public *veillée* or storytelling evening only lingered in the occasional home, most people prefering the attraction of television, the bar or club, or the bingo hall to the folktale.[4] Contexts for traditional singing were likewise replaced, for example, and many customs only survived in memory. While it was possible still to collect large quantities of generic folklore still richly textured, the traditional contexts were very often gone, and the folklore collector could rarely observe such material in natural contexts. But it was always possible to find excellent informants to evoke with clarity and detail the reality of such contexts, if they had experienced them to begin with. Today, the Centre d'Etudes Franco-Terreneuviennes has taped and manuscript material from several hundreds of informants; it is possible to cast light on a great number of cultural phenomena that have now all but disappeared.

Against this very roughly sketched but necessary backcloth let me now consider manifestations of begging rituals existing or having existed amongst the French of the Port-au-Port Peninsula. And I shall begin, as does the title of this paper, at Christmas, with the custom of mumming or mummering, which occurs during the twelve days of Christmas. Christmas mumming amongst French Newfoundlanders fits fairly precisely into the typology established by

Herbert Halpert in his essay in *Christmas Mumming in Newfoundland* jointly edited with G. M. Story (Halpert 1969:34–61). In Halpert's typology the French tradition corresponds to the Informal House Visit (A1a) in which a)"The visitors are an informal group of varying composition," b)"Members of the group attempt complete disguise," c)"The behaviour of the disguised visitors tends to be uninhibited and the reverse of normal," d)"The hosts attempt to penetrate the disguises by a form of guessing-game, sometimes accompanied by roughness; unmasking by the visitors usually, though not invariably, follows successful identification," and e)"The unmasked figures return to their normal social roles and are usually offered, and accept, food and drink," consumed on the premises. This, according to Halpert, is the predominant pattern in Newfoundland, and French-Newfoundlanders clearly conform to this pattern.

Apart from numerous but scattered and often fragmentary reports collected from French Newfoundlanders, I can personally attest to the still vigorous tradition, having witnessed a visit of two mummers to my lodgings in Cape St. George in January 1973. The home I was at was not then receptive to such visits; the two mummers stood at the kitchen counter, refused offers of "syrup," though they would probably not have refused alcohol or beer, and they refused to admit the accuracy of the guesses made as to their identity. When they spoke, they disguised their voices, and they were dressed in sexually indeterminate clothing. At Christmas 1975–76, I went mummering at Mainland with a band of young adults; reverse dressing, masking, unbridled behaviour, guessing of identity, offerings of food and drink were involved. Finally, in 1986 I was given a copy of a video report made at Rousseau Rouge/Red Brook by James Bamber, working for Radio-Canada.

In all reports, the element of the offering of food and drink is a relatively minor part of the proceedings; only rarely was food or drink actually begged for, at least in recent years, and then by the rowdier elements for whom the alcohol might have been an important inducement, when faced with the intense seasonal cold, of course. Older informants, some now dead, said that mummering at Christmas was not an old French custom but had been adopted from the growing number of anglophones, many of whom were resettled in the 1930s on the Port-au-Port Peninsula and had an important influence, because of geographical proximity, in the French communities of Mainland and Winterhouses/Black Duck Brook. Mummering nonetheless is a still popular activity amongst the French.

La Chandeleur, or Candlemas, which falls on February 2, officially marks the Purification of the Virgin Mary in the calendar of the Roman Catholic church. Evidence of the tradition in French Newfoundland communities shows little or no religious observance associated with the custom which had, when I began research in 1970, apparently died out at least ten or fifteen years before. But it was possible to elicit descriptions of the custom, which are remarkably uniform. In the days before Candlemas, a group of young men choose a king. The king, identified by a pole, and his retinue go from house to house begging for contributions in kind—of potatoes, turnips, meat, cabbage, milk, tea, salt, for example. For each house that contributes, a coloured ribbon is attached to the pole. On the night of Candlemas, the local youths meet at a designated house to which the various contributions have been brought and prepared; at an appointed time there is a loud rapping at the door. Someone announces "Here comes Candlemas—the King behind!" at which point the King, his ribbon-bedecked pole sticking out of his pants, enters with his followers and begins the dance. Later the food and drink is consumed, the dancing continues to fiddle or accordeon music, and would continue until supplies and energies alike were exhausted—sometimes several days later.

This generalised description, based on recollections, was all I had to go on until 1974 when, acting as a consultant for CBC, I was asked to set up something particularly visual. It was March, but seasonally appropriate, and a number of my informants were more than happy to reenact the arrival of the King and the start of the dance for the cameras. However, the following year, it seems, the custom was spontaneously revived, though with what changes I am unable to say. As it was described, however, the custom seems particularly close to Acadian versions reported by Anselme Chiasson (1961) and, particularly, Georges Arsenault (1982).

Shrove Tuesday—or, even in some English traditions now, Mardi Gras—is today celebrated primarily by the eating of crêpes or pancakes in both French and anglophone traditions in Western Newfoundland; usually, too, symbolic objects are incorporated into the pancakes, the significance of which is collectively to predict the occupation of one's future husband; such symbols would seem then to be of more interest to women than to men. In former times—perhaps no less than twenty or thirty years ago—young adults would go mummering, as they put it, following their evening meal of pancakes. They would disguise themselves and behave in much the same fashion as at Christmas, save that they specifically asked for pancakes at each house they visited, and were thus most clearly begging.

At Mainland, they also used to make a straw man known as "Mardi Gras" which they carried from house to house, until they had a sufficiency of pancakes, at which point they carried the straw man to the river, into which they would toss it, thereby "drowning Mardi Gras." A begging song, alluded to though not recorded in Mainland, usually accompanied the ritual, close parallels to which were reported from late nineteenth-century Brittany and elsewhere in France.[5] As with Christmas and Candlemas, the common factor is the disguising and passage from house to house. Such similarity of the documented French customs of Candlemas and Mardi Gras to the English Christmas mummering must have allowed an easy adoption of mummering at Christmas.

Finally, in this overview of begging customs, a word on Hallowe'en. Informants in all the French communities were unanimous in attributing to American servicemen stationed at Stephenville after 1940 the introduction into the region of "Trick or Treat." Older informants warmly recalled the generosity of GIs who would visit communities in the region at appropriate seasonal festivals bearing gifts for the children and, in many cases, for the womenfolk to whom they became attached. Between 1940 and 1966 several hundreds of local women married American servicemen, returning with them to the U.S.A. But it was the children who were the apple of the American eye, and it was the Americans who introduced them to the begging house visit, in disguise. It was only much later that ready-made, store-bought costumes and accessories became available; and much later, too, that the "trick" element seems to have very largely fallen by the wayside, even as the custom as a whole has become more the domain of pre-teens. There was a time, perhaps as late as the early sixties, when young adults customarily played tricks on people, tricks such as blocking pathways, cutting clothes-lines or dirtying gates or door handles with tar, manure, or seal fat, or even blocking a chimney from the rooftop and filling the house with smoke; and, without the actual begging, the acquisition of plundered chickens subtilised from coops or vegetables spirited out of gardens. Both kinds of activities have been reported from Cape St. George and Mainland.

It will be clear by now, most emphatically in the case of Hallowe'en, less so for the other customs referred to, that each has been marked by the influence of a group of people external to the original French settlements. The Christmas mummering carried out by the French is almost a mirror image of the Anglo-Irish tradition in Newfoundland as characterised by Halpert and was adopted no doubt late in the nineteenth or, more probably, early in the twentieth century. There is no hard evidence permitting the establishment of a precise chronology.

But while mummering at Christmas seems to have come directly from the anglophone tradition, the basic elements of disguise and begging were not alien to the French. Both features exist or existed in Franco-Newfoundland tradition but were associated with the variably defined period of Carnival and Lent. Arnold van Gennep marshalled all available evidence of begging and disguising rituals in France over the Christmas period, including the Old French word *Mômeries* to describe a late fifteenth-century Alsatian edict forbidding begging and disguises (Van Gennep, 1937, vol. 3; 1938, vol. 4; 1943–1958, vol. 1, parts 1–7, all published; vol. 1, part 7, pp. 2874 ff.). Nevertheless, it is clear that by the mid to late nineteenth century most such traditions were defunct or extremely attenuated in France, associated where they survived with children, as are Hallowe'en traditions in North America today, or with specific age or occupational groups. A description reported by van Gennep of a New Year's begging ritual, with parallels elsewhere in France, has much more in common with the Franco-Newfoundland Candlemas tradition than with mummering; there is communal begging with song, at the end of which the young people, carrying a flag, congregate in a hall or large room to eat and drink what they had collected, and to dance (Van Gennep 1958:2882). This is the custom known in Québec as the *guignolée* (Dupont and Mathieu 1986:15). It was, in a multitude of variations, widespread in France, though in general decline by the end of the nineteenth century. It was throughout the nineteenth century, of course, that French settlement began in Newfoundland, often by young, single men, the age group most likely to want to maintain such a boisterous tradition. The eventual discovery of mummering at Christmas merely afforded a new occasion to indulge in recognisable activities.

In France, as van Gennep clearly demonstrated, the period of masking and begging rituals *par excellence* is that of Carnival/Lent. Carnival is of course the period during which meat was permitted, Lent, the period beginning the fortieth day before Easter, in which both alimentary and sexual interdictions prevail. Mid-Lent, the twentieth day before Easter, was initially a brief suspension of interdictions and abstinence. Van Gennep stresses however that in tradition no such calendrical rigidity prevailed, rather that extreme chronological variation was the rule. Depending on the location, the period of Carnival could begin as early as Christmas and last as late as Ash Wednesday.

That French Newfoundlanders should have adopted Candlemas (February 2) as the beginning of Carnival is not surprising; there were many precedents in France. But most significantly, Candlemas was also the date on which it was celebrated in Acadia, as was first reported by Anselme Chiasson for Chéticamp, on Cape Breton Island (Chiasson 1961:211–16); Georges Arsenault's *Courir la Chandeleur* is an extensive survey of the custom amongst Acadians of Prince Edward Island (see Arsenault 1982). The Acadian tradition is very close in detail to that recorded in Newfoundland; it is safe to attribute the Franco-Newfoundland custom to the influence of neighbouring Acadians, with whom many Frenchmen intermarried. Indeed, it was the Cormier family at Cape St. George that volunteered to put on a Candlemas "run," and the Cormiers are, of course, Acadian.

Mardi Gras customs today are simplified, seemingly confined to the eating of pancakes with or without symbolic ingredients. Certainly in my fieldwork I did not encounter ritual begging in disguise nor the drowning of a straw effigy of Mardi Gras. This tradition, however, is one which seems most closely related to areas of France from which many of the earliest deserter-settlers seem to have come. Van Gennep refers to the straw man Mardi Gras carried by four young men in the Dinan region of Brittany (Van Gennep 1947:939); the straw man could be burned or drowned depending on the region. Versions of the song associated with the Mardi Gras custom occur in Sébillot (1965:301–302) for Brittany and Carmen Roy's study of St. Pierre and Miquelon traditions (Roy 1966:145–46).

Disguises similar to those of Christmas mummers are commonly associated with mid-Lent in Acadian tradition, with informal house visits and attempts at guessing the identity of the guisers (Chiasson 1961:213). But there is no mention of a straw man nor its drowning or cremation. Insofar as the custom has survived at all, it would seem in Newfoundland to be more directly associated with France rather than Acadia. I need not take up Hallowe'en again, since its introduction to the Newfoundland French is relatively recent.

All of these begging customs share similarities, though differences also exist. While Franco-Newfoundland tradition owes something to France, to Acadia, to anglophone Newfoundland, and to the U.S.A., while each tradition is practiced in more or less attenuated form, the element of begging remains, explicitly or implicitly. As van Gennep points out, the obtaining of gifts is not simply a question of economics; at Christmas and the New Year the good wishes accompanying the giving of gifts are for good fortune; the clearest indication of this can be seen both with the mummers and at Hallowe'en (Van Gennep 1958:2874ff.). Mummers, especially if refused entry, might damage the property of the refusing parties; the refusal of a treat at Hallowe'en at one time meant a real "trick," and less clearly, but in similar vein, the theft of chickens or vegetables from specific individuals in the pre-Trick-or-Treat tradition can be interpreted as a sublimated curse aimed at those who have incurred the ire of the young people. It was a form of traditional sanction clearly akin to the vengeful actions associated with the mummers in many parts of Newfoundland.

Now while all these begging rituals are associated with Christian festivals—Christmas, Candlemas, Shrove Tuesday, Hallowe'en—the high degree of chronological and textual variation apparent geographically also supports van Gennep's contention that the whole cycle of begging rituals probably predates Christianity. The magical elements underlying the good wishes and the tricks or pranks is one clue; the transfer of wealth, not simply the good Christian virtue of sustaining the poor but also, since the most frequent participants were young, unmarried people, is another; van Gennep notes that the associated festivities often led to marital unions. I am sure Alan Dundes would not fail to point out the obvious phallic significance of the King of Candlemas's pole sticking out of his pants. Thus a veneer of Christianity overlaps old and fundamental community values and practices. It would take another paper to discuss the significance of elements of begging rituals and disguising which remain, and those that have disappeared, but in which evolving functions would reflect the evolution of contemporary society and its needs.[6]

Notes

1. Official census figures include francophones in the Labrador section of the Province, as well as those living in St. John's. Labrador francophones are from Quebec chiefly; the St. John's French include Europeans, Acadians, Québécois, and West Coast French. The last census for which figures are available is that of 1986, which gave a global figure of 564,005 for the Province as a whole, a figure of 2,170 for the francophone element in the Province, and 1,090 francophones for the Port-au-Port Peninsula.

2. See, for a detailed account of the development of the French fishery in North America, de la Morandière (1962, 1966).

3. Two particularly useful perspectives on Acadian history are Massignon (1962) and Poirier (1984).

4. See for this specific point Thomas (1976:192–201); for the influence of television on narrative, Thomas (1980:343–51); and for a comprehensive study of the folktale tradition of the French, Thomas (1983).

5. See Sébillot (1965:301–2). Sébillot reports the custom of drowning Mardi Gras,

with the song sung to the accompaniment of the accordeon:
    Mardi-Gras, ne t'en vas pas,
    J'f'rons des crèpes et t'en mangeras.
    Mardi Gras s'en est allé
    J'f'rons des crèpes sur n'un gal'tier.

6. All uncited references draw on collections deposited in the Centre d'Etudes Franco-Terreneuviennes, Department of Folklore, Memorial University of Newfoundland. Much of the material on Franco-Newfoundland customs was incorporated in an unpublished manuscript entitled "Folklore franco-terreneuvien (contes, chansons, costumes, croyances)," which I compiled in 1984–85; the 101-page manuscript was subsumed in Dupont and Mathieu (1986).

References

Arsenault, George
    1982 *Courir la chandeleur*. Moncton: Les Editions d'Acadie.
Chiasson, Anselme
    1961 *Chéticamp, Histoire et Traditions acadiennes*. Moncton: Editions des Aboiteaux.
Dupont, Jean-Claude and Jacques Mathieu, eds.
    1986 *Héritage de la francophonie canadienne—traditions orales*. Québec: Presses de l'Université Laval.
Halpert, Herbert
    1969 A Typology of Mumming. In *Christmas Mumming in Newfoundland. Essays in Anthropology, Folklore, and History*. Eds. Herbert Halpert and G. M. Story. Toronto: Univ. of Toronto Press.
de la Morandière, Charles
    1962, 1966 *Histoire de la pêche française de la morue dans l'Amérique septentrionale*. 3 vols. Paris: Maisonneuve and Larose.
Massignon, Geneviève
    1962 *Les parlers français d'Acadie*. 2 vol. Paris: Klincksieck
Poirier, Michel
    1984 *Les Acadiens aux îles Saint-Pierre et Miquelon 1758–1828*. Moncton: Les Editions d'Acadie.
Roy, Carmen
    1966 *Saint-Pierre et Miquelon. Une mission folklorique aux îles*. Ottawa: Musée national du Canada, bulletin 182, No. 56 de la série anthropologique (2 versions).
Sébillot, Paul
    1965 *Le Folk-lore des Pêcheurs*. Paris: Maisonneuve & Larose.
Thomas, Gerald
    1976 A Tradition under Pressure: Folk Narratives of the French Minority of the Port-au-Port Peninsula, Canada. In *Studia Fennica* 20, *Folk Narrative Research* (Helsinki). Pp. 192–201.
    1980 Other Worlds: Folktale and Soap Opera in Newfoundland's French Tradition. In *Folklore Studies in Honour of Herbert Halpert. A Festschrift*. Eds. Kenneth S. Goldstein and Neil V. Rosenberg. St. John's: Memorial University of Newfoundland. Pp. 343–51.
    1983 *Les Deux Traditions: Le conte populaire chez les Franco-Terreneuviens*. Montréal: Bellarmin. (English translation by the author: *The Two Traditions:*

The Art of Storytelling Amongst French Newfoundlanders. St. John's: Break water Books, 1993.)

Van Gennep, Arnold
  1937, 1938, 1943–58. *Manuel de folklore français contemporain.* 4 vols. Paris: Picard.

LANGUAGE AND PERFORMANCE

Dialect and Verbal Art in Newfoundland Oral Narrative

J. D. A. Widdowson

NEWFOUNDLAND has a rich heritage of oral narrative and of many other traditions originating from England, Ireland, Scotland, and France. These remained relatively unchanged in coastal enclaves although modified by their new environment. The early English settlers came predominantly from the West Country, and later they were joined by immigrants from Southern Ireland. Admixtures from Scotland, and the French-speaking tradition, together with those of the indigenous native peoples, the Inuit, the Montagnais, the Naskapi, and the Micmacs, contributed to the breadth and depth of the unique amalgam that constitutes the linguistic and cultural inheritance of the Province of Newfoundland and Labrador.[1]

All the immigrant communities scattered around the coast had to be self-sufficient, and much of the work in the fishing grounds and in the lumberwoods often kept groups of men together in relative isolation for periods of time and gave opportunities for maintaining storytelling and singing traditions in addition to many other traditional activities commonly practised in the home.

Newfoundland has therefore preserved many aspects of English and Irish folk tradition, some of which are apparently no longer active in the countries of their origin and are now also under the threat of extinction in the province. Among these is the telling of the longer folktales, which were discovered during exploratory fieldwork in various parts of the province by Herbert Halpert and myself, together with some of our colleagues and students, in the 1960s and 1970s. A total of 150 recensions and 15 fragments of these tales have been transcribed, analysed, and annotated (see Halpert forthcoming). The tales were collected from 65 individuals in 40 communities over a period of some 14 years from 1964 to 1978, and 137 of the texts were transcribed from tape recordings.

Their themes and motifs are international and represent more than 80 AT Types. The aim of the transcription has been to preserve the actual speech of the storytellers, along with many features of their oral styles. It is an attempt to explore how far it is possible to set down in written form not only the exact words of speakers but also some idea of the structure of the narrative as indicated by pauses, emphases, and other linguistic and rhetorical features.

Quite apart from the immediacy of the spoken texts, the collection reveals the rich variety of the older Newfoundland narrative tradition. In their stories and songs, Newfoundlanders prove themselves to be part of a highly oral culture, rich in inventive language, colourful names, vivid proverbial sayings, ingenious riddles, and other forms of verbal art. For theirs is a verbal art—a dramatic art—and for that reason hard to capture on paper.

The storytellers recorded in the field were mainly between forty and ninety years old, most being over sixty, but some of the shorter tales contributed by students were from a much younger age group, including a few in their twenties. The majority of the tellers represent the everyday working occupations of Newfoundlanders. Those who had retired when we recorded them had mostly spent their lives in the seasonal tasks of fishing and woods work. One teller had been a blacksmith, and two others had been captains of ocean-going vessels. Most of those interviewed were of English or Irish descent and retained many features of their parent dialects in their speech. A notable exception was the Bennett family, whose ancestors were French (some branches of the family maintaining the older surname Benoit) but whose speech is now predominantly West Country English in its distinctive features, which they share with inhabitants of the Great Northern Peninsula communities in which they live. They also had a reputation as storytellers in their communities, sometimes restricted to their families, friends, and neighbours. Almost all of them had repertories that included legends, riddles, personal experience narratives, songs, and information on local history and the ways of life in their community.

The rapid cultural changes following confederation with Canada in 1949 reduced the need, the opportunities, and even the venues for storytelling sessions. However, once the collectors asked for such tales, narrators whose once extensive repertories had been inactive for many years became encouraged to try to "get the stories together" as they put it. This process of recall sometimes took days rather than hours, though some tellers first sketched the story out and then suddenly remembered and told it in full. Others told the tales hesitantly, piecing them together, and were able to improve them in later retellings. In so doing, their enthusiasm for the story and renewed confidence in their ability to tell it brought back the old fire and vividness into the narration.

During the fieldwork, the collectors became aware of the extraordinary flexibility in the narrative texts, which allows the storyteller to exercise ingenuity and creativity in different ways at each performance. Such flexibility is much more possible in a story than a song, since the narrator retells the basic structure of a tale, though not necessarily including all the same motifs or presenting the episodes in the same order, each telling being unique and the variants differing in detail if not in more substantial ways. As one narrator put it: "You never hears two stories alike. Never hears one feller tell . . . one story the same. Always a little different." Narrators such as the Bennetts from whom more than one telling of the same story was recorded obviously felt free to vary motifs and episodes, and to omit, combine, and recombine them at will. Since the individual styles of storytellers and the contexts of performance also vary, each interpretation reflects this. A teller may expand or contract the narrative according to a variety of constraints such as audience response, problems of recall, tiredness, and numerous other factors.

Individual styles of storytelling in Newfoundland and Labrador range from the measured, leisurely pace of some narrators, through the animated delivery and colourful dialogue of others, to the extraordinarily breathless pace of one particular man, all of whose stories are a tour de force of what Robert Hollett has termed "allegro speech" (Hollett 1982:124–70). All of this man's stories, incidentally, are of a remarkably even length, their average duration being seven minutes, 32 seconds, with the longest (eight minutes, four seconds) taking only one minute, 22 seconds more to tell than the shortest. This contrasts markedly with the much wider variation in the duration of tales by other narrators and with the deliberately unhurried delivery of those tellers who utilise frequent and lengthy pauses. The timing of the duration of oral narratives reveals important differences between individual storytelling styles, quite apart from what it can tell us about the average timespan of various narrative genres performed in different situational contexts.

While there is demonstrable continuity of the oral tradition in the transmission of folk narratives in Newfoundland, it seems likely that a few of the tales were originally learned from printed sources. For example, close textual parallels between two recensions of one particular story, together with the formulaic delivery of each, suggest that the tale's origins may well lie in the relatively fixed form of a recitation. On the other hand, of course, formulaic delivery is part of the oral narrator's stock-in-trade. Many of the tales begin with a traditional opening formula, some of the simple "Once upon a time" variety, and others more elaborate, such as those of Albert Heber Keeping of Grand Bank:

> Once upon a time and a very good / time / it was_not in your time_'deed [i.e. indeed] in my time_in olden times. (When) quart bottles hold half a gallon an' house paper[ed] with pancakes_an' pigs run about, forks stuck in their ass_see who wanted to buy pork.[2]

The same is true of end-formulas, which range from down-to-earth variants of "For I had a cup o' tea an' left for home" to the more complex rapid-fire runs such as those with which our allegro speaker ends his stories:

> An' they got married an' if they didn't live happy I don't know who did. They had children in baskets_(hove outdoors) [in] shelffuls_sent to the sea to make seapies an' the last time I seen 'em I wished 'em goodbye an' I haven't seen ar one sunce.

Formulaic elements in the body of a tale occasionally take the form of a rhyme or may simply consist of segments or phrases, often repeated, which are uttered with a markedly strong rhythm. Such elements have parallels with the verse/song sections of the cante fable. They break up the text and give variety on one hand, and they allow the audience to recognise and respond to certain core sections of the story on the other. In this respect they resemble the refrains of ballads, especially when they include repetition. They are focal points with which the audience can identify, and which the narrator may well use as markers on the cognitive map necessary for remembering and telling the tale. Like the "runs" characteristic of Irish tales, their formulaic nature, which at times leads to their being intoned almost ritually by the teller, may be one way in which he continues to remember the tale. Just as the repetition of actions, quests, and other elements is governed by Olrik's "Law of Three," the formulaic passages provide both teller and audience with set pieces which mark stages in the development of the plot and are part of the underlying structure of the tale.

Many of the narratives, and especially those of the longer Märchen type in which Jack is the protagonist, are frequently characterised by certain underlying patterns of structure and plot that by their very repetition establish in the minds of both listener and reader a certain predictability about the course of the given story. With only the most superficial analysis, for example, one becomes aware of certain recurrent basic patterns such as:

(beginning formula) + unpromising hero (+ meeting futurebride) (+ encounter with adversary) (+ assistance (human or supernatural)) + task/quest accomplished (+ recapitulation) + denouement/resolution (+ end formula).

This is a generalised schema, and the sequence of episodes is not fixed. The elements in parentheses are optional, whereas the remainder, in whatever sequence, are typical of many of the tales and might be regarded as core episodes, if not essential ones.

The quest/test element frequently involves a journey or a voyage and provides a point of stability in the narrative that lends itself to the generation of a variety of journeys, voyages, and difficult or impossible tasks. Structurally it is a pivotal point in the narrative in which the teller may exercise his ingenuity in developing the plot in a number of different ways. It therefore provides a focus for studying variation between recensions and may well offer clues about the development of new oicotypes. It also offers opportunities for the hero to demonstrate his skills and capabilities, and since the action in each narrative centres on him, he is the prime focus of the audience's attention. His character and his activities are essentially the vehicle through which the worldview implicit in the tales is communicated. Since the audience for the most part identifies with his character, or is at least in sympathy with it, these deeper levels of meaning in the tales are readily apprehended and absorbed by the listeners, whether consciously or unconsciously.

The characterisation of the hero and his interaction with both helpers and adversaries is heavily dependent on the high proportion of lively and informative dialogue, which also adds colour and animation to the tales. It is largely through the dialogue that the audience gets to know about the protagonists. Its immediacy and dramatic quality allow the listeners to become as it were eyewitnesses to the events as they happen. Its appeal is instant and direct since it incorporates all the vernacular conventions such as greetings, leavetakings, and countless other idioms of the local speech with which the audience is familiar and with which it identifies. It is often through dialogue and brief comments spoken to the audience aside from the narrative that the storyteller conveys much of the humour inherent in the tales. The mixing of direct and indirect speech, which is typical of many of the narrative styles illustrated in the collection, also has the effect of bridging from past to present time, especially in recapitulation. This again makes the events appear more immediate and gives the impression that what took place earlier in the story is in fact happening at the present moment. Indeed the way in which time is handled by the narrators would repay further investigation. For example, they rarely employ specific time references such as *soon, directly, presently*, but prefer much less precise local usage such as *by an' by* or the marking of the end of a given episode with *very good, anyway, all right*, etc. The passage of time is signalled by references to having breakfast or supper, going to bed, etc., the next morning often marking a new stage in the development of the plot. Major forward movements in time, however, are often more specific, being prefaced by such phrases as *after ... nine months, 'bout a ... twelvemonth afterwards, in a hundred and one year.*

Iterative constructions are frequently employed to convey a sense of time passing or of distance travelled: *she cooked away and cooked away; an' he rode all day. Rode all day; walked away again; she walked an' walked, walked on again an' walked on.*[3] The passage of time is also of course implicit in a sequence of events such as when three brothers in turn undertake journies or quests that imply that time elapses, even though the timespans are usually vague and indeterminate.

In Newfoundland many stories are told with a degree of verisimilitude more typical of the novella or the legend, in that they are deliberately set more in the real world than might be expected of international Märchen and include correspondingly fewer elements in which magic or "wonder" plays a significant part. The shift from the wonderful to the realistic is emphasised by the localising of many episodes, elements, and details, including of course the use of familiar vernacular words and idioms. However, the storytellers rarely deviate significantly from their normal speech style during performance. With few exceptions, they make little or no attempt, for example, to mimic the voice quality of a woman when speaking the dialogue of a female character in a story.[4] Instead they content themselves with varying the speed, pitch, stress, and pause structure of the narration, for the most part within the limitations of everyday speech.

The linguistic cues that signal the passage of time and the forward movement of the narrative appear to be similar in both the English- and Irish-based narrative traditions in Newfoundland. However, the Irish tradition may have penetrated more deeply into Newfoundland storytelling than may at first appear from the comparatively few Irish tales in the collection. For example, it is interesting to note the use by the predominantly English narrators on the west coast of the Great Northern Peninsula of certain superficial Irish linguistic forms such as *begar/begobs, don't be talkin'*, etc. Furthermore, like many other narrators from predominantly West Country English speaking communities in the province, these storytellers also knew a number of tales about the Irish comic characters Pat and Mike. It therefore appears that the West Country English and the Anglo-Irish storytelling traditions in Newfoundland have much in common, even down to the lexical level. It is mainly at the phonological level that the two traditions differ, and most of this distinction is lost in any non-phonetic transcription.

The texts presented in the collection are not literary reworkings but transcribed verbatim from oral tradition. As such, they include all the normal characteristics of spoken usage, such as false starts, re-encodings, unstable "sentence" structure, and various pause and intonation patterns signalled in different and more complex ways that can be achieved by the standard rules of punctuation in written narrative. It is impossible to convey every nuance of the variety and complexity of such spoken usage in print, but the transcriptions attempt to give as much of the authenticity and flavour of the speech as is feasible in the circumstances. The aim here is essentially to extend to English language texts some of the conventions of verbatim transcription, analysis, and commentary employed so successfully by the translators and editors of tales collected from the oral tradition of many native peoples. This at least provides a starting point for more objective and rigorous analysis in the future, which will in due course no doubt reveal much about the form, structure, and conventions of oral narrative style and provide a key to its universal appeal.

The transcriptions employ a system of conventions that permits the original speech to be transferred verbatim to the printed page but that is not so complex as to hamper accessibility. By means of this system, it is possible not only to provide an accurate rendering of the language itself—including many features of pronunciation, vocabulary, grammar and syntax—but also to convey some idea of the narrative structure, as indicated by pauses, emphases, and other linguistic and rhetorical means. One immediate effect of this more detailed system of transcription is that it reveals numerous linguistic forms that invite further attention. As lexical items from these tales were excerpted for the *Dictionary of Newfoundland English*, the linguistic notes to the collection complement and extend the record of local usage available in that work (see Story, Kirwin, and Widdowson 1982). At the same time they demonstrate how the creativity and versatility of Newfoundland storytellers have adapted these older international tales to the local culture, environment, and idiom.

The Newfoundland storytellers are so skilled that they are able to hold the attention of their audience even if they make mistakes or omit or vary the sequence of episodes. They concentrate their efforts on holding the audience's attention, come what may, and seem less concerned than scholars might think about telling a story consistently, fully, or accurately to conform with some preconceived "ideal" or "complete" version. They themselves are usually aware that they have made a mistake or omission and occasionally even apologise for so doing. However, the audience is equally responsive whether or not such errors or omissions occur. The listeners do not usually question the minutiae of motivation or plot but are well content simply to listen to the performance. Minor hiatuses cause little difficulty to the audience, whose attention is maintained by the overall flow of the narrative, and any brief, temporary difficulties are soon forgotten. Even the coughs, hesitations, and other hindrances to reading the transcriptions are often significant in that they involuntarily delay the progress of the spoken narrative and are sometimes used deliberately by the teller as a means of creating suspense, humour, and expectation.

The transcriptions reveal a plethora of misencodings and indistinguishable speech from storytellers whose narratives are not only dramatic and entertaining but also quite understandable to the audience in context. When the voice drops to make some ironical or other "aside," the listeners get the point, but the tape recording may give only a muffled reproduction of vowels and consonants whose meaning can often only be guessed at. The problem is compounded by the fact that the speakers are using their local dialect. Older speakers may not enunciate words clearly or may turn aside to address another member of the audience (and so lose clarity in the recording) or otherwise, as they put it, "swallow their words."

In transcribing the Newfoundland audiotapes, it proved impossible to do more than hint at the many nuances of vocal expressiveness used by tellers, especially in the dialogue. For example, the hero Jack's blatant, cocksure manner when he denies facts which the audience already knows and which his opponent also has correctly guessed, is clearly indicated during performance by subtle changes in the voice quality, speed of delivery, pitch levels, stresses, and other linguistic and stylistic devices. These can only be apprehended by the ear (and incidentally the ear of someone familiar with the dialect) and cannot be represented in a written recension. The transcriptions are analogous to a musical score, the flesh being put on the bones only in an actual performance, in which the interaction between teller and audience essential for this verbal art form generates the combination of factors that give it its unique flavour and power.

Since the language of folktales is essentially simple and the lexical range is limited, tellers are proportionally restricted in the means at their disposal to provide emphases and contrasts and otherwise exploit the rhetorical devices in their repertory. Instead they must rely for much of their impact on subtle variations of intonation, pause, rhythm, and tone of voice. Such features are therefore of crucial importance in the interaction between teller and audience. To some extent they are predictable because of the basic simplicity of the narrative structure, with its usually straightforward syntax, simple vocabulary, and transparent form. Its very simplicity and directness make for a certain consistency and predictability; there is no hidden, covert, or obfuscating use of language. Its stereotyping gives both hearer and reader useful clues about the ways in which it is to be told, read, heard, and interpreted. The only problems in interpreting the language arise from dialectal usage or from misencodings and similar inaccuracies of narration and articulation.

As anyone who has attempted to transcribe spoken usage will attest, there are numerous and ultimately insuperable problems in setting oral narrative down on paper. It is readily apparent, for example, that the more detailed the transcript, the more misencodings, repetitions, and hesitations are represented. While these may be a hindrance to the reader, who may respond by identifying what he sees as deficiencies in the storytelling style, such responses seriously misjudge the very nature of the oral tradition. In the actual storytelling context, as noted above, the misencodings are scarcely noticed by the audience. The repetitions often serve as punctuating devices, and the hesitations have the advantage not only of giving the teller time to collect his thoughts but also of allowing the audience to anticipate the clarification that usually follows. The audience present at a storytelling event has the incomparable advantage of being able to follow and respond to all or most of the largely untranscribable linguistic and paralinguistic features that are an essential part of the interaction between teller and audience and for which there is no substitute, especially in print. In reading verbatim transcriptions of speech we must therefore adopt a completely different approach that not only puts aside much of our habitual response to printed texts, and especially to works of literature, but that also accepts the transliteration of the oral tradition and its context as valid and important in its own right. The Newfoundland storytellers themselves emphasise that it is the manner of telling— or, as they put it, "the way he's told"—that makes a story successful.

As for the language itself, the lexis and syntax are essentially simple and straightforward, apart from such items as *quintal*, ['kaentl] (a measure of fish, usually = 112 lbs.) the spelling of which offers no immediate clue to pronunciation. Phonological and grammatical features, on the other hand, may cause difficulties for the listener, and even the reader, unfamiliar with the dialect.

The monosyllabic nature of much of the narrative is striking, the proportion of monosyllables on occasion being as high as twenty words in an utterance of twenty-two or twenty-three words. As a corollary to this, many of the longer words such as *abed, adown, afore, bestraddled, bluejackets, bosom, consent(ed), damsel, forsaken, guineas, merchandise, pacified, passion* (fury), *perished* (died), *recommend, satisfied* (agreeable), *twelvemonth,* and *yonder* and such monosyllables as *ails, aught, breeze* (strong wind, gale), *eyed* (observed, looked at), *poll* (head), *scoff* (mock), *slay, steed, strand* (shore, country, etc.), and *sway* (control) are more typical of formal and/or archaic literary usage and are part of an often somewhat selfconsciously-used wordstock also found, for example, in folksong and traditional drama.

Allied with the straightforwardness of the vocabulary is a marked restraint in the use of risque or vulgar expressions. Expletives and exclamations, for instance, are usually kept strictly within the limits of decorum and, with very few exceptions, euphemism is employed, often coupled with innuendo and humour, to maintain propriety, especially with reference to sexual matters, e.g., *to have a time with*, *lay around with*. Some of these euphemisms, e.g., *to get aboard*, are drawn from a wide range of nautical expressions that are characteristic not only of these tales but of Newfoundland speech in general. This is very natural in such a maritime environment, but it is particularly interesting to note that many of these words and expressions have been transferred from a nautical to a general usage in the province. Examples in the stories include *all hands* (everyone), *crew* (crowd, company), *grog* (drink of rum, spirits), *grub* (food), *hatch* (trapdoor), *rig* (clothes, dress), *ship* (hire, employ, etc.), *sing out* (shout), *skipper* (respectful term of address to older man), *stow away* (hide), *turn in* (go to bed). Many more of these expressions and their vernacular counterparts are of course used with their normal reference in the numerous accounts of voyages and other seafaring activities in the tales.

Attention has already been drawn to the importance of intonation in storytelling, much of the impact of a tale depending on subtle variations in vocal tone. Nowhere is this more evident than in the frequent passages of direct speech, punctuated by the ubiquitous *he/she said*. The frequency of the latter often causes ambiguity in that the referent or antecedent is not always clear, especially when the teller uses *he* with a female referent and vice versa and when *he* or *she* is substituted for *they*. The confusion of *he* and *she* is often precipitated by two principal factors: (i) the teller's anticipation of a change of speaker in the dialogue from male to female or female to male; and (ii) the intrusion of a male character into the narrative at a point when a female is speaking, or vice versa. The situation is further complicated by the fact that *he* and *she* may also refer to inanimate items, and that *un* (it, him, her) may apply to male, female, and inanimate referents. As is the case with most regional dialects, the reader will therefore find that the pronominal system is more complex than that of Standard English and that this complexity is accompanied by a greater variety of verb forms and their nonstandard inflections.

An aspect of intonation worthy of note is the syllable stress in certain disyllabic and polysyllabic words that differs from standard British or Canadian usage. Examples include: *cannonball*, *godsend*, *gullentined* (guillotined), *hotel*, *insane*, *interested*, *Portuguee* (Portuguese), *Queebec* (Quebec), separated, and also in the phrasal compound *inside clothes* (underwear). Of those, *interested* and *separate(d)* suggest Anglo-Irish influence, the malapropistic *gullentined* maintains the French stress on the final syllable, and the stress in *godsend* is almost equally strong on each syllable, the second perhaps being marginally more prominent.

Phonology

In the absence of a comprehensive phonological description of Newfoundland speech, it is useful to draw attention here to some of the more prominent features commonly found in these narratives, and in particular those that differ from Standard (British) English and/or general (world) English. They include the following:

1. Aphesis

The loss of the initial syllable of words is a recurrent feature in both the West Country English and the Anglo-Irish dialects of Newfoundland. Examples include *'board* (aboard), *'bout* (about), *'canter* (decanter), *'cause* (because), *'cordin'* (according), *'cquainted* (acquainted), *'cross* (across), *'deed* (indeed), *'fore* (before), *'gain(st)* (again(st)), *'gar* (begar, begorrah), *'gree(d)* (agree(d)), *'greement* (agreement), *'lectric* (electric), *'long* (along), *'longed* (belonged), *'longside* (alongside), *'lowed* (allowed, supposed), *'magine* (imagine), *'nitials* (initials), *'nother* (another), *'pose* (suppose), *'self* (herself), *'sleep* (asleep), *'spects* (expects), *'stead* (instead), *'stificate* (certificate), *'tween* (between), *'ward* (towards), *'way* (away), *'while* (awhile). It is interesting that a majority of these forms begin with *a-* in Standard English, and that others, e.g., *before*, *between*, formerly had alternative first syllable forms with *a-* which are now archaic. To the above list one might add the following, which, being phrases, are not strictly aphetic but which manifest the loss of an initial unstressed vowel: *'tis(n't)* (it isn't), *'twas(n't)* (it was(n't)), *'twill* (it will), *'twont* (it won't), *'twudden* (it wasn't), *'twould(n't)* ['twudn] (it wouldn't). The initial consonant is also lost in *'ee* (thee, ye) in the speech of the West Country English narrators in the collection.

2. Consonants

a. Initial: The deletion of *h* is extremely common in word-initial position, though inconsistently from speaker to speaker. The aspirate is also added initially in words beginning with a vowel, usually for emphasis; the addition of *h* is also inconsistent and is far less common than its deletion. For practical reasons it has not been possible to indicate these features in the transcriptions.

Fricative consonants in initial position are sporadically voiced by a few of the West Country English narrators, this feature being almost entirely absent in the Anglo-Irish speech. This characteristic feature of West Country English is in rapid decline in Newfoundland, and in these stories is largely confined to only four of the speakers.

Initial voiced *th-* is realised as /d/ in such words as *that*, *the*, *them*, *there*, *this*, *these*, *they*, and *those*, in both speech types, and voiceless *th-* is realised as /t/ in *thick*, *thievin'*, *think*, *thought*, *thousands*, etc., apparently borrowed from Anglo-Irish into the West Country English speech variety.

b. Medial: Medial /t/ is normally voiced by the West Country English narrators, but much less so in the Anglo-Irish type of speech in which it often has a breathy quality. The medial consonant is lost in *e'er*, *ar* (a, a single, any), *ne'er*, *nar* (no, not a, not one), and *whe'r* (whether); /d/ is lost in *shoulder*, /n/ is realised as /l/ in *chimley*, voiced *th-* as /d/ in *father*, *mother* and as /t/ in *bathing*.

Glottalisation and/or gemination sometimes occur medially in *twothree*. Intrusive /t/ is found before /f/ in *infants*, /s/ follows /r/ in *cerstificate* and is retained as the first sound in the aphetic form *'stificate*, /h/ follows /r/ in *overhalls* (perhaps through folk etymology (overhauls)), and the on-glide /j/ precedes the final vowel in *livyer(s)* (inhabitant(s)), *mowyers* (mowers). Metathesis of /k/ occurs in *aks* (ask) and of /r/ in the distinctively West Country English *gert* (great) and *perty* (pretty). Syncopation is found in *bimeby* (by and by), *spose* (suppose), and many other words and phrases in allegro speech. Before nouns beginning with a vowel, the preferred form of the indefinite article among the West Country English type storytellers is *a* where standard English would have *an*. Examples include: *a aunt, a awful, a axe, a egg, a eye, a hour* (no initial aspirate), *a office, a old*.

c. Final: Newfoundland speech is predominantly rhotic, and the /r/ continuant occurring finally in syllables strongly colours the preceding vowel. In the tape-recorded narratives, however, there is little evidence for the survival of the retroflex continuant -*r*, with its characteristic pharyngovelar quality in word-final position which is typical of much West Country speech in England. On the other hand, narrators of the Anglo-Irish type retain the distinctive breathy quality of word-final or penultimate retroflex continuant -*r*, for example in such words as *her, sir, stirred, sure*.

In the speech of West Country English type, frictionless continuant -*r* also occurs finally in *feller* (fellow), *piller* (pillow), and *winder* (window), while in some pronunciations of *tomorrow* the final syllable is assimilated. Unlike British English, there is no assimilation in the first syllable of *forecastle*, which is invariably pronounced with the full three syllables. Final "-*ng*" is normally realised as /n/ in present participles and other words ending in "ing."

Among the West Country English narrators, glottalisation of /t/ occurs frequently in syllable-final and word-final position. Offglides /t/ and /d/ are fairly common in final position, e.g., *acrosst* (across), *clifft* (cliff), *revolverd* (revolver), *sermont* (sermon), *townd* (town), *underneatht* (underneath), *unknownst* (unknown—cf. *unbeknownst*), and *wholed* (whole).

3. Vowels and diphthongs

The variety and complexity of the vowel sounds in this collection is such that few valid conclusions can be drawn concerning dialect boundaries. While it is clear, for example, that the Anglo-Irish narrators commonly use a centralised form of the half-open back-rounded vowel, e.g. in *her*, and *sir*, in contrast with the West Country English pronunciation which has schwa, the pronunciations of the diphthong /ei/ in such forms as *beat, cleaned, grease*, and *speak* are more problematical since their origins may well lie both in English and Irish dialects. Among the vowels and diphthongs of stressed syllables that have clear parallels in the dialects of West Country English one might note the following /i:/ in *his, in, shin*; /i/ in *been, catch, climb, crutches, keep, meets, such, weasel*. It must be emphasised, however, that these pronunciations are by no means consistent among the West Country English storytellers.

The vowel of the definite article is usually elided before a following vowel: *th' attic, th' axe, th' end, th' evening, th' island, th' office, th' old, th' only, th' other(s), th' owner*, and *th' under*, including those words in which initial *h-* is absent in pronunciation: *th' hammer, th' harbour, th' heart, th' hole, th' horse, th' house*. In all these pronunciations, the initial consonant(s) of the determiner effectively become the initial consonant(s) of a single unit of speech. Alternatively, if elision does not take place, the transition from *the* to the initial vowel of the following word is effected by brief glottal closure. There are occasional instances of the reduction of *the* to /t/, e.g. *t' other*. A similar elision is also found in the preposition *to*: *t' heaven*.

As one might expect, the versions of tales from manuscript sources convey comparatively few dialectal features, especially as regards phonology. Much of the vernacular pronunciation and lexis has been filtered out by the collectors, in response to the conventions of written usage, and the attempts by student collectors to represent dialectal forms are sometimes idiosyncratic and/or questionable.

Lexis

The simplicity of the lexicon in these tales is of course characteristic of folk narratives in all languages. Technical and complex words are singularly absent, and this in itself makes such stories maximally accessible. Those lexical items in the transcripts that are unusual or may cause difficulty in reading and/or interpretation are glossed in the text. Virtually all these items are dialectal, and since the speech of the majority of the storytellers is of the West Country English type, most of the unfamiliar words are characteristic of dialects in the southwest of England. Typical examples are *abroad* (in pieces), *arg* (argue), *crunnick* (weather-beaten tree), *drivin' works* (causing a commotion), *duckish* (dusk), *either* (any), *empt* (v) (empty), *flux* (snatch), *handy* (near), *handier* (nearer), *livyer* (settler, inhabitant), *lodge* (put, place), *neither* (none), *planchin* (floorboards), *skirred* (flew rapidly), *spell* (pause for rest), *the once* (directly, right away), *turn* (load).

Anglo-Irish examples include: *begar* (begorrah), *begobs* (by god), *boniffs* (piglets), *gutter* (mud), *rightified* (corrected, put right), and perhaps also *boy* (pronounced bye), as an informal term of address for males, and *scords* (gashes). Rather more problematical are a number of dialectal items that could be either of English or Irish origin. As with the phonology, in establishing the provenance of individual items it is often difficult to distinguish between the two principal sources, West Country English and Southern Irish, because of the longstanding historical links between the two, both in their places of origin and also in New-foundland. The problem is compounded by the fact that a number of these words are also well attested in other regional dialects of English. Among these items are *(al)lowed* (supposed, reckoned), *dodge* (move slowly, saunter), *flat* (level piece of ground), *forelaid* (lay in wait for, got there ahead of), *frounge* (?complain), *gawks* (fools—friendly term of address), *gugglin'* (gurgling), *hypocrite* (cripple), *intermined* (determined), *learn* (teach), *oreweed* (seaweed), *persuadance* (persuasion), *rattle* (rustle), *rampsin'* (tumbling, romping with), *scrunchins* (fried cubes of pork fat), *siss* (hiss), *twothree* (two or three), *trickled* (raised—to facilitate movement), *uncle* (respectful term of address to older man), *unstrip* (undress), *without* (unless), *wonderful* (great, tremendous).

The long history of settlement in Newfoundland has given rise to numerous terms which are particularly associated with the province, many of them having a specifically local reference and/or a somewhat different meaning in their adopted environment. Among these are: *blackguard* (vulgar, risque), *buddy* (this man/ fellow), *chinched* (full, tightly packed), *country* (inland area, interior), *cracky* (small mongrel dog), *dagger* (whetstone), *fitout* (outfit, equipment), *flake* (raised wooden platform for drying fish), *heelstick* (wooden last for mending shoes), *lunch* (snack eaten between meals), *marshberries* (small cranberries), *mug up* (cup/mug of tea), *scattered* (occasional), *scribbler* (exercise book), *smart* (in good health), *smopped* (drew—at a pipe), *stage* (covered wooden platform for processing fish), *tilt* (temporary shelter, hut), *time* (party, celebration).

To the reader unfamiliar with the dialect, the vocabulary of course contributes to the somewhat archaic flavour of the narratives and helps distance them from the real world. The reader's impression that the tales are set in another time and another place is strengthened by the frequent use of archaic and/or specialised words and phrases, some of which have also been retained in other regional dialects of English, while others were once part of the standard language but have become obsolescent or fallen into disuse. They include *bide* (stay, remain), *clergy* (clergyman), *daybed* (couch), *dout* (put out—candle, etc.), *fresh* (not salty—of food), *heighth* (height), *little small* (small), *make away with* (kill, remove), *mind* (remember), *minded* (inclined, disposed), *put up* (put away), *pitched*, (land(ed), alight(ed)), *puncheon* (large wooden cask), *quintal* (a measure of fish), *right* (very), *sack* (hit, beat), *shift* (change (clothes)), *slack o' the poll* (nape of the neck), *start naked* (naked), *take (re)marks* (observe, take notice), *tant* (tall), *turned (the door)* (closed). A few alterations of a malapropistic nature also occur, e.g., *grand aviser* (?grand vizier), *gullentined* (guillotined), *manogany* (mahogany).

The pronominal system in Newfoundland retains many archaic and dialectal features, notably in the West Country English speech type. In these narratives, for instance, we find *her, 'ee, us, ye, yous* and *'em* in subject position: *where her was, have 'ee got ar 'nother son, how's us goina get, how long are ye here, yous'll be killed, how is 'em goin' to find out, what would 'em do, where's 'em to*; and *I, 'ee, he, she, un, ye, yous, they* may occur in non-subject position: *only got I, no more of I, get aboard 'ee, give 'ee three chances, got he shaved, that wasn't he, the devil can have he, you'll always mind he, he'll kill he, didn't know she, dig she up, try to get she out, soon bring she to life, give she a lot, pilot un in, nobody couldn't save un, never see un no more, lost a needle into un, keep ye awoke, there's no men like yous, two o' we, stay with we, had they goin', 'tis not they, one/some/three o' they*. A rare example of *you* as a vocative in sentence-final position occurs in *sure take all night sure [to] cut it off, you.* Most of these non-subject forms occur under strong, secondary, or tertiary stress. It must be emphasised that the examples here, as elsewhere in this section, are selected for their deviation from the standard. Many of them are found comparatively rarely, as alternates for their more standard equivalents.

As mentioned briefly above, the third person singular pronouns *he* and *she* may have both animate and inanimate referents. Typical of the latter are the use of *he* with reference to *barn, basket, chain, chest, kettle, newspaper, ring, story* (*I learned he*), and of *she* with reference to *chest* and of course attributively with *boat, ship,* etc. This extends to the object forms *him* with such referents as *egg,* and *her* with such referents as *Devil* and *gun.* The pronoun *un* may be substituted for all three non-subject case forms of the third person singular pronouns, *him, her, it,* though substitution of *un* for *her* is less common. Occasionally, *it* has a plural referent, e.g., *clothes.* The forms *ar, e'er, either, arn, ne'er,* and *neither_(one)* function as positive and negative indefinite pronoun substitutes, meaning *a, any, not a, none*—a semantic grouping that is further complicated by double or multiple negation. The reflexives *meself, hisself, ourselfs, theirselfs/theirselves* are augmented by *me own self,* and *his own self,* especially in emphatic utterance. These last are evidently Anglo-Irish but are also found in the speech of the West Country English narrators.

The demonstrative *those* is sometimes replaced by *them* or *they: them fellers, them two, they cakes/candles/three.* The function of *this* is pronominal or adverbial in *we leaved this,* i.e., this place here. The plural forms *these* and *those* may have different time reference from that of their use in the standard language, *those days/times* referring to the present and *these days/times* (or *them days/times*) referring to the past. Also of note are the preposition *into* (in), the prepositional phrase *off o',* the preposition and adverb *'gain* (against), and the intensifiers *awful, right, terrible,* and *wonderful.*

Grammar

As in any regional dialect of English, the speech of Newfoundlanders preserves numerous grammatical features that have been lost or become obsolescent in the standard language. In the following summary account attention is drawn to some of the more outstanding of these features in the narrators' speech.

1. Nouns

A few nouns whose singular form ends in -*st* retain -*e*-, pronounced as schwa, in the plural inflection, e.g., *beastes, locustes, toastes,* and a double plural common in many other regional dialects is found in *belluses* (bellows). Isolated examples of a similar phenomenon occur in marking the possessive singular: *Jackses, motherses, worldes.* On the other hand the possessive marker is absent in *Paradise', Pierce'* and in one instance of *horse'* (horse's); a parallel example is the lack of plural marker in *corpse* (corpses), *mile, storey, year,* and in single instances, e.g., *cow, question.*

2. Verbs

Many archaic and dialectal verb forms are found in the speech of the storytellers and reflect the extent and variety of such features in Newfoundland usage as a whole. In the simple present tense the *-s* inflection is predominant throughout the paradigm in all three persons, singular and plural, in both of the speech types identified above: *I comes, you carries, we wants, they pitches*. The verb *have* may also add *-s* in the present tense. Occasionally, the *-es* form is retained, e.g., *you askes, (he) knockses, you wantes*. The various forms of the verb *be* also warrant attention, e.g. the Anglo-Irish *don't be talkin', I don't be tellin'*, and the West Country English variants, *I is, I's, I aint* (I am not), *so be I, aint I, aint 'ee* (aren't you), *you'm, you is, is you/ya, he be, we'm, we's, is we, they bes, they is*. Dialectal present tense forms include *he do, How much do the moon weigh?, she/it don't, you does, I ant*, (I haven't), *up to the pigeon*. The absence of final "-ng" in the present participle *being* leads to difficulty in distinguishing it from the past participle *been*. Occasional instances of the *a*-form of the present participle are found, e.g., *agoin', asingin'*.

A major characteristic feature of Newfoundland dialect, and especially of the West Country English speech type, is the high proportion of nonstandard forms in the past tense and past participle of verbs. This feature is well illustrated in the texts. Several categories of nonstandard past tense forms may be distinguished:

i. forms that lack a final marker of tense, such as *ask, bake, become, begin, blind, bring, build, catch, climb, come, drift, eat, fit, get, give, happen, hide, hold, invite, keep, leave, light, live, load, meet, persuade, point, pound, post, ride, send, slip, spit, start, stoop, twist, visit, want*.

Of these, some two-thirds end in a dental or alveolar consonant, notably /t/ and /d/. Final *-ed* following these consonants is very susceptible to assimilation. It should also be borne in mind that many of these unmarked past tense forms alternate with marked forms in the speech of the narrators. Furthermore, the frequent switching of tenses, especially from past to present in dialogue, encourages the blurring of inflectional distinctions between the two. In a number of cases at least, therefore, verb forms embedded in a predominantly past tense context of utterance may be construed as "vivid present" in function if not in form.

ii. forms with nonstandard additional past tense marker, often alternating with another variant: *beated, bursted, drowneded, owneded*.

iii. forms in which the historically "strong" or "mixed" classes of verbs have followed the "weak" pattern with dental suffix: *blowed, buyed, catched, choosed, comed, creeped, drawed, drinked, eated, falled* (fell), *flied* (flew), *gid* (gived, gave), *growed, hided, knowed, leaved, meaned, rised, runned, seed* (saw), *shined, sleeped, swimmed, throwed, winned*.

iv. one or two verbs that, in contrast with the standard language, indicate tense by vowel change, in much the same way as "strong" verbs: *bid* (stayed, waited), *hod* (hid), *hove* (heaved), *ris, rose* (raised), *sot* (sat), *sove* (saved), *sprod* (spread), *squez* (squeezed), *upsot* (upset).

v. occasional instances of past tense forms with the prefix *a-*: *abroke*, *afalled* (fell).

Other nonstandard past tense forms include (*I*) *been, begun, builded, confound* (confined), *done, fled* (flew); (*he*) *have been, heared, laid* (lay) *losed, maked, rung, seen(ed), sond* (sent), *sung; he/she were; you/we/they was*. Such past continuous forms as *was stood* also occur.

Nonstandard past participles appear to be rather more limited in number in these narratives but have a great deal of affinity with the past tense verb forms outlined above. Examples include *beat, borned, broke, cutted, drowneded, eat, frit* (frightened), *gi(ve), growed, leaved, lied* (lay), *lineded, look, paste, runned, sot* (sat), *saven, sove* (saved), *stole, took, tore, wore*. More significant, however, is the comparatively large number of past participles prefixed by *a-*, such as *abarred, abeen, ablowed, abought, aburned, acome, acured, adone, adrinked, afeared, afind, afired, afound, agive, agot, aheard, ahung* (hanged), *akilled, aknowed, aleaved, alost, aput, arobbed, aruined, ascared, aseen, aserved, aslep', asold, astalled, astart(ed), astole, astruck, atold, atook, atried, awent, aworked*. The frequency of such forms raises tantalising questions about adverbs in such phrases as *apast me labour, to make asure*, and *keep ye awoke*; the second of these perhaps allows such alternative transcriptions as *to make sure* and *to make her sure*.

3. Adjectives and adverbs

The archaic weak inflection *-en* survives in *glassen*, and nonstandard adjectival forms are found in the double comparatives *more contenteder, more handier, more hungrier*, and the superlatives *beautifullest* and *firstest*. Uninflected adjectival forms occur in adverbial position, e.g. *he spoke cross, he gets un done good*. The *-s* inflection persists in certain adverbs and adverbial phrases: *anyhows, anywheres, a long ways, somewheres*.

Syntax

Much of the syntax in these Newfoundland narratives is characterised by short, simple sentences. This is especially evident in the compression and economy typical of many of the storytelling styles, as the following examples demonstrate: *Soon have enough; Got the ring; Mixed up a big cake; Still couldn't learn; Lost everything; Off jacket; Sat down; Wasn't enough see; Go across ocean; Just got in port; Went over; She found out; So they left; Come to my turn; Got up; Bed empty, nobody in; No breakfast; Frightened her; Went on up; Next man came; Looked everywhere; Went home; Come ashore; Sot up*. The numerous sentences and clauses of this type are often used as a kind of rhetorical shorthand by the narrators to sketch in some of the pivotal points in the forward movement of the plot. Their elliptical form is reminiscent of various types of block language such as that used in telegrams in which not only are function words frequently omitted but also adverbs, and especially the pronominal subject of the utterance.

Ellipsis is also of course inevitable in allegro speech, in which determiners, prepositions, connectives, relatives, auxiliaries, and pronouns are sacrificed without detriment to overall communication. Typical examples of each are *in boat, in cabin, knock me in head, in ship, what is into orange, practisin' with gun, get little mare, course* (of course), *what's goina happen us, had plenty money, dout they ten . . . candles the one shot, one thing another, the man* [*who/ that*] *done it, the feller* [*who*] *was with me; I* [*was*] *tryin' to catch her, he wouldn't* [*have*] *done it, What* [*did*] *Pa(ppy) say, She mixed* [*it/un*] *up, brought* [*it/un*] *down, she put* [*them/they*] *on the step*. With reference to these latter three examples, the omission of the object pronoun after *brought* and *put* is common and, as with *mixed*, it may be due in part to the assimilation of it with the final /t/ of the verb. The subject pronouns *he* and *she* are often lost before *said* in the structural framework of direct speech, and the definite article is sometimes omitted before the modifier or head of a noun phrase, e.g., *Other fellow*.

The syntax of the verb phrase invites further investigation. It must suffice here simply to draw attention to a few of the more interesting features. Those storytellers whose speech is of the Anglo-Irish type continue to employ the construction: auxiliary + *after* + present participle, used of a completed action in the past tense, which is a translation from Irish and is a hallmark of the English spoken in Ireland. Examples include: *they were after being' out in the barn; we were after droppin' our beans; the poor old horse is after eatin' oats; I been after fallin'; he was after gettin' a berth; I was after gettin' jammed in; they're after growin' that tall; we're after killin' our brother; he's after makin' a bad job of it; the boy was after overhearin'; he was after sellin' hisself; you're after sleepin' longer than you thought; I'm after spendin' a very weary night here*. Occasionally, as mentioned earlier, narrators of the West Country English speech type also use this construction. Other verb phrases that seem to be exclusively used by the Anglo-Irish storytellers are seen in the elliptical *without be cuttin'* (without being cut) and *I suppose be a Welsh* (I suppose would be a Welsh).

Among our West Country English-speaking storytellers there is some ambiguity in the pronunciation of *used to* and *was to* which often fall together and are indistinguishable. Certain verb phrases have the form auxiliary + participle + *of*: *they were eatin' of it; beans is hurtin' o' me; I'm not stealin' of it; she was takin' of it all down*. This construction can lead to some unusually complex syntax: *if you're tellin' of me a lie; I was tellin' of ya about today*. By contrast, *of* is lacking in *she took un hold, he got the door hold,* and *goin' to catch me hold*, but with similar effects on the syntax as in the examples immediately above. Also of note are the frequent use of the archaic purposive *for to* before infinitives, and such constructions as *I'd like for, he had like to kill 'em*, and *I don't think* (I don't think so). At times the syntax can be simultaneously complex and cryptic, contrasting sharply with the normally straightforward structure of clauses and sentences. Typical examples are: *more I don't* (nor do I); *more can't you* (any more than you can); *they missed un gone* (they noticed he was missing). Once in a while the normal rules of syntax are strained, no doubt partly as a result of the teller's striving to remember, articulate, and concatenate a complex string of forms under the stress of the performance and its context. Even here, however, the audience has no difficulty in unravelling the syntax and apprehending the meaning and may even respond to the rhetorical effect of the suspension of sense by means of which the resolution of the utterance is postponed until the final word of the utterance, as in *there was goin' to be three o' the prettiest fish was in the sea caught.*

Mention must be made of the remarkably large number of double negatives in these texts, in both the West Country English and the Anglo-Irish speech types. Indeed one becomes so used to them in hearing the tales or reading the texts that it is easy to forget that such negative constructions have long ceased to be used in the standard language. Examples are so plentiful that it must suffice merely to offer a sampling of them here to illustrate their range and variety: *don't know no stories, don't eat/do it/fire/tell no more, don't want no dinner, didn't make no matter, couldn't get no further, can't eat/don't know nothing, couldn't learn un nothing, don't know/won't take/won't tie up none, don't miss ne'er step, couldn't get nar drink, couldn't see no one, don't/ wouldn't let nobody, aint been nowhere, nobody is not going to, nobody couldn't save un, nobody don't recognise him, nobody never done it, nobody never came/could catch, never let nobody know, never done/fired/got/had/ stole/thought nothing, ain't got/didn't know/haven't done/won't know nothing, never made no noise, never thought no more, never had nar punt, no other man'll never live here.* Multiple negatives are rare but such forms as *No, never seen nobody* occur occasionally, as does the archaic *or no* (or not): *whe'r 'tis he/you or no.*

Note also, among many other phrases typical of local usage: *(a)way to go* (off we go, let's go); *last going' off, on the last of it, in (the) latter end* (finally); *pod auger days* (bygone times); *they'd take week on week* (they'd take turns on alternate weeks); *where's he to?* (where has he gone (to)? where is he?); *knocks to the door* (knocks at the door); *(ac)cordin' as; so big as; so well as; 'stead on* (instead of); *light in/make in a fire;* and that dates normally have *and* between the century and the year: *eighteen and ninety six.*

Even within the comparatively restricted conventions of the traditional fictional narrative, Newfoundland speech proves to be an extraordinarily rich and vibrant expressive medium. It is a matter of regret that so little of it has yet been studied in depth. We must hope that the opportunities for such research offered by the Departments of Folklore, English, and Linguistics at Memorial University will attract a new generation of students to this important topic. The excellent facilities of the University's Folklore and Language Archive, and English Language Research Centre provide excellent resource bases for such study. As linguists and folklorists, we should actively encourage our colleagues and students to join us in studying the unique varieties of linguistic usage and the wealth of oral traditions that remain vibrant and essential features of the living speech and culture of Newfoundlanders today.

Notes

This is a revised and shortened version of a paper presented in the panel on Newfoundland English at the Annual Meeting of the American Folklore Society and the Folklore Studies Association of Canada in St. John's, Newfoundland, in 1991. Both versions of the paper are based on material co-authored by Herbert Halpert—a kind of joint distillation over many years of fruitful collaboration. I gratefully acknowledge here not only his major contribution to this paper but also his enthusiastic encouragement, guidance, and friendship over more than thirty years.

1. For an account of settlement patterns in the province, see Mannion 1977.

2. Corrected misencodings are set within obliques, editorial interpolations and emendations are in square brackets, parentheses mark putative transcriptions of unclear speech, and the symbol "_" indicates a brief pause.

3. This iteration is also characteristic of narratives in the French-speaking tradition in Newfoundland; see Thomas 1991, pp. 39–47.

4. This is in strong contrast with the performance style of such storytellers as Emile Benoit in the Newfoundland French tradition; see Thomas, op. cit.

References

Halpert, Herbert and J. D. A. Widdowson
    Folktales of Newfoundland: The Resilience of the Oral Tradition, a publication of the American Folklore Society, forthcoming.

Hollett, R.
    1982 Allegro Speech of a Newfoundlander. In *Languages in Newfoundland and Labrador*, 2nd version, ed. H. J. Paddock. St. John's: Department of Linguistics, Memorial University of Newfoundland. Pp. 107–45.

Mannion, J. J.
    1977 *The Peopling of Newfoundland: Essays in Historical Geography, Social and Economic Papers* 8, St. John's: Institute of Social and Economic Research, Memorial University of Newfoundland.

Story, G. M., W. J. Kirwin, and J. D. A. Widdowson, eds.
    1982 *Dictionary of Newfoundland English.* Toronto: University of Toronto Press; 2nd [revised] edition [with Supplement], 1990.

Thomas, Gerald
    1991 The Aesthetics of Märchen Narration in Franco-Newfoundland Tradition, *Lore and Language* 10(2):59–66.

A SELECTED LIST OF THE WORKS OF AN UNCONVENTIONAL SCHOLAR: KENNETH S. GOLDSTEIN

Prepared by Stephen Winick

ONE OF the many conventions in producing or editing a festschrift to honor an academic colleague is the inclusion in that work of a complete list of the scholar's books, articles and other pertinent publications and productions. What is one to do, however, when the honoree is hardly conventional in any sense of the word? Kenny Goldstein is that unconventional honoree. Though he authored or edited a fair number of books, monographs, and articles published in scholarly journals, as well as notes, reviews, etc., he never allowed himself to be restricted to or limited by the typical media or genres of scholarly publication. He has also written for normally non-academic publications, like textbook modules, popular music magazines, folkmusic and storytelling festival programs, and backliners and booklets containing descriptions, analysis, commentary and annotations for records and tapes. In addition, he was responsible for recording, editing, producing and/or annotating more than five hundred long-playing records and tapes (many designed for potential classroom use), as well as for serving as co-producer and/or editor of film, radio and television programs. All of the above productions he sees as legitimate media for achieving his primary goal of informing, communicating about, and educating students of folklore, members of an interested general public, or any others he wishes to convert to what he acknowledges as his true religion and favorite cause: folklore. To carry this metaphor one step further, his sermons and homilies in the classroom and on the public stage are also carefully produced to achieve such conversion. Though he never thought of himself as a performer (he claims the only instrument he can play is a tape recorder), as an award-winning teacher he knows how to engage his audience by the use of anecdote and tale, complemented and illustrated by a phenomenal range of field recordings. These presentations (he calls them "set lectures") take more time to research, author, and produce than do most writings that see the light of day through print in books and articles. Some of these set lectures eventually *do* reach print though rarely with the powerful effect of the oral presentations of his lectures and of his field recorded informants. Because it is the hope of many of us, who have heard or have even borrowed from his lectures in our own teaching, that these field recordings and the lectures of which they are a part will eventually be produced in a "hard" format (as articles and publicly available recordings), a selected number of these set lectures have also been listed in this bibliography.

Because it would be nearly impossibile to prepare a total listing of his productions (he has never kept a record of or prepared such a list even for his curriculum vita), and because an attempt to do so just of his commercially issued recordings would require more pages than the rest of this festschrift, we have decided to publish here (A) a short and selected list of his publications, (B) a similarly select list of his recordings, (C) a list of his "set lectures," and (D) a listing of some works in progress and projected future works that health and time permitting he will produce upon retirement.

A. Publications

1. BOOKS (Authored and Edited) & OTHER PRINTED PUBLICATIONS

A Guide for Field Workers in Folklore. Memoirs of the American Folklore Society, volume 52. Philadelphia, Pa., 1964; Turkish edition, Ankara, Turkey, 1977; Chinese edition, Taiwan, 1982.

Two Penny Ballads and Four Dollar Whiskey: A Pennsylvania Folklore Miscellany (edited with Bob Byington). Pennsylvania Folklore Society, 1965.

Thrice Told Tales: Parallel Tales from Three Continents (edited with Dan Ben-Amos). Loch Haven, Pa., 1970.

Folklore: Performance and Communication (edited with Dan Ben-Amos). The Hague, Netherlands, 1975.

Monologues and Folk Recitation (edited with Robert D. Bethke). Special Issue of *Southern Folklore Quarterly* 40:1 and 2, 1976.

Canadian Folklore Perspectives (editor), St. John's, Newfoundland, 1978.

Folklore Studies in Honor of Herbert Halpert (edited, with Neil Rosenberg and Maggi Craig). St. John's, Newfoundland, 1979.

By Land and By Sea: Studies in the Folklore of Work and Liesure Honoring Horace Beck on his 65th Birthday (edited, with Roger D. Abrahams and Wayland D. Hand). Hatboro, Pa., 1985.

2. ARTICLES, NOTES, & INTRODUCTIONS

More of the Unfortunate Rake and his Family. *Western Folklore* 18 (1959).

Folklore Recordings as Bibliographical Entries. *Midwest Folklore* 9 (1959).

Folklore in the Northeast of Scotland. *Fulbright Courier,* February 1960.

Ghosts, Witches and the Devil in Northeast Scotland. *Fulbright Courier,* March 1960.

Preface to *The Broadside Ballad: A Study in Origins and Meaning,* by Leslie Shepard. London, 1962.

William Robbie: Folk Artist of the Buchan District, Aberdeenshire. In *Folklore in Action: Essays in Honor of MacEdward Leach.* Philadelphia, Pa., 1962; reprinted in *Chapbook: Scotland's Folk-Life Magazine* 3:3 (1966).

Foreword (with Arthur Argo) to *Folk-Song of the North-East,* by Gavin Greig. Hatboro, Pa., 1963.

Riddling Traditions in Northeastern Scotland. *Journal of American Folklore* 76 (1963).

The Collecting of Superstitious Beliefs. *Keystone Folklore Quarterly* 9 (Spring 1964).

The Texas Rangers in Aberdeenshire, Scotland, In *A Good Tale and A Bonny Tune.* Publication of the Texas Folklore Society, vol. 32, 1964.

The Ballad Broadside. *Keystone Folklore Quarterly* 9 (Summer 1964).

Robert "Fiddler" Beers and His Songs: A Study of the Revival of a Family Tradition. In *Two Penny Ballads and Four Dollar Whiskey,* edited by Kenneth S. Goldstein and Robert H. Byington. Pennsylvania Folklore Society, 1965.

Foreword to *Traditional Singers and Songs from Ontario,* by Edith Fowke. Hatboro, Pa., 1965.

The Ballad Scholar and the Long-Playing Record. In *Folklore and Society: Essays in Honor of Benjamin A. Botkin,* edited by Bruce Jackson. Hatboro, Pa., 1966.

The Induced Natural Context: An Ethnographic Folklore Field Technique. In *Essays on the Verbal and Visual Arts: Proceedings of the American Ethnological Society,* 1967.

Experimental Folklore: Laboratory vs. Field. In *Folklore International: Essays in Honor of Wayland D. Hand,* edited by D. K. Wilgus, Hatboro, Pa., 1967.

Bowdlerization and Expurgation: Academic and Folk. *Journal of American Folklore* 80 (1967).

Harvesting Folklore. In *Our Living Tradition,* edited by Tristram P. Coffin. New York, 1968; reprinted in *The Maorilander* 1 [New Zealand, 1972], and *Folklora Dogru* no. 34 [Turkey, 1975].

The Verse Competition Jest in Northeast Scotland. *Journal of American Folklore* 83 (1970).

On the Application of the Concepts of Active and Inactive Traditions to the Study of Repertoire. *Journal of American Folklore* 84 (1971).

Strategy in Counting-Out: An Ethnographic Folklore Field Study. In *Sources for the Study of Games,* edited by B. Sutton-Smith and Elliott M. Avedon. New York, 1971; reprinted in *Folk Groups and Folklore Genres: A Reader,* edited by Elliott Oring. Logan, Utah, 1989.

Labor's Place in American Folk Culture. In *1972 Festival of American Folklife* program booklet, Smithsonian Institute, Washington, D. C., 1972.

Foreword to *American Ballads and Songs,* by Louise Pound. Reprint edition, New York, 1973.

Introduction (with Dan Ben-Amos) to *Folklore: Performance and Communication.* The Hague, Netherlands, 1975.

The Telling of Non-Traditional Tales to Children: An Ethnographic Report from a Northwest Philadelphia Neighborhood. *Keystone Folklore* 20 (Summer 1975).

Monologue Performance in Great Britain. *Southern Folklore Quarterly* 40:1 and 2 (1976).

Songs from the Repertoire of James Patrick Kelly, Marystown, Burin Peninsula. *The Livyere* 1:2 (1981).

Songs from the Repertoire of Leander Roberts, Cartwright, Labrador. *The Livyere* 1:3 and 4 (1982).

The Impact of Recording Technology on the British Folksong Revival. In *Folk Music and Modern Sound,* edited by William Ferris & Mary Hart. Oxford, Mississippi, 1982.

Four Songs from the Repertory of Dorman Ralph, St. John's. *The Livyere* 2:1 (1982).

Introduction (with David Buchan) in Part I: Overview; Part II: Methodology & Fieldwork; Module 4: Folksong; Module 5: Recitations & Monologues; Module 6: The Ballad (with David Buchan), in *Folk Literature: A Folklore/Folklife Educational Series,* series editor Larry Small. St. John's, Newfoundland, 1983.

Faith and Fate in Sea Disaster Ballads of Newfoundland Fishermen. In *By Land and By Sea: Studies in the Folklore of Work and Leisure Honoring Horace Beck on his 65th Birthday,* edited by Kenneth S. Goldstein *et al.* Hatboro, Pa., 1985.

A Collector's Personal Aesthetic as an Influence on the Informant's Choice of Repertory. In *Ballades et Chansons Folkloriques. Actes de la 18th session de la Commission pour l'etude de la poesie de tradition orale de la S.I.E.F.,* edited by Conrad Laforte. Quebec, 1989.

A Report on Continuing Research into "Treason Songs": A Private Newfoundland Folksong Tradition. In *Studies in Newfoundland Folklore: Community and Process,* edited by Gerald Thomas and John D. A. Widdowson. St. John's, Newfoundland, 1991.

Notes Toward a European-American Folk Aesthetic: Lessons Learned from Singers and Storytellers I Have Known. The first MacEdward Leach-Stith Thompson Lecture of the American Folklore Society. *Journal of American Folklore* 104 (1991).

A Future Folklorist in the Record Business. K. S. Goldstein interviewed by Neil Rosenberg. In *Transforming Tradition: Folk Music Revivals Examined,* edited by Neil Rosenberg. Urbana and Chicago, 1993.

Unit 6. Folksong, and Unit 7C. Recitation and Monologues. In *Folk Literature: Voices Through Time,* general editors Bill Butt and Larry Small. St. John's, Newfoundland, 1993.

B. Recordings (A Short Selection from over 500 Records and Tapes)

American Street Songs: Harlem Street Spirituals (Rev. Gary Davis) *and Carolina Street Ballads* (Pink Anderson). Riverside Records RLP 12-611, 1956.

The English and Scottish Popular Ballads (Ewan MacColl and A. L. Lloyd), 9 LPs. Riverside Records RLP 12-621- RLP 12-629, 1956.

Matching Songs of the British Isles and America (Ewan MacColl and Peggy Seeger). Riverside Records RLP 12-637, 1957.

Banjo Songs of the Southern Mountains (Various Singers). Riverside Records RLP 12-610 [field recordings], 1957.

Folksongs and Ballads of the Southern Mountains (Various Singers). Riverside Records RLP 12-617 [field recordings], 1957.

Folksongs from the Great Smokies (Various Singers). Riverside Records RLP 12-649 [field recordings], 1958.

The Cowboy: His Songs, Ballads, and Brag Talk (Harry Jackson). Folkways Records FH 5723, 1959.

The Singing Streets: Children's Songs and Rhymes from Scotland and Ireland (Ewan MacColl and Dominic Behan). Folkways Records RW 8501, 1959.

The Unfortunate Rake and His Descendents: A Study in the Evolution of a Ballad (Various Singers). Folkways Records FS 3805, 1960.

Lucy Stewart: Traditional Singer from Aberdeenshire, Volume 1. Folkways Records FG 3519, 1961.

Songs from Robert Burns' Merry Muses of Caledonia (Ewan MacColl). Dionysius D1, Folk-Lyric Records, 1962.

Sara Cleveland of Brant Lake, New York. Folk Legacy Records 33, 1968

The Kilfenora Ceili Band. Transatlantic Records TRA 283, 1974.

Joe Heaney: Come All Ye Gallant Irishmen. Philo Records 2004, 1975.
Sara Cleveland. Philo Records 1020, 1976.

Music from South Turkey Creek (Bascom Lamar Lunsford, George Pegram, and Red Parham). Rounder Records 0065.

C. Illustrated "Set Lectures"

Sexual Metaphors, Euphemisms, and Motifs in Anglo-American Obscene and Erotic Songs: A Study in Socio-Psychological Meaning and Functions.

A Typology of Occupational Songs.

A Model for Variation and Change in American Songs: An Explication and Extension of Tom Burns' Model.

Anglo-American and Western European Singing Styles.

The Other Genres of Folksong: Lyric and Descriptive Songs.

From First Foot to Last Rites: Calendar Celebrations and Life Cycle.

Customary Practices in Britain, Ireland, and America.

A Structural Analysis of Lyric Songs of Unrequited Love.

The Folklore of Scottish and Irish "Tinkers" and other Travellers.

Ethnic Jokes and Counter-Jokes in Newfoundland and Ireland.

Skin Stories and Sensitivity Sessions: Boasting, Exaggeration, Fantasy, and Wish Fulfillment in Gender Based Personal Experience Narratives of Anglo-American and Canadian Adolescents and Young Adults.

Genres and Sub-Genres of Anglophonic Prose Narrative.

D. Works Projected and in Progress

The Ballads and Songs of Sara Cleveland.

A Sailor's Garland: The Louis Jones Mid-Nineteenth-Century Manuscript Collection of Songs from East Hampton, Long Island.

Bawdy Ballads and Dirty Ditties: Erotic and Obscene Songs from Canada (with Edith Fowke).

The Canadian Colored Jubilee Singers and Their Songbook: The Spiritual Repertory of American Slaves and Their Descendents in Upper Canada.

Edited and annotated edition of four thousand Newfoundland and Labrador songs collected between 1978 and 1992.

The Songs and Ballads of Lucy Stewart of Fetterangus, Aberdeenshire.

The Ballads and Songs of Dorman Ralph, Newfoundland (with Peter Narvaez).

Traditional Storytellers in the English Language. A series of ten tapes or CDs, of which four have been edited for production:
1. A Miscellany of Tales and Tellers
2. Tales and Belief Stories told by Sara Cleveland
3. Tales and Legends told by Belle and Alec Stewart
4. Somerset Tales and Legends told by Ruth Tongue.

Songsters and Song Broadsides: Feeding the Stream of the American Song Repertory.

CONTRIBUTORS

Roger D. Abrahams is the Hum Rosen Professor of Folklore and Folklife at the University of Pennsylvania, where he has been teaching for the last nine years. The author or editor of twenty-some books on African- and Anglo-American folklore, forms of festive expression, and children's folklore, he has recently turned his hand to topics in American history. His latest work deals with the history of folklore studies and with the folkloric events as they enter into the American historical experience.

Dan Ben-Amos is Chairman of the Department of Folklore and Folklife at the University of Pennsylvania.

Tristram Potter Coffin is an emeritus professor of English and Folklore at the University of Pennsylvania. He is the author of *Folklore of the American Holidays* (second edition, 1991).

Henry Glassie is College Professor of Folklore at Indiana University. He has served as president of the American Folklore Society. His books include *Pattern in the Material Folk Culture of the Eastern United States, Folk Housing in Middle Virginia, Passing the Time in Ballymenone, The Spirit of Folk Art,* and *Turkish Traditional Art Today.*

Herbert Halpert is Henrietta Harvey Professor of Folklore Emeritus at the Memorial University of Newfoundland. He has completed a book of Newfoundland folktales and is working on an annotated collection of New Jersey supernatural legends.

David J. Hufford is Professor of Medical Humanities and Director at The Center for Humanistic Medicine at Penn State College of Medicine, and Adjunct Professor of Folklore and Folklife at the University of Pennsylvania. His work, grounded in the experience-centered study of belief, addresses both theoretical issues and applications in health care. This is illustrated by the thematic issue of *The Journal of Philosophy and Medicine,* "Nonorthodox Medical Systems: Their Epistemological Presuppositions," which he recently

(1993) co-edited with K. Danner Clouser. He most recent book, *Being without Bodies: An Experience-Centered Theory of Supernatural Belief*, continues the theory development begun in *The Terror That Comes in the Night* (1982).

Dell Hymes is Commonwealth Professor of Anthropology and English at the University of Virginia in Charlottesville. His research focusses on ethnopoetic patterns in narrative, both Native American and English. Recent studies include "Use All There Is to Use" in *On the Translation of Native American Literatures*, ed Brian Swann and "Notes Toward (an Understanding of Supreme) Fictions" in *Studies in Historical Change*, ed. Ralph Cohen.

Virginia Hymes is a lecturer in Anthropology at the University of Virginia in Charlottesville. Her research focusses on the Sahaptin language and narrative patterns in Sahaptin and English. "'How long ago we got lost': A Warm Springs Sahaptin Narrative" will appear in an issue of *Anthropological Linguistics* in honor of the late Florence Voegelin.

Barbara Kirshenblatt-Gimblett is Professor of Performance Studies and Professor of Hebrew and Judaic Studies at New York University. She received the Ph.D. in folklore from Indiana University and taught for many years in the folklore programs at the University of Texas and the University of Pennsylvania. Her forthcoming books, *Confusing Pleasures* and *Destination Museum*, deal with tourism, heritage, and public culture.

Margaret A. Mills is UPS Foundation Term Associate Professor of Folklore and Folklife at the University of Pennsylvania. Author of *Rhetorics and Politics in Afghan Traditional Storytelling* and co-editor of *Gender, Genre and Power in South Asian Expressive Traditions*, her next major project is a book on the life and repertoire of an Afghan woman verbal artist. Other research in progress concerns education development and women's expressive lives in northern Pakistan.

Peter Narváez has a Ph.D. in folklore from Indiana University and is an associate professor of folklore at Memorial University of Newfoundland. A former president of the Folklore Studies Association of Canada and the Association for the Study of Canadian Radio and Television, he has edited two books, *Media Sense: The Folklore-Popular Culture Continuum*, with Martin Laba, and *The Good People: New Fairylore Essays*, and has published articles on a variety of folklore and popular culture topics including Newfoundland culture, occupational folklife, vernacular song, and African-American blues. He is presently a co-convener, with Lori Taylor, of the Popular Music Section of the American Folklore Society.

John W. Roberts is an associate professor of Folklore and Folklife at the University of Pennsylvania where he also serves as Director of Afro-American

Studies. He is the author of *From Trickster to Badman: The Black Folk Hero in Slavery and Freedom* as well as numerous articles dealing primarily with African American folklore, literature, and culture. He currently chairs the State of the Profession Committee of the American Folklore Society, which is working on the development of initiatives designed to enhance minority participation in the field of folklore and folklife studies.

Dan Rose, Professor of Anthropology and Landscape Architecture at the University of Pennsylvania, authors artists books and makes sculpture in addition to writing social science. His most recent projects include seven papers on capitalism, corporations, and the rhetoric of the marketplace, and a single artist's book entitled, "Choice Quality," a phrase taken from the prose on the Camel cigarette pack.

Neil V. Rosenberg is a professor in the Department of Folklore at Memorial University of Newfoundland. He is the author of *Bluegrass: A History* and the editor of *Transforming Tradition,* a collection of essays examining folk music revivals.

Robert Blair St. George is associate professor of Folklore and Folklife at the University of Pennsylvania, and formerly was visiting Dittman Chair in American Studies at The College of William and Mary. His publications include *Material Life in America, 1600-1860* (ed.), and a forthcoming study, *Conversing by Signs: Place and Performance in Early New England Culture.*

Brian Sutton-Smith is a professor emeritus of the University of Pennsylvania. He has held professorships in psychology at Bowling Green State University (Ohio) and at Teachers College, Columbia University, and in education and folklore at the University of Pennsylvania. He has published extensively in the fields of children's toys, play, games, stories, folklore, gender, and sibling relationships. He is an editor of *Children's Folklore: A Source Book.*

John F. Szwed is Musser Professor of Anthropology, African-American Studies, and American Studies at Yale University. His interests focus on contemporary Afro-American culture, but he has also done work in Newfoundland and the West Indies. Among his publications are *Afro-American Anthropology, After Africa,* and the forthcoming *Sun Ra: Afro-Saturnian Nationalist.*

Janet Theophano is the associate director for Graduate Studies at the College of General Studies and adjunct assistant professor in the Department of Folklore and Folklife at the University of Pennsylvania. She has taught courses in folklore and aging, food and culture, regionalism, and multiculturalism at the University of Alaska, the University of Cincinnati, Penn State University, and Rutgers University as well as at Penn. She has published numerous articles on food, women's work, and ethnicity.

Gerald Thomas is a professor in the Departments of Folklore and French at Memorial University of St. John's, Newfoundland. He is former head of the Folklore Department and past president of Folklore Studies Association of Canada. He has been studying French Newfoundlanders since the early 1970s. Among his publications are *The Two Traditions: The Art of Oral Storytelling Amongst French Newfoundlanders* and *The Tall Tale and Phillipe d'Alcripe,* a reworking of his 1977 masters thesis.

J. D. A. Widdowson is Professor of English Language and Linguistics at the University of Sheffield. He is the Director of the Centre for English Cultural Tradition and Language, Co-Director of the Institute for Folklore Studies in Britain and Canada, and editor of *Lore and Language.*